Child Development
and Education
in Japan

A Series of Books in Psychology

Editors
Richard C. Atkinson
Gardner Lindzey
Richard F. Thompson

Child Development and Education in Japan

Edited by
Harold Stevenson
Hiroshi Azuma
Kenji Hakuta

W. H. Freeman and Company
New York

Library of Congress Cataloging-in-Publication Data

Main entry under title:

Child development and education in Japan.

(A Series of books in psychology)
"Based on a conference sponsored by the Center for
Advanced Study in the Behavioral Sciences . . . [et al.]"

1. Child development—Japan.   2. Child rearing—
Japan.   3. Education—Japan.   I. Azuma, Hiroshi,
1926–   . II. Hakuta, Kenji.   III. Stevenson,
Harold Williams, 1924–   . IV. Center for Advanced
Study in the Behavioral Sciences (Stanford, Calif.)

V. Series.
HQ767.9.C4436   1986   305.2'3'0952   85-16085
ISBN 0-7167-1740-9
ISBN 0-7167-1741-7 (pbk.)

Printed in the United States of America

1 2 3 4 5 6 7 8 9 0   MP   4 3 2 1 0 8 9 8 7 6

This book is based on a conference sponsored by the Center for Advanced Study in the Behavioral Sciences; the Japan Society for the Promotion of Science; and the Joint Committee on Japanese Studies of the American Council of Learned Societies and the Social Science Research Council. The program of the Joint Committee is supported by the Ford Foundation and the National Endowment for the Humanities.

Contents

Introduction

The intense interest in comparisons between eastern and western approaches to business practices, religion, and daily life has recently been extended to include an interest in the rearing and education of children. Part of this interest is a result of reports of children's academic achievement, where Japanese and Chinese children have been found to outperform American children in international comparisons of achievement in areas such as mathematics and science. Interest comes, too, from the desire to understand the personal components of the astounding economic, scientific, and technological advances that have been made in parts of Asia during the past three decades.

Perhaps by knowing more about the rearing and education of children in a country such as Japan, westerners can obtain new insights and perspectives on the rearing and education of their own children. How adults respond to children involves practices, and beliefs and expectations deeply embedded within a culture, and there is no ready transfer of such responses from one culture to another. Nevertheless, one of the best avenues to understanding the strengths and problems within such a complex domain as the rearing and eduction of children is through knowing how members of another culture have coped with these problems. For this purpose Japan is especially important. Among contemporary industrial societies, it is the one that differs most completely from the other societies in its history and culture. Open to interaction with other countries for little more than a century after several centuries of isolation, much of the traditional culture of Japan remains. The approaches to child rearing and education that have continued and the changes that have been initiated in Japan should be especially informative to members of other industrial societies and societies currently undergoing industrialization.

Plans for this volume began at the Center for Advanced Study in the Behavioral Sciences, where we were fortunate to spend a year in 1982–1983. Through many lively discussions of children in Japanese and American societies, the content of this volume began to take shape. It rapidly became evident that there is a great disparity between what Japanese behavioral scientists and educators know about western writings and research literature and what westerners know about issues being discussed in Japan. Whereas many Japanese scientists have a good reading knowledge of English, few westerners are sufficiently fluent in Japanese to read Japanese journals and books. Further, there is active translation of important western writings into Japanese, but few Japanese books dealing with children and families have been translated into English. We hoped that a volume such as this would help overcome the disparity in sophistication between the two groups.

This volume is written for the general reader as well as the specialist. We have attempted to avoid technical jargon and statistical discussions so the book could be read, not only by professionals in related fileds but also by persons who are interested in Japanese society or who seek new insights about child development and education. We sought to present a comprehensive coverage of the cultural and historical backgrounds, as well as contemporary research and thinking. To write the chapters, we invited scholars from several disciplines, including psychology, education, sociology, and anthropology, who are involved in research in Japanese child development, education, and family life. The Japanese authors are specialists in the field and the American authors have conducted research in Japan. The authors are able, therefore, to present authoritative statements about topics covered in their chapters. A brief biographical statement about the professional background of each author appears at the end of the book.

The chapters are grouped into three major sections. The first section offers information about Japanese children, their roles in society and in Japanese culture; how children are reared; and about the Japanese family, education, and the Japanese language. In the second section, summaries of a number of empirical studies are discussed. In several cases the development of Japanese children is contrasted with that of American children. The contrasts between Japanese and American children appear, not because of selectivity, but because the major cross-cultural studies involving Japanese children frequently include comparisons with American children. Several chapters dealing primarily with conceptual issues complete the volume.

Many books have been written about Japan during the past decade, but none of them include information about Japanese children that is as comprehensive or detailed as that which is presented by the authors of the chapters in this volume. We hope this book will provide a firmer and broader source of information.

> Harold Stevenson, Ann Arbor
>
> Hiroshi Azuma, Tokyo
>
> Kenji Hakuta, New Haven

December 1986

Child Development
and Education
in Japan

PART ONE

BACKGROUND

I | Why Study Child Development in Japan?

Hiroshi Azuma

Many arguments can be advanced for studying psychological development in different cultures, for only through such studies can principles of psychology be cast into a generalizable form. Cross-cultural studies introduce concepts and approaches developed in many different contexts. As I have discussed elsewhere (Azuma, 1984), different cultures attend to different aspects of the same phenomena. Concepts and methods for understanding human behavior are attuned to the culture from which they arise. They are also more accurate, better articulated, and more finely differentiated in regard to the behavior domains with greater relevance to personal and interpersonal adjustment in that particular culture. In behavioral science the conceptual repertoire has been created predominantly within Europe and the United States and is attuned to the value structure of those cultures. To overcome this limitation, it is important that researchers of different cultural origins interact and cooperate.

In particular, Japanese child development has attracted the interest of cross-cultural investigators in recent years. There are several reasons for this interest. One is that several studies have shown Japanese children as a group to be among the highest achievers in international comparisons of educational attainment. Also, a number of studies (Caudill & Weinstein, 1969, Doi, 1981, and Lebra, 1984) suggest that the Japanese child-rearing culture provides a natural experiment that may suggest alternatives to the western model of child-rearing practices.

Pioneering studies conducted by cultural anthropologists have increased our awareness of cultural variations in traditions and practices of child rearing. Studies of child development in different cultural settings offer important contributions to our understanding of psychological development. During the last two decades, cross-cultural studies of psychological development have stimulated reformulation of major theories and contributed new concepts of child rearing and education.

A limitation of such studies is that cultural variables covary with the degree of industrialization of the society which, in turn, affects the standard of living, family structure, levels of nutrition and education, and often even the available means of living. This covariation makes interpretation of observed facts difficult, especially when the interactions among child rearing, education, and intellectual development are under consideration. Also, if the output of a culture is less effective in assuring the population's basic welfare—for example, if a social system keeps people ignorant, poor, and near starvation—it would be more difficult to influence the concepts and orientations of the mainstream science by studying that culture.

Studying child development in Japan is of special value as a complement to this limitation. Japan equals any western country in terms of industrialization, per capita income, education, and employment; yet it has its own traditional culture of child rearing and education. East and West are two cultures, and pre- and postindustrialization also represent two different cultures. In Japan, we can observe the interaction of these two sets of cultures. Japanese culture is a complex system of many finely differentiated regional, occupational, sociocultural, and generational subcultures that are, nevertheless, integrated into a distinct culture.

A less mentioned, but equally important reason for studying child development in Japan, is that the country is undergoing rapid and drastic sociocultural change. To be sure, every culture is in transition. But the extent of change that Japan has experienced during the last 100 years—a shift from quasi-feudalistic tranquility to the furious pace of a future-oriented industrial center—is perhaps unparalleled among industrialized nations.

In dealing with cultural phenomena like education and child rearing, the interaction between the treatment and its broader cultural background must be taken into account. A treatment may be badly misinterpreted if it is reported without its cultural context. Consider the case of a young child who stubbornly refuses to eat a helping of vegetables. After several attempts to make the child eat, Japanese mothers will often say, "All right, then, you don't have to eat it" (Azuma, Kashiwagi & Hess, 1981). When I discussed this case in my class, a Chinese mother remarked that she would have said the same thing. Asked to explain herself, she answered: "Because I don't think that the child must eat particular kinds of food. There are other things which I can offer." This explanation agreed with our American colleagues' interpretation of such statements by Japanese mothers when we discussed how to code the protocols—that the mothers did not feel very strongly the child should eat the vegetables. In fact, such mothers were the ones who felt most strongly about their child eating the vegetables. The assertion, "You don't have to obey me," was actually a very powerful threat. One mother said that it always worked. It carried the message: "We have been close together. But now that you want to have your own way, I will untie the bond between us. I will not care what you do. You are not a part of me any longer." This message was effective because the child had assimilated the *amae* culture in which interpersonal dependence is the key. If, however, an American mother borrowed this method, her child would happily leave the table. Thus, methods of education and socialization are not readily exportable. Theoretical and structural insight into universals and cultural specifics are prerequisite to generalization. With that in mind, I shall discuss some characteristics of Japanese culture that are relevant to understanding the psychological development of the Japanese.

The Formation of Japanese Culture: A Quick History

One interesting characteristic in the history of Japan's interaction with other cultures is its cyclic alternation of open and closed periods. People came to Japan in prehistoric times via Korea, Southeast Asia, and perhaps the Pacific Islands. Before the third century, however, interaction among these regions was limited. Few contemporary Chinese documents mention islands to the east of Korea. In the third century, an official Chinese history documented a visit by Japanese delegates. Then came a period of massive importation of learning from the continent which laid the foundation for the future civilization. A writing system was brought from China to Japan in the sixth century. With it came Mahayana and other sects of Buddhism, as well as various schools of Chinese philosophy. During this period substantial numbers of educated and skilled Koreans and Chinese settled in Japan. They were welcomed as mediators of civilization. An official collection of genealogy published in 814 (Shinsen Shoujiroku) listed about 30 percent of the prominent families of central Japan as descendants of these immigrants. This influx was accompanied during the seventh and eighth centuries by a massive flow of Chinese culture into the country. A period of relative isolation followed; regular visits to the Chinese capital by Japanese representatives were terminated toward the end of the ninth century. Although commercial relationships and some diplomatic contacts continued, Japan remained an essentially self-contained culture for the next several centuries.

By the fifteenth century, however, it again began a period of active international contact. As the ruling power of Ashikaga Shogunate declined, regional powers sought to establish their own diplomacy. A limited but still significant influence came to Japan directly from Europe in the middle of the sixteenth century when Catholic missionaries, including Francis Xavier, opened missions. By 1639, however, only remote villages secretly observed the Christian faith.

The Japan Sea, which separated Japan from the Asian continent, served an important role in fostering Japanese culture. It allowed Japan to close itself off from time to time, thus moderating the impact of foreign cultures by allowing the Japanese to be selective about what arrived from abroad. These periods of relative seclusion permitted foreign influences to be assimilated and Japanized and old influences to be preserved.

In 1854, with the reopening of the country, efforts were begun to absorb western civilization as efficiently as possible. Deliberate moves were made to westernize Japan's legal, governmental, economic, and educational systems. This cultural reform was more powerful than any the Japanese people had ever experienced. The mechanisms by which Japan had assimilated foreign influences for centuries continued to function, however; it was often stressed that people should stay Japanese in spirit, morals, and manners in spite of intellectual mod-

ernization. I personally recollect that the Japanese pre-World War II ultrana-
tionalism had in it the same spirit of isolationism that was the modus operandi
whenever the influence from abroad became overwhelming.

But by far the strongest impact on Japan came with the post-World War II
internationalization. This latest form of outside influence differed from previous
incarnations because it occurred when the Japanese were at their lowest ebb,
experiencing the full misery of a defeat accompanied by starvation and hard living
conditions. The feeling of attachment to the national tradition was weak, and
the sea provided no barrier to airplanes. Fueled by the subsequent economic
success, sociocultural reform has continued at a rapid rate.

Japan is not, therefore, a cultural Galapagos, ideal for a natural experiment.
Many elements of western culture are evident in Japan, but these exist alongside
of elements from the period of almost perfect isolation that ended only a little
more than 100 years ago.

The Structure of Japan's Child Rearing: Maternalistic *Hon-ne* under Patriarchical *Tatemae*

Mothering is a logical starting point for a discussion of child rearing. Far eastern
family culture in general has been commonly understood to be patriarchical.
Possessing systems and ethics imported from China, the Japanese family did not
deviate from this norm. The head of the family usually was the senior male
member, and the male heir succeeded him in this position. The legal status of
women was weak. For example, in the Tokugawa era, not bearing a child after
three years of marriage constituted a sufficient reason for divorce. A woman, it
was said, should obey her parents when she was young, her husband when she
was married, and her son when she was old. This saying illustrated the basic
belief that women existed within the family only to bear children and to serve
its head.

Whether these principles were either actually or regularly enforced is another
question. In Japan, people often distinguish between *tatemae* and *hon-ne*. *Tatemae* is how things should be according to the officially recommended ideology;
hon-ne is the state of affairs that, although it contradicts the *tatemae*, represents
what people actually want. This dualism was one of the factors that contributed
to Japan's flexibility in assimilating thoughts and ideologies introduced from
abroad. The ideology from abroad was accepted as *tatemae* and represented more
advanced civilization, but the coexistence of the indigenous *hon-ne* was quietly
tolerated until the two accompanied each other. The Confucian-influenced statements about women were *tatemae*. As an officially-defended *tatemae*, of course,
they exerted sufficient influence to make the lives of many women miserable, but
hon-ne often went against the strict application of such principles. Before the

introduction of Chinese thought in the sixth century, though still not quite ma-triarchical, Japan was probably less patriarchical than it later became. Although little is known about the social system at that time, scattered signs in myths and old legends suggest evidence for this interpretation. The mythical ruler of heaven, Amaterasu, was a woman from whom, according to legend, the imperial family was descended. Another woman, the legendary Jingu Kogo, was said to have led the country in an invasion of Korea in prehistoric times. Himiko, the ruler of an unidentified part of Japan in the third century and the first Japanese whose name appears in the official history of China, was also a woman. Later, in the written history, the genealogical table of the Japanese imperial family included many legally enthroned female mikados. In contrast, throughout the long history of China, no woman was legally enthroned as the country's ruler, although a number of famous women did hold great power. They exerted it, however, because of their position as wife or widowed mother of the emperor, not as legitimate ruler.

Turning to common practice, in Japan, a woman takes the husband's family name when she marries. In China and Korea, a woman retains her maiden name (although children of both sexes take the father's family name). From a contem-porary viewpoint, the latter practice may appear to be more progressive, yet in the context of the strong family-centered traditions of these countries, it is not. In Japan, the woman leaves her family and becomes a full member of her hus-band's family. In China, she is not, so to speak, a full family member. From these and other signs, we may conclude that, although the rigorous patriarchism of China was introduced to Japan, it first coexisted and then was incorporated into an indigenous, not strictly male-centered, culture.

The unique position of the woman in the family may have influenced the characteristics of Japanese motherhood. Based on extensive interviews with con-temporary Japanese mothers, Lebra offers an interesting argument. Until the birth of a child, the bride is regarded as a womb loaner. Then, as the child is seen as the child of the family, the new mother is bound to the family. Her position in the family becomes strong and stable, and she often develops into the most in-dispensable member of the household. (Her position is also strengthed because it is believed that men should not concern themselves with household affairs.) Such a personal implication of motherhood, Lebra says, "refers to the subjective meaning penetrating the core of a woman's self-identity in an existential sense." Most of Lebra's informants were intensely filocentric. One young woman even said that, when rearing her children, a woman does not need a husband except as a supplier of money. The child is her first priority. Thus, a neglected or abused wife might quietly endure her condition if immediate divorce were deemed harm-ful to the child.

The mother's devotion and indulgence evoke a strong sense of dependence in the child; he or she senses what pleases the mother and behaves accordingly. Doi has elaborated the concept of *amae* ("the feeling of dependency coupled with the expectation of indulgence") as a basic concept for understanding Japanese interpersonal relationships. In interpersonal relationships defined by *amae*, a person may forget about *tatemae* and live with *hon-ne*. Mothers' and other caretakers' indulgent devotion socializes children into *amae* relationships. Thus socialized, a child may be demanding, even tyranical, at home but at the same time remain sensitive to the caretaker's desires and feelings. The child also learns to discriminate *uchi* ("inside"), where *amae* will be accepted and rewarded, and *soto* ("outside"), where *amae* will not be so readily tolerated. The mother's dependency on the child is both emotional and existential. In a sense she establishes her control over the child through devotion and indulgence.

In many families the position of the father is peripheral. The formal head of the family, he is accorded respect. However, this respect is symbolic; in reality he does not exert much control. Having been conditioned to an *amae* dependency toward his own mother, he generalizes it to his wife. For her part, she sees him as another child, one that is somewhat more burdensome and harder to control than other children. It is still often said that "A good husband is one who is healthy and stays out of the home." According to *tatemae*, the father is the head of the household, but according to *hon-ne*, he is psychologically dependent. Kawai (1976), a Jungian psychologist, suggests that Japanese culture is basically matriarchical. Sasaki (1985), a clinical psychologist, has recently argued that there is not, nor has there ever been, a substantial father figure in the Japanese family. The post-World War II reform of Japanese family law weakened the binding power of the family over individual members. Paradoxically, as a result, the sense of mother-child inseparability became even stronger. Formerly, the child had belonged to an extended family and was shared by the mother-in-law and other members. Now the mother became the only caretaker in the nuclear family. Some of the effects of this change have been negative. Thus, a number of psychologists maintain that the recent increase in behavior problems among young adolescents originate in part during this overly prolonged period of inseparability.

The emphasis on *amae* dependency in the structuring of social values and social roles differs from western practice, where parents try to make their children independent as early as possible (Azuma, Kashiwagi & Hess). Japanese parents want to keep the child closely interdependent with them. The feeling of interdependence helps the child assimilate the hopes and values of the parents, thus enhancing the child's educability. In the past, when people were expected to follow rules and traditions rather than to become independent individuals, this was an ingenious way of socialization. Social institutions designed for different age levels gradually shifted the object of the child's dependency from mother to peers and then to community. It is conceivable that with social modernization, and its emphasis on individual initiative and interpersonal competition, this subtly gradated transition may no longer be possible.

Many foreign observers, ranging from sixteenth century Jesuit missionaries to contemporary American anthropologists, have noted that young children in Japan, though "indulged," are, nevertheless, generally well behaved. Hara and Wagatsuma (1974) report that in many parts of Japan people used to believe that, because a child came from another world and was not yet deeply settled in this world until age 6 or 7, he or she had to be treated with indulgence and tenderness up to then. Otherwise, it was said, the child would soon go back to the other world. Six hundred years ago, Zeami, a noh master, wrote that young children in the families of noh players should not be forced to learn to perform until around age 6. He recommended waiting until the child started to imitate spontaneously. Even after the child began to imitate, Zeami warned against offering any evaluative comments. Such a tradition fits well into the scheme of indulgence-dependence-identification-controlability.

The system which implicitly presupposes this mechanism may be difficult for those raised in a different culture to understand. The Japanese school system has followed the western model for more than 100 years. Today, what takes place in a typical Japanese classroom does not differ greatly from that of a traditional American school. Nevertheless, Japanese schools remain Japanese in many subtle ways.

It has often been pointed out that Japanese attitudes toward self-expression are quite different from western attitudes. Nagashima (1973) has pointed out that in contrast to the West, where it is the sender's responsibility to produce a coherent, clear, and intelligible message, in Japan, it is the receiver's responsibility to make sense out of the message. For a Japanese to express himself or herself too clearly is impolite. It shows deficient empathy; the listener puts the speaker in the position of having to express his or her own opinions too explicitly. Such an attitude helps avoid confrontation, an adaptation well suited to people destined to live for generations in a restricted area without much room for mobility. In the classroom this view of the nature of messages characterizes the interaction process. The teacher avoids excessive prescriptiveness. The student may ask questions but should not force the teacher to confess ignorance.

In recent years many Japanese children have been raised and educated outside Japan because of their parents' jobs. Such children provide an interesting glimpse into the differences between cultures, for their education after returning has become a major problem in Japanese education. More troublesome than obvious problems like language handicaps are the scripts, or schemata, the returnees have acquired abroad about how to deal with peers, adults, teachers, and school classes. If a child's first schooling was in the United States or England, he or she would have acquired, for example, a script for success in school, emphasizing independence, explicitness, and uniqueness—quite un-Japanese values.

Minoura (1984) has followed up children who attended schools in the United States for several years and entered Japanese schools in their teens. One of her cases is a boy named Jiro, who moved to the United States at age 6, returned to

Japan at age 13½, and went back to the United States at age 16½. Jiro developed a sound understanding of both cultures and had clear feelings of identity as a Japanese, yet he found the American way more agreeable. His first frustration when he returned to Japan after 6 years of schooling in the United States involved the lack of clarity with which his friends expressed themselves. In part, some of his difficulty may have been caused by problems with the language, his achievement in Japanese was below average by three grade-equivalent points. At age 13, however, this deficit would not have signified a serious handicap in oral communication. Jiro said that he thought his American friends expressed themselves much more clearly. He discovered another source of frustration in the pressure to conform, symbolized by school uniforms and the custom of respecting upper graders for their seniority alone. These were also the most frequent complaints by teen-age returnees from English-speaking countries in a survey we have conducted (Azuma, Nakazawa & Yamawaki, 1981). When Jiro was interviewed again as a high school student in the United States, he compared Japan and the United States in the following way:

> In Japan you will not be acceptable unless you keep up with others. In the U.S. there is a lot of diversity. It is all right if you are happy with it. Things don't go that way in Japan. When I returned to the United States I felt relieved. I thought that now I could assert myself without worrying about conforming to others. But on the other hand, it was difficult. Here you have to make decisions yourself. There is no set pattern like there was in Japan. Looking back, it was easy in Japan. Others tell you what you should do and you just do that. The table is ready and you will even be helped with chopsticks. Here in the U.S. you should always be alert and support yourself, or you will drop out. (Minoura, pp. 137–42)

Jiro's statement describes the typical climate of Japanese schools—maternalistic protection and indulgence on the one hand and pressure to conform to the group on the other. Another characteristic of Japanese schools, which is often pointed out, is the severe competition for achievement. In Japan, everyone is supposed to be equal; therefore, it is the effort expended to pass the hard examinations that proves one's merit for better positions. This mixture of protectiveness, conformity, and competition may make the schools effective in some circumstances but highly stressful in others.

Conclusion

In the preceding two sections, I have presented a crude sketch of the heritage and practices that I think relevant to understanding the psychological development of the Japanese. Certainly, none of them is truly unique to Japan. Concepts like *tatemae*, *hon-ne*, and *amae* may be as useful in describing the behavior of westerners. We can find English words similar to them, though not without differences of nuance. Also, the values and functions of these concepts in the total structure of the culture are different. It is intriguing to think how such differences are reflected in the process of psychological development. For example, *tatemae* and *hon-ne* differ from the concepts of "principle" and "convention." *Tatemae* is "the way things should be," and, thus, it would appear to be equivalent to the concept of "principle." But, at the same time, it is conventional and not deeply internalized. It can be willfully lost in the family, in the company of friends, or in *bureiko* drinking parties, where participants are supposed to forget about social ranks and roles. *Hon-ne* and *tatemae* can coexist consciously. Taken together with the weakness of the father figure, the subtleties of this coexistence offer good reasons for personality theorists to look into the self-development of the Japanese.

A less-explored but potentially rich field for cross-cultural comparison between Japan and western countries is the influence of such cultural differences on cognitive development. As Jiro noted, learning is a matter of personal initiative in the United States, but it is a matter of receptivity in Japan. The role played by the self is different. A recent study (Azuma, Kashiwagi & Hess) has demonstrated that receptive diligence assessed during the preschool period was by far the strongest predictor of later school success in Japan. In the United States, curiosity and originality were more important predictors. Careful analyses of the abilities and knowledge structures formed within each of these different schema should provide fertile ground for testing the predictions of various educational theories.

References

Azuma, H. (1984). Psychology in a non-Western country. *International Journal of Psychology, 19*, 45–55.

Azuma, H; Kashiwagi, K.; and Hess, R. D. (1981). *Hahaoya no taido koudo to kodomo no chiteki hattatsu* [The effect of mother's attitude and behavior on the cognitive development of the child: A U.S.–Japan comparison]. Tokyo: University of Tokyo Press.

Azuma, H.; Nakazawa, Y.; and Yamawaki, N. (1980). How returnee children feel about Japanese schools. *Proceedings of the Faculty of Education, University of Tokyo, 20*, 159–72.

Caudill, W., & Weinstein, H. (1969). Maternal care and infant behavior in Japan and America. *Psychiatry, 32*, 12–43.

Doi, T. (1981). *The structure of dependency.* New York: Kodansha International. (Originally published in Japanese in 1966.)

Dore, R. P. (1976). *The diploma disease: Education, qualification, and development.* London: Allen & Unwin.

Hara, H., and Wagatsuma, H. (1974). *Shitsuke* [Socializing discipline]. Tokyo: Kobundo.

Kawai, H. (1976). *Bosei shakai Nippon no byori* [The pathology of Japan: A maternalistic society]. Tokyo: Chuo Koron-sha.

Lebra, T. (1984). *The Japanese woman*. Honolulu: University of Hawaii Press.

Minoura, Y. (1984). *Kodomo no ibunka taiken: Jinkaku keisei katei no shinri-jinruigaku-teki kenkyu* [Children's experience of other cultures: A psycho-anthropological study of the process of personality formation]. Tokyo: Shisaku-sha.

Nagashima, N. (1973). "A reserved world: Or is it?—The Japanese way of communication and their attitudes towards alien cultures." In *Models of thought*, edited by R. Horton and R. Finegan. London: Faber & Faber.

Sasaki, K. (1985). *Hahaoya to Nippon-jin* [Mother and the Japanese]. Tokyo: Bungei Shunju-sha.

The Social and Cultural Background of Child Development In Japan and the United States

Harumi Befu

The comparative study of child development is an ambitious undertaking and, at least from a psychologist's point of view, a novel one. In most psychological studies, the subjects are from one culture, and they are compared on the basis on such variables as age, sex, socioeconomic status, family size, and birth order. These factors can all be varied or controlled fairly easily. But when analysis involves comparison of two different cultural groups, psychologists opt for methodological surrender rather than attempting to assess the effects of culture. The vast, nebulous concept called *culture* seems so shapeless, so incomprehensible, and, at the same time, so trite. "You can't do anything with it," the psychologists complain.

But methodological surrender may be a bit premature. A more imaginative and unconventional approach (which to compulsive methodologists may appear but a flimsy excuse for abandoning the rigor that has made psychology, psychology) may salvage cross-cultural comparison for the psychologists. It is in this spirit that the present paper has been undertaken. It may appear presumptuous to many psychologists for an anthropologist to claim to answer a question from which psychologists abstain. They may be right. Yet I would hope that dissatisfaction with the present effort will not deter psychologists from considering other efforts at cross-cultural analysis.

My discussion is divided into two sections. In the first section, which examines social factors, I consider a variety of family structures in the United States and in Japan and ask how they may affect child development. In the second section, which examines cultural factors, I discuss conceptions of personhood and sex roles in the two societies. Before I begin, however, a couple of cautionary points are in order.

The first is that one should not idealize any culture, either one's own or another's. Caught up in ardent praise for the Japanese educational system, which produces students with higher achievement scores in mathematics and science than American schools, we often ignore the toll this system exacts on its children: middle school violence, paint-thinner and glue sniffers, children who refuse to leave home to go to school, and so forth. Japan does not have all the answers, obviously. Those it does have been achieved at some cost. Also, it is vital to remember that the arrangements allowing for these answers are embedded in a particular cultural and social setting. It is most unlikely they can be removed from that setting and transplanted wholesale to another culture.

The second, and related point, is that we must be wary of steryotyping. It may be impossible to eliminate stereotyping altogether even from scientific discourse. The question is, therefore, how to use stereotypes and how to interpret them when used by others. That Americans believe in free will, for example, does not mean that they exercise it all the time or that their actions are based exclusively on it. Similarly, the truism that the Japanese are group oriented does not mean that all Japanese are or that group orientation is the only form of relating Japanese recognize. Of course, some of the time some people act stereotypically. On which occasions they do, depends on the situation, which scholars must do their best to specify.

Social Factors

Social Coalitions

One salient difference between the Japanese and the American nuclear families with enormous impact on child development is the emotional alignment of family members. In Japan, very often there is a coalition of mother and children against father. By contrast, in the American pattern, the tie between husband and wife remains the basic coalition even after children appear on the scene. This difference does not mean that the Japanese mother loves her children more than the American mother or that American husbands and wives love each other more than their Japanese counterparts. What it does mean is that the quality of the typical father-mother-child triad differs in the two countries. Vogel (1963), one of the first ethnographers to report on mother-child coalitions in Japan, puts the case succinctly, if extremely: "Father is treated in many ways as a high-status guest in the home, a welcome, friendly, and even jovial guest, but one who stands on the periphery of the intimate circle of a mother and children" (p. 212). Vogel acknowledges that this mother-child versus father alignment is neither permanent nor equally solid in all families; other alignments appear from time to time, but the alignment of mother and child versus father remains the dominant pattern.

The structural isolation of husband-father in Japan results in part from his authority. According to a 1980 survey by the Japan Broadcasting Corporation, 80 percent of the men and 74 percent of the women agreed with the statement, "If a husband and wife disagree on something, the husband shoud make the final decision." Only 40 percent of American men and 34 percent of American women agreed with this statement (NHK Hoso Yoron Chosajo, p. 53). There is a marked age split in Japanese responses, with younger respondents less likely to agree than older ones—a possible indication of changing social norms. In the United States, by contrast, educational level is a more salient factor in determining response than age; the higher the educational level, the less likely the respondent was to agree that the husband should have the final decision.

The unchallenged authority of the Japanese father not only requires others to treat him with deference and respect, it makes them also be circumspect in their dealings with him. The mother reinforces this pattern by threatening to tell the father when the children misbehave, a threat that relieves her from being a disciplinarian and the dispenser of negative affects; and, at the same time, creates an image of the father as an ogre and further isolates him from his children.

This alignment is evidenced, as Vogel (p. 213) points out, in "the reserve of the wife and children in the presence of the father, the secrets that they keep from him, the plots of the mother and children for dealing with him." It is also seen in the allocation of family resources, which are divided between the father's expenses and the rest of the family's. A Japanese husband has social obligations to his colleagues and business associates that compete with family needs. A wife is generally given her husband's monthly pay and entrusted with managing the family finances. She usually spends little on herself and tries to maximize the funds available for the needs of the children and the household. In allocating funds, she is acutely aware of the competition between her husband and the rest of the family (Vogel, p. 213). In a wage earner's family, like those Vogel studies, "the cleavage between father and family is accentuated by the amount of time the mother and children spend together without the father" (p. 213).

Vogel's study of "new middle class" families was done around 1960. In the last 25 years, the authority of the father probably has to some extent decreased. It seems safe, however, to assume that the predominant coalition is unchanged.

In the United States, by contrast, the conjugal coalition is extremely strong. That it is not unshakable is attested by the high incidence of divorce. Normatively, however, the conjugal tie between husband and wife keeps a marriage and a family together. Indeed, the brittleness of American marriage may be attributable to the enormous importance placed on romantic love between husband and wife as its basis. An American couple who defined their marriage, not on the basis of mutual love, but on a commitment to raising children or achieving an economic goal would be regarded as an anomaly. Of course, the importance of the conjugal bond does not mean that American parents love each other at the expense of their children. Child custody fights between divorcing parents show that both parents have strong interests in their relationship with the children.

The ideology of the American family prevents an alliance from developing between the children and one parent against the other parent. The doctrine of equal responsibility for child rearing in some abstract sense governs the parent-child relationship in America. One-sided alliances are frowned upon. If such alliances develop, they usually do not involve all the children and one parent, but a cross-sex or unisex pair, namely, father-daughter, mother-son, father-son, or mother-daughter. These alliances seem to be psychologically motivated, without the institutional and normative underpinnings they have in Japan. Which type of alliance occurs depends on psychodynamic considerations peculiar to individual families.

When grandparents reside in the same household as the nuclear family, a different coalition develops. According to the survey by the Japan Broadcasting Corporation cited previously, 37 percent of the Japanese respondents with living parents were living with those parents in a three-generation household. A mere 4 percent of Americans were living in this fashion. Thus, the role that American grandparents play in the daily affairs of growing children is much smaller than it is in Japan.

How significant the role of Japanese grandparents is, of course, varies from family to family. Their role has diminished considerably in recent decades. A couple of generations ago, the grandfather was often described as the final arbiter, until he retired, when much of his authority was relinquished to his heir. As the grandfather's personal authority waned, however, his emotional bond with his grandchildren often waxed.

The presence of grandparents cannot help but affect Japanese family dynamics. Frequently, their presence results in a transgenerational coalition, with grandparents and grandchildren forming an alliance against the parents. Because grandparents lack authority, they develop affective ties unencumbered by the need to exercise authority and control. As with the mother-child coalition, the transgenerational coalition often results in grandparents doing favors for the children, such as giving them candy, money, or other items unauthorized by the parents. This practice may annoy the parents, but, in general, they tend to see favors done for their children by grandparents as something to appreciate—as long as the betrayal of parental authority is neither blatant nor extreme. This division of roles allows grandparents to provide the children with otherwise unavailable emotional gratification. The grandparents may even serve as a haven if parental authority becomes unbearable.

The patterns of alignment that develop in a three-generation family in the United States may be quite similar. At least, there seems to be the potential for a similar pattern since the authority structure in American families, in which grandparents have virtually no say in discipline or decision making for the children, is very similar to that of Japanese families. It is my impression, however, that American grandparents do not enjoy the right to the kind of semiconfidential relationship with their grandchildren so widely accepted in Japan. In the United States, parents are likely to reprimand grandparents for transgressing the permitted boundaries. Any attempt by American grandparents to develop a coalition against parents is likely to provoke strong opposition and to be frustrated at every turn. At any rate, since so few children live with their grandparents in the United States, there are not many children for whom such a coalition is a possibility.

Self-Employed versus Wage Earner Families
in Japan

William Caudill (1963) made a useful distinction between two types of Japanese families. Where the father is independent, or self-employed, the workplace and residence are typically in the same location, whereas the salaried husband-father is a wage earner who leaves home each day to work. The former is sometimes identified with the "old middle class," or *chusan kaikyu*, the latter with the "new middle class," or *chukan kaikyu*. Vogel's 1963 book, *Japan's New Middle Class*, is precisely about white collar wage earners and their families. The Tokyo neighborhood that Bestor (1983) has written about is an old middle class neighborhood, where about one-half of the households are independent.

The distinction between these two occupational statuses is important for child development. In the new middle class families, the father often leaves home in the morning before the child wakes up, especially if he has a long commute, as is often the case. On some days he may return by 7 or 8 P.M., which allows him some brief interaction with his children, but on many evenings he is home after they have gone to sleep. In such families, the children barely see the father on weekdays. On weekends, too, he is likely to have commitments away from home, such as an obligatory company outing. Children, then, are primarily raised by the mother, and the mother-child coalition is strengthened.

According to the 1982 Japan Statistical Yearbook (p. 41), households headed by wage earners numbered roughly twenty-three million in 1980, constituting 67.8 percent of all "ordinary" households, an increase of 7 percent since 1965. Given this predominance, the mother-child coalition seems likely to remain a prominent feature of Japanese family life.

I would emphasize, however, that the mother-child alliance results from a cultural propensity in Japan not entirely attributable to the absent father-husband. Otherwise, we would see as many mother-child coalitions in American wage earner families. The reason we do not is that the norm of equal responsibility for the children prevailing in American culture mitigates against the development of a one-sided coalition. That this norm exists is evident in the criticism made when a one-sided coalition does appear in an American family.

In an urban, self-employed family in Japan, the residence is usually above or behind the family-owned business. The business may be a retail store or a small factory, as described in Wagatsuma and Devos' *Heritage of Endurance* (1984).

Where there is *such* a family business, the father tends to be with his children much more of the day than a father who is wage earner. Other family members, especially the wife, work alongside him. These two factors inhibit the formation of a mother-child alliance. The father's continual presence in the immediate vicinity tends to offset the emotional bond between mother and child. Moreover, if the wife assists in the family business, as often happens, she is less accessible to the child than a full-time mother. If a full-time mother neglects her child, she has reason to feel guilty, but a mother who has to help her husband cannot be expected to attend to her child's every whim. In the Japanese view, ideally, a mother should be a full-time mother, but once she is working, she is justified in not looking after her children to her own satisfaction. The combination of these two factors suggests that in self-employed families, the mother-child coalition is weaker than in wage earner families.

About 7.8 million Japanese households were headed by self-employed persons in 1980. Although the percentage of households with self-employed heads has been decreasing (from 34.4 percent in 1965 to 22.9 percent in 1980), the absolute number has remained roughly the same for the past 15 years. Moreover, 22.9 percent, though less than a quarter of Japanese households, is still a sizeable proportion. Also, for tax and other legal reasons, many family businesses have in recent years been incorporated, the family head becoming a salary-drawing president of a company with one or two employees, who, more often than not, are family members. Because these "presidents" are reported in censuses as wage earners, the number of self-employed household heads is underreported, and correspondingly, the number of wage earners is inflated. At any rate, mode of employment in Japan is a significant variable in the Japanese family, potentially affecting parent-child relationships.

Working Mothers

Even though women, including a large percentage of mothers, constitute almost one-half the work force in Japan, the Japanese still tenaciously adhere to the basic norm that the male head of household should be the sole breadwinner and that the mother should stay home and devote herself to the care of household and children. This belief is held much more emphatically in Japan than the similar belief is in the United States.

Thus, the term *working mother* has a very different connotation from *working father*. The latter is redundant—fathers are supposed to work; a nonworking father is even more anomalous than a working mother. *Working mother*, on the other hand, connotes misfortune; mothers should stay home and look after their children unless they have to work. The real reason for working may not be economic survival, especially in middle class family, but the term *working mother* suggests economic necessity. In the United States, the more generalized movement toward equal opportunity has resulted in an alternative norm, which accepts working women, including mothers. Although there are individual women in Japan with successful careers in business or in education, if they have children at home they are still unlikely to meet full societal approval.

If a Japanese mother has to work away from home, the arrangement is tolerated only to the extent that she does not neglect her principal duty—at home. It is definitely regarded as unfortunate if the child has to be in the care of someone else while the mother works. If a grandparent or another close relative can serve as the caretaker, the misfortune is lessened. However, the desire to enjoy higher standards of living has created a variety of child care arrangements in Japan that serve working mothers—from "baby hotels" (where infants are cared for while parents work) through day care centers to nurseries and kindergartens. These institutions are consciously used by many working mothers primarily for baby-sitting and only secondarily for educational or socialization purposes.

Thus, massive numbers of Japanese mothers are working while feeling guilty in varying degrees for transgression of the societal norm that urges them to stay at home and be full-time mothers. Whether or not the discrepancy between the norm and the actual behavior will lead to a change in the norm, only time will tell.

Time Away from Children

Although a variety of institutions has sprung up to meet the needs of working mothers, one American institution, that of the babysitter, has made no inroads in Japan. Here, I refer to teen-agers who baby-sit in the evening and on weekends and professional, licensed baby-sitting agencies, as well as neighborhood mothers' baby-sitting co-ops. Why baby-sitting has never emerged as an institution in Japan is an enigma. It cannot be because parents are wary of leaving their children with strangers, for they do entrust them to day-care organizations of all kinds—including some with dubious reputations. Furthermore, Japanese teen-agers engage in all kinds of part-time work.

Whatever the reason, the absence of individualized baby-sitting and the availability of institutionalized group care only during weekday working hours means that, after school and on weekends, most couples are without a means of separating themselves from their children for any length of time.

In the United States, parents can be free in the evening and on weekends, leaving their children with sitters, so they can relax and enjoy themselves together—a reaffirmation of the conjugal bond. The emotional, and possibly cognitive, impact of the sheer number of hours children spend away from their parents is probably not negligible. But probably more important than sheer time is the attitude of the parents and the society at large. American parents don't doubt their right to enjoy themselves away from their children. In Japan, leaving children with outsiders for such a frivolous reason would be frowned upon. Young couples may wish they could leave their children for an evening, but societal attitudes still remain conservative. Young couples must worry about the sanctions of their parents, relatives, and neighbors, who constitute the conceptual social unit called *seken*, or *mawari*. Japanese society has made a concession to material needs in providing child care institutions during working hours, but it has not allowed parents to enjoy themselves at what is considered the expense of their children.

"Anomalous" Families

In addition to the normatively approved family forms, there are many "anomalous" families in both Japan and the United States, such as single-parent families, those resulting from second marriages, and so forth. Whereas the number of such families is small in Japan, they constitute a significant percentage of all American families. The dynamics of parent-child interaction in such families depart considerably from those in the normative family.

For the past 15 years, about 1,000,000 American children every year have been involved in the divorce of their parents (Bureau of Census, 1980, p. 83). In 1980, 8,236,000, or 14.4 percent of American families were headed by women, and an additional 1,655,000, or 2.9 percent, were headed by males without a spouse. Altogether, some 9,891,000 families were headed by single parents, if we assume all these families involved children (Bureau of Census, p. 45). In 1979, of 62,389,000 American children under 18 years of age, 16.9 percent, or 10,544,000, lived with their mothers only, and 1.6 percent, or 998,000, lived with their fathers only (Bureau of Census, p. 52).

In Japan, the number of motherless two-generation households is 1980 was 297,276; in comparison, the number of fatherless two-generation households was 1,755,677. Although these figures are small in proportion to all households (.9 percent and 5.11 percent, respectively), they are on the rise—up 30 percent and 20 percent, respectively, from 1965. In these households, obviously, we cannot speak of a mother-child coalition against the father. Emotional patterning and cognitive development would of necessity be quite different in them. When parents divorce, children bear the brunt of marital conflict, with emotional and, possibly, cognitive consequences.

Using single parent as a catchall disguises that having only a father is very different from having only a mother. It also matters whether the parent is the same or the opposite sex. If the custodial parent is the opposite sex, the child lacks the appropriate sex-role model at home.

Although the number of children involved in the remarriage of a parent is unknown, 548,000 cases of remarriage for the wife were recorded in 1978 alone (Bureau of Census, p. 83). Most of these cases (448,300) involved women aged between 14 and 44, whose children were most likely to be relatively young. If divorced men are at least as likely to remarry as women, the total number of parental remarriages would be significantly greater.

If a child is brought into a remarriage, the child must adapt to the parent's new spouse, who will act as parent-surrogate in varying ways and degrees. How difficult this adaptation is and what sort of effect it has on the child's development depends on such factors as the child's age and sex and the sex of the parent-surrogate. Two problematic issues may be mentioned here: (1) the child has to establish a new relationship with the parent-surrogate; this relationship cannot be the same as the one with the biological parent. Unless the child is very young, the new relationship is, inevitably, less intense and less deep emotionally; and, (2) parent-surrogates may be unable to play the parental role fully. Even when they are, the style of parenting is likely to be different, and the child must adjust to this new style. In any case, readjustment is likely to entail at least some degree of trauma for the child, with consequent impact on emotional and cognitive development.

Summary

To summarize, I have pointed to a number of structural considerations that affect children, primarily at the level of emotions but most likely at the cognitive level as well. Some have to do with Japanese/American differences, for example, in the internal dynamics of the father-mother-child triad. Some have to do with differences in the distributon of various family types, as well as with structural variations within Japan and the United States. All of these differences point to a diversity of patterning in child development. Awareness of this diversity offers one way to avoid stereotyping of child development.

Cultural Factors

I now turn to several cultural concepts that may affect emotional and cognitive aspects of child development. These are normative ideas, that is, beliefs about how the world—social or otherwise—is constituted. When we speak, for example, of self-reliance as an American cultural concept, we do not mean that Americans always behave in self-reliant ways or that they never accept help from others. What we mean is that Americans believe that, ideally, they should help themselves, not rely on others.

The reason I wish to discuss these concepts is, first, they are powerful, fundamental concepts, held by a great majority of the population. Second, since they are broadly espoused throughout the population, parents of children also espouse them. To the extent that parents belive in them, these concepts have an impact on their children. Since American and Japanese concepts regarding the nature of personhood are so radically different, these differences must be reflected in the parents' interactions with their children. Third, growing children must somehow internalize cultural concepts. What impact parents' espousing these concepts have on their children and how children learn to espouse them should be of interest to students of child development.

Individualism in American Culture

Individualism is one of the cornerstones of American society. Indeed, the social structure must accommodate the peculiarly American definition of the individual. Included in the concept of individualism are notions such as self-reliance, independence, freedom, and free will (Spindler, 1983; Vogel, 1963; Riesman, 1950; Hsu, 1981). Each of these concepts has its own semantic domain, though, naturally, they overlap. Together, they occupy a significant place in defining American culture. Thus, individualism is but one component in a cluster of closely related cultural concepts. It has been selected for discussion because of its contrast with Japanese *interpersonalism*, which will be discussed below.

When Americans speak of individualism, without saying so they often mean *rugged individualism*, with its implications of the pioneering spirit, the lone wolf, a competitive person, and the like. Inculcating children with the values surrounding individualism is of paramount importance in American culture. Telling children to "make up your mind" about what clothes to wear or what flavor ice cream to order, even when they are too young to exercise such judgment, is common. American parents seem to coax their children to become independent even before they are ready. Parents say to their children, "You have to make up your own mind; it's your decision." This same expression is repeated constantly in adult life. The final responsibility for making a decision is left to a person; if its consequence is adverse, the decision-maker, not someone else, is responsible. If the decision has a successful outcome, he or she is credited with making the right decision. In reality, of course, decision making is influenced by the views of many other persons. Even if no one other than the decision maker has made an explicit contribution to a particular decision, it is still affected by the views and values of parents, peers, teachers, among others. Such influences, however, are discounted when the idealized American self is under consideration.

Personhood in Japan

In discussing Japan, *personhood* seems a much more appropriate word than individualism in referring to the definition and identity of self. The Japanese concept of personhood embodies at least three separate dimensions: "interpersonalism," or *jinkaku shugi*, and role perfectionism. "Interpersonalism" is a rough translation of what Hamaguchi (1977) called *kanjin shugi* (see also Kimura, 1972), or the definition of self in terms of the relationship one has with others. Americans laugh when a person is identified as someone else's girlfriend, ex-husband, or wife's brother because such an identification implies that that person has no individual identity. In Japan, a young woman is identified as a matter of course as X's former student (even though the last time she took a course from X might have been decades ago), the son of a prominent writer, or a brother of the president of a well-known company.

In the Japanese view, it is the interconnectedness of persons and the quality of this interconnectedness that determines who one is. Connectedness is not merely a matter of knowing someone; it also expresses moral commitment to reciprocal support, whether instrumental or expressive. This commitment is expressed in such cultural concepts as *on* and *giri*, which have been discussed at length in the anthropological literature on Japan since the writings of Benedict (1946).

Interpersonalism as a normative orientation in Japan has the following characeristics:

(a) **Particularism.** Human relations vary, depending on the person with whom one is interacting. The concepts of role and status are, of course, predicated on that assumption: a friend is necessarily the friend of a friend; a father is necessarily the father of a child. Particularism in interpersonalism refers not to this truism, but to the value component of the relationship, namely, that those who are connected have a commitment to one another, and this commitment varies, depending on the relationship that obtains between them.

(b) **Mutuality of Trust.** Trust is extended to particular individuals in Japan to a degree considered not quite normal among Americans. For example, in obtaining a loan from a bank, a person often enlists a relative or a friend to serve as a guarantor, someone responsible for the loan in case of default. When beginning a new job or entering a school, a person must also name a guarantor, someone to vouch for his or her character. Should such a person act contrary to normative expectations, the guarantor may be called in to explain or rectify the situation. Serving as guarantor obviously assumes mutual trust.

(c) **Interdependence.** Persons in a relationship of mutual trust depend on and, are obliged to, assist each other. What degree of burden one can impose on the other is a subjective decision but is normally well understood by both parties. When a person asks someone to do him or her a favor, the request is based on the assumption that it will be honored. To have a request refused means a loss of face. The favor-seeker should be able to divine what the other person is willing and able to do, given their particular degree of mutual commitment. Demands should not be made that the other person would feel uncomfortable meeting or be unable to carry out. The person from whom a favor is requested is, of course, aware of the consequences of refusal and will normally try to honor the request, even if it results in inconvenience, diminution of privacy, or loss of time.

In America, by contrast, it is perfectly all right to ask a favor that may be refused, precisely because the other person has the right to refuse it. Being refused brings with it no shame or loss of face in the United States. This attitude is predicated upon American individualism, which gives a person the right to look after his or her own interest first. In Japan, one important consequence of a refusal is that a favor cannot later be asked of a person whose request has been turned down.

Thus, the identity of a person in Japanese culture is defined to a great extent in terms of the particular relationships with specific others and in terms of the relationships of mutual trust and reciprocal obligation with significant others.

Self-Discipline

Personhood in Japan is not totally defined by interpersonal relationships. Another important component is based on the quality of self, for which there is no English equivalent. "Self-discipline" may be used as a kind of rough shorthand as long as it is understood to express the complex set of concepts described here (Rohlen, 1977, Chap. 9; Kondo, 1982, Chap. 2). Japanese believe that a person's character is shaped by a mental substance called variously *ki, kokoro, tamashii,* and *seishin. Ki* refers to the basic life force that gives a person the vitality to live. *Kokoro,* often translated as "soul," is not a neutral soul but a sympathetic and empathetic one. *Tamashii* is "elan vital," including the determination to overcome all odds. *Seishin,* sometimes clumsily translated as "spirit," is a mental attitude that helps a person tackle a task. These noncorporeal substances—and they are conceived of as substantive—make self-discipline possible.

But a substance needs to pass through the crucible of experience before self-discipline is achieved. The experience necessarily involves hardship (*kuro*), endurance (*gaman, nintai, shimbo, gambaru*), effort (*doryoku*), and the utmost self-exertion (*isshokemmei*). "If you try hard, you can do it" (*yareba dekiru*) is a well-worn phrase used to exhort people to try against all odds because spiritual substance will make it possible to overcome material hurdles—but only by trying very hard. Lebra's survey (1976) of the sentence completion test demonstrates this emphasis on self-discipline. Over 70 percent of Japanese respondents—youths and adults, men and women—attributed success to diligence, effort, and endurance (Lebra, Appendix A, Table 8). The English words *endurance, perseverance,* and *hardship* do not connote the strong positive value inherent in the Japanese equivalents, which, in effect, exhort Japanese to undergo Spartan experiences, defined as good in themselves.

Experience in self-discipline is often conceived of as training. It used to be said that to become a mature person, a person has to "eat someone else's rice," that is, to be away from home and living in a setting where it is necessary to defer to others and to endure psychological and material hardships. At present, companies send their employees to training institutes, where self-discipline is a major component of the curriculum.

Role Perfectionism

Lebra (p. 82) discussed the strong Japanese commitment to developing particular roles. DeVos (1973, Chap. 17) calls this "role narcissism." I prefer "role perfectionism" because I regard this phenomenon as a cultural concept, that is, a value-laden idea, although I do not deny underlying psychodynamic processes. The Japanese commitment to a role is a commitment to do well against all odds. The implication is also that, no matter how lowly the role might be, it is worthy of a person's utmost efforts. This attitude contrasts sharply with the American view of "menial" tasks. But to make a total commitment to a role that may seem unworthy, such as janitorial work, is hard. This is where self-discipline comes into play. The cultural ideal of endurance enables a person to overcome the feeling that a role is unworthy. Thus, role perfectionism is supported by the cultural ideal of self-discipline. It is possible to hypothesize that the motivation of Japanese children to do well in school is at least in part derived from the cultural value placed on self-discipline and role perfectionism.

How does role perfectionism relate to child development? First, we must ask how a child learns the cultural value of role perfectionism. One answer is that Japanese mothers themselves engage in role perfectionism. That Japanese women take their maternal role with utmost seriousness is proverbial. Of course, motherhood has a sacred aura in many cultures, but the point here is the normative devotion of the mother to the mother's role. American mothers are pulled by competing roles as wife and career woman. Professionalism applies to almost anything but motherhood and being "merely" a mother, as opposed to being a professional, is equated with failure by many women.

In contrast, the Japanese define motherhood as an entirely worthwhile and satisfying calling. Japanese women take motherhood as seriously as American career women take their jobs, perhaps even more seriously. Doing a good job as a mother is widely regarded as a full-time occupation in the United States, too. But a woman's other interests and commitments are viewed as having equal, or nearly equal, claims on her time. Consequently, she must decide on her own priorities. At times her commitment to her children must be compromised, for example, she may also need to go to work, attend school, have time with her husband, and see her friends. All these activities are considered legitimate in American culture. For Japanese women, on the other hand, the rank order of their various commitments—to motherhood, to being a wife, to fulfilling personal goals, and so forth—is clear-cut and absolute: motherhood comes first. Neglect of one's responsibility as a mother is inexcusable under any circumstances.

I should remind the reader we are talking about cultural ideals and the disposition to fulfill those ideals. Though many people fail to reach these goals, the strong positive value placed on attaining them is, nonetheless, unmistakable.

Summary

How these conceptions of personhood are related to child development remains unclear. Somewhere along the road from childhood to maturity, the child acquires them. Surrounded by adults with these cultural conceptions of the self, children are bombarded daily by stimuli manifesting them. Since these are cultural concepts with inherently positive values, children are necessarily rewarded by accepting, internalizing, and acting in accordance with them. Concepts of the self must, therefore, be powerful molders of the adult the child will become.

References

Benedict, R. (1946). *The chrysanthemum and the sword: Patterns of Japanese culture.* Boston: Houghton Mifflin.

Bestor, T. C. (1983). *Miyamoto-cho: The social organization of a Tokyo neighborhood.* Unpublished doctoral dissertation, Stanford University.

Caudill, W. (1963). *Sibling rank and style of life among Japanese psychiatric patients.* Proceedings of the Joint Meeting of the Japanese Society of Psychiatry and Neurology and the American Psychiatric Association. Tokyo, Japan.

DeVos, G. A. (1973). *Socialization for achievement.* Berkeley: University of California Press.

Hamaguchi, E. (1977). *'Nihon rashisa' no sai hakken* [Rediscovery of 'Japaneseness']. Tokyo: Nihon Keizai Shimbunsha.

Hsu, F. (1981). *American and Chinese: Passage to differences.* Honolulu: University Press of Hawaii.

Kimura, B. (1972). *Hito to hito to no aida [Interpersonal relationships].* Tokyo: Kobundo.

Kondo, D. (1982). *Work, family and self: A cultural analysis of family enterprise.* Unpublished doctoral dissertation, Harvard University.

Lebra, T. (1976). *Japanese patterns of behavior.* Honolulu: University Press of Hawaii.

NHK Hoso Yoron Chosajo. (1982). *Nihonjin to Amerikajin [Japanese and Americans].* Tokyo: Nihon Hoso Shuppon Kyokai.

Prime Minister's Office, Statistics Bureau. (1982). *Japan statistical yearbook.* Tokyo: Japan Statistical Association and Mainichi.

Riesman, D., Denny, R., & Glazer, N. (1950). *The lonely crowd: A study of changing American character.* New Haven: Yale University Press.

Rohlen, T. P. (1977). *Harmony and strength.* Berkeley: University of California Press.

Spindler, G., & Spindler, L. (1983). Anthropologists view American Culture. In B. Siegel (Ed.), *Annual review of anthropology* (pp. 49–78). Palo Alto: Annual Review.

U. S. Department of Commerce, Bureau of Census. (1980). *Statistical Abstract of the United States.* Washington, D. C.: U. S. Government Printing Office.

Varenne, H. (1977). *Americans together: Structured diversity in a Midwestern town*. New York: Teachers College, Columbia University.

Vogel, E. (1963). *Japan's new middle class*. Berkeley, Ca.: University of California Press.

Wagatsuma, H., & DeVos, G. A. (1984). *Heritage of endurance: Family patterns and delinquency formation in urban Japan*. Berkeley, Ca.: University of California Press.

3

The Child in Japanese Society

Yoshiaki Yamamura[1]

How does one make general comparisons of the special characteristics and conditions pertaining to children in different societies? Perhaps the most common way is to base investigations on statistical data describing such aspects as birth rate, health, family relations, entrance and advancement in school, delinquency, academic achievement, or attitudes prevalent in the society being examined. There is another method, however, which focuses not on the concrete phenomena surrounding the children themselves, but on the underlying, fixed attitudes toward children entertained by adults in the society. Once these attitudes are clearly identified, they serve as a basis for further investigation of problems related directly to children.

If any society, adults protect their offspring, evaluate their actions, attempt to guide them in desirable directions, and influence their development in a variety of other ways. These actions are based on tacit assumptions, which may or may not be conscious, concerning the nature of children. These assumptions are at work when a parent decides the proper time to begin toilet training, when a teacher begins to correct a child's word usage, or when society in general begins to define a child's actions as "delinquent." Viewed from this perspective, problems related to children in society can be defined in terms of adult actions, arising from preconceived notions of what children are and children's responses to those actions.

The cultural conception of children is a widely accepted definition of what children are and how they should behave. It is strongly connected to overall concepts of human nature. The nature of the concept naturally can be expected to differ from society to society and to change within a single society over time. Despite these variations, however, it is a fundamental aspect of human life, formed through historical processes and closely bound to the daily activities of the population. Because of its fundamental nature, the social view of the child is rarely formulated consciously and is highly resistant to modification. Using Kluckhohn's terminology, it is part of the "implicit culture."

There also exists a body of scientific research on children, studies in education, and various conscious formulations of human nature comprising a systematized knowledge of child behavior. This kind of knowledge can be termed ideological, and it is less fundamental than the traditional, common-knowledge view of children, defined by the culture. This is not to say that the common-knowledge view of children cannot be influenced by the academic view, but it seems safe to assert that the latter can never entirely replace the former.

We face a problem, however, in attempting to represent this basic, traditional conception of the child. Not being a historian, I am unable to present research results on the same scale as Phillippe Ariès (1960). Instead of trying to examine the actual treatment of the child in various sociohistorical periods, I would like to approach this task in a cultural context. Therefore, I shall be dealing with a general understanding of Japanese cultural norms as well as describing studies and materials on Japanese children. I shall examine various fragmentary descriptions of Japanese children, represented in folklorist and historical accounts, and then construct the cultural conceptions of the child as an ideal type which seems to best explain the observed phenomena. Next, I shall consider the relationship between the traditional concept of the child in Japanese society and its modern manifestations.

Since the term *cultural conception of the child* covers a broad area, we must begin by specifying the particular aspects to be examined. I propose the following four topics as useful themes in clarifying the special characteristics of the Japanese conception of the child: (1) how Japanese society distinguishes between adult and child; (2) the process of birth itself and how it is viewed; (3) how children are assigned their place in society; and (4) the view of the child's fundamental nature as reflected in rearing practices.

The Distinction between Child and Adult

The first theme concerns the maturation process and how stages of development are defined as the child grows into adulthood. As Ariès pointed out, a child living in Europe during the middle ages was considered a small adult. There was no concept of childhood as a distinct developmental period. It was not until the late seventeenth and early eighteenth centuries that children began to be viewed as beings with separate, special characteristics. This *discovery of childhood* was accompanied by the notion that children needed to be coddled, that they were dependent, naive beings requiring protection and training.

In Japan, this latter view of the child can also be found. The trend toward protecting and fostering children has grown particularly with the development of family sentiment and the institution of school systems. But this view has also been evident in the traditional behavior of the upper classes throughout many centuries of Japanese history. However, it seems doubtful that it underwent the same kind of development as in the West, with a clear distinction between medieval and modern modes of thought, such as Ariès describes.

The concept of the child as an object of love has roots in ancient Japan; numerous examples of parental love can be cited from classical literature. Ya-manoue Okura's poems in the eighth century *Manyoshu* collection or the *waka* of Fujiwara Kanesuke in the tenth century immediately come to mind; in the twelfth century, we have a general expression of adult love for children in the Ryojinhisho, while noh plays of the fourteenth and fifteenth centuries depict the deep bonds between parent and child in such plays as *Sakuragawa, Sumidagawa*, and *Miidera*. As we move toward the modern period, examples proliferate.

A common theme in the early plays, such as *Sakuragawa*, is that of a mother, half-crazed in search of a lost child. There is a common mentality behind this theme: the idea that parents can become so attached to their children that they become *lost*, a condition which, according to Buddhist doctrine, is considered tainted with earthly desire (*kobonno*). When such strong attachment is coupled with the idea of children as potential successors, who will eventually assume responsibility for family support, the tendency for parents to treat their offspring as flawless jewels (*ko-dakara*) becomes even more pronounced. The overprotectiveness and indulgence toward children often observed in the nuclear families of today's affluent society can be interpreted as extensions of these historical propensities.

Such treatment of children was not confined to the parents, but became institutionalized in Japanese society as a whole. In contrast to Ariès's description of the western child, who was thrown into adult society as soon as it was clear he or she no longer needed protection, the Japanese child was gradually led to adulthood through a series of socially systematized stages, established on the basis of age. Ariès tells us that the organization of age-groups within a community was a classical phenomenon which broke down under the apprenticeship system of the middle ages. In contrast, Japanese society preserved age-group organization, with its well-defined rites of passage, until as recently as World War II. Details of this orientation varied, depending on location and era, but studies in Japanese folklore have made clear the following general pattern.[2]

A child was christened at a name-giving ceremony 7 days after birth (*nazuke iwai*). At the age of about 1 month, the child was brought to the family shrine to be blessed (*miyamairi*). After 100 days, the first solid food was given to the child (*kuizome*). The first birthday was celebrated at one year (*hatsutanjo*). In the third year, the *obitoki* ceremony marked the child's first use of an *obi*, or "kimono sash." At age 4, the young child was permitted to wear *hakama*, or "formal, divided skirts." This ceremony was, for the most part, restricted to males. At age 6, the child was officially admitted as a member of the clan. As can be seen, the early years of life, then, were replete with celebrations, each commemorating a new stage of development.

The most important stage came at age 6; at this time the child was first recognized as an independent human being and member of the community. "The first six years are in the hands of the gods," or so the traditional saying goes, referring to the instability of life during this first period. Once having safely crossed this threshold, the child began to participate in the working life of the community and to learn about production and household affairs. The change in status occurring at age 6 thus marked the boundary between infancy and childhood.

The next milestone occurred at 12 years; boys were given their first *fundoshi* ("loincloths") and girls the first *koshimaki* ("underskirts") in a ceremony formally recognizing the emergence of sexual differences. Another series of rituals and celebrations followed at age 14 or 15. At this time, boys were initiated into manhood (*genpuku*) and permitted to wear *eboshi* ("formal hats"), and girls were similarly initiated into womanhood with the ceremony of *kanetsuke*, literally, "tooth blackening," derived from the court custom during the Heian period of blackening teeth for cosmetic purposes. Although these ceremonies signified a coming of age, the young initiates were not yet treated as full-grown adults. Instead, boys and girls were segregated and expected to continue their training— a maturation process which finally culminated in marriage.

A comparison of this folklorist information with Ishikawa's (1949) historical research on warrior families brings no major discrepancies to light. This work, analogous in many ways to that of Ariès, deals with similar issues and represents a preeminent example of Japanese scholarship. Ishikawa's description of the rites of passage essentially mirrors the outline given above: an important milestone at age 6, when education and training begin; a period lasting until age 12, during which the child is not personally responsible for his or her actions and is, therefore, not subject to legal punishment; a coming-of-age ceremony at around age 14, followed by training which leads to the attainment of full adulthood at 16 or 17.

Upon reflection, it seems that this premodern series of stages leading to adulthood is not too far removed from modern practice. The basic progression remains as it was in classical times, although our coming-of-age ceremony now comes later, at age 20, and recognition as a mature adult now occurs with marriage and/or employment. Age 6, when the child enters grade school, still represents an important milestone, dividing infancy from childhood. Age 12 marks entry into junior high school, with compulsory education ending at age 15, corresponding to the old coming-of-age ceremony. The high school years, from ages 16 to 18, mark the period in which young people first take an active part in society—corresponding to the final training years of the classical system. The ages considered important in development from child to adult have, thus, been preserved from the middle ages to the present day.

To summarize this first aspect of the Japanese cultural conception of the child, we can note that premodern Japanese conceived of children as objects of affection needing protection and training, that there existed a period of *childhood* which divided infants from adults, and that this period was traversed through a series of developmental stages. Modern attitudes toward children may then be interpreted as clarified, strengthened versions of the premodern conceptual tendencies.

From Birth to Giving Birth

The second aspect of the Japanese conception of the child concerns the birth process itself. The birth of a child is an awesome and a mysterious event. Since there is never a guarantee that the child will be healthy, various petitions to the gods (both Buddhist and Shinto) have evolved, and a strong sense of the child as a divine blessing has been preserved in the Japanese mentality until very recently. This conception has further reinforced the tendency for parents to take the task of child rearing seriously.

However, with the development of scientific knowledge concerning pregnancy and the introduction of modern contraceptive techniques, traditional views of childbirth have undergone inevitable changes. Birth control, in particular, has become extremely widespread, reflecting Japan's lack of religious taboos in this area, and the birthrate has rapidly declined. This trend has benefited those who would otherwise be burdened either spiritually or financially with unwanted children. But it has also resulted in a change in parental attitudes. Offspring have ceased to be gifts from the gods; they are now willfully created in a planned, artifical way. The decision whether or not to have a child is now made with a variety of factors taken into consideration, including housing, the financial burden, the nature of the prospective parents' sexual relationship, and the consideration of their life as a couple. In other words, childbirth has become dependent on the convenience and inclination of the parents. This attitude has, in turn, led to an increased abortion rate and to a general change in the attitude toward human life. Some evidence for this change in attitude can be seen in the decline of the custom of having Buddhist services for children lost through miscarriage. Planned parenthood has brought with it, perhaps, a certain arrogance; there is a tendency to treat not only childbirth itself, but also child rearing, as artificial activities, dependent on the convenience of the parents.

From Communal to Private Property

The third aspect to be dealt with concerns the child's assignment to a place in society. Regardless of the circumstances of birth—planned or accidental—biologically, children belong to their parents. However, this does not always correspond to the social view of the parent-child relationship, which includes concepts of the caretaker and the cared-for, the protector and the protected. It is useful, then, to look more closely at the discrepancy that traditionally existed between biological parenthood and social customs.

In Japan, emphasis has traditionally been placed on the social relationship rather than the biological, as shown by the work of Yanagida (1946) and Ariga (1945). These researchers found that the word "parent" (oya) in Japanese was used to indicate one who had the right to direct labor, while "child" (ko) referred to someone functioning as a unit within a labor group directed by an *oya*. Thus, the terms "parent" and "child" gained a wider, social meaning that transcended the actual biological connection and were used to indicate a more generalized bond relationship of leader to follower. This concept contributed to the formation of the *ie* (house or clan), which is the traditional form of Japanese family organization and includes "relatives" who are not actually blood related. It was also responsible in part for the widespread system of *karioya*, or "quasi-parent/child relationships," which has traditionally thrived in Japan. Under this system, a child had a "taking-up" parent (the midwife), a "name-giving" parent (the godfather), a "milk-giving" parent (the wet nurse), a "hat-bearing," or "tooth-blackening" parent (present at the coming-of-age ceremony) and a "house" parent (present during the period prior to marriage, when boys and girls lived in segregated quarters). All these "parents" took their place beside the biological ones, watching over the child and contributing to his or her development.

Undoubtedly, the role played by these social, nonrelated "parents" was crucial in enabling the biological parents to become totally absorbed in their children. Indeed, such a social creation of the parent-child relationship (*oyakonari*) was virtually fused with the ceremonial process described previously. If we look at the way in which these ceremonies were conducted, it also becomes clear that these rituals served to define the child in terms of the community as a whole, with all mature community members taking an active interest. Thus, the child was not viewed in the light of a single set of parents, biological or otherwise, but as a member of the community, with responsibility for child rearing lying with it.

What then, were family relations like between a child and his or her real parents? Naturally, the biological bond remained strong. However, in the *ie* system there was no place for the parents as individual entities, since child rearing was considered the responsibility of all adult members in the household. The child was the successor who would assure the continued prosperity of the *ie*; as such, he or she belonged to the *ie* more than to the parents. In the same way, each *ie* was in turn embedded in the community as a whole, vertical and horizontal associations making up the village.

This traditional view of the child has undergone a radical change in today's society. Common-sense knowledge and implicit cultural behaviors are in their very nature resistant to modification, but when their supporting base erodes they, too, must adapt to new conditions. As we have discussed, the concept of the child as a gift from heaven changed in response to increasingly widespread knowledge and use of contraceptives; in much the same way, this third aspect of the Japanese conception of the child has undergone a transformation in response to the changes in social structure which have led to the collapse of traditional village communities.

With economic development has come a strengthening of individual families that operate independently from the community at large; the result has been a weakening of the community structure and of its regulating power. At the same time, the organization of the traditional *ie* has crumbled, with independent, nuclear families coming to the fore. The concept of the child as a member of the general community has thus ceased to function, while loosening relationships within the *ie* system itself have confined the child to the individual family and to the biological parent-child relationship. The child is now thought of as the product and property of the parents as individuals; the result has been a strengthened sense of identity between parents and their children. The *kobonno* tendency described previously—that of parents becoming totally absorbed in their progeny—continues to play an active role, but there are no longer the counterbalancing controls formerly supplied by the *ie*. The change may explain the increase in the number of parents who overprotect and spoil their children. This, combined with the concept that children are properly subject to parental will goes a long way in explaining how the so-called "child care neurosis" has been fostered in Japanese society.

To give a concrete example of this attitudinal transformation, let us examine the phenomenon of *sutego* ("abandoned children"). Under the old, communal system, parents who were unable to support children would "abandon" them with the tacit understanding that some other *ie* would take them in and raise them. The other *ie* shared in this understanding and could not refuse the responsibility of rearing the child. The unspoken pact was strong enough to be considered a true social system, based on mutual emotional responsibility. In a society composed of independent households, however, an abandoned child is *literally* abandoned.

This change in mentality is also reflected in the dramatic increase in the modern period of *oyako-shinju* ("a parent's killing the child before the parent's own suicide"). When parents have formed an entirely private bond of identity with their child, there can be no hope that, after a parent's death, members of the community will take it upon themselves to look after the child left behind. For such a parent, the only course remaining is to take the child's life as well. This drastic solution is not as surprising as it may first appear. For one thing, Japanese society has no religious tradition of viewing suicide as a sin; for another, double suicides, usually between lovers, have been traditionally romanticized in the popular imagination.

The Inherently Good Nature of Children

The final aspect to be discussed concerns how the intrinsic nature of children is defined. This does, of course, tie indirectly with a society's view of human nature. What will be treated here in particular are the unconscious assumptions that form the basis for an adult's actions when dealing with a child. Hatano (1969) identified

Calvinism and philanthropism as representing two distinct points of view about children, but these are intellectual constructs. For our purposes, it is more profitable to consider the question from a more basic perspective, making distinctions on the basis of whether the nature of the child is considered inherently good or inherently evil.

The first view asserts that since children are inherently good at birth, there is no need for strict discipline; left to their own devices, they will naturally come to understand the surrounding world. The opposing view asserts that, unless strict discipline is administered from an early age, children will be unmanageable when they grow up and fall naturally into evil ways. Yet a third view compares newborns to pieces of white paper, neither good nor evil. However, in discussing the implicit conception of the child, it is convenient to set up a contrasting dichotomy.

Applying this basic distinction, we find that Christian cultures, with their view of human beings as fallen creatures, who can regain an honest life only a little at a time and with divine assistance, seem to regard human nature as inherently evil. The same may be said for Freudian concepts, with their identification of sexual desire and aggressiveness in children.

In contrast, the Japanese tend to think of children as inherently good. It cannot be denied that scholars, such as Ishikawa or Hatano, have pointed to a line of thought in Japanese society expounded by Kaibara Ekken that defines human nature as evil, even as the opposite line can be found represented by Nakae Toju. However, even taking into account Kaibara's assertions were offered as a criticism of popularly held beliefs, it seems safe to conclude that, on the implicit cultural level, the most generalized Japanese concept of human nature is one of moral goodness.[3]

"The first 6 years are in the hands of the gods." This saying has more than one implication. Certainly, it suggests the instability of life in the early years, but another implication is also present: the recognition that a child possesses a divine nature. According to the folklorists, among them Yanagida Kunio, children were historically considered the gods' mediums and played an important part (yorimashi) in local religious festivals when the gods were supplicated.

This sanctification of the child is important to understanding the way children are viewed by Japanese society in general. It is true that a pure and innocent vision of the child exists in America and Europe as well, (see Mead & Wolfenstein, 1955), particularly in the mass media, but there is an important difference in that the Japanese concept of purity goes hand-in-hand with that of adult inferiority. As Sato (1966) has pointed out, Japanese films tend to contrast the noble spirit of children with the worthlessness of their parents, representing the young as the embodiment of the purity and virtue which adults have lost. The kind of relationship often found in western films—the wise adult educating the child in the ways of society—rarely occurs in their Japanese counterparts. On the contrary, in Japanese films, the adult is purified and given new strength through interaction with the child. Moreover, adults rarely exhibit clear, positive feelings or confidence about their own lives; instead, there is a tendency to feel shame or guilt in front of offspring.

Clearly, the Japanese conception is more complicated than a simple objectification of the child as the center of parental attention or as a differentiation of the transitional step on the way to adulthood. The fundamental nature of the child is perceived to be both different from, and superior to, that of an adult; the transition from childhood to adulthood is considered a step down. Although the exact age of this transition is variable, it can probably be linked to the coming-of-age ceremony and marriage, or, in today's industrial society, with the commencement of full-time employment. In this sense, childhood is considered a period of grace, in clear contrast to the western point of view. Even after the seventeenth-century recognition of *childhood* as a distinct period in human development, westerners still considered adults and children to be on the same plane in the eyes of God, with the same fundamental human nature.

Since the Meiji period (1868 to 1912) and the overall modernization of Japanese society, the importation of western concepts has weakened the sanctified Japanese view of the child. However, the optimistic confidence in children's essential goodness has gone unchanged; if anything, it has strengthened the idea that adults are inferior. This may account for the indulgence Japanese society shows toward its children. The Japanese adult's sense of inferiority brings out the overprotectiveness characterizing the parent's relationship to the child. Parents neither tend to demand respect from their offspring, nor do they forcefully scold them, for fear that to do so would bring out undesirable traits.

This positive view of the child has been affected by the dissemination of modern psychological knowledge. Although the first part of the older view relating to the innate goodness of children has remained intact, the second part, proposing that a child will come to understand his or her world naturally, if given time, has had to be discarded. The intensification of educational competition, coupled with a rise in juvenile delinquency accompanying the high-level industrialization of Japanese society, has resulted in a new emphasis on the disciplinary aspects of education during the early years. In such circumstances, a shift from positive to negative in the Japanese attitude toward the child seems likely.

One important consideration, however, works against such a change in attitude. This is the belief that since children are essentially good in nature, all people, of any age, possess a virtuous side, hidden though it may be. The fall of adults into a state of unworthiness is perhaps an inevitable outcome due to acquired habits and environmental influences. But because the condition is seen as externally imposed, individual variation can occur. Value is placed on an attempt to preserve and develop as much of the individual's original nature as possible.

Thus, a two-part notion has developed, predicated, first, on a belief in universal equality at birth and, second, on a belief in the positive value of effort in maintaining the virtue with which all human beings are born. This notion has contributed to the preservation of the positive conception of the child in Japan to the present day.

Such an appreciation of effort is reflected in our research, which centers on Japan's notorious entrance examination system. Parents' and teachers' responses are amazingly consistent in their emphasis on effort, regardless of whether the child in question has any aptitude for study (Yamamura, 1983). If it were generally believed that children possessed innate differences in ability, one would expect more students to drop out of the competition. Parents' and teachers' strong emphasis on effort implies a belief in equality at birth, with success or failure entirely dependent on how hard the child tries. This phenomenon can be considered a corollary of the traditionally positive Japanese conception of the child.

In conclusion, certain aspects of the Japanese traditional view of the child, those of the birth process and of the child as property, have undergone dramatic changes. Others have proven appropriate to modern circumstances without modification, such as the differentiation between child and adult and the view of the child's nature as essentially good. To understand the many problems concerning the child in modern Japanese society, it is necessary to consider both specific changes and overall loss of balance within this traditional view.

Notes

1. This chapter is an adaptation and extension of my "The modern Japanese conception of the child" [Gendai Nihon no kodomo kan], appearing in *Modern Society and the Child* [Gendai shakai to kodomo], (1970), pp. 23–56, Tokyo: Toyokan, (1970). The reader may consult this earlier article for further information.
2. See, for example, Tokuzo et al. (Eds.) (1959), *Outline of Japanese folklore 4—Society and folklore II* [Nihon minzoku gaku taikei 4—Shakai to minzoku II]; Takeda Akira (Ed.) (1976), *Japan folklore lecture 2: Social transmission* [Nihon minzoku gaku koza 2, shakai densho]; Ofuji Yuki. (1944). *Koyarai*; and the *Collection of the authentic texts of Yanagida Kunio* [Teihon yanagida kunio shu], volumes 15 and 20, 1962–1963.
3. In literature pertaining to the intellectual life of the warrior clans in the fifteenth and sixteenth centuries, and in particular the *Hundred-day record of Yamamoto Doki* [Yamamoto doki nyudo hyaku nichiroku monjo], reference is made to the inherent goodness of the child's nature. See Yamazumi Masami et al. (1976), *Writings on childrearing I* [Kosodate no sho I]. Tokyo: Iwanamishoten.

References

Aries, P. (1960). *Centuries of childhood—A social history of family life*. (R. Bladick, Trans.). New York: Random House.

Ariga, K. (1945). *The Japanese family system and the tenant system* [Nihon kazoku seido to kosaku seido]. Tokyo: Kawadeshobo.

Hatano, K. (1969). What is a child? A structural approach [Yoji to wa nanika—kozoshugiteki apurochi]. *Thought Shiso*, No. 542.

Ishikawa, K. (1949). *The development of the view of the child in Japan* [Wagakuni ni okeru jidokan no hattatsu]. Tokyo: Shinreisha.

Mead, M., & Wolfenstein, M. (Eds.). (1955). *Childhood in contemporary cultures.* Chicago: The University of Chicago Press.

Sato, T. (1966). *Discussion of films and children* [Eiga kodomo ron]. Tokyo: Toyokan.

Yamamura, Y. (Ed.). (1983). *Thought, behavior, and the examination order* [Juken taisei o meguru ishiki to kodo]. Tokyo: Itochukinenzaidan.

Yanagida, K., (1946). *Reflections on family life* [Ie kandan]. Tokyo: Kamakurashobo.

Child Rearing Concepts as a Belief-Value System of the Society and the Individual

Hideo Kojima

Introduction

This chapter addresses the problem of child rearing in terms of the adult's view of the child as a belief-value system of the society and the individual. The perspective is a historical one. The first part of this chapter discusses Japanese concepts of child rearing and education from the mid-seventeenth to the mid-nineteenth century. Documents written during this period have been analyzed from three aspects: the theory of the child and his or her nature, the goals of child rearing and education, and the theories of child rearing and education.

The second part of this chapter deals mainly with conceptual issues. The concept of tradition is discussed by distinguishing three classes of continuity: no change, change with continuity of functions, and change with continuity of content and form. Then, the concept of tradition in child rearing research is examined in the following three areas: cross-cultural research in child rearing, cultural conflict and assimilation in child rearing, and the ecology of human development. Finally, empirical research on adults' views of the child at the present time is briefly discussed.

Child-Rearing Concepts in Japanese Society from the Mid-Seventeenth to the Mid-Nineteenth Centuries

Historical Background

The medieval feudal system in Japan, shaken by continuing civil war during the latter part of the fifteenth century and broken down by the middle of the sixteenth, was restored in 1590, when Toyotomi Hideyoshi completed national unification. Shortly after, Tokugawa Ieyasu, who established supremacy over Japan in 1600, created a ruling system for the country. He centralized political power at Edo—later to be called Tokyo—and established local feudal control. Efficient and stable, the political system he erected lasted for $2\frac{1}{2}$ centuries.

Up to this time, Westerners had not penetrated the interior. Apart from survivors of a ship, wrecked on the coast of Kyushu a few years earlier, the first western visitors to Japan were believed to be the Portuguese in 1543. The matchlocks and gunpowder they brought interested the Japanese very much, and within a few years large quantities of muskets were being produced in central and western

Japan. These firearms were to play an important part in the national unification process during the latter part of the sixteenth century. Meanwhile, in 1549, Christianity was introduced into Japan by St. Francis Xavier. Christian missionaries successfully proselytized in western and central Japan. The first Japanese rulers watched the process with increasing attention. Hideyoshi, and later Ieyasu, became concerned about growing Christian influence, with Ieyasu's successors banning Christianity and persecuting believers. The Tokugawa shogunate's fear of Christian influence led Japan to isolate itself from European countries around 1640. During the next two centuries, the Chinese and Dutch trading post located on a small island in Nagasaki harbor may have been, besides Korea, the only official window to foreign countries.

By the eighteenth century, the fear of Christianity had receded, and the shogunate relaxed its ban on western books, except for those on Christianity. As a result, interest in western political and social systems and technology increased, and when, in 1858, Treaties of Commerce were concluded with the United States, the Netherlands, Russia, Great Britain, and France; Japan gradually opened itself to the West.

The social structure of Edo-period Japan (1600 to 1867) is particularly important for an historical understanding of Japanese concepts of the child. In an attempt to establish political stability, Hideyoshi had tried to restrict social mobility among the classes. Following ancient Chinese practice, his successor Ieyasu distinguished four social classes, in descending order of rank: warriors (the samurai); peasants; artisans; and merchants. The distinction between the warriors and the other three classes was the most rigid—the artisans and the merchants, who lived in towns, being virtually indistinguishable in terms of social status. Warriors made up about 6 to 10 percent of the population. During the period of peace, which lasted nearly 200 years, they became a bureaucratic class, with a literacy rate probably close to 100 percent.

The peasants, estimated to make up about 85 percent of the total population, formed the fundamental element in the agrarian system. During the second half of the Edo period, the economic situation of rural districts deteriorated, in part, because of the commercialization of the nation's economy. As a result, the gap between rich and poor peasants began to widen, with many peasants becoming seriously impoverished. Meanwhile, the feudal lords and warriors, dependent on rice produced by the peasants, were unable to keep pace with the nation's rapid economic development and occasionally fell into deep debt to the wealthy town merchants. It is within the context of these developments that, by the middle of the eighteenth century, a percentage of the children of commoners (peasants, merchants, and artisans) were educated for three or four years at private elementary schools called *terakoya*. Dore (1965) estimated that during the Edo period about 43 percent of Japanese boys and 15 percent of Japanese girls attended school.

The family, composed mainly of parents, children, and grandparents, functioned as the basic unit of society. Oishi (1973) estimated that, in the second half of the Edo period, almost all peasant families consisted exclusively of members from one hereditary line.

In this world, children had instrumental economic and social value. Hara and Wagatsuma (1974) have pointed out the double loss felt by childless common families: first, loss of additional labor and, second, and perhaps more importantly, the absence of an heir to worship the ancestors. Among warriors, familial succession was even more crucial. If a warrior lacked an heir, his family simply ceased to exist. Wealthy merchants also needed heirs to inherit the family property.

During the Edo period, a number of factors led to the publication of various documents about child rearing. Among the subjects considered were: political and social stability, economic development, the growing literacy rate, the advancement of printing techniques, and bureaucratic concern. It is to these documents that I shall now turn.

Materials for Analysis

In the middle of the seventeenth century, theories and methods of child rearing first became available to the public. It is interesting to note that various books on farming began to be published around this time as well, and illustrated books for children also made their debut. Although it is hard to estimate how extensively child rearing documents were circulated, several factors point to a wide readership. Compared to European countries, the Japanese rate of literacy was rather high; some of the books went through different printings, and the content of the books varied greatly.

More than sixty documents dealing with children were published during the next 2 centuries. Some of these stressed the value system of the warrior class; others were Confucian. Some books and articles were written by warriors, Confucians, or physicians; others by townspeople, peasants, local government officials, economists, and priests. Although almost all these documents had male authors, a few were composed by women.

Besides the documents exclusively about children other materials were reviewed. These included medical books, novels and poems, pictures, and ethnographic data. The results of a content analysis of all of the material is presented in the following sections.

Theory of the Child and the Child's Nature

Most Japanese writers of this period assumed, implicitly or explicity, that human nature was fundamentally good. This notion perhaps had its origin with the

Chinese Confucian Mencius (372–289 B.C.). According to Mencius, all evil in human beings is the result of events that corrupt the originally good nature of the child. A somewhat different role was assigned to experience by Zhu Xi (1130–1200), who contended it actualized the goodness inherent in children. This position was most explicitly stated by Kaibara (1710). He argued that every child was born with a potential for five virtues (humaneness, righteousness, decorum, wisdom, and sincerity) but that these qualities would remain unactualized without the assistance of learning. Kaibara suggested following the model of an idealized sage from ancient times; like such a man, people should perpetually feel a sense that their learning had not been accomplished.

Some writers of the Edo period commented on individual differences among children; they believed these variations to be innate. Most authors emphasized, however, that with a few, unusual exceptions, children were similar to one another in their innate moral character and intellectual abilities and that differences in these qualities could be attributed to environmental factors. (Were these views shared by the general populance? Perhaps not; this can be inferred from one writer's argument against a rival interpretation attributing a son's bad conduct to innate evilness.)

The emphasis on environmental factors to explain differences among children does not mean the Japanese saw them as passive beings in relation to their experiences. On the contrary, they viewed children as autonomously learning organisms. Kaibara believed they learned, especially through imitation, from the earliest period of life; the first learned habits would later become dominant. What these habits were was absolutely critical; it can be said that Japanese writers thought educational intervention necessary to keep the autonomously developing child on the course considered morally right from the standpoint of adult society.

As for writings on child rearing and education, these were concerned with three main problems: How should children, (a) with a certain nature, (b) be reared and educated, (c) toward specific goals? Naturally, arguments were presented to insure consistency among the three components. The writer generally introduced presuppositions about the child's nature, then, explicitly stated the goal of child rearing and education, and, finally, recommended the adoption of specific practices in accord with the work's major themes. We may infer that the writer's main point might be discovered in the recommendation of specific practices.

To effectively persuade readers to adopt a particular practice, the writer often contended that it would lead to the realization of specific goals. Theories about the nature of children were then invoked to support the recommended practice. In reality, I suspect that these theories were selected after the fact to support the pattern of the author's argument. Theories concerned with the children's nature, not only made the writer's argument more persuasive, but also helped parents attach meaning to specific child-rearing practices.

The Goals of Child Rearing and Education

Goals of development were different for each social class and gender. It is true that in a society where each member's status and roles were determined by class, gender, and ordinal position, the concrete goals of development differed, depending on the combination of these various factors. On a more abstract level, however, the goals had some common characteristics: many related to one or the other of the following two values.

First, writers emphasized the value of harmonious human relationships. Confucianism, which stressed ethical human relationships, seemed compatible with the long-held Japanese value of interpersonal harmony. Second, the writers emphasized the importance of knowing one's role, accepting one's place in society, and working hard at one's assigned task. This work ethic was not restricted to the warrior class. Yamana (1784), a peasant, tried to promote the dignity of his particular class by arguing that peasants, by actualizing their wisdom and virtues, could attain respect from other classes. Ishida Baigan (1685–1744), who formulated a practical philosophy for townsmen, insisted that economic activities were neither ignoble nor tainted as people had been led to believe. Ishida stated that making a profit in trade did not differ from working as a warrior. One of his pupils, Wakisaka (1803) wrote that a man's most important goal was the pursuit of his vocation and performance of his role both in the family and the society through the exercise of thrift, honesty, patience, and familial harmony.

So it seems that the value system generally based on Confucianism was strongly recommended in all classes. Yet whether this system pervaded people's thinking and directly determined their ordinary behavior in various social contexts is questionable.

Theory of Process and Method
of Child Rearing and Education

Before discussing various theories of the child, it should be explained to whom they were addressed. Advice on child rearing and education was addressed primarily to fathers and, then, only secondarily, to mothers. In the Edo period, fathers were expected to direct family policy on child rearing and education. As will be seen, this trend was reversed in the early Meiji period. However, even in the Edo period, the mother's strong influence on the child's personality development was recognized. Nakamura (1661) pointed out that even boys spent much time with mothers and were influenced deeply by them when young. He encouraged mothers to train children properly, keeping in mind their power to influence their offspring. Kaibara was more worried about the role of mothers; he was concerned that they tended to resort to temporizing measures and to overindulge children, thus spoiling them.

It was only after the Meiji Resotration (1868 to 1912) that the need for formal education of women was fully realized. The education of good wives and wise mothers, goals based on Japanized Confucian concepts (Hong, 1978), was promoted during the following decades. A the same time, fathers began gradually to turn over child training to mothers. Thus, mothers became trainers, as well as caregivers, of their children.

The basic approach to child training and education was to observe level of maturation and then assign age-appropriate tasks at this level. Though writers stressed the importance of early training, they did not necessarily imply it should begin at the earliest age possible. Rather, they felt training should begin when children were ready. This concept can be traced back to Liji ("Record of Rituals") compiled in China in the first century B.C. Thus, Yamaga (1663–1665) maintained that when training is premature, nothing is gained other than a great deal of work. Keep babies quiet, he urged, and do not stimulate them. Only after behavior emerges from inside can proper guidance begin.

In the welter of documents, it is hard not to admire the recommendations of the physician, Kazuki (1703), who warned against overprotection and overstimulation, emphasizing the importance of responsiveness by caregivers, especially with young infants. In his book on medical care and training for children, Kazuki wrote that 60 days after birth, the pupils of a baby's eyes are formed. As a consequence, the baby is able to recognize people and to smile and vocalize to them. Advising against overstimulation of the sensitive baby, Kazuki stressed mutual talking and vocalizing as a way of encouraging the development of speech and of freeing the baby from fear of strangers. Kazuki also recognized innate differences among children in their proneness to anxiety, expecially on encountering strangers.

Kazuki's writing was based on his clinical experience and descriptions obtained from Chinese medical books. One of the Chinese sources he often quoted was a book on health care by Wang Zhong-yang of the Yuan dynasty (thirteenth to fourteenth century). Wang believed that the age of 2 months marked the beginning of the sensitive period in infant development. Wang operated on a concept of milestones of infant development, which could be traced back to Qianjin Ya-ofang, by Sun Si-miao (compiled in the mid-seventh century). The phase Sun recognized, beginning at 60 days, with smiling and vocalization to people and ending at 360 days, with walking, is essentially the same as that understood by modern researchers and clinicians. Though Quianjin Yaofang is believed to have been brought to Japan at the end of the seventh century by a Japanese envoy to China, 1,000 years elapsed before Kazuki called general readers' attention to the importance of the caregiver's responsiveness to an infant's smiles and vocalization.

Early Japanese writers stressed the importance of both modeling and direct teaching. Kaibira (1710) noted that children did not distinguish between good and bad. Therefore, they imitated everything seen, making the proper selection of models—parents, wet and dry nurses, attendants, and friends—of utmost importance. Yamaga discussed the process now called identification. A young child who believed that his father was the richest, noblest, and most virtuous person in the world would begin to imitate him. Hence, Yamaga said, it was an error to ask a child to behave with restraint if the parents behaved differently.

The basic teaching strategy for older children accorded with the emphasis on observational learning (Hara & Wagatsuma, 1974). Adults did not teach a complex procedure analytically. Instead, they first brought children to, or allowed them to move freely about the place of work. The children were thus provided with opportunities for observation. At the appropriate time, adults demonstrated the performance of the whole task and then asked children to perform it by themselves. Unless the performance deviated greatly from the model, adults did not give corrections at this early stage, expecting isntead that the children would observe the model and learn gradually by themselves.

In later stages of learning, adults, began to give more specific instructions to enable children to attain the criterion of good performance. Still, the instructional method did not articulate behavior control, but stressed internal regulation through the learner's own understanding.

One basic characteristic of teaching in the pre-Meiji period was that no attempt was made to control learners' behavior externally. Instead, learners were encouraged to understand the whole procedure by modeling and expected to regulate their behavior. Chidlren were viewed as autonomously learning beings, very difficult to control completely from the outside. This concept was retained in another method of teaching, that is, direct teaching.

Many Japanese writers recommended mildness in the direct verbal teaching of children. They felt adults should admonish children in a firm but calm manner, and avoiding abusive language or the show of anger or impatience. Such behavior, it was felt, led children after the age of 10 or 11 to resent and, eventually, to disobey the urgings of authority. For the same reason, these writers refrained from recommending excessive praise. They feared it would make children arrogant and resentful of the older person's admonition, thus obstructing their development of abilities and wisdom. On the other hand, the townsman Wakisaka's advice (1803) about the training of a young child was more permissive. He felt the young child was not intellectually developed enough to understand the parents' motives and would come to fear them. For this reason, he recommended that good conduct be praised rather than corporal punishment threatened for misbehavior. The child who was praised would automatically want more praise and, therefore, would naturally move toward proper behavior.

In essence, these writers felt the training of children was not to be imposed, but should stem from the deepest reciprocal relationship between parent and child. The relationship between parent and child was seen as a transactional system.

Mencius wrote, "Between father and son there should be *qin*." *Qin* is a Chinese word meaning "kinlike closeness and affection." Quoting this sentence, Yamaga suggested a reason why Mencius did not use the word "love." Yamaga proposed that "love" was a one-way sentiment, implying favor and selfishness, which could lead to dislike. *Shin* (Japanese pronunciation of *qin*) was a much deeper sentiment, a product of prior interactions, containing, too, the quality of mutuality. The core of this sentiment is a humane, flexible, and considerate relationship between parent and child. Such a relationship was seen as the basic requirement for successful discipline; it was also the central goal of education, to be attained only by mutual accommodation of parent and child. Because of this perspective, the use of abusive language or the showing of anger and impatience by parents was discouraged. The child's resulting counteraggression inevitably established a vicious circle, jeopardizing the proper relationship between the two (Hayashi, 1786).

The foregoing does not mean, however, that overindulgence, or overpermissiveness, was advocated. Physicians and Confucians alike emphasized the need for proper care of infants and children, but, as indicated, counseled against overprotection. Chinese and Japanese medical books and Japanese ethnographic data, regarded young infants as sensitive and unstable beings. For example, loud noises and the presence of strangers around infants were to be avoided, but their exposure to mild noise was thought beneficial. There also existed an excessive fear of overprotecting, or spoiling, children. This could be accomplished by dressing them in thick clothes or through overfeeding, both of which were thought to make infants ill. Kaibara quoted an old Chinese saying, "Thirty percent of hunger and coldness makes a child healthy." With older children, exposure to mild deprivation and hardship was thought to express the parents' true consideration; later, as adults performing adult roles, this earlier experience would enable them to endure hardships. Moreover, as has been discussed, one educational goal was to enable the child to work hard to perform the assigned task faithfully. Therefore, writers considered it important to begin anticipatory socialization very early in the child's life.

The Role of Tradition in Child-Rearing Research

I have not, at this time, completed my analysis of Japanese child-rearing concepts after 1868. Nor have I yet constructed a solid methodology for ascertaining these aspects. However, there is a strong indication of continuity as well as of change within the belief-value system. The following attempts a conceptual analysis of the tradition of child rearing and its relation to developmental research.

Table 4.1
Three Meanings of Tradition in the Adult's View of the Child

		Past		Present
No Change		A A	$\rightarrow$	A
		B B		B
Change with Continuity	Continuity of Functions	A A′	$\rightarrow$	A″
		B B		B
	Continuity of Contents and Forms	A A	$\rightarrow$	A
		B B′		B″

Note: A: areas of contents and forms; B: areas of functions. The symbols ′ and ″ indicate change in each area.
Source: Kojima H. (1982).

The Concept of Tradition and Child-Rearing Research

My conceptual analysis of the adult's view of the child distinguishes three meanings of tradition: no change, change with continuity of functions, and change with continuity of contents and forms (Kojima, 1981) (see Table 4.1). However, another class, that of nontradition (emergence or extinction) should also be considered. Though the content and the form of the adult's view of the child can be distinguished from one other, they may be included in a class, when contrasted with adaptive functions of the adult's view of the child.

No Change.   When the content and the behavioral manifestations, as well as the adaptive function of the adult's view of the child are maintained across time, together, they represent a case of no change. Unless a given society maintains a stable system for transmission of modes of behavior and values from one generation to the next and the circumstances surrounding the society are stable, we cannot expect many aspects of the adult's view of the child to remain unchanged. But, as in the cult of *Jizo* ("a guardian deity of children"), which still flourishes in today's Japan, some beliefs may remain unchanged.

Change with Continuity of Functions.   When the content and behaviorial manifestations of the adult's view of the child change across time, but the adaptive function remains fundamentally unchanged, it represents a case of continuity of functions. If a portion of a society's middle class can sensitively discern the signs of the coming times and adjust their child-rearing practices in anticipation, both goals, and methods of child rearing, that is, content and form, may also change. Even so, child-rearing practices still will aim at enabling children of such parents to attain an advantageous position in society.

Change with Continuity of Content and Form.   This third category occurs when both the content and the behavioral manifestations of the adult's view of the child remain altered, but the adaptive function changes. For example, the belief that differences among children are derived from environmental rather than innate factors has remained basically unchanged for the past 300 years in Japan. In other words, there has been, continuity of content. Moreover, during the Edo period, children were encouraged not to deviate from the ideal of the subgroup to which they belonged. In contrast, today's very young children are trained to compete with each other in the hopes of attaining an advantageous position. In this instance, the social function of the environmentalist beliefs concerning the child's nature has changed.

However, we should be careful in speaking of change of functions. First, the adaptive function of a child-rearing practice at the time of its emergence may be different than at a later period. Second, the adaptive function of a child-rearing practice is not always reflected in the subjective meaning people attach to it. For example, the Russians and the French offer contrasting interpretations, based on each society's perception of the child, of the practice of swaddling (Mead, 1972). Similarly, the ritual of rice cakes on the first birthday has been interpreted quite differently in one district of Japan than in another (Ohtoh, 1969). It is unknown what the true adaptive function of these practices is or if, indeed, any exists. One thing does, however, seem to be probable, the subjective meaning attached by people to some practice may develop a degree of autonomy from its original adaptive function, and may eventually function in the way that is defined by the belief about the meaning of the practice.

The Role of Tradition

To show the usefulness of the historical viewpoint, I shall select three areas of research:

Cross-Cultural Research in Child Rearing

The viewpoint of tradition may be a useful method of interpreting the results of cross-cultural research in child rearing and development. The research by Caudill and his colleagues is an example of this approach. As I (Kojima, 1979) have pointed out, Caudill's view concerning Japanese and American mothers' conception of the infant changed radically between his two articles (Caudill & Weinstein, 1969; Caudill, 1973). In 1969, Caudill wrote: "In Japan, the infant is seen more as a separate biological organism who from the beginning, in order to develop, needs to be drawn into increasingly interdependent relations with others. In America, the infant is seen more as a dependent biological organism who in order to develop needs to be made increasingly independent of others" (p. 15). In his 1973 article, in describing the American mother's view of the child, Caudill used the words, "a potentially separate and autonomous being who should learn to do and think for himself" (p. 43). As for the Japanese mother, she "views her baby much more as an extension of herself, and psychological boundaries between the two of them are blurred" (p. 43).

I have tried to reconcile these two seemingly contradictory views, suggesting that they were coexisting aspects of the Japanese mothers' view of the baby and could be connected with the traditional conception (Kojima, 1979). I have also made an interpretation different from that of Caudill (1973) to explain part of his results. Why was the Japanese mother slower to respond to the infant's unhappy vocalization, than the American mother? Caudill wrote, ". . . for her, there is no need for hurry as the expectation is that she will devote herself to her child without any great concern for time away from him or even for time to be alone with her husband" (p. 43). According to my interpretation (Kojima, 1978, 1981), the Japanese mother listens with strained ears to the infant's fretting, expecting him or her to fall asleep again, for she believes it is very important for an infant to sleep soundly. Only after the baby begins to cry loudly will she sooth, thus making her a slow respondant to the infant's unhappy vocalization. This example indicates how the historical viewpoint may provide a different means of interpreting results of cross-cultural, child-rearing research.

Cross-Cultural Conflict and Assimilation in Child Rearing

What happens when one culture has contact with another culture and receives different ideas and new scientific information? Both on the individual and the group level, an inevitable interaction occurs between the traditional and the new. The process of cultural conflict and assimilation cannot be understood without consideration of a society's tradition. It is, therefore, useful to examine the kinds of foreign ideas and methods that were and were not incorporated into Japanese thought and practices, and, if incorporated, how they were modified.

To ascertain what the Japanese have assimilated about child rearing and education is easier than to discover what they have rejected. Kazuki was deeply influenced by Chinese medical and Confucian books and was eager to introduce new methods that seemed to be potentially effective. But this did not mean that he blindly accepted their complete theory and method. Attaching great importance to his own empirical testing, he reviewed the effectiveness of many of these methods himself, in the process, rejecting some that had never been practiced in Japan, and recommending in their stead, good traditional customs still in use. Kazuki also devoted much study to the question of why particular practices had continued from generation to generation in Japan. Another physician, Kuwata (1853), in the preface of his child-care book also took an eclectic position toward both Chinese and western theories and methods.

Kaibara's curriculum of age-related teaching was based on Chinese theories, too. However, he also based his advice on his own experience and on consideration of the actual circumstances of his readers.

This approach is carried on today, where books on child care are mostly framed by western theories and methods, but the advice in them takes into account what the authors believe is appropriate Japanese behavior. When these authors choose and reject theories and practices or modify them to make them suitable for their readers, they typically consider traditional concepts. Without such consideration, their advice would be ineffective. Because of the value assigned to traditional methods, readers, too, can influence the writer, for what is proposed by an author cannot merely be some theory, independent of the actual practices.

This combination of the old and the new is illustrated by the following recent Japanese newspaper advertisement: "Your newborn baby is cute and delightful! But his potentialities are astonishingly great. He grows on what he absorbs from his environment whether it is good or bad. His makings are vastly influenced by what he absorbs. If you treat him only with love now, you may well feel great repentance some day." This advertisement of educational materials for young children seems to me to successfully combine the traditional environmentalist view of the child (for example, Kaibara) and the findings of recent infant research. As such, it should prove very persuasive to the concerned Japanese parent.

Ecology of Human Development.

Many of the formal aspects of the conceptualization of environment by Bronfenbrenner (1979) are based on Lewinian field theory (Bronfenbrenner, 1977). For Lewin, the environment was a contemporary field of forces, agenetic and simultaneous in nature. Bronfenbrenner relates conceptions of Lewinian environment to the developmental process of an individual, stressing especially, the mutually regulating interactions between developing individuals and their environment. The changing pattern of interrelations between individuals and their environment are discussed as each changes through time within the macrosystem of a society.

Of course, it is possible to say that the past has been incorporated in the present, and we need only study the existing macrosystem. I believe, however, that by understanding the history of the macrosystem, its functions in a given society may be revealed more fully. In addition, this understanding may enable us to predict in a society the macrosystem that will provide the settings for future human development.

The Adult's View of the Child in Developmental Research

Past studies of interpersonal relations, including investigations of parent and child, dealt largely with dyadic relations (Kojima, 1980). Because of this focus, these studies ignored both the internal cognitive and affective factors of the persons involved and the contexts of interpersonal relations. In this sense, they were "studies on the relations of two black boxes in a vacuum."

Recently, I have focused attention on one aspect of what was missing in earlier discussions of mine—the adult's view of the child. This view represents a stable cognitive factor on the part of an adult who is interacting with a child. Figure 4-1 shows a schematic representation of the reciprocally influencing relations of the four classes of factors related to the adult's view of the child and child development. It illustrates that the adult's view of the child is partly a product of socialization. Throughout the formative period, the adult constructs

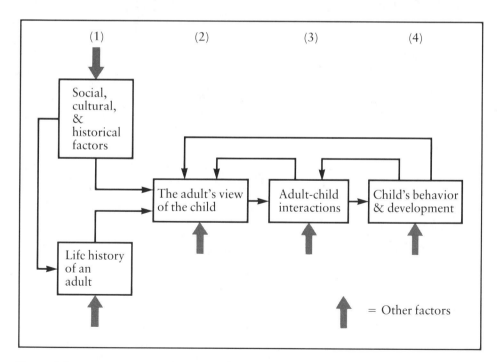

Figure 4-1
Schematic representation of the reciprocally influencing relations among factors related to the adult's view of the child (Kojima, H. [1982]).

a view of the child, adopting suitable beliefs and values from society and modifying them on the basis of personal experience. In this sense, traditional beliefs and values about child rearing and education in a given society may be traced in an individual adult. On the other hand, the child's experience of parent-child interactions also forms a part of his or her life history, and, thereby, becomes part of the process of socialization for parenthood of the next generation. In the long run, adults' experiences as children will influence their views of the child.

Individually, the adult's view of the child may influence adult-child interactions and vice versa. Also, the adult's view of the child is the outcome of a reciprocal relationship, with adult-child interactions working as a mediating factor.

The next step in our research is to select a specific aspect of child behavior and development, as some researchers have already done (McGillicuddy-de Lisi, 1982; McGillicuddy-de Lisi & Sigel, 1977; McGillicuddy-de Lisi, Sigel & Johnson, 1979) [factor 4 in Figure 4-1], and then to deal with reciprocally influencing relations among factors (2), (3), and (4), incorporating the historical viewpoint. Theories of the process of reciprocally influencing relations between adult-child interactions (3) and child behavior and development (4) are badly needed to promote this line of research.

REFERENCES

Bronfenbrenner, U. (1977). Lewinian space and ecological substance. *Journal of Social Issues, 33* (4), 199–212.

———. (1979). *The ecology of human development.* Cambridge, Mass.: Harvard University Press.

Caudill, W. (1973). Tiny dramas: Vocal communication between mother and infant in Japanese and American families. In W. Lebra (Ed.), *Mental health research in Asia and the Pacific* (Vol. 2, pp. 25–48. Honolulu: East-West Center.

Caudill, W., & Weinstein, H. (1969). Maternal care and infant behavior in Japan and America. *Psychiatry, 32,* 12–43.

Dore, R. P. (1965). *Education in Tokugawa Japan.* Berkeley, California: University of California Press.

Hara, H., & Wagatsuma, H. (1974). *Shitsuke* [Cultural background of child rearing in Japan]. Tokyo: Kobundo.

Hayashi, S. (1976). *Fukei-kun.* [Precepts for father and elder brother]. In M. Yamazumi & K. Nakae (Eds.), *Kosodate no sho* [Books on child rearing] (Vol. 2, pp. 58–59). Tokyo: Heibon-sha.

Hong, Zu-xian, (1978). *Juka kyoiku shiso no kenkyu* [Study of Confucian thought in education]. Tokyo: Koryo-sha.

Kaibara, E. (1976). *Wazoku doji-kun* [Precepts for teaching children as the Japanese custom]. In M. Yamazumi & K. Nakae (Eds.), *Kosodate no sho* [Books on child rearing] (Vol. 2, pp. 3–57). Tokyo: Heibon-sha. (Original work published 1710).

Kazuki, G. (1976). *Shoni hitsuyo sodategusa* [Handbook of child care and child rearing]. In M. Yamazumi & K. Nakae (Eds.), *Kosodate no sho*, [Books on child-rearing] (Vol. 1, pp. 287–366). Tokyo: Heibon-sha. (Original work published 1703)

Kojima, H. (1979). Lectures on psychology of parent-child relations, I & II. *Child Study, 33*, 938–955; 1126–143. (In Japanese)

———. (1980). Japanese research in parent-child relations and family. In *Publication Committee on History and Perspectives*, JAEP 20th Convention (Ed.), Symposia on educational psychology (pp. 195–214). Tokyo: Kawashima Shoten. (In Japanese)

———. (1981). Psychological approaches to personality development. In Y. Isogai (Ed.), *The world of educational psychology* (pp. 89–112). Tokyo: Fukumura Shuppan. (In Japanese)

———. (1982). Studies on the adult's view of the child and his development. In T. Saigusa & O. Tabata (Eds.), *Views of the child and education in contemporary time* (pp. 4–41). Tokyo: Fukumura Shuppan. (In Japanese).

Kuwata, R. (1853). *Aiiku Chadan* [On child care]. Edo: K. Okadaya.

McGillicuddy-de Lisi, A. V. (1982). Parental beliefs about developmental processes. *Human Development, 25*, 192–200.

———, & Sigel, I. E. (1977). The effects of spacing and birth order on problem solving competence of preschool children. *Progress Report, Grant RO1 H10686-01, NICHD.* Princeton, N. J.: Educational Testing Services.

———, Sigel, I. E., & Johnson, J. E. (1979). The family as a system of mutual influence: parental beliefs, distancing behaviors and children's representational thinking. In M. Lewis & L. A. Rosenblum (Eds.), *The child and his family* (pp. 91–106). New York: Plenum Press.

Mead, M. (1972, January). A new understanding of childhood. *Redbook*, pp. 49, 54.

Nakamura, T. *Hime kigami*, Book 1. [Precepts for women]. In M. Yamazumi & K. Nakae (Eds.), *Kosodate no sho* [Books on child rearing] (Vol. 1, pp. 177–202). Tokyo: Heibon-sha. (Original published c. 1661)

Ohtoh, Y. (1969). *Koyarai* [Child rearing] (2nd ed.). Tokyo: Iwasaki Bijutsu-sha.

Oishi, S. (1973). *Kindai izen no kazoku: Nippon, kinsei* [Family in the modern feudal Japan]. In M. Aoyama et al., (Eds.), *Kazoku* [Family] (Vol. 1, pp. 76–96). Tokyo: Kobundo. (In Japanese).

Sun, Si-miao. (1974). *Qianjin Yaofang*. Tokyo: Senkin Yoho Kanko-kai. (Original work written in Tang dynasty) (In Chinese)

Wakisaka, G. (1976). *Sodate-gusa* [Child rearing and education]. In M. Yamazumi & K.

Nakae (Eds.), *Kosodate no sho* [Books on child rearing] (Vol. 2, pp. 267–302). Tokyo: Heibon-sha. (Original work published 1803).

Wang, Zhong-yang. *Taiding Yangsheng Zhulun.* (Original work published in the Yuan dynasty)

Yamaga, S. (1976). *Fushi-do* [Precepts for father and son]. In *Yamaga Gorui* [The analects of Yamaga Soko]. In M. Yamazumi & K. Nakae (Eds.), *Kosodate no sho* [Books on child rearing] (Vol. 1, pp. 138–174). Tokyo: Heibon-sha. (Original work published ca. 1663–65)

Yamana, B. (1976). *Noka-kun* [Precepts for the peasants] In M. Yamazumi & K. Nakae (Eds.), *Kosodate no sho* [Books on child rearing] (Vol. 2, pp. 204–222). Tokyo: Heibon-sha. (Original work published 1784)

What Is an *Ii Ko* (Good Child)?

Merry I. White
Robert A. LeVine

An increasing part of psychological research is being done by psychologists of diverse cultural backgrounds whose personal knowledge of their particular languages and cultures make them unlikely to commit the kinds of errors that have often marred cross-cultural research performed exclusively by western researchers in nonwestern settings. Even so, there is still no universal vocabulary to describe interpersonal behavior or mental capacities and their acquisition. In constructing concepts to describe and investigate development, investigators rely on words used in ordinary language to which they give a more precise specification. These words are not only derived from a lexicon with many vernacular connotations, but also carry with them a set of categories based on certain philosophical or folk premises. At this level of analysis, psychologists are operating within the conceptual framework of their own cultures, and the importation of concepts across cultural boundaries is problematic.

The idea of numerous culture-specific psychologies may at first sight represent defeat to many who seek a universal understanding of social development. We propose, however, that a firmer basis for comparative analysis and, ultimately, for universal generalizations, can be derived from culture-specific understanding. Thus, by examining how Japanese parents, teachers, and children categorize the means and ends of child development—including how they put together what our categories take apart and vice versa—we may achieve a clarification, not only relevant to Japan, but to more general questions of how children are and can be socialized. We may then be able to construct more adequate categories for cross-cultural research, categories grounded in at least two cultures and perhaps applicable elsewhere. We shall present here several examples of Japanese concepts that differ from western ones and can be used as starting points for cross-cultural clarification. Our approach follows the example of Doi (1981), who showed that the concept of *amae* ("dependence") more adequately describes Japanese expectancies in several social situations—such as those defined by mother-child and patient-therapist relationships—than the psychoanalytic concept of transference in its classical Freudian definition. Doi also argued that *amae* may have some usefulness as a category for cross-cultural understanding of interpersonal expectancies in countries other than Japan. With this suggestion, he opened up the possibility of a clinical psychiatry not exclusively western in its conceptual apparatus, but striving for transcultural validity from a base in two cultures. Beginning with cultural *mis*understanding and the resistance of concepts to translation, Doi moved toward what Werner and Campbell (1970) have called a "de-centered" position that transcends the limited perspectives of "source" and "target" languages alike.

We call particular attention to Japan terminology concerning the goals of child development and valued means for achieving these goals. In presenting them we do not intend, nor are we able, to give a full semantic or ethnopsychological interpretation—a task we must leave to our Japanese colleagues. Our purpose is simply to stimulate discussion about the conceptual framework and assumptions implied by these terms and how they would be dealt with in comparative research.

Following several recent studies of early childhood education in Japan, including those of Shigaki (1983) and Lewis (1984), as well as many reports and studies treating the relationship of mother and child in a cross-cultural perspective, we note that terms relating to children's development in Japan have been clustered into two groups: terms referring to social embeddedness and terms describing performance qualities in the child. The clustering itself is of interest in considering cultural assumptions about child development, and in it we may discover a western bias. First, what is significant is that, in Japan, all valued qualities have a moral weight: personal performance is seen not only as evidence of *individual* ability, contributing to an identity demonstrated by skills. It is also a way of cementing one's place in the social environment because it provides evidence of moral character and appropriateness to the milieu. Second, the most highly valued qualities make a child *ningen-rashii*, or "human-like" (Shigaki, p. 15), that is, able to maintain harmony in human relationships. Performance qualities are important but are only the visible demonstrations of deeper abilities to be a good (social) person. By contrast, Americans tend to give priority to highly individualized skills and qualities, such as independence, and to see social abilities as more superficial, or as *means* rather than *ends*. This contrast will be pursued in our consideration of the particular virtues designated by the terms we shall examine.

All valued traits and abilities cited in Shigaki and Lewis were seen by them as related to one's connectedness in human relationships. A further distinction should be made between wished-for qualities and skills and characteristics seen as needed in the process of attaining those goals.

The first group of terms, relating to goals for children's growth, add up to a description of an *ii ko* ("a good child"). Usually included in the list are words such as *otonashii* ("mild," "gentle"), *sunao* ("compliant," "obedient," "cooperative"), *akarui* ("bright eyed"), *genki* ("active," "spirited," "energetic"), *hakihaki* ("brisk," "prompt," "clear") and *oriko* ("obedient," "smart"). Such words describe valued qualities that may be produced in a child through appropriate socialization.

The second group of terms describe qualities viewed as helpful in a child's personal and social development. They imply a pedagogical theory and/or describe the active teaching relationship through which the development theory is implemented. These words include *gambaru* ("persist"), *gaman suru* ("endure hardship"), *hansei suru* ("reflect on one's weakness"), *amaeru/amayakasu* ("depend/indulge"), *wakaraseru* ("get the child to understand"), and *rikai-saseru* ("get the child to understand logically"). The terms involve strategies in nurturant and didactive relationships with children that overlap western categories of affective, cognitive, and conative development. A glance at them immediately suggests the existence of markedly different conceptions than western ones regarding the proper training of children—conceptions involving strategies that we have loosely translated as "indulgence" and "patience" toward ends which have been commonly mistranslated as "obedience" and "submission."

In Japanese child development theory, no conflict exists between goals of self-fulfillment and goals of social integration. The two goals are bridged by the type of socialization encouraged in the relationship between mother and child. This relationship is consistent with Japanese ideas of nurturance and "indulgence," and yet always refers to the standards of the larger social unit. Although a mother is expected to recognize and to be sensitive to her child's personality and inclinations, the characterization by or encouragement of individualistic traits is not emphasized. Realizing that a child is spirited and self-willed means also knowing what strategy to use to get him or her to cooperate—it does not mean reinforcing or valuing these qualities in themselves.

The mother's job is to prepare her children for life and to provide a bridge between the home and other environments. She achieves these goals by identifying the children's qualities and by progressively exposing them to the values of social and institutional settings. Throughout the process the mother is alert to the norms of good mothering as reinforced by *seken*, "the measuring community"—neighbors, kin, teachers—whoever will notice her own and her children's abilities and behavior. *Seken* is not something to which you belong, like a family or a school or a workplace; it is a watchful normative presence, the equivalent of "what will the neighbors say?" All valued qualities, either personal or social, are important to *seken*, not just those that explicitly help to bond relationships. Ultimately, all valued qualities are relevant to one's place in the social nexus.

Attending to children's predilections and qualities, socializing them to the values of society while enhancing their abilities and performances, as well as maintaining the proper profile of mothering in the *seken*, are time-consuming tasks that contribute to the cultural definition of mothering as a full-time job. The mother, too, is measured as the *seken* (teachers or examinations) measure her child, and the goal of nurturant development involves her own success as well as that of her children. Her investment in her children, therefore, is an investment in herself.

An analysis of the terms we have selected shows that the line cannot easily be drawn between social and personal qualities or abilities. While this blurring of concepts may appear vague to a westerner, it indicates a wider integration of self and society, permitting highly nurturant indulgence in the mother-child relationship, not only congruent with social discipline and order, but actually contributing to it.

First, let us look at the word *sunao*, frequently translated as "obedient." It would be more appropriate to approach its usage through a cluster of meanings attached to it by mothers and teachers—"open minded," "nonresistant," "truthful," or, as Kumagai (1981, p. 261) says, "authentic in intent and cooperative in spirit." Murase as cited in Kumagai (1974, p. 440), states that "*Sunao* is almost impossible to translate into English. It contains such implications as naturalness, naiveté, straightforwardness, simplicity, frankness, open mindedness, mildness or gentleness and compliance. . . ." One Japanese mother noted the range of meanings for *sunao* available to her by saying, "It means obedient if I see my child as bad; it means autonomous if he is good." She added that most mothers see their children as naturally good, needing only proper treatment to grow up "straight." Kumagai also points out that the English translation "obedience" implies subordination and lack of self-determination and says that *sunao* "assumes cooperation to be an act of affirmation of the self" (p. 261). (Here, Kumagai has converted obedience/compliance to the more Japanese meaning of cooperation which is closer to *sunao*.)

A child is *sunao* has not yielded his or her personal autonomy for the sake of cooperation; cooperation does not suggest giving up the self, as it may in the West; it implies that working with others is the appropriate way of expressing and enhancing the self. Engagement and harmony with others is, then, a positively valued goal and the bridge—to open-hearted cooperation, as in *sunao*—is through sensitivity, reiterated by the mother's example and encouragement.

Another term, related to *sunao*, is, by its seemingly contradictory nature, equally difficult to translate and to understand in the context of western child rearing. This term is *yutaka*, meaning "empathic," "receptive," or "open hearted." Sensitivity and anticipation of the needs of others sound passive and feminine to western ears, but appearances are deceptive, *yutaka* has a very positive, active connotation and suggests a mature vigor. It is hearty and confident, implying both abundant receiving and giving, an enjoyment of life in a social context. Other translations include "having common sense in one's dealing with others" and "being fertile and abundant." It is interesting to note that *yutaka* has recently appeared in official recommendations for educational reform; it is hoped that by liberalizing education, while maintaining the importance of traditional social morality, Japan can produce children with *yutaka na kokoro* ("confident, sensitive hearts"). Like *sunao*, this quality is seen to be encouraged not only by mothers but through schooling as well.

How one achieves a *sunao* child with a *yutaka na kokoro* involves the technique of *wakaraseru* ("getting the child to understand"). As Vogel (1963) and Lanham (1956) have described the processs of *wakaraseru*, or the engaging of the child in the goals the mother has set, the chief principle seems to be *never go against the child.* Where an American might view this manipulation of the child through indulgence as preventing the development of a strong self-will; the Japanese mother sees long-term benefits of self-motivated cooperation and real commitment from her strategy of keeping the child happy and engaged.

A western observer sees a paradox between the use of *amayakasu* ("to indulge") as a technique of socialization and the goal of producing a child committed to and positively engaged in disciplined effort. There may, however, be no contradiction between the device of "indulgence" and the goal of "effort" in Japanese child rearing. Taniuchi (1982) describes a process in which intimacy and supportive attention to a child are used by the mother to teach the child social standards and the need to work hard to achieve and be valued in society. Other investigators (Conroy et al. 1980) cite "Love-oriented" techniques, rather than "power-assertive" methods in disciplining children.

Western beliefs that sparing the rod spoils the child obviously assume that discipline is good not only for the immediate correction of a fault or misdeed, but in the long run as well. "I'm only doing this because I love you" does not need to be said in Japan, although there *is* a similar underlying notion that a child benefits from experiencing hardship. *Kurō saseta hō gaii* ("It's better to make [the child] endure difficulties") is a very common expression. *Kurō* ("suffering or hardship") is said to have a beneficial effect on the self, deepening and maturing it and removing much of its self-centeredness. Without *kurō*, a person cannot be said to have matured. *Kurō* can be psychological, physical, or environmental, and although small children should be protected from it, the *kurō* of intensive study, or the whole-hearted application of energies at the expense of pleasures, is said to be good for the older child. The saying, "Pass with four, fail with five," meaning that if you sleep as much as 5 hours a night you are not studying hard enough, is now prevalent among junior high schoolers. In any case, *kurō* would not result from parental discipline, as in America, but from situations in the wider environment; parents are there to support and aid the child against hardships (Vogel, 1963).

An interesting aspect of Japanese self-discipline, encouraged in school and indeed throughout life, is *hansei*, or "self-examination and reflection." *Hansei* is both personal and social: children are encouraged to *hansei* and look for their own weak points; it is far more preferable to discover these themselves than to have others point them out. Indeed, the cultural avoidance of criticism of others makes *hansei* even more important. When a whole class *hansei*s together, it first examines its relationships, its motivations, the dynamics of its interactions, and its goals and methods. Then the class develops a plan of action to change. Change and reform are implied: *hansei* is oriented toward improvement.

In *hansei*, as in other modes of active socialization, *engagement* is a key to success. As we have seen, the development of valued abilities and qualities in the child implies active participation and whole-hearted commitment to the goals shared by parents and teachers. Engagement is demonstrated by the tone and mode of performances of tasks. The following words describe the evidence of a positive commitment through the style of action.

Hakihaki describes an interesting cluster of desired qualities: "brisk," "active," "quick," and "clear." It also implies that the child can speak forthrightly; it is usually used to describe boys, or in a slightly more negative sense, girls. Other terms are related to it; *tekipaki* ("brisk and positive") and *kichinto* ("accurate and punctilious"), among others. These words describe a child (or adult) confident and engaged in an endeavor. The style of working indicates effective commitment and is considered almost as important as the product of the performance. A crisp, upbeat, cheerful demeanor is highly valued. *Hakihaki*, when simply translated as "brisk" or "active," seems to western ears rather superficial; it conveys neither the Japanese sense of the engagement of the child nor the deeper significance accorded to the style of performance. How this affective engagement, as well as the incentive to achieve and conform to external expectations, is encouraged in the context of an "indulgent" relationship is a topic that needs greater attention.

Translating the terms we have briefly reviewed in an effort to expose more fully the ends and means of child learning and development in Japan would require the multiple-iteration procedure suggested by Werner and Campbell (1970). Included in the multiple paraphrases of each term would be the situational specifications Japanese parents and teachers take for granted when they use it. From the translation exercise could come an understanding of the category system the Japanese use to approach the process of child development. This system differs from the western system of categories in the ways in which cognitive and affect are conceptually packaged and, undoubtedly, in other ways as well. Another developmental agenda is suggested. To recognize differences of this sort is not to conclude that comparability in concepts is unattainable; the best road to comparability runs through the forest of ethnopsychological investigation.

Implications for Education

In this chapter we have focused on the issue of translatability of Japanese terms relevant to child rearing. There are also some interesting points to be made beyond clearly demonstrating the need for greater sensitivity and attention to context in the comparison of terms related to cultural modes and goals of development.

These points reveal differences between Japanese and western definitions and perceptions of the child. They also highlight contexts for the child's development. And all of these express the larger societal contrasts.

First, it is evident that little difference exists in Japan between parents' and teachers' goals for the child. Although the homogeneity of attitudes and beliefs may be overestimated in the literature, Japanese society gives evidence of far greater congruity and agreement in this matter across the population than does American society. Moreover, as Shigaki notes, Japanese society and family have shown great stability over time and great continuity in ideology and values; thus, the terms we have examined are widely understood to be central to children's development.

Second, in Japan, there is less conflict or contradiction between the development and training of the individual's character and abilities and socialization to the group and to society's institutions than is exhibited in western ideology and practice. The congruence between goals for intrapersonal, and interpersonal development in Japan highlights the divergence between our goals for the child and our goals for society. Rohlen (p. 314) has said that "our individualism is an attempt to deny social structure itself." Clearly, Japanese goals for the child can more easily be achieved in the setting of the school than can ours. It might even be said that our ideologies advocate goals inconsistent with what we can actually expect of children. In other words, our goals and ideologies are in conflict with the realities of children's development, regardless of the cultural setting. Moreover, in the United States, the institution of the school has not provided an environment in which our ideologies of child development and the actual qualities valued in the child can be inculcated.

References

Conroy, M.; Hess, R. D.; Azuma, H.; & Kashiwagi, K. (1980). Maternal strategies for regulating children's behavior. *Journal of Cross-Cultural Psychology, 11,* 153–172.

Doi, T. (1981). *The anatomy of dependence.* Rev. ed. Tokyo: Kodansha International.

Kumagai, H. A. (1981). A dissection of intimacy: A study of 'bipolar posturing' in Japanese social interaction—*amaeru* and *amayakasu,* indulgence and deference. *Culture, Medicine, and Psychiatry, 5,* 249–272.

Lanham, B. (1956). Aspects of child care in Japan: Preliminary report. In *Personal character and cultural milieu,* edited by D. G. Haring. Syracuse NY: Syracuse University Press.

Lewis, C. (1984). Cooperation and control in Japanese nursery schools. *Comparative Education Review, 28,* 69–84.

Rohlen, T. P. (1983). *Japan's high schools.* Berkeley: University of California Press.

Shigaki, I. (1983). Child care practices in Japan and the United States: How do they reflect cultural values in young children? *Young Children, 38,* no. 4, 13–24.

Taniuchi, L. (1982). The psychological transition from home to school and the development of Japanese children's attitudes toward learning. Unpublished manuscript, Harvard Graduate School of Education.

Vogel, E. F. (1963). *Japan's new middle class.* Berkeley: University of California Press.

Werner, O., & Campbell, D. T. (1970). Translating, working through interpreters and the problem of decentering. In *A handbook of method in cultural anthropology,* edited by R. Narole and R. Cohen. New York: Natural History Press.

6 | Privatization of Family Life in Japan

Kiyomi Morioka

Introduction

In the 40 years since the end of World War II, the Japanese family has undergone tremendous changes. Frequent discussions of the decay or breakdown of the *ie* "the traditional household pattern of the Japanese" have attempted to summarize these changes. My purpose in this paper is to examine them from a fresh perspective, that of privatization.

The terms *individuation* and *privatization* both refer to a tendency to attach greater importance, not to the objectives and values of a group, but to those of smaller units within it. Individuation implies the increasing independence of smaller units centering on instrumental values, whereas privatization stresses the increasingly secured privacy of a unit, especially its consummatory values. These two trends are closely interrelated, but they do not necessarily proceed at the same rate along a parallel course. Thus, privatization may lag behind individuation. Although a clear distinction must always be maintained between the two concepts, any discussion of privatization entails an occasional reference to aspects of individuation.

Omote versus *Oku*

The *ie* was the predominant, as well as the ideal, household pattern in prewar Japan. Two major characteristics of the prewar *ie* were that the household was supported by a family enterprise, maintained on the basis of the property which belonged to it, and that a successor to the headship of the *ie* stayed with his parents even after marriage, thereby forming a single household. By its existence, household enterprise brought about the differentiation between *omote* ("front") and *oku* ("interior").[1] The *oku* was the private sphere of family life. The *omote*, the arena where enterprise activities took place, formed the sphere of family life open to society. This differentiation between public and private was clearest when the enterprises associated with a household were of considerable size. However, it could also be found in small-scale households, where the *omote* manifested itself in and around the entrance and the *oku* in and around the *nando* ("bedroom")—at least, during sleeping hours.

The marked decrease in the ratio of self-employed workers and the accompanying increase in those working for wages during the past half a century have created on a larger scale a spatial separation of residence and work place, which has consequently cut the *omote* sphere off from *ie* life, where *oku* and *omote* once were united.[2] This separation has occurred even among small business owners and has resulted in a shift of the *omote* sphere from inside to outside the home.

The *ie* as a multifunctional institution depended on a network of mutual aid among neighbors; this network expanded the communal aspects of the *omote* sphere. The differentiation of social institutions, which greatly lessened family dependence on neighborhood aid systems, also contributed to the disappearance of *omote*.

To a young wife, the household headed by her coresident father-in-law was a workplace rather than a home (Sakurada, 1982). For this reason, adult members recognized that a semi-*omote* character prevailed in the private sphere of family life. With the loss of support for the ideal of the multigenerational household, however, this semi-*omote* character has also disappeared from the household, and only the *oku* sphere has remained and expanded.

The *ie* changed decisively when it lost its own enterprise, and when the norm of coresidence, which made lineal succession possible, decayed. A family that has lost these *ie* characteristics has frequently been called a modern family, but I prefer calling it a Japanese conjugal family, paying special attention to the quality of its personal relations.[3] In such a family, the public sphere of life no longer exists; there is only activity in the private sphere. Keigo Okonogi, a respected psychiatrist, refers to the same phenomenon when he says the contemporary Japanese family has lost its social consciousness; and the image of home today representing the world of affectivity of the small nuclear family but nothing social beyond it (1981). What Okonogi really is describing is privatization.

Transformation since the Edo Period

The privatization of the family first became apparent after the Second World War, but it can be traced back to changes in the *ie* since the Edo period (1600 to 1867).

Japanese society in the Edo period was patterned after the *ie* system. The *ie* was not only the basic unit of social structure, but it also functioned as the guiding principle of social organization. *Ie* were tied to each other by the hierarchical relations of head and subordinate, main and branch household, or by the quasi-familial relation of *oya* ("parent") and *ko* ("adoptive child"). A large *ie* comprised a number of smaller, subordinate *ie*. Such an *ie* was active in political, religious, and artistic as well as economic spheres. Consequently, it displayed a strong public character combined with its private function.

The political sphere will serve as an example of how the *ie* worked. The Tokugawa Shogunate was composed of the Tokugawa family, which held the central power, and hereditary local *daimyos* ("feudal lords"), who governed the people in their fiefs under the indirect control of the *Shogun*. Some *daimyos* were the heads of branch, or subordinate, households of the Tokugawa family; others were the *Shogun's* "adoptive" children, or *kobun*. The ritual marking the official formation of the adoptive tie took place during the rite celebrating the coming of age of a daimyo's heir. Among the *Kobuns* of the *Shogun* were such powerful families as the Maeda, the Shimazu, and the Date. Formerly rivals of the To-kugawa, they had become its subjects after being defeated either politically or in battle. The Tokugawa family, then, in the broadest sense, was the primary *ie*, with hundreds of *daimyo* and thousands of *hatamoto* ("retainers") under its direct control. Each *daimyo* family was itself a secondary *ie*, containing hundreds or thousands of retainers' families.

Thus, the texture of the political world in the Edo period was a huge network of households connected hierarchically with each other. The Tokugawa family, as defined in the narrower sense, lived in the Edo castle, which was divided into two sections, *ooku*, or great *oku*, consisting of the *Shogun's* private sphere of life, and *omote*, the governmental offices.

This huge *ie*, spreading over the whole society of feudal Japan, was broken up after the Meiji Restoration through a series of political reforms. Still, the *ie* remained the basic unit of Japanese social structure. In local neighborhoods and communities, small *ie* were connected with each other by the ties of main and branch houses, or that of *oya* and *ko*. But now each network of connecting *ie* covered only a tiny portion of the society in terms of area and social class. In place of a centralized *ie*, modern bureacratic organizations developed into systems which penetrated the entire society. This new, rational principle of social organization naturally aroused resistance from people accustomed to the traditional way of life. To smooth the transition between the old and new, the affective relation of *oya* and *ko* was adopted in interpreting the boss-subordinate relationship.

Managerial paternalism, a family-state ideology, and the idea of the barracks as a soldier's home, only began to be advocated explicitly in the early twentieth century, when the national government took action to reorganize traditional *gemeinschaftlich* bodies that were on the brink of ruin under the impact of the developing capitalistic economy. A barrack was described as an *ie*, with the troop commander as father (Oh'e, 1982); a company or a factory as an *ie*, with the president or the manager as father; and Japan itself as a large family, with the emperor as father. In the context of the history of the *ie*, it is understandable that an analogy of parental relations was used to strengthen the bureaucratic organization. The father-son relation, which had a kind of public nature that did not exist in the mother-child relation was thought particularly useful for this purpose.

After the Second World War, family relations ceased to be the model for social organization, even in the ideal sense. The family became a totally private matter. This trend occurred simultaneously with the breakdown of the *ie* and the emergence of the Japanese conjugal family.

Aspects of Privatization

Privatization is manifest in various aspects of family life.

Legal and Political Aspects.   The Residents Registration Act of 1951 and the Farm Land Act of 1952 presupposed the household as a unit of registration for farming and granted official status to the household head or the cultivator of the farm. In contrast, the current Residents Basic Register Act, formulated in 1967, ordered municipalities to prepare resident cards for individuals and to arrange them according to household, thus paving the way for the government to deal with individuals directly. At present, the family, or the household composed of relatives, is without legal status. It is merely a private group. In this instance, then, privatization has advanced parallel with individuation.

Mate-Selection Aspect.   The major pattern of mate selection shifted in the 1960s from that of *miai* ("arranged") marriages to love matches. This first became apparent in a 1972 opinion poll on women, conducted by the Prime Minister's Office and a 1977 poll on the Japanese married couple, conducted by NKH (Morioka & Mochizuki, 1983).[4] From the results of these polls, it would be an oversimplification to state that there has been a shift in the overall pattern from one form of marriage to the other. Both patterns coexist and function interdependently. Nevertheless, from a macrocosmic point of view, love matches, looked down upon socially in prewar days, became acceptable afterwards and finally gained even greater popularity than "respectable" arranged marriages. This shift suggests a widespread acceptance of the idea that mate selection is basically the private concern of the persons involved. In this context representatives of the public interest are parents, close kin, and concerned others. The trend away from their involvement is one aspect of the privatization of marriage.

Structural Aspect.   A trend toward the small, nuclear-family household has become marked since the war, especially since 1955. According to the national censuses of Japan, the average size of an ordinary household, composed of two or more persons, remained at a level of 5.1 to 5.2 persons for the 35 years from 1920 through 1955. In contrast, the census recorded an extremely rapid decrease in the average size of this type of household, from 5.1 persons to 3.8 persons, during the 20 years between 1955 and 1975. The plateau in the earlier part of the century contradicts the proposition that the size of the family becomes smaller with the progress of industrialization (Greenfield, 1961), but the proposition proves valid for the period from 1920 to the present. The ratios of the number of nuclear-family households to the total number of households composed of relatives remained stable for many years after 1920 (59 percent) but increased remarkably during the 20-year period from 1960 (64 percent) to 1980 (75 percent). The rapid shrinkage of family size was thus accompanied by a nuclearization of family form. This suggests that the contraction was caused, not only by a decrease in the number of coresident children, but also by a corresponding decrease in the number of coresident close kin other than children. The latter factor is closely related to privatization.

The present-day generational coresidence differs greatly from that of former days. The prewar coresidence was a virtually complete sharing of the household by two couples from the same family line. In striking contrast, the contemporary coresidence has an element of separation between generations. The major forms of separation are spatial (bedroom and/or living room reserved for the exclusive use of parents or younger couple) and financing (establishing an independent source of income for the exclusive disposal of each pair). Of course, the extent of separation varies depending on the conditions of coresidents. In recent years, the so-called two-household residence has attracted popular attention. Its very name implies a separation of activities between generations. A partial separation in coresidence effectively provides for the privacy of each couple. This phenomenon, therefore, confirms the ongoing trend toward privatization, despite an estimated decrease in the future nuclear family ratio to the total number of households composed of relatives.[5]

The Functional Aspect.   It has been suggested that a shift in dominant function has occurred in the Japanese family, from the family centered around economic stability in prewar days to the contemporary affection-centered family (Morioka, 1977). This suggestion is supported by the findings of a study on family function, which was conducted twice, in 1969 and in 1972. Of the four functions contained in the survey—rest and relaxation, consumer life, rearing of children, and the conjugal life of the couple—the first mentioned was most popular, gaining even greater popularity in the second survey, where nearly 50 percent of the respondents deemed it the most important part of family life (Nihon Chiiki Kaihatsu Center, 1970). The increased value attached to the function of rest and relaxation relfects a trend of privatization in family life.

Around 1950, the divorce rate in Japan began to decline. During the first half of the 1960s, however, this trend reversed itself, and the present specific divorce rate is 4.5 per million. The recent increase may be attributed partly to the rising earning capacity of married women and to the public financial aid given to fatherless households. Another partial explanation for this increase is the greater significance of affectivity in contemporary family life, in other words, the privatization of family functions.[6]

Religious Aspects.   Privatization can be recognized in ancestor cults as well. The cult of the ancestors was functionally related to the continuation of the *ie*; it was not only a result, but also an objective, of the *ie* continuity. Consequently, it is reasonable to expect the decay of the *ie* would be reflected in a similar decline of ancestor cults. If we use the ratio of households with Buddhist altars as an index of the practice of ancestor cults in the home, we can prove a trend toward decay. According to a survey I conducted in Shizuoka City in 1982, only 56 percent of households with middle-aged heads were equipped with Buddhist altars, although 85 percent of the respondents recalled their presence in parental homes when they were young (Morioka, 1985). In a nation-wide opinion poll conducted in 1981 by the Asahi Press, 70 percent of the middle-aged informants and 63 percent of the total interviewees responded affirmatively to the same question (Asahi Press, 1981). Roughly speaking, then, nearly 90 percent of prewar households were equipped with Buddhist altars; the ratio today is about 60 percent.

Despite the alleged decay of the *ie*, however, the present ratio is higher than expected. Here we can see one manifestation of the latent change in the quality of ancestor cults.

First, a cult for bilateral ancestors has emerged in the decline of the rites for the lineal ancestors of the *ie*. Although the cult for remote ancestors, with whom the contemporary descendants had no personal contact, is on the decline, the rites for close ancestors of both the husband and wife tend to be maintained in warm, personal memory. This represents a change in the object of the cult.

The function of the cult has also altered. Formerly, when memorial rites were performed in honor of the lineal ancestors of the *ie*, semipublic functions dominated, such as those designed to justify the social status of the *ie*, to provide motivation for hard work, and to strengthen clan solidarity. In contrast, the central function of ancestral rites today is private; they serve as a chance for the attendants to recall and have spiritual contact with close relatives who have died. This shift in dominant function also reveals the trend toward privatization.

The ratio of household Buddhist altars tends to rise with an advance in age of the oldest generation in the household. When the member of the oldest generation is a widow, the ratio is especially high. This suggests that widows desire to install household Buddhist altars to keep in daily contact with their dead husbands through rites performed before the altar (Takahashi, 1975). It also suggests that the ratio of household Buddhist altar installation is as high as it is because of the increasingly private function of the rites.

A trend toward privatization is thus evident in various aspects of family life. In the 1960s it became the vogue to express the nature of the contemporary family with the term *mai hōmu shugi*, coined by combining English ("my home") and Japanese (*shugi* = *ism*). The term denotes the behavioral characteristics of today's young urban families, who, in concentrating on the pursuit of personal happiness, leave little time for social concerns and for contacts with relatives and neighbors. Though *mai hōmu shugi* is now used infrequently, privatization has advanced even further since the 1960s.

Door-to-door interviewing has been conducted frequently, and it has contributed greatly toward the advancement of sociological inquiries in postwar Japan. For some time, however, interviewers have complained of the targeted interviewee's frequent refusal to be interviewed. As a result, the national censuses of Japan, once well known for exactness and thoroughness, has suffered from a decline in the accuracy of information. The refusal to be interviewed or the neglect of one's duty to respond to the national census conscientiously is due partly to an increasing consciousness of human rights and, partly, perhaps to a sharpened sense of privacy.

Consequences of Privatization

Privatization of family life is regarded as a factor conducive to the following trends.

The Decline of the Neighborhood Mutual Aid System.   The neighborhood of the past has been broken down, or weakened, in function. Neighborhood relations are kept superficial or are maintained voluntarily. In the past, neighbors visited each other quite often, sitting in the small entrance hallway of the host house to exchange information and to chat. With the disappearance of occupational co-operation and mutual aid in the daily life of neighbors, visiting itself has become rare. Surrounded by a fence with a closed gate, each house is secluded from the outside world. In prewar times, a family shared, even when physically isolated by a tall fence, a functional network of mutual aid with neighbors. Today, even when physically interconnected, as in apartment houses, families are virtually isolated functionally from other families living in the building.

The Decline of Obligatory Kinship.   Obligatory kinship has been replaced by optional kinship or by superficial kin contacts. Formerly, under the normative regulation of the *ie* system, paternal, rather than maternal kinship, was regarded highly because the headship of the household was handed down to the next generation through the eldest son or his substitute. At present, traditional norms regulating the kinship system have lost almost all influence. Today's young nuclear families show greater open attachment to kin on the wife's side, with whom they maintain a substantially meaningful aid relation.

The Increase of the Importance of the So-Called Third Sector of Life.   The major feature of the third sector of life is leisure-time activities. The second sector of life, which centers on activities of production, has public significance. In contrast, the third sector tends to be connected with privatization. The increasing importance of this sector can be inferred from research findings which detail that more and more people meet a spouse-to-be for the first time during their recreational activities. (Women's and Minor's Bureau, Ministry of Labor, 1972).

The Weakening of the Child-Training Function of the Family.   In the *ie*, younger members were disciplined so that they might live successfully in the *omote* sphere of life after reaching maturity. Daughters, who were destined to marry into other existing households and to cope with the difficult tasks of adjustment, received particularly careful training. As a result of the shrinkage or disappearance of the *omote*, the nurturant function has become the dominant characteristic of the *oku* sphere of family life. Meanwhile, the disciplinary function, demanded and supported by the public nature of the *omote*, has waned greatly. Still, even if the *omote* sphere is cut off, the training function may remain at work when some normative behavior patterns which result from a generalized principle are internalized in individuals. In a culture such as Japan's, where behavior is contingent on a particular situation, the disappearance of the *omote* sphere tends to bring about the decline of the disciplinary function of the family. Fathers, largely retired from active participation in child discipline delegate responsibility to mothers, who remain the agents of the nurturant role of child rearing. Frequenty, parents do not train or are unable to train their children. Nor do they attempt to prevent delinquent behavior of another's child. The often noted absence of discipline in contemporary Japan is due at least partially to the privatization of family life.

The Decline of the Father-Son Coalition and the Subsequent Growth of a Mother-Son coalition.   In the self-employed worker's family, where the *omote* sphere of life was significant particularly when the business was handed down from the father to his heir as a family enterprise, the father-son coalition was normatively most important. Although a mother-son coalition may have been psychologically more important, it operated only informally and was in no position to compete with the father-son coalition. The shrinkage of the sphere of *omote* life in the wage-earning family, however, has deprived the father-son coalition of its normative significance and brought the latent importance of the mother-son bond to the surface. A similar shift has occurred in the United States; Maccoby mentions a substantial majority of families are more individuated than previously because the mother-child unit is being detached from the father (1983).

Privatized Family Life Fits a Competitive Society.   The pattern of competition characteristic of Japanese society is, it is said, not so much among individuals as among groups, as represented by interenterprise competition. But the life-long employment and seniority systems, which foster loyalty to the company and, hence, promote intercompany competition, have been modified in most sectors of industry. As the intensity of high school and college entrance examinations illustrates, competition among individuals has, however, become more open than before. Formerly, despite conflicts and contradictions within the *ie*, it was maintained to secure economic stability. In the present affluent society, where the income level has risen, people seek compensation in family life for the frustrations and dissatisfactions caused by intense competition. The high marriage rate in Japan, the concepts of "rest and relaxation" as the most important family function, and the high values given to the concepts of "health" and "family," found in a recent survey are evidence of this turning inward (Prime Minister's Office, 1980).

Unit of Privatization

The family, especially the small nuclear family composed of a husband, wife, and dependent children, is a unit of privatization. When children become independent and marry, they form a new unit of privatization. In this sense, the conjugal couple is the unit of privatization after all. In Japan, where family life is characterized by a mother-child attachment, this dyad might be proposed as the unit, but as long as the issue of gender is at the core of privatization, the marital dyad rather than the maternal dyad should be called the unit. One piece of evidence for this is the increasing ratio of numbers of households consisting only of an aged husband and his wife to the total number of households that contain old people 65 years or over (1975: 13 percent; 1983: 18 prcent). It suggests the possibility of the marital dyad becoming the unit of privatization in the more general cultural milieu of mother-child attachment.

In countries, such as the United States, where the trend of privatization has a long history, the unit is divided into individual persons. This is demonstrated in the high American divorce rate (about 40 percent of all marriages) and also in the high rate of remarriage (two/thirds to three/fourths of all divorces). In Japan, however, where society is based on what Eshun Hamaguchi calls "interpersonalism" (*kanjin-shugi*), rather than on individualism, it is unthinkable that in the near future the unit of privatization will be the individual (Hamaguchi, 1977). Thus, although the ratio of one-person households has increased remarkably—from 5 percent in 1960 to 16 percent in 1980—we cannot assert that this will lead eventually to the individualization of the unit of privatization.

Notes

1. The contrast of *omote* ("front") and *ura* ("back") has received considerable attention in discussions of Japanese culture and personality. What I propose here is to introduce the contrasting terms of *omote* and *oku* to explore the daily life of the Japanese and its changes.
2. Based on the national censuses of Japan, Befu stated that the ratio of ordinary households with heads engaged in self-employed occupations for 1980 was 15.6 percent (1986). The Basic Survey for Health and Welfare Administration, conducted once a year and regarded as the second largest survey undertaken by the national government, classifies the occupation of households according to the kind of job the highest earner among household members has rather than the kind of job held by the household head. This

survey shows that the ratio of households of self-employed workers has decreased from 40 percent in 1955, to 25 percent in 1980, mainly because of the rapid decrease of the ratio of farming households (from 27 percent to 10 percent), whereas the ratio of wage earner's households has increased from 49 percent to 64 percent during the same period.

3. The nomenclature of *conjugal family* does not imply that the family relation is conjugal-dyad centered. Instead, it emphasizes that each family begins with marriage and ends with the death of a spouse; hence, it implies that the notion of family continuation characteristic of the *ie* has almost disappeared. Under the *ie* system, a new household was established with the branching off of a small nuclear family from an existing extended household. Marriage was a procedure designed to take the bride or bridegroom of an heir into an existing household from outside; at the same time, it was a means of having a young member of the household leave her or his parental home.

Young people today usually marry for love after repeated dating over an average of nearly 2 years. Until the birth of the first child, their family life is conjugal-dyad centered in that they refuse parental interference and control and try to attain independence—a neolocal residence being an expression of their desire. After the birth of the first child, however, a mother-child coalition tends to develop. In a wage earner's family, this tendency is especially marked because of the father's commitment to his job and, consequently, the limited length of time he can share with the child at home. Nevertheless, the conjugal-dyad centeredness is still not entirely absent. After all the children have left the parental home, their aging or aged parents enter the empty nest period, unknown in former days under the *ie* system, when parents lived together with their eldest son, his wife, and children. Despite the individuation of the American nuclear family from its kin network (Maccoby, 1983), recent studies demonstrate that the American elderly living part from their children have frequent contact and are usually part of an extended family network (Sussman & Burchinal, 1962; Hill, 1970). In contrast, Japanese aged people living apart usually have only scant contact with adult children and tend to be isolated. In this sort of living arrangement, the conjugal-dyad centeredness comes into being.

In conclusion, a husband-wife coalition exists in families in Japan, but generally speaking, only in young couples in the prechild period, and with old people in the postparental period. For young people the conjugal-dyad centeredness is certainly an ideal, but for the aged it exists by default.

4. The question asked was, "Was your marriage arranged (*miai*) or a love-match (*ren'ai*)?" Informants were requested to choose one of the two forms of marriage. In the survey by the Prime Minister's Office, an intermediate category was introduced, "starting with *miai* introduction but ending up with a love-match."

5. An exclusive use of one room by a child of school-age or over may be regarded as a form of spatial separation between generations. In present-day Japan, parents provide or make efforts to provide children with a separate study-bedroom, sometimes even at the expense of their own living space. A separate living room-bedroom for old parents guarantees the privacy of the two generations but tends to make the parents lonely, particularly in the case of the widowed. The impact of this separate room on children, especially on the formation of their sense of identity, is a problem open to investigation.

6. Imhof maintains in his recent paper that "a revolution in affection and intimacy within the marriage," which has taken place during the last century or so, is closely linked with

"the transition from the more open, more extroverted family life of the past to the more intimate, more introverted, closed, nuclear western family lifestyle of today" (1983).

References

Asahi Press. (May 5, 1981). "Shûkyô-shin to Nihonjin" [Religiosity and the Japanese]. *The Asahi.*

Befu, H. (1986). Social and cultural background for child development in Japan and the United States. Chapter in this volume.

Greenfield, S. M. (1961). Industrialization and the family in sociological theory. *American Journal of Sociology, 67,* 312–322.

Hamaguchi, E. (1977). *Nihon-rashisa no sai-hakken* [*Rediscovery of 'Japaneseness'*]. Tokyo: Nihon-Keizai Press. (In Japanese)

Hill, R. (1970). *Family Development in Three Generations.* Cambridge: Schenkman.

Imhof, A. E. (1983). *From an unsure to a sure lifetime: Implications and consequences of the increase in life expectancy during the last 300 years in Europe.* Paper for German-Japanese Symposium on "Time," Kyoto, Japan.

Maccoby, E. E. (1983). *Issues in socialization.* Paper for the Conference on Child Development in Japan and the United States, Stanford, California.

Morioka, K. (1977). *Kazoku no hendō* [Family change]. In Morioka, K., et al. (Eds.), *Kazoku.* Tokyo: Yūhikaku. (In Japanese)

———, and Ishihara, K. (1979). Waga kuni no kazoku-kōsei no henka to shōrai yosoku. [Changes in family composition and an estimation of the future trend, the Japanese case]. In Tōkei Kenkyū-kai [Association for Statistical Study], Eds., *Shin SNA gata chōki model no kaihatsu* [Exploration of a long-term model of the new SNA type], 61–107. (mimeo.) (In Japanese)

Morioka, K. (Ed.) (1985). *Family and life course of middle-aged men.* Tokyo: The Family and Life Course Study Group.

———, and Mochizuki, T. (1983). *Atarashii kazoku shakaigaku* [A modern introduction to the family]. Tokyo: Baifūkan. (In Japanese)

Nihon Chiiki Kaihatsu Center. (Eds.) (1970). *Nihon-jin no kachi-kan* [The Japanese view of values]. Tokyo: Shiseido. (In Japanese)

Oh'e, S. (1982). *Tennō no guntai* [The Emperor's army]. Tokyo: Shōgakkan. (In Japanese)

Okonogi, K. (1981). *Moratoriam ningen no jidai* [The Age of man in moratorium]. Tokyo: Chūō-Kōronsha. (In Japanese)

Prime Minister's Office. (Eds.) (1980). *Katei kiban no jyūjitsu* [Toward an enriched family life]. Tokyo: Printing Bureau, Ministry of Finance.

Sakurada, K. (October 21, 1982). "San-sedai dokyo no muzukashisa ni nayamu" [The difficulties involved in a three-generation household]. *The Asahi.*

Sussman, M. B. & Burchinal, L. (1962). Kin family network: Unheralded structure in current conceptualization of family functioning. *Marriage and Family Living, 24,* 231–240.

Takahashi, H. (1975). Kazoku-keitai to senzo-saishi [Family type and ancestor veneration]. *Kazoku Kenkyū Nempō [Annals of Family Studies, 1],* 37–52.

Women's and Minor's Bureau, Ministry of Labor. (Eds.) (1972). *Fujin no chii ni kansuru jittai-chosa [A survey on the status of women].* (In Japanese)

7 | School Education: Its History and Contemporary Status

Tadahiko Inagaki

Introduction

Education in Japan has generally been evaluated highly by outside observers. Not only such general works as Reischauer's *The Japanese* (1977) and Vogel's *Japan as Number One* (1979), but studies by more specialized students of Japanese schools, including Cummings's *Education and Equality in Japan* (1980) and Easley's *Math Can Be Natural: Kitamaeno Priorities Introduced to American Teachers* (1982) praise the excellence and superiority of Japanese education. As proof of excellence, they point to such features as a broad and detailed national curriculum; tightly regulated course hours, the abundant time devoted to school, including *juku* ("after-school") education, the quality and availability of school facilities and equipment, the well-disciplined behavior of students, the equality of education, the use of groups in the classroom, and the superior achievement of Japanese students in international comparative studies.

These benefits of the Japanese system can be easily acknowledged. At the same time, however, for the Japanese themselves, there is certain ambivalence about their educational process, stemming from the evident gap between the outsider's positive evaluation and the difficulties they confront as insiders. I refer to such difficulties as the highly competitive nature of entrance examinations for higher education, the high stress and anxiety of both students and parents, the prevailing student mistrust of teachers, and the increasing incidence of secondary school violence. Although the rate of student violence is lower than in the United States, its existence is, nevertheless, an indication of a broad change in attitudes toward teachers and schools.

To convey some sense of the difficulties we face, I wish to discuss two recent Japanese best sellers, both concerned with education in Japan. One is Tetsuko Kuroyanagi's *Totto-chan* (1981), a recollection of the author's elementary school days. Expelled from public elementary school as a first grader because of her unmanageable behavior, Tetsuko entered the private school Tomoe Gakuen. Small and informal, it had inherited the child-centered principles of the New Education Movement of the 1910s. She recalls her student days there with gratitude and appreciation.

The other book, another autobiographical account, is Takanobu Hozumi's *Tsumiki-kuzushi—200 day's war in the family* (1982). It is a portrait of the internal struggles of the Hozumi family, when the author's daughter rebels and becomes a juvenile delinquent.

Totto-chan has already sold a phenomenal 5.5 million copies, and *Tsumiki-kuzushi* is approaching 2.3 million copies. The former may appeal to Japanese as a Utopian dream, in sharp contrast to the formalized education of today; the latter may be read because of anxiety and fear, with lenders worried they may encounter the same situation. The popularity of these accounts and of many other books focussing on juvenile delinquency and school violence, demonstrates the significance of the difficulties and problems facing Japanese education today.

Strange as it may seem, I think these difficulties are closely connected with the very excellence attributed to Japanese schooling by foreign observers. It is, therefore, necessary to look at education in Japan from both the outside and the inside. For this reason, in this article I shall examine it from each of these viewpoints, focussing on their interrelationship through a consideration of two different perspectives.

The first of these is historical and begins with the inception of Japan's modern educational system in 1872. From this perspective, I shall discuss the system's quantitative growth, the various changes in government educational policies, and some specific characteristics of Japanese schooling. My second perspective is contemporary. Using it, I shall make some comparisons between Japanese and American teaching based upon ongoing research projects. Hopefully, these two perspectives will allow for an analysis of both the practical successes and the deeply rooted defects characterizing contemporary Japanese education.

Historical Perspectives

Quantitative Growth and Its Background

Table 7.1 shows the increasing enrollment ratio for students in various age groups since 1875.

In elementary education, the rate of enrollment increased steadily during the 1890s and the early 1900s, this increase coinciding with a period of rapid industrial growth in Japan. Before the Meiji period, of the various kinds of schools, the so-called *terakoya* ("writing school") enjoyed the most popularity. The rate of attendance for elementary school just prior to the inauguration of the new national school system was estimated at 43 percent for boys and 10 percent for girls, not far below the level of 1875 (Dore, 1965).

The first increase in the rate of secondary attendance occurred in 1910. By then, the process of urbanization had begun to accelerate, corresponding to an increase in the size of Japan's middle class. The second significant increase in

Table 7.1
Enrollment Ratio for Students in Various Age Groups

Year	Educational level		
	Elementary	Secondary	Higher
1875	35.2	0.7	0.4
1885	49.6	0.8	0.4
1895	61.2	1.1	0.3
1905	95.6	4.3	0.9
1915	98.5	19.9	1.0
1925	99.4	32.3	2.5
1935	99.6	39.7	3.0
1947	99.6	61.7	5.8
1955	99.8	78.0	8.8
1965	99.8	83.8	14.6
1970	99.8	89.2	18.7
1975	99.9	95.9	30.3
1978	99.9	96.2	34.0

SOURCE: Ministry of Education, Science and Culture, 1979.

attendance rate occurred in the years following the Second World War. During this period, junior high school attendance became compulsory, and enrollment for the senior high schools increased rapidly—the latter change was stimulated in large part by the high economic growth of the 1960s.

In higher education, even more remarkable change has occurred since the 1960s. The rapid increases in secondary and higher education enrollment after 1970 have resulted in growing competition for entrance to senior high schools and colleges, based on an examination system.

Major Educational Policies and Practices

Centralization and Foreign Influences. In 1869, following the Meiji Restoration, feudal domains were abolished and the nation unified, as the new government proceeded to build a centralized government. At the same time, the education system was also centralized and new policies implemented.

First, the new government adopted a single-track system of elementary education, replacing the old dual-track system which had been used to educate both the samurai and the common people. Second, the Meiji government based its new system on western models, particularly that of the United States. Third, the new leaders proposed new educational objectives. The most important was that, since the acquisition of knowledge and the cultivation of talent were deemed essential to a successful life, the school should be recognized as the place to promote these qualities.

To prepare for the new system's construction, the government appointed a special committee to conduct research on its organization, among other things. A majority of committee members were experts in English, French, Dutch, and other foreign studies. Based upon their collective materials, they formulated the so-called Order of Education ("*Gakusei*"), promulgated in 1872 (Figure 7-1).

The influence of the United States on the new system of education was particularly dominant. For example, Marion M. Scott, a former official of the Bureau of Education in San Francisco, was appointed to teach at Japan's first normal school, where he implemented new teaching methods. These methods, centering on group instruction and object lessons, derived largely from the views of Pestalozzi, whose ideas were then popular in the United States. New curricula, textbooks, and materials were introduced along with these methods and distributed throughout Japan. Scott's copatriots, L.W. Mason and G.A. Leland, were responsible for introducing two new subjects, music and physical education, as well as methods to instruct them, into the Japanese curriculum. David Murry, of Rutgers University, also exercised considerable influence, following his appointment in 1875 as National Superintendent and Special Advisor for education in Japan.

These and other changes represented a dramatic departure from the traditional Japanese forms of schooling, which were being gradually replaced by an entirely new and more modern system. By the early 1890s, the new organizational structure was fully developed and it continued to function with only minor modifications until 1947. The new educational ideals, however, were less readily accepted. Liberal utilitarianism, initially advocated by the Meiji leaders, began, after 1880, to be modified by more overtly traditional aims.

Controversies and Institutionalization.   The 1880s were years of controversy in Japan. Discussions about the constitutional model that should be adopted abounded, and basic questions were raised about the political course the nation should follow. A widespread reaction to the changes in the educational system led to quarrels between traditionalists and modernists.

The issue of local autonomy versus centralization in education caused friction. In 1879, Fujimaro Tanaka, then Minister of Education, issued the New Education Order (*Kyoikurei*), replacing the 1872 ordinance. The new order provided much more popular control over education and also lessened requirements for school attendance. In 1880, however, this order was overhauled, largely for political reasons, by the Revised Education Order (*Kaisei Kyoikurei*); the revision resulted in a curtailment of popular control and the reassertion of more centralized authority over education. In the process, the imperial court began to increase its own educationl initiatives.

Japanese education can be said to have become fully established and institutionalized during the 1890s. In 1890, the government issued the Imperial Rescript on Education, setting forth principles which guided education until 1945; the New Elementary School Order (*Shogakko-rei*) and its accompanying detailed regulations for schools and teachers were issued soon after.

The Imperial Rescript on Education stipulated the nation's moral and educational objectives as follows:

> . . . Ye, Our subjects, be filial to your parents, affectionate to your brothers and sisters; as husbands and wives be harmonious, as friends true; bear yourselves in modesty and moderation; extend your benevolence to all; pursue learning and cultivate arts, and thereby develop intellectual faculties and perfect moral powers; furthermore, advance public good and promote common interests; always respect the Constitution and observe the laws; should emergency arise, offer yourselves courageously to the State. . . .

It was during the 1890s that educational instruction and guidance were also formalized. The government, which also claimed authority over the issuance of school textbooks, completely defined the course of study. And the principal of a school now inspected teaching plans and materials to ensure that they conformed to official regualtions.

The course of instruction gradually was formalized according to steps in teaching proposed by Herbartian theory. There was, however, a major difference in the way Herbartian theory was understood and accepted in the United States and in Japan. In the United States, it was the Herbartian theory of curriculum and material construction, incorporating the concept of the methodological unit, which was adopted and developed. In Japan, however, where the government regulated curriculum and materials, the concept of formal steps, specifying the teacher's instructional procedures, was the element adopted.

Innovations and National Schools.   Criticism of the increasing formalization of pedagogical practices had arisen by the late 1890s, caused, on the one hand, by a certain nostalgia for traditional methods, and, on the other, by the infusion of foreign educational trends, such as the New Education Movement and the child-centered movement. The theories of Francis W. Parker, P. W. Search, and John Dewey were introduced during the early 1900s, as were American educational innovations, such as the Gary Plan and the Platoon Systems. Some schools adopted the Project Method and the Dalton Plan. Such concepts as child centeredness, self-activity of children, and flexible curriculum were particularly popular in Japan. but due to the government's strict regulations, these innovations were introduced only into private schools located in large cities or into laboratory schools affiliated with the normal schools. Eventually, the government saw the

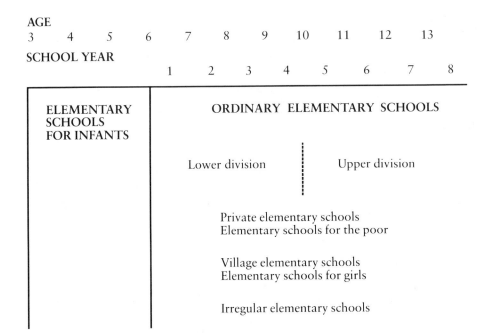

Figure 7-1
The educational system envisaged in 1872 by original provisions of the Educational Systems Order.

growing influence of the new concepts as a threat to established educational practice, and so their use was formally prohibited. Tomoe Gakuen, mentioned earlier, was one of the last of these child-centered schools, until it closed in 1944, to survive.

With the onset of war in 1941, the government reorganized the elementary schools, renaming them "national schools." The aims of education, in turn, took on a more pronounced nationalistic character. The organization of the system was also targeted for change. A new regulation, formally adopted, but never actually put into effect, extended the length of elementary education from 6 to 8 years. Moral instruction and education in history became even more overtly nationalistic than before. On the other hand, through the participation of leading scientists in the revision of the curriculum, science and mathematics education greatly improved. At the same time, efforts were also made to bring greater integration into the curriculum, and the importance of creativity and the scientific spirit received a degree of encouragement. Ironically, the reorganization of the 1940s reflected some of the principles of the earlier New Education Movement.

The introduction of child-centered ideals of education, such as flexible curricula and a developmental approach to teaching, received encouragement as the industrialization and modernization of Japanese society advanced. The urban

AGE
14   15   16   17   18   19   20   21   22   23   24   25
SCHOOL YEAR
9   10   11   12   13   14   15   16   17   18   19

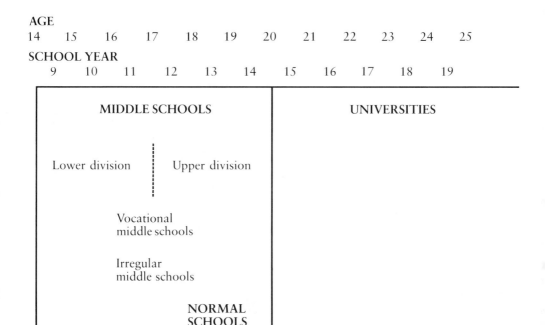

middle class, among whom such ideals and practices prevailed, began at this time to exert considerable influence in the public schools.

The government responded to this movement in two ways. First, it regulated school curricula and materials to prevent any deviation from the existing national standard. Second, and simultaneously, it accepted certain of the new methods, directing them to serve to government's own educational aims.

Post-World War II

In 1947, a new educational system was established in accordance with the new Constitution and new educational principles (see Figure 7-2 and Appendix A).

Since these reforms were carried out under the recommendations of the United States Educational Mission to Japan, naturally, they exhibited a strong American influence. The American 6-3-3-4 system (elementary, junior high, high school and college) was adopted, with attendance for the first 9 years made compulsory. Regulations providing for local control and popular participation were also instituted. Both curriculum and teaching methods reflected the progressive orientation of the United States, and curriculum regulations, in particular, were significantly relaxed.

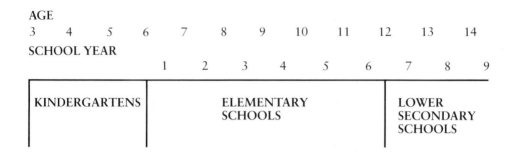

AGE

3   4   5   6   7   8   9   10   11   12   13   14

SCHOOL YEAR

1   2   3   4   5   6   7   8   9

| KINDERGARTENS | ELEMENTARY SCHOOLS | LOWER SECONDARY SCHOOLS |

SCHOOLS FOR THE BLIND
SCHOOLS FOR THE DEAF
SCHOOLS FOR THE HANDICAPPED
   other than the blind and deaf

| Kindergarten division | Elementary division | Lower secondary division |

Figure 7-2
The educational system specified in 1947 by the School Education Law.

However, beginning around 1950, reaction to these reforms set in, with authority over curriculum regulations and other education policies reverting to the central government's control. Since 1960, the rapid increase in enrollment has aggravated the competition for entrance to both high schools and universities and has stimulated the current trend toward formalization in education (Figure 7-3).

Juku

To fully understand contemporary Japanese education, it is necessary to discuss the phenomenal growth and influence of *juku* schooling.

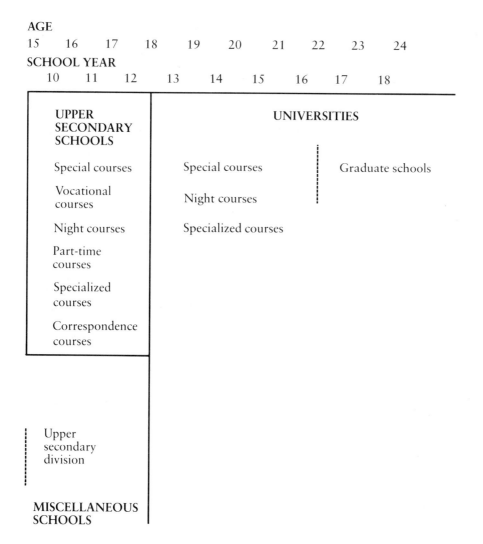

AGE
15   16   17   18   19   20   21   22   23   24
SCHOOL YEAR
10   11   12   13   14   15   16   17   18

UPPER SECONDARY SCHOOLS

Special courses

Vocational courses

Night courses

Part-time courses

Specialized courses

Correspondence courses

UNIVERSITIES

Special courses

Night courses

Specialized courses

Graduate schools

Upper secondary division

MISCELLANEOUS SCHOOLS

The term *juku* referred originally to a study room in the home. Gradually, it came to mean a small private school, practicing individualized instruction, in which the teacher's personal influence was dominant. During the 1890s, with the complete institutionalization of education, enthusiasm grew for *juku*-style education, prompted largely by antipathy toward formalization.

In the last fifteen years, the *juku* has undergone a further transformation and now occupies a dominant position in Japanese education. The *juku* today is mainly concerned with helping students cram for entrance examinations to high schools and universities. Parents' concerns about competitive exams have contributed to this growth. Because of the *juku*'s continuing popularity, they are now called "second schools."

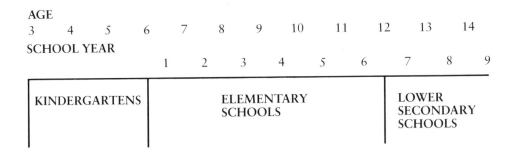

AGE

| 3 | 4 | 5 | 6 | 7 | 8 | 9 | 10 | 11 | 12 | 13 | 14 |

SCHOOL YEAR

| 1 | 2 | 3 | 4 | 5 | 6 | 7 | 8 | 9 |

| KINDERGARTENS | ELEMENTARY SCHOOLS | LOWER SECONDARY SCHOOLS |

SCHOOLS FOR THE BLIND
SCHOOLS FOR THE DEAF
SCHOOLS FOR THE HANDICAPPED
  Other than the blind and deaf

| Kindergarten division | Elementary division | Lower secondary division |

Figure 7-3
The educational system in 1971.

Immediately after the war, child-centered educational ideals were formally recognized by the government. Child centeredness, equality of educational opportunity, and localism of educational administration became the leading principles of the new education.

As discussed earlier, the change in educational policy in the 1950s brought about a reversion to centralization, which resulted in tighter governmental regulation of the course of study and textbooks. Even so, the continuing importance

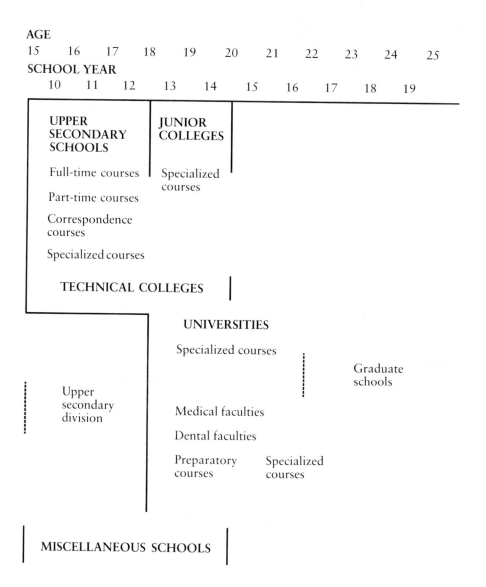

AGE

| 15 | 16 | 17 | 18 | 19 | 20 | 21 | 22 | 23 | 24 | 25 |

SCHOOL YEAR

| 10 | 11 | 12 | 13 | 14 | 15 | 16 | 17 | 18 | 19 |

UPPER SECONDARY SCHOOLS

Full-time courses

Part-time courses

Correspondence courses

Specialized courses

JUNIOR COLLEGES

Specialized courses

TECHNICAL COLLEGES

Upper secondary division

UNIVERSITIES

Specialized courses

Graduate schools

Medical faculties

Dental faculties

Preparatory courses   Specialized courses

MISCELLANEOUS SCHOOLS

of the principle of equal opportunity is evident in the growing attendance at institutions for post secondary and higher education. At the same time, there has been an exacerbation of the competition for entrance into these institutions, especially those perceived as having greater prestige. A result of the heightened competition has been to strengthen he formalization of education by orienting the system toward the entrance examinations. The transformation of ideals, which has stimulated modern Japanese educational development—liberal utilitarianism

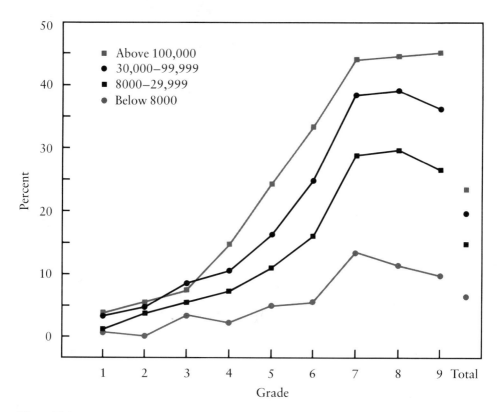

Figure 7-4
Juku attendance ratio by grade (Ministry of Education, 1977).

in the early Meiji period, child centeredness in the Taisho era, and equality after the war—parallels successive stages in the modernization of Japanese society. It also parallels the rise of economic and popular consciousness, as well as mirroring variations in governmental strategy.

Within the Classroom

An Example of Science Teaching.   In order to examine contemporary schooling, I have taken science teaching in the elementary schools as an example. Researchers (Azuma, Inagaki and others) studying science teaching have conducted a comparative study of science teaching in Japan and in the United States, using as examples four classes of fifth graders from each country. This project is an outgrowth of the agreement reached at "the United States-Japan Seminar on Adult's Understanding of Science," held in Honolulu in 1978. The general questions asked in the study were: "How is science taught in schools?" "What are the outcomes of science teaching?" "What are the factors influencing the effectiveness of learning?" Although the study is still incomplete, I shall introduce some of the intial findings for the purpose of clarifying the major characteristics of Japanese teaching.

Curricular Regulations and Supporting Facilities.   Curricular regulations are stricter in Japan than in the United States. In Japan, national standards specify both content and number of class hours for each subject. Similarly, textbooks are written to accord with the national course of study. Organization, content, and textbook materials are less diverse than in the United States. Provisions governing the facilities and equipment for science education have, since 1954, been fully set forth in the special Law for Development of Science Education. Each school has a science laboratory; facilities and equipment are financed under the detailed direction of this law (see Table 7-2).

Characteristics of Teaching.   What are the similarities and differences between Japanese and American teaching?

1   The teaching plans devised by Japanese teachers are more detailed, and, I believe, more sophisticated than those of their American counterparts. The Japanese plans predetermine course content, distribution of time, and questions to be asked.

2   Japanese teachers often follow the *prediction-discussion-experiment* format to stimulate creative thinking and inquiry by students. Influenced by the New Curriculum Movement in the United States, this teaching strategy has prevailed since the revision of the course of study for science in 1968. In contrast, three of the four teachers in our American sample followed the *observation-discussion* procedure, based on an Elementary Science Study program.

3   Japanese teachers are careful to stay within predetermined content and time distribution, and they emphasize *group* interaction during discussions. Teachers in the United States, on the other hand, rely more upon *individual* reinforcement, encouragement, and feedback. Their procedure for questioning students is more sequential and flexible, designed to probe and to develop the students' ideas.

4   There are major differences in classroom procedures between the two countries. At the beginning of a lesson, American teachers explain the experiment to be conducted and the procedures for it. Next, the children start the experiment and record their findings. After completing the experiment, they begin a discussion; in the course of it, teachers accept divergent ideas and proposals, without leading the participants to any predetermined conclusion. In general, then, lessons begin with a prescriptive-directive assignment of the task and end with divergent learning.

Japanese teachers begin with divergent discussion, encouraging children to express their own ideas and predictions. Gradually, however, discussion focusses on major issues or questions that teachers have prepared in advance. Teachers take the leading role in the discussion, guiding students to prescribed conclusions.

Table 7.2
A Comparison of Curricular Regulations, Teacher Guidelines, and
Supporting Facilities for Science Education

	Japan	United States
National/federal	National standards Course of Study* $\begin{cases} \text{subjects} \\ \text{objectives} \\ \text{contents} \\ \text{time} \end{cases}$	No standards
Prefectural/state		Subject (science) "A district shall provide the following coordinated and supervised course of study" (Illinois state)
School district	Some school districts have programs based on national standards.	Course of study or program $\begin{cases} \text{objectives} \\ \text{contents} \\ \text{topics} \\ \text{time allotment} \end{cases}$
School	Some schools have schedules based on course of study and textbook.	Individual schools set their course of study based on "Scope and Sequence" charts or teachers set course of study.
Textbook	Censorship of textbook by Ministry of Education Adoption by textbook district (496 districts)	School district, individual schools, or teacher choose textbook.
Teacher	Teachers use teachers' manual, Akahon‡ and students' workbook accompanying textbook. Regulation for supplementary materials	Teachers use teachers' manual, supplementary books for teacher, magazines, and student workbooks.
Facilities and equipment	Most schools have a science room. Facilities and equipment are provided by Law for Promotion of Science Education. Science Education Center	Science room Science "center" or regular classroom

* 1947; revision 1951, 1958, 1968, 1977.
† 68, 70, 105, 105, 105, 105 classroom hours/year.
‡ "Teacher-proof" typed teacher's manual.

In contrast to their American counterparts, Japanese teachers, then, start by permitting divergence and gradually induce convergence. This procedure has been adopted as a compromise between either centering on the child or on the prescribed body of knowledge to be unparted. Such a teaching strategy, however, often leads to prescribed conclusions and deprives students of the most important and fruitful steps in the thinking process—individual inquiry and the exchange of ideas, which may promote more thorough understanding.

Teacher Constraints and Difficulties.   Japanese teachers face many more constraints in teaching than American teachers, such as stricter curriculum regulation, larger classes, pressures toward comprehensive coverage of the text, parental expectations, shortage of time, and *juku* schooling. These constraints, both structural and cultural, tend to make teaching more shallow than in America. Moreover, teachers' ideals and experimental teaching devices often conflict with them.

Educational policies aimed at greater centralization and regulation, as well as economic demands for a standardized quality of manpower, constitute the main structural constraints on Japanese teaching. Also, certain sociopsychological tendencies of the Japanese themselves—including group orientedness, pressure toward conformity and fear of deviating from the majority, and competitiveness—not only are produced by these structures, but, in turn, help to consolidate them.

Particularly in secondary school, the difficulties students face are exacerbated by the amount of material to be learned, the discrepancies in their abilities and levels of achievement, and the pressure of entrance examinations. The increased attendance at *juku* also promotes the collapse of regular schooling. And although the competitive climate of education does accelerate level of achievement, it also increases the difficulties and problems in education.

This is a general outline of contemporary Japanese education. Among teachers, there have been attempts to improve the quality of education by introducing curricular reforms and developing new teaching materials and innovative teaching methods. It has been difficult, however, in recent years to build a consensus among parents, teachers, and officials about reform proposals. In the end, the rigid structure of the educational system in Japan has made for significant contraints.

Topics for Discussion

Reconsideration of Criteria for Comparison.   The criteria for cross-cultural comparison, particularly concerning the quality of education and its social and sociopsychological background, must be broadened to include intracultural difficulties and problems. When used by persons outside a culture, the criteria for comparison often tend to focus on the outcomes of education or its surface features rather than on the processes and the problems lying beneath the surface.

Table 7.3
Characteristics of Formalization and Deformalization

Formalization	Deformalization
Institutional	Individual
Subject-matter centered	Child-centered
or	
Teacher-centered	
Rigid curriculum and scheduling	Flexible curriculum and scheduling
Restricted decision making by teachers	Decision making by teachers
Centralization	Decentralization by teachers
Transmission from above	Innovation from below

Both points of view, external as well as internal, must be considered in comparative studies.

Formalization and Deformalization of Education.   To analyze the quality of education, I propose a pair of concepts, *formalization* and *deformalization*. The contrasts presented in Table 7.3 can be used to define them.

Formalization has been the dominant trend in advanced countries since the nineteenth century. Nevertheless, since the beginning of this century, attempts at deformalization have gradually increased in reaction to this trend.

The same interaction can be seen in Japanese education. Whereas we can recognize a strong tendency toward formalization in education, we can detect, too, a growing criticism of, and a broadening antipathy toward it. Both the popularity of *Totto-chan* and of books introducing Steiner and other informal schools of education are evidence of this trend.

Finally, it appears paradoxical that the child-centered ideal and the formalization of Japanese education originate from the same source—the modernization of society—and have, nevertheless, produced the conflicts we now face. Some way must be found to introduce innovations into our educational system and to make modernization more compatible with humanization and child-centered ideals. Other industrialized and mass democratic societies share this difficulty. For the Japanese and the Americans, it is a common problem in education.

References

Cummings, W. K. (1980). *Education and equality in Japan*. Princeton, N.J.: Princeton University Press.

Dore, R. P. (1965). *Education in Tokugawa Japan*. London: Routledge & Kegan Paul Ltd.

Easley, J. (1982). *Math can be natural: Kitamaeno priorities introduced to American teachers*. Committee on culture and cognition, University of Illinois at Urbana-Champaign.

Hozumi, T. (1982). *Tsumiki-kuzushi. [200 day's war in the family]*. Tokyo: Kirihara-shoten.

Inagaki, T. (1966). *History of the theories and practices of teaching in the Meiji Period (1868 to 1912)*. Tokyo: Hyoronsha. (In Japanese)

Kaigo, T. (1956). *The history of the relationship between Japan and the United States: Education*. Tokyo: Yoyosha. (In Japanese)

————. (Ed.). (1976). *Educational reform in Japan since 1945*. Tokyo: Tokyo University Press. (In Japanese)

————. (Ed.). (1982). *History of education in Nagano prefecture*. Tokyo: Shinkyo Publishing Co. (In Japanese)

Kuroyanagi, T. (1981). *Totto-chan*. Tokyo. Kodan-sha

National Institute of Education. (1973). *Japanese modern history of education*. (10 vols.). Tokyo: Bunshodo Co. (In Japanese)

Reischauer, E. O. (1977). *The Japanese*. Cambridge, Mass.: Harvard University Press.

Vogel, E. F. (1979). *Japan as number one*. Cambridge, Mass.: Harvard University Press.

Appendix

The Fundamental Principles of Education, promulgated in 1947, contain eleven articles describing the aims and principles of education.

The following seven articles illustrate the major differences from the former system:

ARTICLE 1 *Aim of Education* Education shall aim at the full development of personality, striving for the rearing of the people, sound in mind and body, who shall love truth and justice, esteem individual value, respect labor and have a deep sense of responsibility, and be imbued with the independent spirit, as builders of the peaceful state and society.

ARTICLE 2 *Educational Principle* The aim of education shall be realized on all occasions and in all places. In order to achieve the aim, we shall endeavor to contribute to the creation and development of culture by mutual esteem and co-operation, respecting academic freedom, having a regard for actual life and cultivating a spontaneous spirit.

ARTICLE 3 *Equal Opportunity in Education* The people shall all be given equal opportunities of receiving education according to their ability, and they shall not be subject to educational discrimination on account of race, creed, sex, social status, economic position, or family origin.

The state and local public bodies shall take measures to give financial assistance to those who have, with all their ability, difficulty in receiving education for economic reasons.

ARTICLE 4   *Compulsory Education*   The people shall be obligated to have boys and girls under their protection receive nine year general education.

No tuition fee shall be charged for compulsory education in schools established by the state and local public bodies.

ARTICLE 5   *Co-education*   Men and women shall esteem and cooperate with each other. Co-education, therefore, shall be recognized in education.

ARTICLE 6   *School Education*   The schools prescribed by law shall be of public nature and, besides the state and local public bodies, only the juridical persons prescribed by law shall be entitled to establish such schools.

Teachers of the schools prescribed by law shall be servants of the whole community. They shall be conscious of their mission and endeavor to discharge their duties. For this purpose, the status of teachers shall be respected and their fair and appropriate treatment shall be secured.

. . . .

ARTICLE 10   *School Administration*   Education shall not be subject to improper control, but it shall be directly responsible to the whole people.

School administration shall, on the basis of this realization, aim at the adjustment and establishment of the various conditions required for the pursuit of the aim of education.

8 | The Japanese Language

Susumu Kuno[1]

For the scholar of child development, the grammatical characteristics of a language should be of interest because they tell us something about the interaction between a formal system, language, and psychological functions served by that system. Children must acquire that system in a short period of time. From my own perspective in linguistics, which can be characterized as a "functional" perspective, it is important to demonstrate that properties of grammar are related to the various uses of language by human beings. I regard "performance" and "discourse" factors such as memory and perception, novelty of information, empathy, and point of view to have important bearings on grammar, and I assume that a full recognition of these factors is a prerequisite for successful grammatical analysis. This view is in contrast to those held by many linguists who assume they can isolate that part of the language structure which is autonomous from other human capacities without first understanding what these performance and discourse factors are (see Hakuta & Bloom, this volume, for further discussion of this issue).

In this paper, I discuss seven aspects of the Japanese language that demonstrate the fruitfulness of a functional perspective: the position of relative clauses and conjunctions, word order, deletion of constituents, pronouns, source of information, point of view, and topic marker and multiple-subject constructions. In part, choice of these topics was made because they are seldom found in either grammatical sketches or in reference grammars of Japanese. Other topics, including kinship terms, address terms, deferential expressions and their relationships with social stratification, are found elsewhere (see Suzuki, 1978; Inoue, 1979; Nevstupný, 1979), and thus will not be treated here. Readers interested in obtaining an overall picture of the Japanese language are advised to read Kuno (1978a) together with the present paper.

1. The Position of Relative Clauses and Conjunctions

Japanese is a verb-final language; that is, verbs appear in sentence-final position. Likewise, postpositions, rather than prepositions, represent direct and oblique case relationships. Clause-final, not clause-initial, conjunctions specify the relationship of subordinate and main clauses, and a noun modified by a relative clause follows the clause rather than precedes it. For example, observe the following sentences (nom. = nominative, acc. = accusative, dat. = dative):

(1) *Postpositions:*   Taroo *ga* Hanako *ni* enpitu *de*   tegami o   kaita.
                        nom.   *dat.* pencil with letter   *acc.* wrote
                        'Taroo wrote a letter to Hanako with a pencil.'

(2) *Conjunctions:*   a. Taroo ga ame ga hutte iru *to* itta.
                          rain   falling is that said
                         'Taroo said that it was raining.'
                      b. Ame ga hutte iru *kara* ie ni imasu.
                          rain falling is since home   stay
                         'Since it is raining, I will stay home.'

(3) *Relative*   Taroo ga, [*enpitu de kaita*] tegami o [*matte ita*] hito ni watasita.
    Clauses: pencil with wrote letter waiting was person to handed
                      'Taroo handed the letter [he had written with a pencil] to the
                      person [who had been waiting].'

These characteristics of Japanese conform to the implicational languages universals, originated by Greenberg (1963), that are summarized in Table 8.1. There is a perceptual explanation for the language universals described in Table 8.1 (see Kuno 1974).

Let us assume that the following premises are well justifiable: first, that certain syntactic patterns such as multiple center-embedding and conjunction juxtaposition cause perceptual difficulties. Second, languages can be assumed to embody devices minimizing those patterns causing perceptual difficulties. The hypothesis that multiple center-embedding, but not right- or left-embedding, causes difficulty in comprehension has been in the literature since 1960. It is enough to show the following examples:

(4) a. *Center-embedding:*
       The cheese [the rat [the cat chased] ate] was rotten.

    b. *Left-embedding:*
       [[[[[My friend's] friend's] friend's] friend's] friend] came to see me yesterday.

    c. *Right-embedding:*
       I think that [John believes that [Mary claims that [the earth is flat]]].

Table 8.1

If a language is	It is most likely that it uses
A. Verb-final	Postpositions, clause-final conjunctions, Prenominal relative clauses
b. Verb-initial	Prepositions, clause-initial conjunctions, Postnominal relative clauses

Only (4a) is difficult to comprehend. Neither (4b) nor (4c) cause difficulty in comprehension.

Yngve (1960) was probably the first to claim that juxtaposition of semantically transparent grammatical formatives, such as conjunctions, causes difficulty in comprehension. Observe the following contrasts:

(5) a. *That that the world is round is obvious is dubious.
    b. ?That, if the world is round, the moon must also be round is dubious.
    c. ?That the fact that the world is round is obvious is dubious.

(Following standard linguistic notation, sentences which are grammatically unacceptable to native speakers of the language are marked by an asterisk (*), and questionably acceptable sentences are marked by (?). Acceptable sentences are unmarked.)

All the previous sentences involved double center-embedding, but (5a) is considerably worse than (5b) or (5c). I assume that this is because (5a), in addition to double center-embedding, involves juxtaposition of the same conjunction: *that*.

Clause-Initial and Clause-Final

Having established that both multiple center-embedding and juxtaposition of conjunctions of the same shape or similar grammatical function cause difficulty in comprehension, let us see whether verb-final languages are easier to comprehend with conjunctions in clause-initial or clause-final position. We will examine four hypothetical structures that could yield multiple center-embedding and/or conjunction juxtaposition. In (6), an English sentence illustrates each structure.

(6) a. Subject clause embedded in subject clause:
       That [that [the world is round] is obvious] is dubious.
    b. Subject clause embedded in object clause:
       John says that [that [the world is round] is obvious].
    c. Object clause embedded in subject clause:
       That [everyone knows that [the world is round]] is obvious.
    d. Object clause embedded in object clause:
       John says that [everyone knows that [the world is round]].

Below, I shall reconstruct these structures as they would appear in a verb-final language. There are two possible cases: first, in a verb-final language with clause-initial conjunctions, as in (7), and second, in a verb-final language with clause-final conjunctions, as in (8). "DC" stands for double center-embedding, and "J" stands for conjunction juxtaposition.

(7) *Verb-Final with Clause-Initial Conjunctions*
    a. *That* [*that* [the world round-is] obvious-is] dubious-is.   (DC + J)

   b. John *that* [*that* [the world round-is] obvious-is] says.   (DC + J)
   c. *That* [everyone *that* [the world round-is] knows] obvious-is.   (DC)
   d. John [*that* everyone *that* [the world round-is] knows] says].   (DC)

(8) *Verb-Final with Clause-Final Conjunctions*
   a. [[The world round-is] *that* obvious-is] *that* dubious-is.
   b. John [[the world round-is] *that* obvious-is] *that* says.
   c. [Everyone [the world round-is] *that* knows] *that* obvious-is.
   d. John [everyone [the world round-is] *that* knows] *that* says.   (DC)

Note that (8b) does not involve double center-embedding because the most deeply embedded clause, *the world round-is*, is left-embedded in the larger object clause. Similarly, (8c) does not involve double center-embedding, because *the world round-is* is center-embedded in a left-embedded clause.

These examples show that if verb-final languages used clause-initial conjunctions, as shown in (7), double center-embedding would necessarily ensue whenever one clause is embedded in another. Conjunction juxtaposition is equally likely to result. In contrast, if verb-final languages used the clause-final conjunction, as shown in (8), conjunction juxtaposition would not occur; two conjunctions would always be separated by at least one verb, and the chances of double center-embedding would be small. Comparing (7) and (8), it is clear that, in terms of comprehensibility, language type (8) is superior to (7). Most verb-final languages, including Japanese, have chosen this type.

Relative Clauses

To avoid complex examples, I shall discuss here only the chances of simple center-embedding, which is prerequisite for double center-embedding. Example (9) lists four possible constructions. Example (10) shows how these structures would appear in a verb-final language with relative clauses in a postnominal position. Example (11) illustrates a verb-final prenominal language.

(9) a. Relative clause on subject of intransitive construction:
     The girl [that John loved] died.
   b. Relative clause on subject of transitive construction:
     The girl [that John loved] hated Mary.
   c. Relative clause on object of transitive construction:
     Mary hated the girl [that John loved].

(10) *Verb-Final with Postnominal Relative Clauses*
   a. The girl [that John loved] died.   (C)
   b. The girl [that John loved] Mary hated.   (C)
   c. Mary the girl [that John loved] hated.   (C)

(11) *Verb-Final with Prenominal Relative Clauses*
   a. [John loved] girl died.
   b. [John loved] girl Mary hated.
   c. Mary [John loved] girl hated.   (C)

If verb-final languages used postnominal clauses, as shown in (12), these clauses would be center-embedded. However, the use of prenominal relative clauses, as shown in (11), can largely evade such embedding. Again, for purposes of speech comprehension, (11) is an easier language type than (10). Most verb-final languages, including Japanese, have chosen this option with respect to the position of relative clauses.

Prepositions/Postpositions

Finally, let us examine the choice between prepositions and postpositions in verb-final languages. I show here only those patterns in which case-marked noun phrases are used adjectivally to modify another noun phrase: for example, *the color of the flowers in the vase on the table.* Given that attributive modifiers of nouns, like relative clauses, appear prenominally in verb-final languages, we obtain the following two patterns for the above expression:

(12) *Verb-Final with Prepositions:*
     [of [in [on table] vase] flowers] color

(13) *Verb-Final with Postpositions:*
     [[[table on] vase in] flowers of] color

Note that while (13) involves a straightforward multiple left-branching pattern, which is known to cause no difficulty in comprehension, (12) involves center-embedding of noun phrases within noun phrases. In this instance, like the others, most verb-final languages have chosen the pattern offering greatest ease of comprehension: postpositions rather than prepositions.

2. Word Order

As mentioned above, the Japanese language marks the grammatical functions of noun phrases by postpositions called particles. Word order of elements within a simplex sentence structure is relatively free, except for the requirement that sentences and clauses end with verbs. (This rule, however, is often suspended in main clauses in informal speech, as will be demonstrated next.) For example, observe the following sentences:

(14) a. Taroo ga Hanako ni sono syasin o okutta.   (Sbj - Indir O - Dir O - V)
                    dat. the picture *acc.* sent
        'Taroo sent the picture to Hanako.'
     b. Taroo ga sono syasin o Hanako ni okutta.   (Sbj - Dir O - Indir O - V)
     c. Sono syasin o Taroo ga Hanako ni okutta.   (Dir O - Sbj - Indir O - V)
     d. Hanako ni Taroo ga sono syasin o okutta.   (Indir O - Sbj - Dir O - V)
     e. Sono syasin o Hanako ni dare ga okutta no ka?   (Dir O - Indir O - Sbj - V)
        the   picture   who   sent that Q
        'Who sent the picture to Hanako?'

f. Hanako ni sono syasin o dare ga okutta no ka?   (Indir O - Dir O - Sbj - V)
   'Who sent the picture to Hanako?'

The order of elements in a sentence is determined by the relative degree of their informativeness. The following condition holds for Japanese:

From-Old-to-New Information Flow. Elements in a sentence are ordered on the basis of increasing degrees of informativeness of the elements. In other words: ordinarily, in a given sentence, elements which relate to what has been mentioned in the preceding context appear at sentence-initial position. Those elements conveying new, unpredictable information appear closer to the end of the sentence, with the verb excepted since its position is fixed as sentence-final (Kuno, 1978a, 1978b; Masunaga, 1983).

Of the six different ways to arrange subject, indirect object, direct object, and verb in a sentence shown in (14), there is no doubt that those placing the subject at sentence-initial position are the most natural and do not require any special context to justify their use. Various syntactic and discourse-based tests show that, despite the relative freedom of word order in Japanese sentences, it is possible to see the underlying word order as subject-first and object-second. The relative order of indirect and direct objects is not easily determinable; some evidence indicates the indirect object comes first.

The fact that the unmarked order of Japanese sentences is Subject-Object-Verb, and the fact that the subject and the object are marked with particles *ga* and *o*, respectively, bring up an interesting question of how children at various stages of language acquisition determine the semantic functions of noun phrases in sentences. Is this determination first based on word order or on case marking? This area of research has attracted a considerable amount of attention from psycholinguists. I refer the reader to Sano (1977) and Hakuta (1982).

In (15), (b) and (c) are examples of how in informal colloquial style constituents can be moved so that the unmarked, verb-final word order of (a) is disturbed:

(15) a. Kimi ano hon kaesite kurenai?
         you that book returning give-not
         'Won't you give me back that book?'
      b. Kimi, kaesite kurenai, *ano hon.*
      c. Kaesite kurenai, *kimi, ano hon.*

It should be noted from these examples that in informal speech style, semantically transparent particles can be dropped. Those elements following the verb can be considered afterthoughts, added to confirm the speaker's intended meaning or to provide incidental information. In other words, sentences such as (15b) and (15c) can be uttered only in the contexts in which the speaker originally thought the sentences would have made sense to the hearer without postverbal elements.

(15) b′. Kimi, kaesite kurenai?
      you   returning give-not
      'Won't you give (it) back?'
   c′. Kaesite kurenai?
      'Won't (you) give (it) back?'

The sentence pattern under discussion has the same discourse function as the so-called "right-dislocation" sentence pattern in English:

(16) He is a good man, *Charlie Brown.*

The nonverb-final sentence pattern under discussion never appears in embedded clauses, even in extremely colloquial speech. For example, observe the following sentences:

(17) a. [Yatu ni kane o kasite yatta] toki, arigatoo mo iwanakatta.
       him to money lending gave when thank-you even said-not
       'He didn't even say thank you when I lent him money.'
   b. *[Kane o kasite yatta, *yatu ni*], toki, . . .
       money lending gave him to when

Example (17b) is unintelligible and unacceptable.

As far as I know, no study exists that addresses itself to the problem of the point at which children acquire the discourse principles that determine word order in sentences. Since the word order in Japanese carries information often represented in English with indefinite and definite articles, it will be interesting to compare the Japnese word-order data with the English data concerning indefinite and definite articles.

3. Deletion

In English, deletion of constituents that are recoverable from context is subject to severe syntactic constraints. For example, observe the following sentences:

(18) Speaker A: Where did you put the bananas?
     Speaker B: a. I put the bananas in the freezer.
             b. I put them   in the freezer.
             c. *I put ∅   in the freezer.
             d. *∅ Put them   in the freezer.
             e. *∅ Put ∅   in the freezer.
             f. ∅∅ ∅   in the freezer.

(The null symbol [∅] indicates deletion of the constituent from the fully formed sentence.)

The subject *I* and the object *the bananas/them* are perfectly recoverable from the preceding context; that is, from Speaker A's question. In spite of this, these two constituents cannot be deleted as long as the verb *put* is present in the answer.

In contrast, deletion of recoverable elements in a sentence is much more extensive in Japanese. For example, observe the following exchanges:

(19) Speaker A: Kimi wa banana o doko ni ireta no?
                you   where in put
                'Where did you put the bananas?'

      Speaker B: a. ?Boku wa banana o reizooko ni ireta yo.
                    I   fridge   in put
                    'I put the bananas in the fridge.'
              b. ??Boku wa   ∅   reizooko ni ireta yo.
              c. *∅   Banana o reizooko ni ireta yo.
              d. ∅   ∅   Reizooko ni ireta yo.
              e. Reizooko da yo.
                    fridge   is
                    '(It) is in the fridge.'

As shown here, it is rather difficult in Japanese, and especially in question-answer situations, to retain recoverable elements undeleted, with the exception of (19d), which has the recoverable verb repeated. This repetition does not result in marginality because the verb is needed there to produce a verb-final sentence as an answer to the question. An alternative way of giving a sentential answer with nothing but the minimally required information is shown in (19e). It presents the focus of the answer in the ". . .*da/desu* [(it) is x that. . . .]" pattern.

There are numerous phenomena worthy of mention with respect to both the (19d) and (19e) patterns of deletion. Limitation of space allows me to mention only two of them. First, it is not the case that all recoverable constituents are deletable in Japanese. For example, observe the following exchanges:

(20) Speaker A: Kimi wa Suisu   de tokei o katta no ka?
                you Switzerland in watch   bought
                'Did you buy watches in Switzerland?'
      Speaker B: Un, ∅ katta.
                yes   bought
                'Yes, (I) bought (watches in Switzerland).'

(21) Speaker A: Kimi wa kono tokei o Suisu   de katta no ka?
                you   this watch Switzerland in bought
                'Did you buy this watch in Switzerland?'
      Speaker B: a. *Un, ∅ katta.
                    'Yes, (I) bought (it in Switzerland).'
              b. Un, Suisu de katta.
                    'Yes, (I) bought (it) in Switzerland.'
              c. Un.

Suisu de 'in Switzerland' is a recoverable element in Speaker B's answer both in (19) and in (20). It is possible to delete it and retain only *katta* in (19), but it is impossible to do the same in (20). This must be due to the fact that while (19A) has *katta* 'bought' as the focus of the question, (20A), in the normal interpretation of the sentence, has *Suisu de* 'in Switzerland' as question focus. In other words, while (19A) can be paraphrased as (22a), (20A) cannot be paraphrased as (22b), but as (22c) or (22d):

(22) a.   Did you *buy* or did you *not buy* watches in Switzerland?
      b.   ?Did you *buy* or did you *not buy* this watch in Switzerland?
      c.   *Where* did you buy this watch?
      d.   Was it *in Switzerland* that you bought this watch?

The following exchanges show the same kind of contrast:

(23) Speaker A: Kimi wa syuusen no tosi ni umarete ita no ka?
                  you   end-of-war year in born   was
                  'Were you (already) born the year the war ended?'
      Speaker B: Un, ∅ umarete ita.
                  'Yes, (I) was (already) born (then).'

(24) Speaker A: Kimi wa syuusen no tosi ni umareta no ka?
                  you   end-of-war year   born-was
                  'Were you born the year the war ended?'
      Speaker B: *Un, ∅ umareta.
                  '*Yes, (I) was born ∅.'

This phenomenon can be accounted for by assuming that, in Japanese, there is a constraint on deletion of recoverable constituents with respect to their information contents.

The Pecking Order of Deletion Principle: Deletion of recoverable elements in a sentence should proceed from less important to more important information.

This principle proposes that the order of deletion cannot be conditioned on the basis of a dichotomy between important and unimportant, but must be based on relative degrees of importance. For justification of this claim, see Kuno (1982).

A glance at the corresponding phenomenon in English shows that the same principle applies. For example, observe the following exchanges:

(25) Speaker A: Did you buy watches in Switzerland?
      Speaker B: Yes, I bought some ∅ . (*in Switzerland* deleted)

(26) Speaker A: Did you buy this watch in Switzerland?
                  (with normal intonation)[2]
      Speaker B: *Yes, I bought it ∅ . (*in Switzerland* deleted)

My research shows that the Pecking Order of Deletion Principle applies to many languages and can be legitimately called language-universal. It would be interesting to see at what stage of development children acquire this principle.

The focus-only answer illustrated in (19e) with the copulative verb *da* 'is (informal)' or *desu* 'is (polite)' at the end gives rise to a sentence pattern for which Japanese is well known—the *Boku wa unagi da* pattern.

(27) Boku wa unagi da.
    I   eel   is

Naturally, at some level this sentence can be used as an answer to the question "Who are you?" Alternatively, it can answer an infinite variety of questions, including "What kind of fish have you caught?", "What are you going to eat?", and "Which fish do you all think is the most delicious?" In all these cases, *unagi da* '(It) is an eel' gives the focus of the answer, and the *wa*-marked NP *boku wa* 'as far as I am concerned' sets the answerer off from the rest of the addressees.[3]

English has a less common counterpart of *Boku wa unagi da* in situations like the following:

(28) (At a restaurant)
    Waitress: Who ordered spaghetti? Did you?
    Speaker B: Not me. I'm the cheeseburger.

4. Pronouns

Japanese lacks authentic pronouns for any grammatical persons. Most existing forms that correspond to pronouns in English are derived from nominal expressions:

(29) First Person: *boku*: (your) servant; *watakusi*: personal
    Second Person: *kimi*: lord; *omae*: honorable (person in) front (of me)
    Third Person: *kare*: thing far away; *kanozyo*: far away woman

Third person pronouns are used only in pedantic speech by educated people and in journalistic or literary writing. Japanese also lacks polite second-person pronouns to be used when addressing superiors. *Otaku* 'your honorable house—you' comes closest to such a pronoun, but it is seldom used when addressing one's superiors. The speaker uses either the addressee's proper name plus title or title only, or alternatively, he or she resorts to deletion when the second-person reference is clear. To illustrate:

(30)   *Child*   *to*
      Mother

$\varnothing$	$\varnothing$	ni kore agemasyoo ka.
Watakusi 'I'	okaasan 'mother'	to this shall-I-give
	*anata 'you'	'Shall I give this to you?'
	*otaku 'you'	

(31)   *Father to Small Daughter*
    Papa   to   kaimono ni ikoo.
    Otoosan 'father'   with shopping   let's-go
    ??Boku 'I'   '(Lit.) Let's go shopping with Dad (= me).'
    *Watakusi 'I'

(32)   *Student   to   Teacher*
    Yamada
    *Anata 'you'   ni okiki sitai   koto ga aru n(o) desu ga.
    *Otaku 'you'   to asking (honor) want thing   there-is   but
    Sensei 'teacher'   'I have something that I would like to ask you about.'
    Yamada-sensei
      'Teacher Yamada'

For a third-person reference, zero-form pronouns appear in Japanese where *he* and *she* would appear in English. For example, observe the following sentences:

(33) a. John hates *his* mother.
     b. Taroo wa ∅ okaasan o kiratte iru.
                 mother   hating is
       'Taroo hates (his) mother.'

(34) a. John said that *he* was sick.
     b. Taroo wa ∅ byooki da to itta.
                sick   is that said
       'Taroo said that (*he*) was sick.'

English does not, in general, allow the use of reflexive pronouns when their antecedents are not in the same clause. Japanese does. Observe the following contrast:

(35) a. John married a girl who hated *him/*himself*.
     b. Taroo wa (*kare* 'him') o kiratte iru onna to kekkonsite simatta.
               (*zibun* 'self')   hating is woman with marrying ended-up

       'Taroo ended up marrying a woman who hated him.'

There is a subtle difference in meaning between the pronominal and reflexive versions of (35b). When the pronoun *kare* is used, the sentence can be interpreted as a statement from the speaker's point of view—'Taroo ended up marrying a woman who I know hated him.' On the other hand, when the reflexive pronoun *zibun* is used, the sentence is more a statement from Taroo's point of view—it usually means 'Taroo ended up marrying a woman who, he realized later, hated him.'

I have shown above that Japanese can use a zero-form pronoun, *kare* 'he,' or *zibun* 'self, where English would use *he*. The use of zero-form pronouns is subject to a strong requirement of predictability. For example, observe the following sentences:

(36) a. Taroo$_i$ wa, $\varnothing_i$ sikaketa wana ni teki o obikiyoseta
　　　　　　　　set up　trap to enemy　lured
　　　'Taroo lured the enemy to the trap that (he) had set up.'
　　b. *Taroo$_i$ wa, $\varnothing_i$ sikaketa wana ni otikonde simatta.
　　　　　　　　set up　trap to falling　　ended up
　　　'Taroo ended up falling into the trap that (he) had set up.'
　　c. Taroo$_i$ wa *zibun$_i$* ga sikaketa wana ni otikonde simatta.

A zero-form pronoun referring to *Taroo* can be used in (36a), but not in (36b). This must be due to the fact that while one usually lures one's enemy into the traps that one has set up, one usually does not fall into one's own traps. In other words, that the subject of *sikaketa* 'set up' in (36a) is Taroo is highly predictable; but that it refers to Taroo in (36b) is least predictable, hence, the acceptability of (36a) and the unacceptability of (36b). Similarly, observe the following contrast:

(37) a.　　　Yamada$_i$ ga hisasiburi de kaette　kita　node, $\varnothing_i$ yuusyoku ni yonda.
　　　　　　　　after-long-interval returning came since dinner　　to invited

　　　'Since Yamada came back after a long interval, (I) invited (him) to dinner.'
　　b. ??Yamada$_i$ ga amerika ni itte iru toki, Tanaka ga gakkai de $\varnothing_i$ hihansita.
　　　　　　　　　　to gone is when　　　meeting at　criticized
　　　'When Yamada was in America, Tanaka criticized (him) at a professional meeting.'

It is natural that one would invite a friend to dinner when the latter has returned home after a long absence, in other words, that Yamada is the object of *yonda* 'invited' is highly predictable. Hence (36a) is acceptable. In contrast, in (37b), while Yamada was in America, anything, either related or unrelated to him, could have happened. Therefore, that *Yamada* is the object of *hihansita* 'criticized' is not as predictable as in (37a). Hence (36b) is not as acceptable as (36a).

The predictability requirement for the use of zero-form pronouns can also account for the following contrast:

(38) a. Taroo no okaasan wa Taroo o dare yori mo aisite iru.
　　　　　　's mother　　　　　　anybody than　loving is
　　　'Taroo's mother loves Taroo more than anybody else.'
　　b. *Taroo$_i$ no okaasan wa $\varnothing_i$ dare yori mo aisite iru.
　　　　　　's mother　　　　　anybody than loving is

　　　'Taroo's mother loves (him) more than anyone else.'

(39) Speaker A: Dare ga Taroo o itiban aisite iru no ka?
               who   most   loving is

               'Who loves Taroo most?'
      Speaker B: Taroo$_i$ no okaasan ga $\emptyset_i$ itiban aisite iru daroo ne.
                    's mother   most loving is I-suppose
               'Taroo's mother loves (him) most, I suppose.'

As the unacceptability of (38b) shows, a possessive noun phrase cannot be used as an antecedent for using a zero-form pronoun in major constituent position (such as object). This must be because there is no reason to assume that the possessive noun phrase is the antecedent of the zero-form pronoun in this sentence pattern. That the same sentence pattern becomes acceptable if the context makes it possible to determine the zero-form pronoun is coreferential with the possessive noun phrase, is shown in (39).[4]

It would not be amiss here to say a word about a recent claim by Lust (1980, 1983) concerning the correlation between the direction of anaphora and the direction of branching. The direction of anaphora is "forward" if the pronominal/proverbal element appears to the right of its antecedent, and "backward" if it appears to the left of its antecedent. In languages such as English, which place relative clauses to the right of their head nouns and object clauses to the right of the verbs, the principal branching direction is "rightward." In languages such as Japanese and Korean, however, which place relative clauses before their head nouns and object clauses to the left of the verbs, it is "leftward." Lust hypothesizes the following constraint:

Constraint on Anaphora (Lust): In early child language, the direction of grammatical anaphora accords with the principal branching direction of the specific language being acquired.

The principal branching direction of English is rightward, and therefore, the constraint predicts that speakers of English, in early developmental stages, prefer forward anaphora. This prediction is uncontroversial. The principal branching direction of Japanese and Korean is leftward, and, therefore, Lust's constraint predicts that speakers of Japanese and Korean in early developmental stages prefer backward anaphora.

Lust derives much of her evidence from coordinate structures such as those provided by her examples:

(40) a. John ate and $\emptyset$ read.   (Forward)
     b. John $\emptyset$ and Mary ate lunch.   (Backward)

(41) a. Inu wa hoeru si $\emptyset$ kamituku. (Forward)
         dog   barks and   bites
       'A dog barks and bites.'

b. Sumire ∅   to tanpopo ga saku. (Backward)
   violet   and dandelion bloom
   'Violets and dandelions bloom.'

Lust assumes that (40a) and (41a) contain a zero-form pronoun in the location designated by "∅," and that (40b) and (41b) contain a zero-form pro-
predicate in the location designated by "∅." She observes that English children
have more ease with verb coordination of (40a) than with noun coordination of
(40b), whereas Japanese children have more ease with noun coordination (41b)
than with verb coordination of (41a).

However, as pointed out by both Terazu (1983) and O'Grady (1984), it is
unclear that these sentences involve anaphora at all. Take, for example, the sentence *John and Mary kissed*; if we interpret that they kissed each other, this is
not paraphrasable as *John kissed and Mary kissed*. Furthermore, the conjunction
si used in (41a) is not a semantically transparent verb-coordinating conjunction.
The pattern "A" *si* "B" means something like "the most relevant to the present
discussion are A and B." It is typically used for presenting an explanation or a
premise. Its frequency is very low, even in adult speech. In contrast, the conjunction *to* used in (41a) is a semantically transparent noun-coordinating conjunction, and its frequency is very high. It should not prove surprising that Japanese children have more ease with (41b) than with (41a).

Lust also offers sentences such as the following:

(42) a. Papa$_i$ ga gohan o taberu *to*, ∅$_i$ otya o ireta.   (Forward)
            meal   eat   when   tea   poured
       'When Papa$_i$ ate the meal, ∅ poured (the) tea.'
    b. ∅$_i$ Mado o akeru *to*,   oneesan$_i$ ga kusyami o sita.   (Backward)
       window open when sister   sneeze   did
       'When ∅$_i$ opened the window, the sister$_i$ sneezed.'

She observes that Japanese children have more ease with (42b) than with
(42a) in imitation task and claims that this also supports her hypothesis of Japanese preference of backward anaphora to forward anaphora. However, her conclusion does not necessarily follow. The pattern NP$_1$ VP$_1$ *to* NP$_2$ VP$_2$ means
something like, "When NP$_1$ did VP$_1$, do you know what NP$_1$ noticed? He/she
noticed NP$_2$ did VP$_2$." The clause to the right of *to* must represent an event which
NP$_1$ observed with a feeling of surprise. For this semantic reason, the pattern
normally requires that NP$_1$ and NP$_2$ be different. Therefore, neither (42a) nor
(42b) is acceptable in the interpretation intended by Lust, in which the zero-form
pronoun refers to *Papa/oneesan*. The reading, "When I opened (the) window, do
you know what I noticed? My sister sneezed," (42b) makes an acceptable sentence.
On the other hand, (42a) is unacceptable if read as, "When Papa ate the meal,
do you know what he noticed? I poured (the) tea." It is unacceptable because

the speaker is not expected to describe his or her own action from a third party's perspective. I suspect that Japanese children did better at (42b) than at (42a) in their imitation task because, although both sentences are unacceptable in the interpretation intended by Lust, (42b), but not (42a), is acceptable in an unintended intepretation.

The above two observations cast grave doubt on Lust's interpretation of her experimental data. Furthermore, other experiments conducted on Japanese and Korean children seem to contradict her hypothesis. According to O'Grady (1984), a study of 102 Korean children between the ages of 5 and 11 (Lee, Lee & Ahn, 1982) shows that while cases of forward anaphora are common for all the children of this age bracket, cases of backward anaphora involving ∅ begin to appear only in the speech of children 8 to 10 years of age. O'Grady reports similar results in Sook Whan Cho's 6-month longitudinal study of three Korean children ranging from 2:2 to 2:10 at the project's inception. Fifteen instances of the pronominal element *key* appeared in the speech of the oldest child, and of these, only two were sentence-bound, but both involved the forward pattern. O'Grady also reports on Yoshiko Suzuki-Wei's imitation task experiments with twenty-one Japanese children between 4:7 and 8:8. The results of her experiments also show that cases of forward anaphora were much easier to imitate than cases of backward anaphora.

None of these results are surprising considering that the basic function of anaphora is to avoid the full repetition of what has been mentioned before. To use anaphora in advance, in anticipation of repetition that would otherwise ensue, seems to be a much more difficult task. In any case, as Lust's hypothesis has attracted considerable attention and seems to have gained acceptance in some quarters, further experimentation is required to resolve whether it can be maintained.

5. Source of Information

It is well known that Japanese does not allow affirmative sentences with emotive verbs such as *kanasii* 'be sad,' *uresii* 'be glad,' *tumaranai* 'be bored,' and *onaka ga suita* 'be hungry,' unless such sentences have a first-person subject. For example, observe the following sentences:

(43) a.   Boku wa kanasii.   'I am sad.'
     b. *Kimi wa kanasii.   'You are sad.'
     c. *Taroo wa kanasii.   'Taroo is sad.'

(44) a.   Boku wa onaka ga suita.   'I am hungry.'
     b. *Kimi wa onaka ga suita.   'You are hungry.'
     c. *Taroo wa onaka ga suita.   'Taroo is hungry.'

This situation contrasts with that of English, in which, if the speaker has observed Taroo's sad face, he or she can legitimately say that Taroo is sad. Similarly, if the speaker has some basis for assuming that Taroo is hungry, he or she can say so, using the English version of (44c).[5]

The same observation applies to sentences with the desiderative form of verbs. For example, observe the following sentences:

(45) a. Boku wa sukiyaki ga tabe-ta-i.
                         eat-want-Present
     'I want to eat sukiyaki.'
   b. *Kimi wa sukiyaki ga tabe-ta-i.
     'You want to eat sukiyaki.'
   c. *Taroo wa sukiyaki go tabe-ta-i.
     'Taroo wants to eat sukiyaki.'

Ta-i 'want' is an extremely productive desiderative affix that can be added to any action verb that takes a human subject.

To express what is intended in (45b) and (45c), Japanese uses modals which make clear that the information is based on hearsay. Alternatively, one can add an expression, meaning that the emotive state described is visible or add an affix turning these emotive expressions into action verbs, meaning something like 'show an overt sign of. . . .' For example, observe the following sentences:

(46) a. Taroo wa kanasii *rasii*.
               sad-be   it-seems
     'Taroo seems to be sad.'
   b. Taroo wa kanasiku nai *soo da*.
               sad   be-not I-hear
     'I heard from Taroo that he is not sad.'
   c. Taroo wa kanasi-*soo* da.
               sad appearance is
     'Taroo looks sad.'

(47)   Taroo wa kanasi-gat-te iru.
              sad-show-ing is
     'Taroo is showing an overt sign of being sad.'

Since the speaker is not expected to be able to tell what is going on in the hearer's or third party's mind, (43b, 43c), (44b, 44c), and (45b, 45c) are considered unacceptable. In contrast, (46) and (47) are acceptable because the speaker *can* observe external manifestations of someone else's internal feeling or report what that person has told him or her. In other words, the above phenomenon has generally been treated as a problem unique to expressions representing internal feelings.[6]

More recent work by Kamio (1979) shows that this phenomenon is simply a special case of a more general constraint that can be stated informally in the following manner:

Territory of Information Principle: In Japanese, the speaker can make a direct affirmative statement about a proposition only if he or she has the first-hand nonhearsay knowledge about it, that is, only if the information of the proposition belongs to his or her own territory of information. Otherwise, the speaker must overtly signal the information belongs to someone else's territory.

For example, observe the following exchanges:

(48) (The teacher observes that Taroo is absent and asks his sister Hanako what has happened.)
    Hanako: Oniisan, kaze de netu o dasite, outi de nete imasu.
              big-brother cold by fever having home at in-bed is
              'My big brother, he has caught cold, and has a fever, and he is staying in bed.'

(49) (The teacher observes that Taroo is absent and asks his classmates if they know what has happened.)
    Yoko: a. *Taroo-kun, kaze de nete imasu.
                  'Taroo is in bed with a cold.'
              b. Taroo-kun, kaze de nete iru *soo desu.*
                  'I hear that Taroo has caught a cold and is in bed at home.'

In (48), Hanako's knowledge about her brother's sickness is direct; therefore, she does not use any 'hedging/hearsay' modal. In contrast, in (49), Yoko's knowledge is based on what she has heard, perhaps from Taroo's mother. Even if Yoko is absolutely certain that Taroo's mother was telling the truth, unless she has witnesses Taroo lying in bed with a cold, she must make clear that her statement is based on hearsay by adding *soo desu* 'I hear that. . . .'

Similary, observe the following sentence, an example of Kamio's:

(50) Yaizu no zinkoo wa zyuuman o koeta.
        's population 100,000   exceeded
    'The population of Yaizu has exceeded one hundred thousand.'

Assume that a given speaker lives in a city next to Yaizu but gained the knowledge of the stated fact only by reading one or two newspaper articles. Kamio observes that this speaker can represent the above demographical fact by using (50) if he or she is talking with someone who lives at a great distance from Yaizu— for example, in Tokyo—but not when he or she is talking with a resident of Yaizu. The statement belongs to the speaker's territory because he or she lives near Yaizu, relatively speaking, if he or she is talking with someone who lives far away from the city; the same information does not belong to the speaker's territory, but to the hearer's territory, when the latter lives in Yaizu.

The shrinking and expanding of the speaker's territory of information, depending on who he or she is talking with, recalls well-known facts concerning the domain of honorific and polite expressions. For example, one's superior is a target of deference within the company or within one's section of the company, but not a target of deference when one is talking to an outsider:

(51) Secretary to her boss:
      Butyoo, nanzi ni o-modor-i *ni nar*-i *mas*-u ka?
      director what-time return honorific polite
      'Director, what time are you coming back?'

(52) Secretary to outside caller:
      Butyoo ⎱
      Yamada ⎰ wa, san-zi ni modor-i mas-u
      director 3:00 o'clock at return polite
      'Director ⎱
       Yamada ⎰ will be back at 3:00 o'clock'

In (51), the secretary is speaking with the Director and is appropriately using the subject-honorific form of the verb *modoru* 'return' (o- . . . *ni nar*-) to show respect to the *Butyoo* as the subject of the sentence; she also uses the polite morpheme *mas*- to show respect to the *Butyoo* as the hearer of the sentence. In contrast, in (52), the secretary is speaking with an outside caller, and the *Butyoo* is no longer a target of her deference. Note that she can even use the director's family name without adding an honorific title.

A great deal of work has been, and is being carried out on the use of honorific expressions in Japanese from sociolinguistic points of view, concentrating on various sociocultural factors involving the speaker, the hearer, and the person who is being talked about. I believe that the perspective of 'the speaker's territory of information' will open up a new avenue of sociolinguistic and psycholinguistic research, an avenue, I suspect, will prove as productive as that of honorific expressions. Kamio's hypothesis, if correct, will provide us with linguistic tools for the objective construction of multileveled sociological and psychological 'territory' maps and for observing children's acquisition of territorial boundaries.

Points of View

If Japanese is a language which forces the speaker to make clear whose territory a given piece of information belongs to, it is also a language which, in many, cases, forces the speaker to make clear from whose point of view he or she is speaking. Let me first illustrate, using English, what kind of hypotheses can be formulated regarding point-of-view phenomena in language. First, observe the following sentences:

(53) Assumption: John and Bill are friends, and John criticized Bill.
    a.   John criticized Bill.
    b.   John criticized his friend.
    c.   Bill's friend criticized him.
            (*or* His friend criticized Bill.)

(54) a.   Bill was criticized by John.
      b.   Bill was criticized by his friend.
      c. ??John's friend was criticized by him.
            (*or* ??His friend was criticized by John.)

We can hypothesize that expressions of the form of $f(x)$ (for example, *John's friend*) are chosen by the speaker when placing himself or herself closer to the referent of x than to the referent of $f(x)$. According to this hypothesis, (53b) is a sentence which overtly shows that the speaker has placed himself or herself closer to John than to John's friend, namely Bill. similarly, (53c) is a sentence which overtly shows that the speaker has placed himself or herself closer to Bill than to Bill's friend John.

We can also hypothesize that the speaker uses passive sentences when he or she wants to overtly signal that he or she has placed himself or herself closer to the referent of the old object than to the old subject. According to this hypothesis, (54a) shows that the speaker has placed himself or herself closer to Bill than to John. Sentence (54b) has dual signals that indicate that the speaker has placed himself or herself closer to Bill than to John: first, the use of the term *his (Bill's) friend* in referring to John, and second, the use of the passive sentence pattern to elevate the old object *Bill* to subject status.

Now we are ready to account for the marginality of (54c) in describing the event under discussion. The use of the expression *John's friend* in referring to Bill shows that the speaker has placed himself or herself closer to John than to Bill. On the other hand, the passive construction signifies that the speaker has placed himself or herself closer to the referent of the new subject *John's friend*, that is, *Bill,* than to John. These two positions are mutually exclusive. The marginality of this sentence shows that the speaker has to take a fixed camera position in producing a sentence.

Observe, further, the following sentences:

(55) a.   Next, I hit John.
      b. ??Next, John was hit by me.

(56) a.   Next, John hit an 8-foot-tall boy.
      b. ??Next, an 8-foot-tall boy was hit by John.

The marginality of (55b) seems to show that it is very difficult for the speaker to place himself or herself closer to a third party than to himself or herself. Similarly, the marginality of (56b) seems to show that it is more difficult for the speaker to place himself or herself to a newly introduced object than to an object that he or she has been talking about in the preceding discourse.

Let us formulate the above observations in the following manner:

Empathy. Empathy is the speaker's identification, which may vary in degree, with a person/thing that participates in the event or state that the speaker describes in a sentence.

Degree of Empathy. The degree of the speaker's empathy with x, $E(x)$, ranges from 0 to 1, with $E(x) = 0$ signifying a total lack of identification, and $E(x) = 1$, a total identification.

Descriptor Empathy Hierarchy. Given descriptor x (e.g., *John*) and another descriptor $f(x)$ that is dependent upon x (e.g., *John's brother*):

$$E(x) > E(f(x))$$

Surface Structure Empathy Hierarchy. In passive sentences with a by-agentive, the following hierarchy holds:

$$E(\text{Subject}) > E(\text{By-agentive})$$

Ban on Conflicting Empathy Hierarchy. A single sentence cannot contain logical conflicts in empathy relationships.

Speech-Act Empathy Hierarchy. The speaker cannot empathize with someone else more than with himself or herself

$$E(\text{Speaker}) > E(\text{Others})$$

Topic Empathy Hierarchy. Given an event or state that involves A and B such that A is coreferential with the topic of the present discourse, and B is not, it is easier for the speaker to empathize with A than with B.

$$E(\text{Discourse Topic}) \geq E(\text{Nontopic})$$

The above set of hypotheses makes it possible to account for numerous phenomena in English that otherwise cannot be explained and that I do not have the space to discuss here. I have evidence, however, indicating that the empathy perspective I have outlined is something children seem to acquire early in their development; and that even 6-year-olds seem to have internalized at least some part of it. Also, Karmiloff-Smith (1980) reports that in her story-production experiments, both in French and English, the children in the second developmental stage (6 to 9 years of age) placed the main character of the story predominantly in subject position, and used pronouns only in that position, and those in the third developmental stage (also ranging in age between 6 to 9) sometimes placed nonmajor characters of the story in subject position but limited the use of pronouns to the major character. If we can equate the major character of the story with the target of the speaker's highest empathy, Karmiloff-Smith's results also show that the English and French children begin to acquire the empathy perspective sometime around 6 years of age.

The empathy perspective in Japanese manifests itself most conspicuously in the use of giving verbs. The language has two series of giving verbs, depending upon where the speaker's empathy lies. Observe the following paradigm:

(57)   E(Giver $\geq$ E(Receiver)   E(Giver) $<$ E(Receiver)
     Informal   *yaru*   *kureru*
     Polite   *ageru*   *kudasaru*

All these verbs mean 'give,' and place the giver noun phrase in subject position, and the receiver noun phrase in the dative object position.

Now, observe the following sentences:

(58) a.   Boku ga Hanako ni okane o *yaru.*   *Giver*   *Receiver*
       I   to money give   E(I) $\geq$ E(Hanako)
       'I give money to Hanako.'
    b. *Hanako ga boku ni okane o *yaru.*   *E(Hanako) $>$ E(I)
       'Hanako gives me money.'

(59) a. *Boku ga Hanako ni okane o *kureru.*   *Giver*   *Receiver*
       I   to money give   *E(I) $<$ E(Hanako)
       'I give money to Hanako.'
    b.   Hanako ga boku ni okane o *kureru.*   E(Hanako) $<$ E(I)
       'Hanako gives me money.'
    c. *Taroo ga (Taroo no) imooto ni okane o *kureru.* *E(Taroo) $<$ E(Taroo's
                 's little-sister to money give   sister)
       'Taroo gives money to his little sister.'

Sentence (58b) is unacceptable because *yaru* requires that the speaker place himself or herself closer to the subject Hanako than to himself or herself, a condition not allowed under the Speech Act Empathy Hierarchy. Due to a similar conflict in empathy requirements, (59a) and (59c) are unacceptable.

The camera-angle phenomenon in Japanese does not exclusively concern the giving verb. The two series of verbs just discussed, together with verbs of coming and going, are used extensively, and sometimes obligatorily, as supporting verbs (coupled with the main verbs) to express where the speaker stands vis-à-vis the events that he or she describes in sentences. For example, observe the following sentences:

(60) a. Taroo ga Hanako ni okane o kasu.
                  to money   lend
     'Taroo will lend money to Hanako.'   *Giver*   *Receiver*
   b. Taroo ga Hanako ni okane o kasite *yaru.*   E(Taroo) $>$ E(Hanako)[7]
   c. Taroo ga Hanako ni okane o kasite *kureru.*   E(Taroo) $<$ E(Hanako)

These three sentences are all active sentences, with *Taroo* as subject but are very different with respect to possible discourse contexts. The sentence (60a) is used by the speaker when he or she takes a detached view of the action described. Sentence (60b) is used when the speaker places himself or herself closer to Taroo than to Hanako, while (60c) is used when he or she takes opposite camera angle.

When one of the characters who appears in sentences is either the speaker, or someone close, he or she has to make explicit that the camera has been placed closer (to the speaker). For example, observe the following sentences:

(61) a. *Taroo ga kinoo boku o tazuneta.
  yesterday I visited
  'Taroo visited me yesterday.'
 b. Taroo ga kinoo boku o tazunete *kureta*.
  yesterday visiting gave
 c. Taroo ga kinoo boku o tazunete *kita*.
  yesterday visiting came

(62) a. *Taroo ga yuube boku ni denwa o kaketa.
  last-night I to phone called
  'Taroo called me up last night.'
 b. Taroo ga yuube boku ni denwa o kakete *kureta*.
 c. Taroo ga yuube boku ni denwa o kakete *kita*.

Kureta and *kita* in the above (b) and (c) sentences do not mean 'gave' and 'came,' but only signal that the sentences are from the receiver's point of view. Note in particular that (62c) does not mean that Taroo phoned and came, it simply means that he phoned the speaker. For further discussion on empathy and syntax, see Kuno and Kaburaki (1976) and Kuno (1978b).

It would be interesting to examine at what stage Japanese children begin to acquire the use of giving and coming/going verbs to overtly state their camera positions for sentence productions.

7. Topic Marker and Multiple-Subject Construction

The Japanese language has a special grammatical device for marking the topic of a sentence. The particle *wa* performs this function. For example, observe the following sentences:

(63) a. *Taroo ga* kite inai.
  nom. coming isn't
  '(Oh, look!) Taroo isn't here.' *or* 'It's Taroo who isn't here.'
 b. *Taroo wa* mada kite inai.
  yet coming isn't

'Speaking of Taroo (who you must be wondering about/who is relevant to the present situation), he isn't here yet.'

(64) a. Boku mo, *kono hon o* yonda koto ga aru.
   I   too   this book   read experience have
   'I, too, have read this book.'

   b. *Kono hon* WA, boku mo yonda koto ga aru.
   'This book, I, too, have read.'

(65) a. Boku wa, *Tanaka-san no* okusan ni sika atta koto ga nai.
                      's wife   to only met experience haven't
   'I have met only Mr. Tanaka's wife.'

   b. *Tanaka-san* WA, boku wa, okusan ni sika atta koto ga nai.
   'Speaking of Mr. Tanaka, I have met only his wife.'

Sentence (63a) presents an event arising out-of-the-blue, or alternatively, fills in the gap in, 'It is ( ) who isn't here.' In either case, the *ga*-marked subject represents new, unpredictable information in a sentence. In contrast, (63b) is a statement about Taroo. It is used when it can be assumed that Taroo, or the set of which Taroo is a member, is in the consciousness of the hearer. Sentence (64a) describes the speaker's experience. In contrast, (64b) characterizes the book as one the speaker, too, has read. Sentence (65a) describes the speaker's lack of experience of meeting anybody relevant, other than Mr. Tanaka's wife. In contrast, (65b) characterizes Mr. Tanaka as someone whom the speaker has not met personally—he or she has met only his wife. In all these sentences, the *wa*-marked noun phrase at sentence-initial position represents the topic of the sentences.

Let us now examine the grammatical functions that the *wa*-marked noun phrases perform in these sentences. In (63b), the *wa*-marked topic corresponds to the nominative subject of (63a). In (64b), it corresponds to the accusative object of (64a). In (65b), *Tanaka-san wa* corresponds to the possessive noun phrase of (65a). In this way, the topic-noun phrase usually performs some grammatical functions in the rest of the sentences. However, there are sentences in which the *wa*-marked topics do not play any grammatical function other than that of topic. For example, observe the following sentences:

(66) a. *Sakana wa*, tai ga itiban oisii.
   fish   porgy   most delicious-is
   'Speaking of fish, porgies are the most delicious.'

   b. *Hankoo-basyo wa*, okunai-setu ga attooteki datta.[8]
   crime-place   indoor-theory   predominant was
   'Speaking of the place of the crime, the 'indoor theory' was predominant.'

There are no particles that can be used in the place of *wa* in these sentences to specify the grammatical functions of the topic noun phrases.

In addition to the topic-subject construction illustrated in (66), Japanese has what can be legitimately called a multiple-subject construction. For example, observe the following sentences:

(67) a. Nihon no dansei no heikin-zyumyoo *ga* itiban mizikai koto wa yoku sirarete iru.
       Japan 's male 's average-life   most short-is that   well known is
       'The fact that the average life-span of Japanese males is the shortest is well known.'
    b. Nihon no dansei *ga* heikin-zyumyoo *ga* itiban mizikai koto wa. . . .
       'The fact that Japanese males—their average life-span is the shortest is. . . .'
    c. Nihon *ga* dansei no heikin-zyumyoo *ga* itiban mizikai koto wa. . . .
       'The fact that Japan—its males' average life-span is the shortest is. . . .'
    d. Nihon *ga* dansei *ga* heikinzyumyoo *ga* itiban mizikai koto wa. . . .
       'The fact that Japan—its males—their average life-span is the shortest is. . . .'

Sentences (67b) and (67c) have two *ga*-marked noun phrases, and sentence (67d), three. We obtain such multiple *ga*-marked noun phrase constructions when the first noun phrase is the possessive of the second, as shown between (67a) and (67b), and between (67b) and (67d). Various syntactic tests show that all these multiple *ga*-marked noun phrases display the characteristics of subjecthood, and, therefore, we can call them multiple-subject sentences. Details can be found in Kuno (1973, 1978a, 1983).

As far as I know, research in children's acquisition of Japanese sentence patterns has thus far focused primarily on the study of simple nominative-accusative sentences and has not extended to topic sentences or to multiple-subject sentences (see Hakuta and Bloom, this volume). My speculation is that children first acquire the subject-object-verb word order but without the nominative particle *ga* and the accusative particle *o*, following the noun phrases. It is most likely that at this stage, the subject-noun phrase, which is not marked with any particle, is the topic of the sentences. Recall Karmiloff-Smith's observation that the English-speaking and French-speaking children, at their second stage of development, always place the topic of this narration in the subject position. I conjecture that at the developmental stage under discussion, the unmarked noun phrase in sentence-initial position in Japanese performs the same function. It is most likely that Japanese children acquire the covert topic construction before learning the nominative subject construction. They probably next learn to mark the topic with *wa* and to mark the nontopic subject (which represents out-of-the-blue information) with *ga*. The use of topic noun phrases for nonsubject functions and the use of multiple subject constructions come much later. But this is only speculation and must either be proved or disproved by careful analysis of collected data.

Conclusion

I have discussed seven aspects of the Japanese language with the view that they might, either directly or indirectly, provide scholars in child development with new areas of research. In my view, language acquisition research in Japanese has been disproportionately centered around (1) deferential expressions, and (2) case marking and grammatical relations. It is hoped that this brief paper will contribute to the initiation of new research efforts in other important and challenging areas, ones which may well be equally rewarding.

Footnotes

1. Research discussed in this paper has been supported in part by a grant from the National Science Foundation to Harvard University (Grant No. BNS-82-14193). The representation of Japanese in this chapter follows the traditional system of Romanization used in Japan and departs from the more phonetically based system used in other chapters of this volume.

2. In sentences with conspicuous stress in nonfinal position, the focus shift to that stressed element. Therefore, in (25a), if *buy* is stressed, it becomes a question as to whether buying took place or whether borrowing or stealing took place.

3. In fact, if, for example, a man goes to a restaurant alone, sits at a table, and is asked by a waitress what he is going to order, he would be unable to use (27) unless he is contrasting himself with customers at other tables who have placed their orders with the waitress. This shows that *boku wa* in (27) is performing the function of setting off the answerer from the rest of the addressees.

4. See Kuno (1983) for more discussion on this subject.

5. But see footnote 6.

6. It seems that this constraint exists in English, too, albeit to a much lesser degree. For example, compare the following sentences:

(I) a. Look! John is hungry. Let's go eat.

b. Look! Professor Johnson is hungry. Let's go eat.

It seems as though (a) is perfectly acceptable, whereas (b) is a little impolite, that is, to Professor Johnson, whose internal feeling the speaker is verbalizing. It is more likely that the speaker will use, instead:

(II) Look! I am sure that Professor Johnson is hungry now. Let's go to eat.

7. Although *yaru* as an independent giving verb requires only that E(Receiver) not be higher than E (Giver) (note the equality sign in (57)), *yaru* as a supporting verb requires that E(Giver) be higher than E(Receiver) (note the absence of an equality sign in (60b)). Justification for this difference is given in Kuno (1978b).

8. This example is Akira Mikami's.

References

Greenberg, J. H. (1963). Some universals of grammar with particular reference to the order of meaningful elements. In Greenberg, J. H. (Ed.), *Universals of language*. Cambridge, Mass.: MIT Press.

Hakuta, K. (1982). Interaction between particles and word order in the comprehension and production of simple sentences in Japanese children. *Developmental Psychology, 18*, 62–76.

Inoue, K. (1979). Japanese: A story of language and people. In T. Shopen (Ed.), *Languages and their speakers*. Cambridge, Mass.: Winthrop Publishers.

Kamio, A. (1979). On the notion Speaker's Territory of Information: A functional analysis of certain sentence-final forms in Japanese. In G. Bedell, E. Kobayashi, & M. Kuraki (Eds.), *Explorations in Linguistics: Papers in honor of Kazuko Inoue*. Tokyo: Kenkyusha.

Karmiloff-Smith, A. (1980). Psychological processes underlying pronominalization and non-pronominalization in children's connected discourse. In J. Kreiman & A. E. Ojeida (Eds.), *Papers from the parasession on pronouns and anaphora*. Chicago Linguistic Society.

Kuno, S. (1973). *The structure of the Japanese language*. Cambridge, Mass.: MIT Press.

———. (1974). The position of relative clauses and conjunctions. *Linguistic Inquiry, 5,* 117–136.

———. (1978a). Japanese: A characteristic OV language. In Lehmann, W. (Ed.), *Syntactic typology*. Austin: University of Texas Press.

———. (1978b). *Danwa no bunpoo* [Grammar of discourse]. Tokyo: Taishukan Publishing Co. (In Japanese)

———. (1982). Principles of discourse deletion: Case studies from English, Russian and Japanese. *Journal of Semantics, 1,* 61–93.

———. (1983). *Sin-Nihonbunpoo kenkyuu* [New studies in Japanese grammar]. Tokyo: Taishukan Publishing Co. (In Japanese)

Kuno, S., and Kaburaki, E. (1976). Empathy and syntax. *Linguistic Inquiry, 8,* 627–672.

Lust, B. (1980). Constraints on anaphora in child language: A prediction for a universal. In S. Tavakolian, (Ed.), *Language acquisition and linguistic theory*. Cambridge, Mass.: MIT Press.

Lust, B., & Mangione, L. (1983). The principal branching direction parameter in first language acquisition of anaphora. In P. Sells and C. Jones (Eds.), *Proceedings of ALNE 13/NELS, 13,* 145–160.

Masunaga, K. (1983). Bridging. *Proceedings of the XIIIth International Congress of Linguists, Tokyo 1982,* 455–460.

Nevstuphý, J. V. (1978). *Post-structural approaches to language*. Tokyo: University of Tokyo Press.

O'Grady, W. (1984). Directionality and language learning: Data from Korean and Japanese. Presented at the Nitobe-Ohira Memorial Conference in Japanese Studies, University of British Columbia.

Sano, K. (1977). An experimental study on the acquisition of Japanese simple sentences and cleft sentences. *Descriptive and Applied Linguistics, 10,* 213–233.

Suzuki, T. (1978). *Japanese and the Japanese: Words in culture.* (A. Miura, Trans.). Tokyo: Kodansha International.

Terazu, N. (1983). Comments on the paper by Lust. In Y. Otsu, H. van Riemsdijk, K. Inoue, A. Kamio, & N. Kawasaki (Eds.), *Studies in generative grammar and language acquisition: A report on recent trends in linguistics.* Tokyo: International Christian University.

Yngve, V. H. (1960). A model and a hypothesis for language structure. *Proceedings of the American Philosophical Society, 104,* 444–446.

PART TWO

EMPIRICAL STUDIES

9 | The Role of the Personal Framework of Social Relationships in Socialization Studies

Keiko Takahashi

Though it is a truism in the psychology of socialization that children are born into a social world composed of multiple social figures, empirical studies on the effectiveness of socializing agents continue to use the traditional dyadic paradigm. That is, to understand the nature of the influence of a given agent on the acquisition of socially valued competence, researchers usually examine dyadic relations between children and only one socializing agent. Most often, this agent is the mother or an experimental model, who is often described in terms of selected attributes or behavioral characteristics.

There are three lines of research on the issue of socialization. The first type or study is based on the assumption that the mother is the primary, and the most important, figure for all children. Researchers attempt to show that children who attach securely to and establish an emotional relation with the mother will be easily socialized by her (for example, Ainsworth & Bell, 1974; Sroufe, 1979; Yarrow, Rubenstein & Pedersen, 1975). The second type of study emphasizes the relation between the mother's teaching skills and the child's cognitive development (for example, Hess & Shipman, 1965; Price, Hess & Dickson, 1981). In this type of study, researchers have assumed that the mother is the primary figure, the most influential person in fostering child development, and they have paid little attention to variations in the emotional relations between mother and child. The third line of research relies on laboratory studies: a model, who is a stranger to the child—a neutral social agent—initiates experimental interactions with the child. Researchers conducting this type of study have shown that children more readily imitate the behavior of a nurturant model than that of a nonnurturant or neutral model (for example, Bandura, Ross & Ross, 1963; Bandura & Huston, 1961).

There are three difficulties with both the assumptions and the research strategies of these traditional dyadic studies of social relationships and their outcomes. The difficulties all arise from a failure to theorize about and manage what may be called the ecological reality of development. For a person is not merely a social being—that is, a definitive member from birth of a social network, who is acted upon simultaneously by multiple members. Even an infant selects significant others and mentally organizes a personal social network, constructing a personal framework for social relationships.

The first difficulty arises from the unrealistic assumption that the mother is the primary agent in the socialization of all children. Some children may attach themselves to someone other than the mother—for example, becoming grandmother's boy or daddy's girl. Though, in research, these children are not separated from their mother-attached counterparts, the mother must be less powerful for them than for those whose mothers do play the most significant role in their personal framework. This loosening of mother-child attachment would occur, not necessarily because of any lack of sophisticated teaching or other inadequacy, but because the mother has been assigned a secondary role as a socializaing agent by the child.

The second difficulty comes from an "optimistic" assumption: that a single primary figure functions as the most important, or effective agent, in all domains. In daily life, a child, even an infant, has social relationships with many others besides the primary figure: it should be emphasized that the primary figure is only one of many significant others. For instance, Yamada (1982) reported that a 14-month-old boy had several different, well-articulated relationships with his family members. He appeared to assign what he perceived as the most appropriate role to each of them. Observations of his home situation suggested that the mother was the primary figure, and she was often asked to care for him when he was drowsy; the grandmother was regarded as the person who gave him special cakes; the grandfather was an important person who repaired his toys; his sister was a playmate, and so forth. Thus, an essential characteristic of the personal framework is that the role of each figure, including the primary one, is determined interdependently with those of others. In other words, the role of each figure complements every other figure. Therefore, even when the mother has been assigned the role of primary figure, this does not necessarily imply she is the person of sole importance to her children. Since a child is surrounded with many people, each having different areas of competence, it is probable that he or she finds a more effective person than the mother as a socializing agent in one or more domains. A secondary figure, for instance, the father, may be more powerful in the socialization of some kinds of cognitive development than is the mother.

Laboratory studies using strangers as social models seem to be ideal from the perspective of experimental control of the social situation. However, the difficulty with this type of study is that the relationship between the model and any child, even though the two are strangers to one another, must be influenced by the child's personal framework. It is unrealistic to assume that subjects can ever start new personal relationships with a clean slate. To the contrary, our studies on attachment to different kinds of strangers suggest that only strangers having similarities to the primary figure—gender, a friendly manner of interaction, and age, for example—could have effective contact with 2-year-olds (Takahashi, 1982; Takahashi & Hatano, 1982).

To obtain more accurate information on the reality of social influences from studies of transactions between socializing agents and children, we must understand the individual frameworks in which social relationships are established before studing the dyadic transactions among subjects. This research strategy should lead to clearer findings than have been obtained from the traditional types of studies.

I would like to propose a model describing the individual framework of interpersonal relationships. After this, I shall describe the instruments used to assess the personal framework based on the model and two empirical studies in which these instruments were used.

The Conceptual Model and Research Instruments

As a social animal, a person has a variety of human relationships, ranging from the purely affectional to the wholly instrumental. Here, I examine the individual framework consisting of the most significant and important agents in socialization, that is, the core of interpersonal relations, which we may term attachment relations.

In constructing the model of attachment relations, I began by examining the nature of attachment in adults, rather than in young children, because during infancy and young childhood the primary caregivers take such prominent roles in socialization that other people are relegated to distinctly secondary roles. A second reason for beginning with adults is the methodological difficulty of studying mental processes in children. Attachment has been described in terms of the following four properties:

1. *The attachment figures to whom the attachment motive is directed.* A person possesses many such figures.

2. *The psychic function of each attachment figure.* These functions vary, from a central one of deep psychic support to those that are purely instrumental.

3. *The mode of attachment behaviors by which the attachment motive are expressed.* Attachment behavior may be symbolic (that is to say, indirect), direct but distal, or direct and proximal.

4. *The strength of the attachment motive and the accompanying intensity or frequency of attachment behavior to each attachment figure.* It is generally assumed that all human beings have an attachment motive (Ainsworth, 1982; Bowlby, 1969; Takahashi, 1974; Weiss, 1982). It is believed to be unnecessary—and also impossible—to measure the total strength of this motive.

To assess the conceptual model, using both college students and mature adults as subjects, I constructed two instruments: an Attachment Questionnaire (Att-Q) and an Attachment Sentence Completion Test (Att-SCT) (Takahashi, 1974).

Table 9.1
Number and Type of Attachment Structure
among College Students

Type	Female	Male
One-focus	57	120
Mother	15	2
Love object	28	99
Closest friend	4	9
Respected person	8	9
Father	1	1
Sibling	1	0
Multifocus	106	152
Two-focus	40	74
Three-focus	40	54
Four or more foci	26	24
Undifferentiated focus	5	5
Total	168	277

The Att-Q consists of twenty-four statements describing concrete situations and the means by which certain functions are fulfilled (for example, "When I have a sad or bitter experience, I think of X." "When I have a pleasant experience, I want X to be the first to know about it.") For each situation, separate ratings are made on a 5-point scale for each of six figures (mother, father, one sibling, the closest friend, love object, and a respected person). The strength of the attachment motive toward each figure is obtained by summing over the twenty-four items. According to the attachment score, one or more primary figures, called the foci, are designated.

The Att-SCT consists of sixteen items concerning attachment figures supporting each subject and the function of each possible figure in the subject's personal life. The Att-SCT was designed to check whether or not the primary figure of the Att-Q is considered by the subject to be a truly important figure.

The studies using college students as subjects (Takahashi, 1974; 1980) indicated that the subject had several attachment figures, including parents, siblings, closest friends of the same sex, a love object of the opposite sex, and respected persons. Modes of attachment behaviors were varied, depending upon the attachment figures and the occasions, and there were clearly articulated psychic functions between figures. The subjects had a primary attachment figure who supported the most important part of their self; they also had a few figures for the next most important part and many other figures for less important parts.

I term the above differentiated attachment figure-function pairs "attachment structures."

Table 9.1 shows several types of attachment structures, differing in who was assigned a central role (though all types had the three common structural properties mentioned).

Using the mature-attachment structure as a model for the final state of development, the inner framework of social relations for each earlier period of development may be described as less mature or less structured. Each stage of interpersonal development involves a transformation of the attachment structure.

Though there are methodological difficulties inherent in studying the inner framework among young children through this conceptual model, I constructed a Picture Attachment Test (PAT), for use with young children (Takahashi, 1978). The PAT consists of two parallel sets of eight to thirteen cards, one set designed for girls and one set for boys. As shown in Figure 9-1, each card illustrates a daily life situation in which attachment behaviors to another person may be induced in young children.

During the test session, the child is asked to suppose the major figure in the picture is himself or herself. The child is shown each card and asked to answer each question with the name of a person. The relative strength of the motive toward each significant figure is the total frequency with which the person is named in all the cards. The function of each figure is inferred from the situations in which the given figure is selected. In the PAT, the modes of attachment behaviors are not asked because of young children's limited verbal abilities.

Children 4 to 6 years of age are interviewed individually; elementary school children are asked to answer a reduced-size edition of the PAT in groups. In the case of 1- to 3-year old children, primary caregivers are asked how the child would respond to the PAT based on what they have already observed in the child's daily life.

Figure 9-1
Item from Picture Attachment Test.

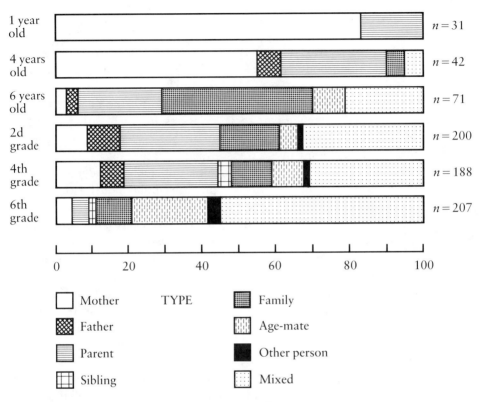

Figure 9-2
Developmental changes in types of attachment.

Studies with children 1 to 12 years of age (Takahashi, 1983) indicated that, as shown in Figure 9-2, all, even 1-year-olds, had individual differences in their personal framework; children began to extend their attachment figures beyond the primary one before the age of 2. For instance, though 4-year-olds were attached primarily to the mother, about half selected the father as a cobathing partner, and 70 percent chose peers as play partners. It is likely that in such situations the mother was not as competent as the father or the peers. The percentage of mother-attached subject decreased from almost 100 percent at 1 year of age as the child grew older. Correspondingly, the percentage of agemate-attached type subjects increased. Even among children of kindergarten age, 10 percent were classified as being attached to agemates.

Empirical Studies

Next, I present two empirical findings illustrating the importance of personal framework in understanding social influences.

Life Histories among College Students

Eighty-four sophomore women were tested two or three times during a 6-month period by the Att-Q and Att-SCT. They were also asked to write their own life histories, spending at least two hours covering 113 items which concerned relations with parents, siblings, grandparents, peers or friends, and teachers in five periods from early childhood to present. The average length of the personal histories was about 2100 words.

Fifteen cases, each judged to have one or two stable primary attachment figures as foci through two or three measurements were selected for analysis. Ten of them, whom we call the family-attached type, selected the primary figures only from the family, five cases selected the mother, three selected both the mother and the father, and two selected the mother and sibling. The remaining five, referred to as the agemate-attached type, chose only from agemates, three cases selected a boyfriend, one selected the closest woman friend, and one selected both a boyfriend and the closest woman friend. The personal histories of the two types were checked against the list of imporant items as to whether they had referred to each item positively or negatively, or neglected it. As Table 9.2 shows, there were clear differences in descriptions between the types of attachment structures. Family-attached type students, who assigned the most important psychic role to family members and did not have close relations with agemates, referred positively and vividly to relations with family members throughout all developmental periods; they reported that they were called "mama's girl" in young childhood and had many difficulties in adapting to school from an early age and in making friends. They also felt strong influences from family members, even in selection of the college they attended and in their future plans. One of them wrote that she would marry in order to give a grandchild to her mother.

On the other hand, agemate-attached type students consistently wrote their life histories mostly in relation to peers and friends, including those of the opposite sex. Even in kindergarten, they reported that they had enjoyed their life with peers rather than with their mothers. They recalled pleasant scenes in kindergarten and very easy adaptation to school. They had boyfriends and planned their future life on their own, that is, independent or parental assistance. Care must be taken in interpreting these findings because life histories are apt to be colored by students' present emotions toward these same important persons, as suggested by Bower (1981). However, we are sure that the personal framework of relationships must mediate new encounters and play an important role in establishing successive personal frameworks which will mediate coming encounters. While I do not subscribe to the so-called childhood determinism, I do believe that an early-established personal framework play an important part in the transactional modification of a later framework. It is necessary to assume the continuity of stable individual characteristics in the developmental process of social relationships.

Table 9.2
Differences between Family-Attached Type and Agemate-Attached Type in Life Histories

Items in each period	Family-attached type*		Agemate-attached type†		χ^2
	Positive description	Negative, neutral description	Positive description	Negative, neutral description	
In early childhood,					
I was an active child.	1	9	5	0	7.81‡
I had many friends.	0	10	3	2	4.22§
In elementary school,					
I was an active girl and took leadership in school.	1	9	5	0	7.81‡
I had many friends.	4	6	5	0	1.90
I liked at least one of my teachers.	4	6	1	4	1.84
In junior high school,					
I was an active girl and took leadership in school.	1	9	3	2	2.59
I had many friends.	1	9	3	2	2.59
I loved my family members.	7	3	1	4	1.64
In high school,					
I was an active girl and took leadership in school.	6	4	5	0	1.07
I had close friends.	0	10	5	0	10.84‡
I had friends of the opposite sex.	0	10	4	1	7.20‡

Table 9.2 (*continued*)

Items in each period	Family-attached type*		Agemate-attached type†		χ^2
	Positive description	Negative, neutral description	Positive description	Negative, neutral description	
I loved my family members.	4	6	0	5	1.07
I liked at least one of my teachers.	4	6	0	5	1.07
At the present,					
I have close friends.	0	10	4	1	7.20‡
I have a lover.	0	10	4	1	7.20‡
I like my family members.	8	2	0	5	5.66§

* $n = 10$
† $n = 5$
‡ $P < .01$
§ $P < .05$

A Study of Cooperation

Using the PAT, the attachment structures of sixty-four 5-year-old children were measured two or three times during the 7 months after their entrance into kindergarten (Nagata & Suzuki, 1983). Two groups of children were selected: five children, called the agemate-attached type, who selected peers dominantly and stably; and five children, the mother-attached type, who consistently expressed closer contact with the mother than with peers through two or three measurements.

Each child was asked to build a house, using forty pieces of colored blocks in cooperation with another child who had been selected as a moderate type. Moderate-types were defined as having relatively good relations with both peers and mother. They also belonged to another kindergarten class and had not been in close contact with the target child in daily play sessions.

Each play session, five minutes in duration, was videotaped. Large differences were found between the two types of children. Agemate-attached children cooperated well with an agemate, even when the partner was unfamiliar to them. These children often offered to cooperate verbally, took the initiative in building blocks, or accepted the ideas of the partner. They played actively and seemed to enjoy the tasks of joint problem solving. In five minutes' interaction, four out of the five pairs were able to build one house.

In contrast, their mother-attached type counterparts were weak in interactions with agemates. Sometimes, they played so egocentrically that their play partners hesitated to touch the blocks. We were impressed by one mother-attached girl, who gathered all the blue blocks, even though her partner had been using some of them, and built her own house very far from the partner. In fact, all pairs with mother-attached type children built two separate houses, disregarding the instructions.

These results suggest that, although children of this age may have actively interacted with peers and been influenced by their agemates in daily life situations, the nature of the relationship with the peer-partner in the experimental situation—specifically, the interaction behavior with the peer-stranger—was clearly affected by each child's inner framework. As I stated earlier, children could not begin their interactions as a blank slate. Consequently, the products of the interactions were strongly influenced by the social network they carried from prior social experiences.

I should emphasize that I have been referring to the importance of the personal framework—that is, the inner social network—not to the external social network, which surrounds a person as environment, like the one Lewis and Feiring (1979) have investigated. Though the inner social network naturally reflects the external one, the two are not the same. The former is constructed by each person as an individual framework, even though its contents are usually selected from the components of the latter. Sometimes, and especially for adolescents and adults, a personal framework may include figures beyond our possible coverage of the external social network; for example, it may include symbolic figures, such as God, dead persons, authors of books, foreigners, and others whom the person has never met.

I assume that this personal framework actually mediates both input and output in social interactions. The two empirical studies supported this assumption: the family/mother-attached type subjects showed different social behaviors from that of their agemate-attached type counterparts. We observed clear differences when the subjects were separated according to their personal framework. It may be concluded that researchers on the susceptibility to social influences should pay particular attention to their subjects' prior personal framework of social relationships.

Once we obtain the knowledge of a given child's personal framework, we can understand and predict more precisely both the degree and the contents of social influences on him or her from another person. It is unrealistic to assume that the mother is assigned the primary figure role by all children; it is also not always true that, as the primary figure, she is the most influential socializing agent. Therefore, the effectiveness of the mother in socialization can be examined more clearly among children who have a personal framework where she is assigned the primary figure role and is more influential in the target domain.

Similarly, even if agemates are expected to act as the important socializing agents in the classroom, all children do not readily interact and affect one another; each must assign different status to peers or friends within his or her personal framework. Therefore, we shall get a better grasp of the reality of agemate influence, when we study socialization by classifying subjects according to the relative importance of the roles within the subject's personal framework.

Even in predicting social interactions with a stranger who has no place in a child's current personal framework, our knowledge of that framework will be valuable. Children infer the characteristics of the stranger from those of figures, already present in it, who had similar salient properties to those of the unfamiliar person. In fact, we are finding that we can understand 2-year-olds who interact positively with a male adult stranger and others who show fear, if we incorporate knowledge of their personal framework in which males, such as their father, uncle, or cousin played important roles.

Although researchers agree that a child is a member of a social group, few have attempted to go beyond dyads and to observe triads and larger interpersonal interactions among family members (Lewis & Feiring, 1982). Both observations and analyses of the interactions beyond dyads are too complicated to be managed by the techniques at hand. The research strategy I have proposed measures subjects' personal framework and classifies them by its contents. Hopefully, this approach will enable us to advance our understanding of children's social acquisitions.

Reference

Ainsworth, M. D. S. (1982). Attachment: retrospect and prospect. In M. Parkes & J. Stevenson-Hinde (Eds.), *The place of attachment in human development*. New York: Basic Books.

Ainsworth, M. D. S., & Bell, S. M. (1974). Mother-infant interaction and the development of competence. In K. J. Connolly & J. Bruner (Eds.), *The growth of competence*. London & New York: Academic Press.

Bandura. A., & Huston, A. C. (1961). Identification as a process of incidental learning. *Journal of Abnormal and Social Psychology, 63*, 311–318.

Bandura, A., Ross, D., & Ross, S. A. (1963). A comparative test of the status envy, social power, and secondary reinforcement theories of identificatory learning. *Journal of Abnormal and Social Psychology, 67*, 527–534.

Bower, G. H. (1981). Mood and memory. *American Psychologist, 36*, 129–148.

Bowlby, J. (1969). *Attachment*. New York: Basic Books.

Hess, R. D., & Shipman, V. C. (1965). Early experience and the socialization of cognitive modes in children. *Child Development, 36*, 869–888.

Lewis, M., & Feiring, C. (1979). The child's social network: social object, social functions, and their relationship. In M. Lewis & L. A. Rosenblum (Eds.), *The child and its family*. New York: Plenum Press.

———. (1982). Some American families at dinner. *Monograph of Educational Testing Service*, Princeton, N. J.

Nagata, C., & Suzuki, M. (1983). *Development of interpersonal relationships among kindergarten children*. Unpublished thesis, Kunitachi College of Music, Tokyo. (In Japanese)

Price, G. G., Hess, R. D., & Dickson, W. P. (1981). Processes by which verbal-educational abilities are affected when mothers encourage preschool children to verbalize. *Developmental Psychology, 17, 554–564*.

Sroufe, A. (1979). The coherence of individual development: early care, attachment, and subsequent issues. *American Psychologist, 34* (10), 834–841.

Takahashi, K. (1974). Development of dependency among female adolescents and young adults. *Journal of Psychological Research, 16, 179–185*.

———. (1978). The measurement of attachment among young children. Paper presented at Annual Meeting of the Japanese Psychological Association.

———. (1980). Development of attachment among male students. *Monograph of Kunitachi College of Music, 14, 113–142*. (In Japanese)

———. (1982). Attachment behavior to a female stranger among Japanese two-year-olds. *Journal of Genetic Psychology, 140, 299–307*.

Takahashi, K., & Hatano, G. (1982). Extension of attachment objects among Japanese toddlers. *Annual Report of Research and Clinical Center for Child Development*, 1980–1981, 9–17. Sapporo: Hokkaido University.

Takahashi, K. (1983). The development of personal relationships, In K. Miyake, J. Murai, G. Hatano, & K. Takahashi (Eds.), *Handbook of child psychology*. Tokyo: Kaneko-shobo. (In Japanese)

Weiss, R. S. (1982). Attachment in adult life. In C. M. Parkes & J. Stevenson-Hinde. (Eds.), *The place of attachment in human behavior*. New York, Basic Books.

Yamada, Y. (1982). Expressions of request and rejection, and the emergence of self in infancy. *Japanese Journal of Educational Psychology, 30, 38–48*. (In Japanese)

Yarrow, L. J., Rubenstein, J. L., & Pedersen, F. A. (1975). *Infant and environment: early cognitive and motivational development*. New York, John Wiley.

Japanese Studies of Infant Development

Shing-jen Chen
Kazuo Miyake

This chapter deals with major empirical studies concerning infant development in Japan during the last 30 years. We do not presume to provide a comprehensive review of the field. Instead, we concentrate on selected topics which describe cultural factors with important implications for the study of infant development and point out methodological preconceptions currently in existence. Through a historical sketch of this area of reserach in Japan, we make some practical suggestions concerning some important factors in the process of infant development and its study. In accordance with the theme of this volume, we chose to discuss comparative studies of mother-infant interaction and infant development in Japan and in the United States. Since Japanese child rearing differs from that of the United States and Europe in some important ways, studies involving Japanese mothers and infants should make a special contribution to our understanding of infant development (Azuma, 1982; Caudill & Weinstein, 1969).

Cross-cultural comparison of child rearing and later personality development has a long history. It was the chief point of interaction between psychology and anthropology before cross-cultural cognitive psychology became popular. The American interest in the psychology of the Japanese, motivated during World War II, was based on practical concerns of the time and probably represented the beginning of modern psychological stuidies of the Japanese. Under the influence of Freudian theory, infancy and child-rearing practices became important topics in the cultural anthropological studies of a given society. Caudill began the first empirical study of early interaction of the Japanese mother and infant in the early 1960s. Subsequent development of this line of research in Japan seems to reflect the influence of both his initial study and the contemporaneous research trends in western—and especially American—psychology.

Comparative studies of infant development in Japan and the United States have increased in number in recent years. Among the infant development studies, mother-infant interaction has attracted recent interest in Japan (Chen, 1983; Niwa, 1982; Tajima, 1982; Takahashi, 1977; Yamada, 1982). Another topic receiving attention is the study of infant temperament. Freedman (1979) suggested that among the Oriental newborn and young babies that he studied, Japanese were more irritable than either Navajo or Chinese but were not at the level of irritability seen in Caucasian babies. Other recent studies have shown behavioral differences of newborns among ethnic groups (Hsu et al., 1981; Kato et al., 1984; Ohyama, Murai & Nihei, 1982). The possibility of behavioral differences of different ethnic groups has implications for other research areas, such as the assessment of attachment and the interpretation of this concept (Miyake, Chen & Campos, in press). However, thus far, such studies are not without problems, and further research, using more rigorous controls and analyses will be necessary before more definite conclusions can be drawn.

We begin with a description of Caudill's studies. His findings and conclusions are reviewed with some comments from the point of view of cross-cultural methodology. A discussion follows of Azuma and Hess's studies of the relations between maternal variables and the cognitive development of the child. Miyake's research project on attachment, infant temperament, and mode of interaction will then be introduced, before we turn to a review of infant temperament studies now in progress.

Caudill's Studies

Psychological studies of the Japanese personality began during World War II through interviews with Japanese-Americans (Benedict, 1946; Caudill, 1952). Caudill inaugurated the first empirical study of Japanese infant-mother interaction in 1961. Our description of infant development studies in Japan starts with Caudill, not only because of his historical priority, but also because of the profound influence his studies have had on subsequent investigations of mother-infant relationships in Japan.

Caudill was trained as an anthropologist at the University of Chicago. He first became interested in Japanese personality development through his attempts at understanding the remarkable adjustment to life in Chicago by many of the 20,000 Japanese-Americans who had spent a few years in the relocation camps during the war years (Caudill, 1952). Caudill published more than twenty research papers concerning the Japanese; those comparing maternal care and infant behavior in Japan and in the United States are the ones for which he is most remembered. These papers all stemmed from one research project he and his coworkers carried out from 1961 to 1964. This study involved thirty Japanese and thirty American first-born, middle-class infants and their mothers. Data were obtained through naturalistic observations made on two consecutive days, covering one morning and one afternoon and totalling 290 minutes (4.8 hours), including a 5-minute break every 10 minutes. In one of his papers (1969) he summarized the findings as follows:

> In summary . . . the findings by culture in the earlier analysis show a basic similarity in the biologically rooted behavior of the infants in two countries regarding the total time spent in intake of food (sucking on breast or bottle and eating of semi-solid food) and in sleep, and also show a basic similarity in the behavior of

the mothers in the two countries in the time spent in the feeding, diapering, and dressing of infants. Beyond these similarities, however, the American infants have greater amounts of gross bodily activity, play (with toys, hands, and other objects) and happy vocalization; in contrast, the Japanese infants seem passive, and only have a greater amount of unhappy vocalization. The American mothers do more looking at, positioning the body of, and chatting to their infants; the Japanese mothers do more carrying, rocking, and lulling of their infants.

Caudill sought the explanation of the cultural differences in the structural variables of mother-infant interaction.

With these empirical findings, he proceeded to confirm his hypothesis concerning the difference in mother-infant interaction. In another study carried out by Caudill and Frost (1973), the same strategy, comparison of maternal care in infant behavior among Japanese-American and Japanese families, was adopted in an attempt to address the problem of whether the differences in infant behavior and maternal care between Japan and the United States could be ascribed to genetic or to cultural differences. It was argued once again that the great activity and happy vocalization of the American baby in contrast to the Japanese baby were not genetic in origin. Caudill and Frost emphasized both cultural change and cultural persistence as influences on behavior of the mothers and the infants. The former aspect was supported by the finding that Japanese babies learned to behave in ways that reflected the cultural style of their parents.

By the time of Caudill's death in 1972, the coding of data from the observations at age $2\frac{1}{2}$ had been finished and some tentative analyses begun; however, the coding and analyses of the data gathered when the children were 6-years-old were left almost undone (Caudill & Schooler, 1973). There had been no further attempts either by Japanese or American developmental psychologists to continue Caudill's work until 1980, when replication of Caudill's observational study was carrried out with forty 3-month-old infants and their mothers (Sengoku, 1981). In 1982, another group of American and Japanese researchers conducted a replication (Otaki et al., 1982). However, these studies were only partial replications of Caudill's work.

Though often quoted, Caudill's works have rarely been subject to serious criticism by psychologists or anthropologists. One exception is a monograph by the anthropologist Hara and the social psychologist Wagatsuma (1974). However, these authors confined themselves to a criticsm of the methodology of modal personality and the type of study under the influence of the so-called cultural and personality theory current in the 1960s and earlier. To be sure, Caudill's implicit theory was not without its problems. However, he was among the earliest researchers to investigate the relation between infant behaviors and maternal-interactional behaviors. Caudill did not seem to be aware of earlier studies on mother-infant interaction by researchers, such as Ainsworth (1963), Moss and Robson (1967), and Sander (1962).

In regard to methodology, Caudill's method of naturalistic observation seemed, on the one hand, too contrived in comparison with traditional anthropoligical field methods; and, on the other hand, too limited and lacking in control when compared with the traditional psychological study in the laboratory. As an anthropologist, he seemed to pay particular attention to the effect of context on human behavior. Yet the possibility that the very presence of an observer in a mother-infant interaction context could have created significant behavioral differences between the two nationalities seems to have escaped his attention. This possibility is unconsidered in any of Caudill's papers on the subject. It is hardly a minor point in a cross-cultural comparative study of mother-infant interaction; the Japanese attitude toward a stranger observing mother-infant interaction would necessarily bias the observation of maternal behavior, as well as that of the infants.

The question of physical setting—the size and the layout of Japanese houses are different from American houses—is also closely connected with this issue. To explain why American infants had more vocalization, Caudill argued that, in the American mother's relationship with her baby, her pace of interaction was "livelier." She tended to move in and out of the room and provided more naturally occurring opportunities both to speak to the baby and for him or her to respond vocally when approached (Caudill & Weinstein, 1969). Caudill considered a cultural difference in maternal attitude toward the infant the ultimate explanation for the differences observed. However, American mothers' behavior can also be interpreted as a result of the phsycial setting of the American home, where more rooms are usually available and the infant is more likely to have his or her own room. Under such conditions, it is natural for the mother to leave her baby alone in his or her room and only to check on the infant's condition from time to time, thus creating what Caudill described as the "liveliness" that resulted in interaction.

As a methodological strategy, cross-cultural study of early interaction has merits as well as limitations. For example, it can produce hypotheses leading to more quantitative assessment of differences between groups. However, cross-cultural comparison does not usually yield a *cause* for the behavioral differences between the groups. As a first step in cross-cultural comparison of early interaction patterns between the United States and Japan, Caudill's research has generated some hypotheses concerning early infant behaviors, maternal care style, mother's attitude toward child rearing, and common views about the infant and child (*jidokan*). A satisfactory explanation of Japanese and American differences in early interaction and early infant development has to address the reasons for these differences.

Kojima (1979, 1981, 1982) has shown that the Japanese view of infant development does indeed differ from that of the American; the Japanese consider sleep and prompt satisfaction of desire the primary needs of young infants, rather than an ability to exert themselves verbally. Based on his study of the traditional Japanese *jidokan*, Kojima offered an alternative interpretation of Caudill's results. He suggested that, for example, the Japanese mother's tendency to touch her sleeping infant or her slow response to the baby's unhappy vocalization, could stem from a different view of infant development, not necessarily from a lack of sensitivity (Kojima, 1982).

Indeed, views of infant development are only a reflection of differences in the entire affective systems that operate within families, and which, in turn, determine many aspects of infant development. In comparing parental attitudes or views of infant development between Japan and the United States, it is important to note that, in Japan, where mothers are usually responsible for housework as well as child rearing, they are always held responsible for their young infant's unhappiness, whether it is expressed in sickness, fussing, or crying. To avoid criticism by husband or neighbors, Japanese mothers do whatever is possible to keep the infant calm and happy and, thereby, avoid disturbing others. These concerns are present long before the mother has developed her own view about the development of the infant. They seem to be the result of the traditional status of the female in Japan—as well as to be related to the crowded living conditions in which most Japanese families find themselves. In view of this, it is understandable that Japanese mothers tend to avoid stimulating their babies, prefering them to be quiet rather than active.

Maternal Variables and the Cognitive Development of the Child

The next major project addressing itself to cross-cultural differences between Japan and the United States is the collaborative project of Azuma, Kashiwagi and Hess (1981). Although this project is not a study of infants, we include it here for several reasons. First, as an empirical study involving actual observation of mother-child interaction, it can be considered a continuation of Caudill's work. Caudill was, in fact, one of the participants in the conference held at Stanford in 1971, where the project originated. Second, the study by Azuma et al. is the first collaborative effort between Japanese and American psychologists to contribute independently to a common goal. Third, their findings aroused the interest of researchers in pursuing the topic further. Finally, some conclusions of this research have implications for future study of infant and child development by using the method of cultural comparison.

The study of Azuma et al. reflects two trends in recent developmental psychology: the rise of general interest in cognitive development and the increasing emphasis on the influence of parental attitudes on behavior on children's language and cognitive development (Bernstein, 1971; Hess & Shipman, 1965, 1967). Several papers, articles, and one book (in Japanese) have been published as a result of the project (Azuma & Hess, 1976; see Azuma, Kashiwagi & Hess, 1981, for detailed references).

The study involved seventy-six Japanese and sixty-seven American mother-child pairs. The average age of the children was 44 months at the start of the study. Both mothers and children were observed in various situations, either individually or in interaction with each other. In addition, observations involving a teacher, a teacher-child pair, as well as an interview with the teacher were carried out.

Several of the findings of this study may have implications not only in the period of childhood under investigation (that is, 4 to 6 years) but also for an earlier period. Further, some of these findings relate to our point made earlier in connection with Caudill's study—the difference in basic attitude and performance between American and Japanese parents and children in response to experimental situations. The following discussion of the conclusions drawn by Azuma and his colleagues will be conducted with these considerations in mind.

Verbal communication between the Japanese mother and child is not necessarily lower in frequency or simpler in content, as was suggested by Caudill and Weinstein (1969). The difference appears to lie in the content of communication. Japanese mothers are found to be characterized by a tendency to emphasize the experience and emotional state of the speaker and listener as related to the topic. They explain the situations surrounding the problem, rather than communicate about the problem itself, as American mothers tend to do.

Another finding bears upon the difference mentioned earlier, in basic attitude or performance during an observation situation. The pattern of interaction was observed in a free-play situation. In general, Japanese mothers tended more often to intervene and to direct the child, while American mothers tended toward less control and more toward paying attention to the child's ability and behavior. They also praised the child more. The authors pointed out that this was related to the observation that, in an experiment situation, Japanese mothers tended to be nervous and less spontaneous in their behavior.

In relation to sex differences, significant differences between boys and girls occurred more frequently in Japan than in the United States in the relationship between maternal variables and the children's cognitive development. This finding seems to suggest a greater difference in the cognitive socialization process between the sexes in Japan.

Although there are differences associated with social class in both Japan and the United States, the patterns of the two countries revealed an interesting contrast. In the United States, mothers of lower socioeconomic status (SES) tended to adopt a direct command, appealing to status, whereas this style of discipline tended to be adopted by mothers from higher levels of SES in Japan. This conclusion is not in agreement with either the findings of the Chicago studies of Hess and Shipman (1967) or with that of Bernstein. The authors suggested that the strategy of mothers of lower SES was more characteristic of the traditional Japanese style of discipline, whereas that of the mothers of the higher SES indicated a tendency to move away from the traditional style and toward that of the West.

The age at which various aspects of development were expected to occur in childhood differed between the two countries. In Japan, emotional maturity, compliance to adults, and etiquette were expected from an early age. In the United States, verbal self-assertion and social skills in making friends were expected to occur early.

Attachment and Infant Temperament

Interest in the differences between children and mothers in the two countries soon resulted in a research proposal for a longitudinal comparative study, from the newborn period to 3 or 4 years of age. The research project began in 1980 with Miyake as the principal investigator. The data collection of two cohorts is underway, and a preliminary report for the first year of the first cohort has been finished and will be published soon (Miyake, Chen & Campos, in press).

In these two longitudinal studies, the main objectives are to study the antecedents of attachment at 12 months, the consequences of attachment, and the interaction between infant temperamental disposition and mode of interaction. Special reference is also made to the cultural factors involved in emotional communication between mother and infant.

Sixty mother-infant pairs from middle-class nuclear families in the city of Sapporo are involved in the two studies. Interviews were conducted during the last two months of pregnancy and observational assessments were made of both the newborn infant and their mothers during the lying-in period.

The two cohorts differ slightly in the number of items assessed and in timing, mainly because the first cohort served as a pilot study. However, major assessments and their time of administration were the same.

The major findings from data collected in the first 12 months are:

1. There is a strong correlation between the tendency for a baby to be either rated or observed as "irritable" in the first 3 months and the tendency for that baby to be classified as a "C" baby in the Ainsworth Strange Situation at 12 months.

2. In addition to "irritability" in the first 3 months, "C" baby classification seemed to relate to the mother's mode of interaction; that is, if an "irritable" baby was accompanied by a mother whose mode of interaction was characterized by more "intrusiveness," the possibility was higher that the baby would be classified as "C."

3. A substantially higher proportion of "C" babies was observed in the Japanese sample than were found in the American. This tentative finding was interpreted as reflecting two possibilities: (1) a particularly Japanese mode of early infant-mother interaction, characterized by close physical contact and a symbiotic emotional relationship between them, and (2) a tendency in Japanese infants toward distress.

These two longitudinal studies are being caried out at a time when the study of the mother-infant or mother-child relationship emphasizing the role of the infant or child is receiving greater attention in the United States (Bell, 1968; Lewis & Rosenblum, 1974; Bell & Harper, 1977). In one sense, we are involved in a controversy concerning the antecedents of attachment and its consequence. However, because we acknowledge the existence of one temperamental disposition—that is, early irritability—in the formation of attachment does not mean that we are seeking to emphasize temperament. What we are stressing is the importance of the maternal mode of response to the baby as influenced by infant characteristics.

Another issue attracting our attention in analysing data from the first cohort sample and collecting data on the second was infants' compliance to maternal commands. Under the name of "prohibition tasks," a series of comparative studies are being carried out between researchers at Hokkaido University and in the United States. Preliminary observations indicate that differences exist in the ways mothers introduce prohibitions in both public and private settings. Japanese infants around the age of 11 months tended to show a more delayed response when their mothers make a vocal signal mimicking anger.

Infant Temperament Studies

In 1980, we saw the beginning of an increase in infant temperament studies in Japan. Kosawa and his colleagues, in what is now known as the Tokyo study, compared fourty-five Japanese newborn babies with fourty-five Boston newborn babies studied by Tronick (Kosawa et al. 1980). The greatest difference was found between the two groups in orientation to an adult's voice and to a rattle. Sex differences were observed in the relationship between maternal affectionate contacts and the infants' scores on physical maturity and self-control. These were two of four factors of the Brazelton Neonatal Behavioral Assessment Scale (BNBAS) resulting from Kosawa's analysis, the other two being irritability and orientation responsiveness (Kosawa et al., 1978). Another research project employing laboratorylike structured observation and assessment of newborn and young infants was carried out at Hokkaido University (Chen & Miyake, 1981). This study observed infants' expression of negative emotions. Although the sample was small, consistency was observed between neonatal irritability—defined by a consistent full-blown crying response to interruption of sucking (Bell, Weller & Waldrop, 1971)—and a higher frequency of crying and/or fussing episodes at 1 and 3 months (Miyake, et al., 1983).

Currently, there are several research groups studying infant temperament by using the questionnaire developed by Carey and McDevitt (1978). The standardization of the Japanese version of this questionnaire has been undertaken by Shoji and Maekawa (1981). One current study aims at a comparison of results using Carey's questionnaire with samples in Taiwan and the United States, (Ohyama, Murai & Nihei, 1982). Another American-Japanese comparative study of neonatal behavior using BNBAS has been conducted by pediatricians and medical personnel (Kato, et al., 1984). This study reported that, as compared with the American sample, Japanese newborn babies showed significantly less decrease of response or quieting to the sounds of a rattle and a bell but greater orientation to auditory stimuli, a result comparable to Kosawa's, mentioned previously.

Recent Developments

The recent increase in studies of infant development in Japan seems to owe much to the participation of pediatricians and other medical personnel. It is quite common in Japan for research concerning newborn babies or young infants to be conducted soley by medical researchers. Only relatively recently have psychologists been actively involved in these studies. One large interdisciplinary research project on early infancy encouraging cooperation between medical personnel and psychologists began in 1979. This project is under the sponsorship of the Japanese Ministry of Welfare and Health; a well-known professor of pediatrics, Dr. Noboru Kobayashi, is the principal investigator. Conferences are held twice a year in Tokyo, and some of the research results are beginning to be published (Ministry of Welfare and Health, 1981, 1983). This operation appears to have promoted interest in interdisciplinary research in Japan.

Efforts such as that headed by Kobayashi will, hopefully, encourage the participation of Japanese developmental psychologists in more studies of socially significant issues. This will, in the long run, benefit both the community of Japanese psychologists and the community at large. Research topics that are popular among researchers in the West usually engender, sooner or later, a Japanese version, and the study of infant development is no exception. However, Japanese studies in this field have had little impact either on theory or methodology in infant development studies, a situation deplored by Japanese psychologists (Miyake, 1980; Nagano, 1981). It is hoped that, as Japanese psychologists become more aware of their own potential, they will make their share of contributions.

References

Ainsworth, M. D. S. (1963). Development of infant-mother interaction among the Ganda. In B. M. Foss (Ed.), *Determinants of infant behaviour* (Vol. II, pp. 67–104). London: Methuen.

Azuma, H. (1982). Current trends in studies of behavioral development in Japan. *International Journal of Behavioral Development, 5,* 153–169.

Azuma, H., & Hess, R. D. (1976). Influence of linguistic environment between mother and child on child's cognitive development. *Annual Report of Japanese Educational Psychology Association: 1966,* 87–92. (In Japanese)

Azuma, H., Kashiwagi, K., & Hess, R. D. (1981). *Maternal attitude, behavior and child's cognitive development: A Japan-U.S. comparative study.* Tokyo: Tokyo University Press. (In Japanese)

Bell, R. O. (1968). A reinterpretation of the direction of effects in studies of socialization, *Psychological Review, 75,* 81–95.

Bell, R. W., Weller, G. M., & Waldrop, M. F. (1971). Newborn and preschooler: Organization of behavior and relations between periods. *Monographs of Society for Research in Child Development, 36,* 1–2.

Bell, R. O., & Harper, L. V. (1977). *Child effects on Adults.* New York, New York: John Wiley.

Benedict, R. (1946). *The chrysanthemum and the sword: Patterns of Japanese culture.* Boston: Houghton Mifflin.

Bernstein, B. (1971). Class, codes and control. *Vol. 1: Theoretical studies towards a sociology of language.* London: Routledge & Kegan Paul.

Bronfenbrenner, U. (1979). *The ecology of human development.* Cambridge: Harvard University Press.

Carey, W. B., & McDevitt, S. C. (1978). Revision of the infant temperament questionnaire. *Pediatrics, 61,* no. 5, 735–739.

Caudill, W. (1952). Japanese-American personality and acculturation. *Genetic Psychology Monographs, 45,* 3–102.

———. (1972). Tiny dramas: vocal communication between mother and infant in Japanese and American Families. In W. P. Lebra (Ed.), *Transcultural research in mental health: Mental health research in Asia and the Pacific* Vol. 2, pp. 25–48). Honolulu: The University of Hawaii.

Caudill, W., & Frost, L. (1973). A comparison of maternal care and infant behavior in Japanese-American, American and Japanese families. In W. P. Lebra (Ed.), *Research in Asia and the Pacific,* (Vol. III). Honolulu: East-West Center Press.

Caudill, W., & Weinstein, H. (1969). Maternal care and infant behavior in Japan and America. *Psychiatry, 32,* 12–43.

Caudill, W., & Schooler, C. (1973). Child behavior and child rearing in Japan and the United States: An interim report. *The Journal of Nervous and Mental Disease, 157* (5), 323–328.

Chen, S. J. (1983). Early Mother-infant interaction. *Annual Review of Japanese Child Psychology,* Volume 22 (pp. 155–170). Tokyo: Kaneko Shobo. (In Japanese)

Chen, S. J., & Miyake, K. (1981). *On the relationship between infant temperamental characteristics and maternal behavior in the first three months.* RCCCD Annual Report 1979–1980 (pp. 45–51). Sapporo: Hokkaido University.

Freedman, D. G. (1979). *Human Sociobiology: a holistic approach.* New York: Free Press.

Hess, R. D., & Shipman, V. C. (1965). Early experiences and socialization of cognitive modes in children. *Child Development, 36,* 860–886.

———. (1967). Cognitive elements in maternal behavior. In J. P. Hill (Ed.), *Minnesota Symposia on Child Psychology, Volume 1* (pp. 57–81). Minneapolis: University of Minnesota Press.

Hsu, C.-C., Soong, W., Stigler, J. W., Hong, C., & Smetana, J. G. (1981). The temperamental characteristics of Chinese babies. *Child Development, 52,* 1337–1340.

Kato, T., Takahashi, E., Amino, T., Kato, N. & Kobayashi, N. (1984). *A Japan-United States comparative study based on BNBAS.* Paper presented at the 87th Conference of the Japanese Association for Pediatrics No. 274. (In Japanese)

Kojima, H. (1979). The psychology of mother-child relationship: Parts I and II. *Child Psychology, 33,* 938–55; 1126–1143. (In Japanese)

———. (1981). Approach to personality development. In Y. Isogai (Ed.), *The world of educational psychology* (pp. 87–112). Tokyo: Fukumura Shuppan. (In Japanese)

———. (1982). An introduction to the study of the views about children: its significance and methods. In T. Sagusa & T. Tahata (Eds.), *Modern views about children and education* (pp. 15–52). Tokyo: Fukumura Shuppan. (In Japanese)

Kosawa, Y. (1980). The influence of the infant upon the early development of mother-child relationships. Unpublished doctoral dissertation. Tokyo: Tokyo University. (In Japanese)

Kosawa, Y., Takahashi, M., Fukumoto, S., Ishii, F., Fujisaki, M., Amaiwa, S., & Fujida, M. (1978). *Mother-child interaction in early development: Neonatal individual characteristics and mother-child relationship.* Paper presented at the annual convention, Japanese Association of Educational Psychology. (In Japanese)

Lewis, M., & Rosenblum, L. A. (1974). *The effect of the infant on its caregiver.* New York, N. Y.: John Wiley.

Maccoby, E., & Masters, J. C. (1970). Attachment and dependency. In P. H. Mussen (Ed.), *Carmichael's Manual of child psychology: Volume 2* (3rd ed.). New York: John Wiley.

Ministry of Welfare and Health (1981, 1983). Reports concerning *Studies on mother-child interaction from the point of view of clinical, psychological, psychobehavioral and social pediatrics.* Tokyo: Ministry of Welfare and Health. (In Japanese)

Mishler, E. (1979). Meaning. *Harvard Educational Review, 49,* 1–19.

Miyake, K. (1980). *The so-called infant studies.* Annual Report of Educational Psychology in Japan, *20,* 70. (In Japanese)

Miyake, K., Chen, S. J., & Campos, J. J. (in press). *Infant temperament, mother's mode of interaction, and attachment in Japan: an interim report.* To be published in I. Bretherton & E. Waters, (Eds.), *Monographs of Society for Research in Child Development.*

Miyake, K., K. Chen, S. J., Ujiie, T., Tajima, N., Satoh, K., & Takahashi, K. (1983). *Infant's temperamental disposition, mother's mode of interaction, quality of attachment, and infant's receptivity to socialization—interim progress report.* RCCCD Annual Report 1981–1982 (pp. 25–49). Sapporo: Hokkaido Univerisity. (In Japanese)

Moss, H. A., & Robson, K. S. (1967). Maternal influences in early social visual behavior. *Child Development, 39,* 401–408.

Nagano, S. (1981). Overview. *Annual Review of Japanese Child Psychology, Volume 20* (pp. 12–19). Tokyo: Kaneko shobo. (In Japanese)

Niwa, Y. (1982). Infancy and early experiences. In T. Takuma & F. Iijima (Eds.), *The unfolding of developmental psychology.* (pp. 351–362). Tokyo: Shinyosha. (In Japanese)

Ohyama, M., Murai, N., & Nihei, Y. (1982). *A follow-up study of temperament and development: cross-national comparison and sex differences.* Paper presented at the annual meeting of the Japanese Association for Educational Psychology. (In Japanese)

Otaki, M., Durret, M. E., Richards, L., Nyquist, L., & Pennebacker, J. W. (U.D.). Maternal and infant behavior in Japan and America: A partial replication.

Sander, L. W. (1962). Issues in early mother-child interaction. *Journal of the American Academy of Child Psychiatry, 1,* 141–166.

Sengoku, T. (1981, September 29- October 10). The changed infants: A Japan-U.S. comparison of the three month old infants. *Yomiuri Shinbun.* (In Japanese)

———. (1983). Mother-child relationship in Japan and the United States through behavioral observation. *Journal of Perinatal Medicine, 13* (12), Supplement, 501–504.

Shoji, J., Maekawa, K. (1981). Infant temperament: Its significance and the method of assessment. *The Journal of Pediatric Practice, 44* (8), 1225–1232. (In Japanese)

Tajima, N. (1982). Family relationships and development. In *Annual Review of Japanese Child Psychology,* (Vol. 21, pp. 135–168). Tokyo: Kaneko Shobo. (In Japanese)

Takahashi, M. (1977). Studies of infancy. In *Annual Review of Japanese Child Psychology* (Vol. 16, pp. 27–50). Tokyo: Kaneko shobo. (In Japanese)

Wagatsuma, H., & Hara, H. (1974). *Shitsuke* [Childhood discipline]. Tokyo: Kōbundo. (In Japanese)

Yamada, Y. (1982). The abilities of the infant. In *Advances in child psychology* (Vol. 20, pp. 107–134). Tokyo: Kaneko Shobo. (In Japanese)

Zaslow, M., & Rogoff, B. (1981). The cross-cultural study of early interaction: Implications from research on Culture and Cognition. In T. Field, A. M. Sostek, P. Vietze, & P. H. Leiderman (Eds.), *Culture and early interaction.* Hillsdale, N.J.: Erlbaum.

Family Influences on School Readiness and Achievement In Japan and the United States: An Overview of a Longitudinal Study

Robert D. Hess, Hiroshi Azuma,
Keiko Kashiwagi, W. Patrick Dickson,
Shigefumi Nagano, Susan Holloway,
Kazuo Miyake, Gary Price, Giyoo Hatano,
and Teresa McDevitt

This chapter describes the findings of a longitudinal study that began when the children of the American and the Japanese families involved were preschoolers and included a follow-up phase when the children were in the middle grades. A number of papers have already reported various features of the findings; others are in preparation. This chapter summarizes major findings of the project and discusses the national differences and similarities in socialization for achievement that appear in the family environments of young children in the two countries.

A comparison of Japanese and American groups has several advantages for an analysis of family effects on school achievement. Both nations value education, as is indicated by compulsory schooling and a high level of literacy in each of them. Japanese and American societies differ, however, in important ways—language, family roles, social norms—that affect family interaction and, possibly, its influence on children's achievement in school.[1] It is also well established that Japanese students perform at higher levels on tests of science and mathematics (Husén, 1967) and that these differences emerge in the early grades (Stigler et al. 1982). It is a cultural truism that experience in one institution within a society prepares the individual for experience in another. Differences between Japan and the United States are thus especially important, for they suggest that children in the two countries are prepared by their families for somewhat different roles as students. Observations of classrooms in the two countries support this interpretation, for they suggest that students in Japan are more likely to be engaged as groups (Easley & Easley, 1981), spend more time on-task (Stevenson, this volume), and are more compliant and ready to undertake the tasks the teacher offers (Azuma, 1984; Lewis, 1984) than are students in the United States (Kedar-Viovodas, 1983; Kikuchi & Gordon, 1970). We assume that these aspects of the role of pupil are dependent on expectations of both the family and the school in each culture. Family antecedents of successful performance in Japan might thus be quite different from those that contribute to successful performance in the United States.

Background of the Study

This project began in 1972, following a cross-national conference at the Center for Advanced Study in the Behavioral Sciences in Stanford, California, sponsored by the Japan Science Foundation and the Social Science Research Council.[2] Interest in a comparison of cognitive socialization in Japan and in the United States came partially from research on maternal teaching styles and partially from writings, especially those of Basil Bernstein, on language and educational achievement.

The central purpose of the preschool study was to identify family variables associated with school readiness in each country, compare these results across the two countries, and describe the socialization processes involved (Azuma, Kashiwagi & Hess, 1981). A follow-up study was conducted when the children were in grade five in Japan and in grade six in the United States. These longitudinal data offer an opportunity to see whether family influences found in the preschool data persisted into the middle school years.

The project was actually two parallel studies, directed and funded separately but with full collaboration on design, instrument development, coding procedures, and statistical analyses. The Japanese component of the project was directed by Hiroshi Azuma of the University of Tokyo; Robert Hess was responsible for the work in the United States.

Methods and Procedures

Mothers and children in the study were first involved in data collection when the children were 3 years, 8 months of age, within a limit of 1 month. Sixty-seven white families from a range of socioeconomic backgrounds participated in the United States. In Japan, fifty-eight families from equally variable socioeconomic backgrounds formed the preschool study group. The children were mostly first born; in each country there were roughly equal numbers of boys and girls.

When the children were in fifth grade in Japan and sixth grade in the United States, families were located for a follow-up interview. In the United States, forty-nine of the original sixty-seven families were found. Of the forty-eight who agreed to be studied, we were able to interview forty-seven. In Japan, children of forty-four of the original fifty-eight families were interviewed; various practical factors reduced the number of participating mothers to twenty-four.

Data-Gathering Schedule

During the first data collection phase, which lasted three years, mothers were interviewed about their child-rearing beliefs and behavior and their children's social and cognitive development. Tests of cognitive ability and school-relevant skills were given to the children at ages 4, 5, and 6. At the follow-up phase, information about student achievement in mathematics was gathered by tests and from teachers' ratings. Interviews were conducted with both mothers and children about their explanations for the children's level of performance in mathematics. In Japan, interviews covered achievements in other subjects as well. Space does not permit a full description of instruments and variables; thus, only the relevant measures will be described as results are discussed.

Data-Gathering Techniques Used with Mothers— Preschool Phase

Maternal Interview. Mothers were interviewed and administered instruments designed for the study when the children were 3 years, 8 months, 4 years, 5 years, and 6 years old. The interview included questions about the parents' expectation for the child's education and occupational attainment; responses to (hypothetical) indications that the child was not doing well in school or wanted to drop out; attributions about the probable causes of the child's success in school (parents' help, teachers' help, natural ability, luck); and more general questions about the home environment and what the mother was doing to prepare the child for school.

Developmental Expectations Questionnaire. Mothers were asked to indicate the age at which they expected their child to master each of thirty-eight different developmental skills (Hess et al. 1980).

Maternal Control Strategies Instrument. Mothers' views of discipline and techniques for influencing the child's behavior were elicited by asking how they would respond to six hypothetical situations many mothers believe call for maternal intervention (Conroy et al. 1980).

Unstructured Game. When the children were age 4, they and their mothers were asked to engage in three interaction tasks. All three tasks were videotaped. The first was an unstructured session of 10 minutes, in which the mother and child were seated at a table and given a pegboard set. The mother was asked to " . . . play with the child for a time until he or she gets accustomed to this room." She was told that they could use the materials in any way they liked (Hatano, Miyake & Tajima, 1980).

Block-Sorting Task. The second session was a block-sorting task in which the mother was asked to teach her child to sort blocks on two dimensions—height of block and mark (*X* or *O*) on top of the block (Hess & Shipman, 1965). After the mother thought that the child had grasped the sorting concepts, the staff member administering the task was called. She gave the child two additional blocks, asked him or her to place them with matching blocks and then requested a verbal explanation of the principle on which they were sorted. This task required about 15 minutes (Price, Hess & Dickson, 1981).

Referential Communication Game. The third task was similar to other referential communication tasks, except for using push buttons connected to a light to provide immediate feedback to the speaker about the accuracy of the listener's response. The instrument consisted of two notebooks with sets of four pictures in a row. Referent sets ranged from simple nameable pictures to abstract figures, designed to require the expression of various dimensions, such as size, quantity, and spatial relationships. During the first half of the game, the mother gave a description, and the child pressed buttons to indicate choice of what he or she thought was the figure being described. The first half consisted of three practice items and twelve scored items. During the second half, the notebooks were reversed. The child described each of fifteen items while the mother pressed the buttons. The task required about 15 to 20 minutes (Dickson et al. 1979).

Children's Measures—Preschool Phase

Several measures of children's cognitive ability and problem-solving style were used during the preschool part of the study. This report describes only the measure of school readiness.

School Readiness. School-relevant skills were assessed by several tests administered when the children of the study were ages 5 and 6: letter recognition, ability to count, number recognition, a series of questions requiring the child to show knowledge of the concepts of *half*, *more*, *as many*, *fewer*, a simple addition task, and the ability to write his or her own name. At age six, the school-readiness measure was a composite of the number and the letter recognition subtests of the Metropolitan Readiness Test (Hildreth, Griffiths & McGauvran, 1964). For the Japanese sample, an adaptation of the Metropolitan Readiness Test was used. Scores were combined within age levels; a total readiness score was an equally weighted composite of the scores at the two age levels.

Follow-up Instruments

Interview about Beliefs. In the follow-up phase, mothers and children in the United States were interviewed at home separately, about the children's achievement in school, particularly in mathematics. Interviews included questions about the causal explanations that mothers and children offered for the children's level of performance in mathematics. Both mothers and children were asked to indicate on a 6-point scale how well the children were doing in school. They were then asked to assign ten chips (in Japan, 100 points) across five alternative explanations for why the children were doing as well as they were (United States) or why they were not doing better (both countries). The five alternatives in Japan were: lack of ability, lack of effort, lack of training at school, luck, and difficulty of the task. The five alternatives used in the United States were similar, except that "lack of training at school" was used in place of task difficulty (Holloway & Hess, 1984).

Measures of Achievement in School.   Children in the United States were also given the mathematics concepts and vocabulary subtests of the Iowa Tests of Basic Skills (ITBS) (Hieronymus, Lindquist & Hoover, 1978). In Japan, mothers and children were given similar interviews to those conducted in the United States, and the children were administered the Japanese version of the WISC-R (Wechsler, 1974). Teachers were asked to rate the children's performance across academic and nonacademic subjects.

Results

Cultural Differences in Maternal Behavior

One of the purposes of the original study was to compare mothers in the two countries on their interaction with children during a teaching task. The interaction sessions yielded a number of variables, some selected for discussion here.

Four types of maternal teaching variables are described: (1) requests for verbal responses; (2) elaboration of child's response; (3) recycling in responses to child's errors; and, (4) directiveness in regulating the child's problem solving. These variables were computed on several different bases—total number of message units, number of task-specific messages, number of requests for verbal responses, and so forth. The percentages across different measures thus do not necessarily accumulate to 100.

Requests for Verbal Responses.   One variable represented the number of *requests for the child to produce verbal responses*, computed as a percent of the mother's task-specific messages. A second variable represented *requests for generative responses*. This was a measure of the mother's tendency to use questions, requests, and commands that invited child-generated verbal responses, taken as a proportion of all message units in which the mother expressed a question, a request, or a command (Price et al.).

Elaboration as Feedback.   In reaction to children's attempts to place blocks or to respond to requests, mothers might elaborate by extending the information originally provided, describing the dimension or attribute of the block in a different or more detailed way or offering analogies from the children's experience that might help them grasp the sorting principle. *Elaboration* was the proportion of elaborations as a percent of all task-specific messages to the child.

An example of elaboration was:

M: "This block is short and has an X. And this one (showing a tall block with an O on top)?"
C: "Tall."
M: "Tall O."

Recycling.   When the child made an error in placing the block or in attempting to explain the principle in the sorting task, the mother might repeat the instruction in words rephrasing the original instruction—in effect, repeat the question or the request. This measure was the proportion of such "recycling" types of feedback from the mothers to the children's errors.

Examples of recycling to an error:

M: (Shows a block with an O on top) "What is this?"
C: "X."
M: "*What is it?*"
C: (No response)
M: "*Look again.*"

Recycling in response to an incomplete answer:

C: "It's an O."
M: "*And what else?*"

Directiveness.   These measures indicated the mother's tendency to direct the child's problem-solving activities in the block-sorting task. *Direct commands* were the use of direct commands in instructional features of the interaction as a percent of requests for response (for example, "Put this block where it should go.") rather than inviting participation, asking questions, or using modified demands. *Moderated commands* were commands softened by requests or polite forms of address, (for example, "Please," "Let's do this next, . . . " "How about . . . ").

The comparison of Japanese and American mothers on these variables showed a clear difference in the tendency to encourage children to make verbal responses during the teaching task. American mothers were much more likely to ask for verbal responses in their attempts to help the child solve the problem (see Table 11.1). This tendency was even more evident in messages that were not directed at the instructional task.

It is of interest that the children in the two countries also differed in performance on the sorting task itself. Scores on the task were recorded as success

Table 11.1

Teaching Styles of Japanese and American Mothers in the Block-Sorting Task
(Means and Standard Deviations)

Variable	United States N = 67	Japan N = 58	p <
Requests for verbal response (as percentage of task-specific messages)	52.96 (17.22)	41.53 (18.41)	.001
Requests for child-generated responses (as percentage of mother's requests for verbal responses)	38.68 (16.70)	37.34 (16.91)	NS
Elaboration (as percentage of total feedback to child)	15.33 (6.94)	26.61 (9.35)	.001
Recycling (as percentage of responses to incorrect answers)	35.04 (21.15)	16.57 (11.34)	.001
Direct commands (as percentage of requests for response)	22.29 (12.01)	25.17 (11.66)	NS
Moderated commands (as percentage of all commands)	46.50 (16.28)	33.18 (18.82)	.001

at *placing* blocks and at *verbalizing the two sorting principles*—height and mark on the blocks. The two groups of children did not differ on placement scores (Japanese group, X = 1.71; United States group, X = 1.65, of a possible 2.0), although the Japanese children had slightly higher scores. American children, however, were more successful at verbalizing the principle on which the sorting task had been based (American: 2.12, Japanese 1.53, of a possible 4.0—two principles used to sort each of the two blocks). This difference was statistically significant ($t = 2.28$, $p < .025$). The result is consistent with data from other measures which suggest that American mothers tend to encourage verbal assertiveness in their young children more than Japanese mothers do.

Another distinction between the two groups of mothers in the teaching task was their use of elaboration and repetition ("recycling") in the sorting task. Japanese mothers were more likely to elaborate instructions in response to incorrect, partially correct, or even correct answers by the child. These differences (shown here only for all message units) were quite large and highly significant as seen in Table 11.1.

On the other hand, mothers in the United States were much more likely to "recycle" the instructions, that is, to repeat them in about the same form as the original request when the child made an error or offered a partially correct answer. This might be interpreted as a form of directness—pressing a child for a response by repeating the question, command, or request. Such direct presentation of a problem or request for performance to an individual child is consistent with the behavior of teachers in classrooms in the United States, where the sequence of *teacher asks question — child responds — teacher evaluates child's answer* is typical. This behavior is less customary in Japanese schools, where group responses and group problem-solving are more common. Again, the differences between the two groups of mothers were quite large, especially when the child made an error.

American mothers tended to use more commands (as a percent of all message units) than did Japanese mothers (18.83 percent versus 15.14 percent), although mothers in the United States tended more often to modify their commands. The two groups of mothers used direct commands equally often. Stated in different terms, Japanese mothers used commands less often than American mothers, but when they did, their commands were as likely to be direct. Consistent with this pattern, Japanese mothers more often made statements that did not need a reply from the child. As noted above, *when a reply was requested*, the two groups of mothers asked for a child-generated response at about the same proportion of all requests (American, 38.68 percent; Japanese, 37.34 percent).

In summary, Japanese mothers called less often on the child to perform verbally. If he or she made an error, the mother was more likely to give the correct information or additional information about the task. The style of the mothers in the United States was to provide information and ask for verbal responses and, if the child made an error, to present the request (problem) again.

Hatano (1982) has suggested that Japanese mothers more often emphasize procedural aspects of the task, whereas mothers in the United States stress the conceptual grasp of the sorting principles. The performance of children on the sorting task is consistent with such an interpretation. The emphasis of mothers in the United States on understanding the sorting principles and on an ability to explain them is congruent with a teaching style oriented toward instructing/explaining. It is as if American mothers must receive a testimony from the child that the concept has been grasped. Conversely, Japanese mothers seem to accept the child's placement of the block as sufficient evidence that the procedures for sorting were understood or, perhaps, would be understood.

These differences also suggest that Japanese mothers first attempt to get the child to adopt the appropriate procedure in its correct form. They then expect the child to infer the correct principle, or concept, of the task by repeating the correct behavioral form. This style of teaching can be traced to traditional Japanese training methods combining cognitive and performance skills ("from form to mind"), that are used extensively for training in the classic arts, such as noh, *Kyogen*, and flower arrangement.

Referential Communication Accuracy

Mother-child pairs in the two countries differed only slightly in their accuracy scores on the referential communication task administered when the children were 4 years of age. The mean number of errors for mother-as-sender and child-as-sender conditions in the United States was 13.03; in Japan, it was 14.84, a non-significant difference. The scores for the mother-as-sender conditions did not differ between the two countries, but scores obtained in the child-as-sender condition did (Japan = 5.82, United States = 4.33; $t = 2.72, p < .01$). The combined communication score was moderately, but significantly, correlated with SES in both countries (Japan: $r = .34$; United States: $r = .27$). The correlation between the combined score and mothers' I.Q., available only in the United States, was .23—significant but low. Communication accuracy scores were associated at the same level in both countries with children's I.Q. at age 4 ($r = .60$) (Dickson et al.). As we shall note later, communication scores were also correlated with other measures of school-related skills at both preschool and follow-up phases of the study (McDevitt et al. 1984). Correlations with school-relevant measures remained significant when the effects of SES and children's mental ability at age 4 were accounted for by partial correlation techniques.

The ability to communicate information accurately about abstract figures may contribute to cognitive growth in several ways: (1) it may foster direct communication of information from parent to child; (2) the greater precision in conveying information may assist the growth of vocabulary for young children; (3) parents who communicate accurately offer a model for their children's communication skills; (4) children who develop good communication skills may interact more effectively with teachers in the classroom; and, (5) children who develop good communication skills at an early age help create a richer verbal environment for themselves in their conversations with others (Dickson et al.).

Strategies of Control and Regulation

The mothers' orientation toward issues of control was assessed in the maternal interview by presenting six hypothetical situations in which the mother would be assumed to want to alter the behavior of the child: (1) disrupting customers in the supermarket; (2) drawing on the wall; (3) hitting another child with a block; (4) refusing to eat vegetables at dinner; (5) refusing to brush teeth; and, (6) refusing to take medicine. Each situation was described; the mothers were then asked to imagine that the child was present and say what they would tell the child in response to the situation described.

Responses were coded into four major categories: (1) appeals to *authority*, where the reason for complying is the mother's authority or power (for example, "I told you not to do that"); (2) appeals to *rules*, where the reason is an impersonal rule (for example, "walls are not for drawing; paper is for drawing"; "blocks

Table 11.2
Mother's Rationale for Disciplinary Action (Percentages)

Rationale	Japan N = 58	United States N = 67
Mother's authority	18	50
Impersonal rules	15	16
Feelings	22	7
Consequences	37	23
Other	8	4

are for building"); (3) appeals to *feelings* (for example, "How do you think I will feel if you don't eat the vegetables I cooked for you?"); and (4) appeals to *consequences* (other than punishment) (for example, "If you eat your vegetables, you'll be strong and healthy").

Analysis of interview protocols showed marked cultural differences in the mothers' handling of encounters calling for discipline and control (Conroy et al.). Japanese mothers relied more on appeals to feelings than did American mothers (see Table 11.2). In the United States, mothers appealed much more to their own authority.

The distribution of responses on this category in the two countries showed little overlap. Many mothers in Japan used no appeals to their authority as mothers; this was the modal response. Mothers in the United States used this appeal in more than half of the disciplinary situations. This approach emphasizes the status relationship between mother and child by using authority without explanation, a parental style which appears to have deleterious cognitive consequences, at least in the United States study (Hess & McDevitt). Japanese mothers appealed to feelings rather than to authority; in contrast, more than 40 percent of American mothers used no such appeals.

Informal observations of child rearing suggest a national contrast in the way a mother responds to the child in situations where he or she resists her requests. At such times, Japanese mothers may practice what they call "yielding." If the child is obstinate, they will give in rather than injure the relationship. Protecting feelings of closeness is an important goal of Japanese mothers. This contrasts with the advice often given American parents—to be consistent, to not lose a battle with the child, to be firm, and to follow through on requests made of the child. These differences in types of appeal do not necessarily indicate that American mothers are more "controlling" than Japanese mothers, only that they approach this parental function differently. A distinction should thus be made between the types of control strategies used by mothers and their effectiveness. We suggest that Japanese mothers are more effective in getting their children to comply with maternal expectations, possibly by using techniques which lead to internalization of adult norms and expectations when the children are very young. The closeness of the mother-child tie is a familiar theme in studies of Japanese families (Caudill & Weinstein, 1966; Dore, 1958). Indeed, a greater explicit emphasis on the use of external authority by mothers in the United States may indicate some concern about or, perhaps, ineffectiveness in eliciting compliance.

Developmental Expectations

Early Mastery of Developmental Skills. Mothers in the two countries differed in their views about the age at which children should master specific developmental skills. Responses were elicited by the Developmental Expectations Questionnaire (DEQ). This technique presented thirty-eight skills to mothers and asked them to indicate the age at which they expected their child to master each of

Table 11.3
Maternal Expectations for Early Mastery of Developmental Skills in Japan and the United States

Behavioral clusters	Means		Difference between Japan and United States
	Japan (N = 58)	United States (N = 67)	
Emotional maturity ("does not cry easily")	2.49	2.08	.41**
Compliance ("comes or answers when called")	2.16	1.96	.20*
Politeness ("greets family courteously")	2.49	2.30	.19
Independence ("plays outside, no supervision")	2.02	1.86	.16
School-related skills ("can tell time up to quarter-hour")	1.24	1.35	−.11
Social behavior ("takes initiative in playing with others")	1.86	2.18	−.32*
Verbal assertiveness ("asks for explanation when in doubt")	1.73	2.18	−.45**
Mean of all items	1.98	1.98	0.0

Note: Scale: 1 = age 6 or older; 2 = age 4 to 6; 3 = younger than age 4. T-Tests: * = .01, ** = .001.

them: (a) before age 4; (b) between ages 4 and 6; and, (c) after age 6. A score of 1 was assigned to the oldest age range, a score of 2 to the next range, and a score of 3 to the youngest category. The thirty-eight items were grouped (by judgment of staffs of the two research teams) into seven areas of behavior: (1) verbal assertiveness (for example, "asks for an explanation when in doubt"), (2) politeness (for example, "greets members of the family courteously"), (3) compliance (for example, "comes or answers when called"), (4) independence (for example, "takes care of own clothes"), (5) emotional maturity (for example, "does not cry easily"), (6) school readiness (for example, "can tell time up to quarter hour"), and (7) social skills (for example, "takes initiative in playing with others"). Scores were computed for each of the subgroups and for the total set of items.

Responses to the DEQ showed no difference on means computed across all items taken together, but there were sharp differences in emphasis for several areas of the child's behavior. Japanese mothers expected compliance, politeness, and emotional maturity at an earlier age; American mothers expected verbal assertiveness and social skills with peers at an earlier age (see Table 11.3). In Japan, mothers emphasized orienting the child toward proper behavior with adults; in the United States, they stressed developing effective behavior with peers (Hess et al.).

The results may reflect a contrast in the concept of "good child" in the two countries. In Japan, a child is thought to be good if he or she is "obedient" (*sunao*), "mild and gentle" (*otonasii*), and "self-controlled" (*jiseishin ga aru*). In the United States, the "good child" is assertive, socially competent with peers, and courteous.

Expectations for Achievement.   Mothers were also asked about expectations for their children's academic and occupational attainment. Other questions asked about the mothers' reaction to hypothetical situations in which their children were not doing well academically or wanted to drop out of high school. Other questions concerned school-relevant goals for the children's development during the preschool years.

These items were combined with items from the DEQ to form a *Expectations for Achievement* composite. As we shall describe later, this composite is associated with both school readiness and follow-up scores (see Table 11.4).

Beliefs about the Causes of Success and Failure

During the preschool phase of the project, mothers were asked to assign 100 points across four alternatives which expressed their belief about the contribution of different sources to children's success in school. The mothers in the two countries gave significantly different patterns of response. Mothers in Japan put more emphasis on children's natural ability (42 percent) than did mothers in the United States (31 percent) ($t = -1.92$, $p < .06$). American mothers placed significantly

Table 11.4

Correlations of Maternal Behavior Assessed at Preschool Phase with School Readiness at Ages 5 and 6 and Performance on Scholastic Tests in Grades 5 and 6

Maternal measures	Ages 5 and 6 School readiness		Grades 5 and 6 Test scores	
	Japan ($N = 58$)	United States ($N = 67$)	Japan ($N = 44$)	United States ($N = 47$)
Teaching styles				
requests verbal response	.13	.30*	.22	.27*
requests child-initiated response	.14	.47*	.16	.21
elaboration (total)	−.31*	−.29*	−.25*	−.26*
recycling (incorrect responses)	−.09	.03	−.05	.11
direct commands	−.32*	−.37*	−.16	−.23
moderated commands	.25*	.24*	.10	.25*
Communication efficiency				
combined score	.44*	.59*	.33*	.36*
Control appeals				
to authority	.19	−.26*	.19	−.37*
to feelings	−.25*	.15	−.47*	.08
to rules	.01	.31*	.19	.23
Developmental expectations				
Total score	.22*	.35*	.26	.15
school skills	.23*	.34*	.15	.15
social skills	.25*	.19	.23	.06
verbal assertiveness	.28*	.39*	.36*	.19
Expectations for achievement composite	.33*	.54*	.44*	.32*
Beliefs				
parents responsible for child's success	.02	.24*	.08	.24*
belief that failure due to lack of effort	—	—	.35*	.18
Affect and tact in interaction				
sensitivity (unstructured interaction)	.26*	.19	.34*	.19
negative affect (teaching)	−.16	−.37*	−.11	−.30*
SES	.51*	.37*	.44*	.21
Correlation for $p < .05$	.22	.20	.25	.24

* Significant at .05.

Table 11.5
Attributions of Children and Mothers in Japan and the United States for Low Performance in Mathematics

| Attribution | Japan | | | | | | United States (N = 47) | | | |
| | Follow-up mothers (N = 24) | | Back-up mothers (N = 39) | | Children | | Mothers | | Children | |
	Mean	S.D.	Mean	S.D.	Mean	S.D.	Mean	S.D.	Mean	S.D.
Lack of ability	1.48	(1.46)	1.45	(2.26)	1.93	(1.92)	2.62	(2.66)	3.38	(2.50)
Lack of effort	6.17	(2.35)	5.63	(3.65)	3.58	(2.37)	3.09	(2.56)	1.98	(2.12)
Training at school	0.77	(1.08)	1.05	(2.01)	0.93	(1.10)	2.26	(2.24)	1.30	(1.96)
Bad luck	0.50	(0.72)	0.76	(2.08)	1.02	(1.65)	0.38	(1.05)	1.94	(2.20)
Difficulty of math	1.04	(1.08)	1.14	(1.82)	2.53	(1.91)	—	—	—	—
Training at home	—	—	—	—	—	—	1.66	(1.52)	1.40	(1.79)

more weight on the contribution of parental encouragement (37 percent) than mothers in Japan (22 percent) ($t = 5.14$, $p < .001$). Theses differences seem consistent with the Japanese view of the responsibility of the individual to try to achieve the goals of the group. They suggest that Japanese mothers put more confidence in internal factors, expecting the child to assume responsibility for performance in school. Mothers in the United States see their own role as more important, expecting their children to be supported by external guidance.

In the follow-up phase of our study, mothers and children were asked to distribute ten chips to any of five sources of relative success ("Why does your child do as well as he/she does?") or relative lack of success ("Why does your child not do better?") in mathematics in grade 5 (Japan) and in grade 5 (U.S.).[3] The results for mothers showed a dramatic contrast between the two cultures (see Table 11.5). In Japan, poor performance in mathematics was attributed to lack of effort; in the United States, explanations were more evenly divided among ability, effort, and training at school. Japanese mothers were less likely to blame training at school as a cause of low achievement in mathematics (.77 percent in Japan, 2.26 percent in the United States). Their children generally shared this view of things. Of the ten points assigned to the five alternatives, Japanese children gave 5.6 to lack of effort; children in the United States gave only 1.98. We note also that causes for poor performance in Japan are those that attribution theorists usually take to be under the child's control. Effort is not fixed; presumably, it can be changed. It is subject to control. However, ability and training at school are generally unsusceptible to change. Events which are seen as not subject to one's control induce a sense of helplessness and inefficacy; those thought to be controllable may enhance a sense of efficacy (Weiner, 1980).

Affective Features of Mother-Child Interaction

Although this project emphasized cognitive, rather than social and affective elements of interaction between mothers and children in the two countries, the analysis of the three interaction tasks did include categories indicating both positive and negative exchanges. Although these brief glimpses of affective expression should be understood to represent only a limited range of the relationship between mothers and children, they are, nonetheless, relevant.

The data comes from observations of interaction tasks or from analysis of transcripts of verbal exchanges. The measures discussed here are observations of two categories of maternal behavior: *negative affect*, a summary of negative comments across the teaching task, and *sensitivity*, a rating of the mother's responsiveness during the unstructured interaction session. Indications of a link between affective behavior and cognitive performance, which appeared in these data (see Table 11.4), are supported by a more comprehensive analysis of the influence of the affective relationship between American mothers and children. A rating based on interviews, interaction tasks, and responses to the disciplinary questions showed a correlation of .34 with school readiness and .47 with test scores at grade six (Estrada et al. 1984). These correlations remained significant after the effects of SES, maternal I.Q., and children's mental ability scores at age 4 were taken into account.

These results, although based on analyses not included in the original design of the study, suggest that affective features of the mother-child interaction may play an important role in children's school achievement. The descriptions of a remarkably close bond between mother and child in Japan raise the possibility that affect plays a different role in socialization in the two countries. This possibility is further supported by the contrast in correlations (see Table 11.4) whereby sensitivity is associated with children's performance in Japan, and negative affect is associated with performance in the United States. Measures of negative affect were thus linked with child outcomes in America; measures of positive affect were linked with these outcomes in Japan. An additional bit of evidence is consistent with this distinction. A composite measure of mothers' use of praise in the interaction tasks was significantly associated in Japan with school readiness ($r = .25$) and later test scores ($r = .34$) but was not significantly correlated with outcomes in the United States.

Association of Maternal Behavior with Performance in School

Several areas of maternal behavior assessed during the preschool phase of the study were associated with children's performance on tests of school readiness and skill in mathematics and vocabulary in the middle grades. (Kashiwagi, Azuma & Miyake, 1982; see also Hess et al. 1984). Correlational data from some variables of interest are presented in Table 11.4.

Several features of these results should be mentioned briefly. First, quite different areas of maternal behavior are associated with both school readiness and later achievement on scholastic tests. Second, the pattern of correlations for the two groups is generally similar for three types of variables; requests for verbal responses and other variables in the teaching task, communication efficiency, and expectations for achievement. In other areas, the pattern is not so similar. Orientation toward authority shows a distinct national difference; it is associated with achievement negatively in both countries, but different aspects of control are associated with school performance in the two groups. In the United States, appeals to authority have a negative correlation with school-relevant outcomes in both preschool and later performance; in the Japanese group, appeals to feelings are negatively correlated. The association between beliefs and outcomes also seems to differ, although more evidence is necessary to establish this point. The limited evidence on affective behavior suggests that affect may be used in different ways as a socializing influence in the two countries.

Third, although teaching styles are linked with school readiness, they show less relationship with outcomes in the elementary grades. Perhaps this reflects a greater specificity of the measures of teaching in the task used at preschool. Comparable measures that assessed parental behavior in more contemporary problem-solving situations might have been more closely associated with achievement.

It should also be noted that measures of socioeconomic status correlated with outcomes at both preschool and follow-up phases of the study. SES was also associated with several types of maternal behavior.

Summary and Discussion

Several features of these results offer particular interest for the comparison of the influences of families on school achievement in the two countries. Mothers in both countries have high aspirations for their offspring; their developmental goals during the preschool years are generally similar. In both countries, too, the maternal behavior we observed during the children's preschool years is correlated not only with school readiness, but with school-relevant performance several years later. Even so, families in the two countries offer different socialization experiences to prepare the children for work in the classroom. Analyses underway, but unreported here, suggest that the influence of family background may affect performance in school to a greater degree in Japan than in the United States. In both groups, however, maternal variables contribute to achievement over and above measures of mental ability at age 4.

There were also differences between the groups in their socialization and teaching styles. Our results are consistent with the view that Japanese mothers interacted with their children in ways that promote internalization of adult norms and standards, whereas American mothers were more oriented toward application of external authority and direction. American mothers relied more on verbal explanations and on the use of techniques encouraging verbalization by children. Japanese mothers seemed to emphasize more following the correct procedure as a route to understanding; the concept of "from form to mind" seems to fit their behavior in teaching tasks.

Japanese mothers also appeared to place higher confidence in efficacy of effort than did American mothers. Perhaps the Japanese mothers were thus expressing a belief that problems are susceptible to persistence and hard work and that responsibility for achievement lies with the individual. Despite the individualism that presumably characterizes American culture, mothers and children in the United States seemed to be less oriented toward internal sources of achievement. They emphasized the role of parents in children's success in school, were more likely to place blame on the school for the children's failure, and appealed more to authority than to internal states in attempts to persuade children to conform.

It may also be interesting that social variables—orientation toward control, beliefs and expectations, affective relationships—continue to show an association with children's achievement over time. In the preschool phase of the study, maternal teaching techniques were correlated with school readiness. The longitudinal analysis, however, shows an apparently increasingly important role of social features of the interaction. Maternal beliefs and expectations, orientation toward control, and affective relationship with the child all seem to have continuing relevance for achievement in both countries.

Some areas of maternal behavior appear to have roughly similar association with child outcomes; expectations for achievement, teaching styles, and communication efficiency. Yet there are differences in the effects of teaching styles, orientation toward control, and beliefs about the utility of effort to avoid failure. Perhaps more detailed studies will describe the processes involved in each country and contribute to a more general theory of family influences on school achievement.

Footnotes

1. There is a large and growing literature on socialization in both Japan and the United States that is relevant to a study of cognitive socialization in the family. Much of it is discussed in other chapters of this volume. A summary of literature about family influences on school achievement appears in Hess and Holloway (1984). We acknowledge this literature, but space limitations do not permit a discussion of its relevance to the study described here.

2. This study was supported by grants from the Japanese Science Foundation, the Spencer Foundation (through the Social Science Research Council), and the National Science Foundation (Grant #NSF BNS 91-07542). Others who participated in the study in Japan are Kayoko Inagaki, Chiba University; Yoko Kuriyama, Internatinal Christian University; Hiromi Ohno, Tokyo Woman's Christian University; Naomi Miyake, Aoyama Gakuin, Woman's Junior College; Nobumoto Tajima, Tokyo University of Foreign Studies; Hiroshi Usui, Hokkaido University of Education; Keiko Watanabe, Kanagawa University. Other participants in the United States included Mary Conroy, San Jose State University; William Arsenio, Stanford University; Peggy Estrada, Stanford University; and Eleanor B. Worden, Stanford University.

3. The follow-up study in Japan included twenty-four of the mothers of the original group. To obtain confirmatory data on attributions, interviews were taken with an additional group of thirty-nine women and their fifth-grade children. Table 11.4 shows data for these groups separately.

References

Azuma, H. (1984). *Socialization and motivation: Some thought about "receptive diligence" implicity encouraged in Japanese education*. Paper presented at the annual convention of the American Educational Research Association, April, 1984, New Orleans.

Azuma, H., Kashiwagi, K., & Hess, R. D. (1981). *Maternal attitudes, behaviors and childrens' cognitive development—Cross-national survey between Japan and the U.S.* Tokyo: University of Tokyo Press. (In Japanese)

Belsky, J. (1981). Early human experience: A family perspective. *Developmental Psychology, 17,* 3–23.

Caudill, W., & Weinstein, H. (1966). Maternal care and infant behavior in Japan and America. In R. Konig & R. Hill (Eds.), *Yearbook of the International Sociological Association* (pp.1–24).

Conroy, M., Hess, R. D., Azuma, H., & Kashiwagi, K. (1980). Maternal strategies for regulating childrens's behavior: Japanese and American families. *Journal of Cross-Culture Psychology, 11* (2), 153–172.

Dickson, W. P., Hess, R. D., Miyake, N., & Azuma, H. (1979). Referential communication accuracy between mother and child as a predictor of cognitive development in the United States and Japan. *Child Development, 50,* 53–59.

Dore, R. P. (1958). *City life in Japan: A study of a Tokyo ward.* Berkeley: University of California Press.

Easley, J., & Easley, E. (1981). *Kitamaeno school as an environment in which children study mathematics themselves.* Address to the Faculty of Education, University of Tokyo, May, 1981.

Estrada, P., Arsenio, W., Hess, R. D., & Holloway, S. D. (1984). *The affective tone of the mother-child relationship and later school achievement.* Unpublished paper, Stanford University, Calif.

Hatano, G. (1982). *Should parents be teachers too?: A Japanese view.* Unpublished paper, Dokkyo University, Japan.

Hatano, G., Miyake, K., & Tajima, N. (1980). Mother behavior in as unstructured situation and child's acquistion of number conservation. *Child Development, 51,* 377–385.

Hess, R. D., & Shipman, V. C. (1965). Early experience and the socialization of cognitive modes in children. *Child Development, 36,* 869–886.

Hess, R. D., Kashiwagi, K., Azuma, H., Price, G. G., & Dickson, W. P. (1980). Maternal expectations for mastery of developmental tasks in Japan and the United States. *International Journal of Psychology, 15,* 259–271.

Hess, R. D., Holloway, S. D., Dickson, P. W., & Price, G. G. (1984). Maternal variables as predictors of children's school readiness and later achievement in vocabulary and mathematics in sixth grade. *Child Development, 55* (5), 1902–1912.

Hess, R. D., & Holloway, S. D. (1984). Family and school as educational institutions. In

R. Parke (Ed). *Review of Research in Child Development* Vol. 7, pp. 179–222. Chicago: University of Chicago Press.

Hess, R. D., & McDevitt, T. M. (1984). Some cognitive consequences of maternal intervention techniques: A longitudinal study. *Child Development, 55*(6), 2017–2030.

Hieronymus, A. N., Lindquist, E. F., & Hoover, H. D. (1978). *The Iowa tests of basic skills.* Boston: Houghton Mifflin.

Hildreth, G. H., Griffiths, N. L., & McGauvran, M. E. (1964). *Metropolitan readiness tests.* New York: Harcourt Brace & World.

Holloway, S. D., & Hess, R. D. (1984). Mothers' and teachers' attributions about children's mathematics performance. In I. E. Sigel (Ed.) *Parental belief systems: Psychological consequences for children,* pp. 177–199. Hillsdale NJ: Lawrence Erlbaum Associates.

Husén, T. (Ed.). (1967). *International study of achievement in mathematics: A comparison to twelve countries.* Vols. 1 & 2. New York: John Wiley & Sons.

Kashiwagi, K., Azuma, H., & Miyake, K. (1982). Early maternal influences upon later cognitive development among Japanese children: A follow-up study. *Japanese Psychological Research, 24,* 90–100.

Kedar-Voivodas, G. (1983). The impact of elementary children's roles and sex roles on teacher attitudes: As interactional analysis. *Review of Educational Research, 53,* 414–437.

Kikuchi, A., & Gordon, L. V. (1970). Japanese and American personal values: some cross-cultural findings. *International Journal of Psychology, 5,* 183–187.

Lewis, C. C. (1984). Cooperation and control in Japanese Nursery Schools. *Comparative Education Review, 28*(1), 69–84.

McDevitt, T. M., Dickson, W. P., Miyake, N., Azuma, H., & Hess, R. D. (1984). Communication accuracy of American and Japanese mother-child pairs and later scholastic achievement: A follow-up study (Unpublished paper).

Price, G. G., Hess, R. D., & Dickson, W. P. (1981). Processes by which verbal-educational abilities are affected when mothers encourage preschool children to verbalize. *Developmental Psychology, 17,* 554–564.

Stigler, J. W., Lee, S-y., Lucker, W., & Stevenson, H. W. (1982). Curriculum and achievement in mathematics: A study of elementary school children in Japan, Taiwan, and the United States. *Journal of Educational Psychology, 74,* 315–322.

Weiner, B. (1980). *Human motivation.* New York: Holt, Rinehart & Winston.

Wechsler, D. (1974). *Wechsler Intelligence Scale for Children (rev. ed.).* New York: The Psychological Corporation.

Personality Development of Adolescents

Keiko Kashiwagi

Two phenomena have recently been noted as serious problems for Japanese adolescents. The first is related to the large percentage of adolescents attending higher educational institutions. In 1982, nearly 40 percent of high school graduates enrolled in colleges or universities. At present, Japan ranks second to the United States in number of students enrolled in universities (Ministry of Education, 1983). Associated with this rapid spread of higher education is the strong pressure for academic achievement and success in entrance examinations exerted by parents. Entrance "examination hell" (*shiken jigoku*) exists throughout the school-age period. The result of this pressure has been to distort students' motivation as stress is placed on extrinsic and instrumental objectives for learning.

The second problem is the increasing frequency over the last decade of various kinds of juvenile delinquency. Recent juvenile delinquency exhibits several unique features: one is the acting out of violent behavior toward parents, especially the mother, and another is school-phobic activity. The incidence of both these behavioral patterns has increased greatly over the past 10 years and they differ from earlier types of delinquency in many respects, particularly in relation to familial and personal backgrounds. In contrast to earlier patterns, problem behavior now occurs among students who have generally excellent scholastic achievement and have been regarded as "good" children by teachers and parents prior to their symptomatic behavior. Moreover, children from middle-class families and children of parents with higher educations seem particularly vulnerable to these new types of delinquency. (Akō, 1981; Imaizumi, 1982). Also, for the first time, there has been an increase of delinquency in the younger generation. Although the rate of crime has gradually decreased, for the overall population as can be seen in Figure 12-1, the percentage of juvenile delinquency has drastically increased, especially among junior-high school students (Ministry of Justice, 1983).

Background of Problem Behaviors in Japanese Adolescents

Clinical psychologists and psychiatrists point out several common social and psychological factors in recent problem behaviors. Compared to "classic" delinquency, which was seen as closely related to family backgrounds in which children

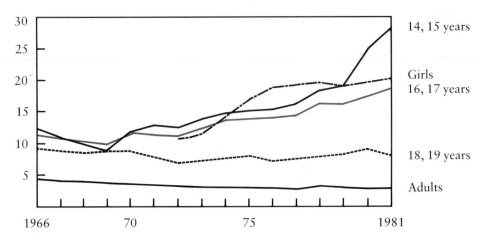

Figure 12-1
Percentage of crime at different age groups.

Table 12.1
Percentage of "Yes" Replies of Children in Six Countries

	Country					
Item	United States	England	Thailand	France	Korea	Japan
My parents plan for my future.	94.4	84.6	93.7	83.8	86.5	72.1
I have someone I'm proud of among my relations.	94.0	77.4	86.2	55.2	65.7	52.1
I'm sometimes thanked by people outside my family.	94.5	85.5	86.9	71.7	82.2	54.8
I'm counted on by my friends.	90.3	77.3	58.4	94.8	72.4	60.9
I can finish anything if I really try.	96.3	89.3	95.0	84.9	73.2	82.9
I'm doing quite well in school.	92.7	91.0	51.8	76.9	61.9	36.6
I'm talented in sports, playing musical instruments, singing, etc.	77.8	74.4	62.6	64.7	52.1	62.3
I usually win in fights.	39.7	30.7	28.5	18.3	41.7	32.4

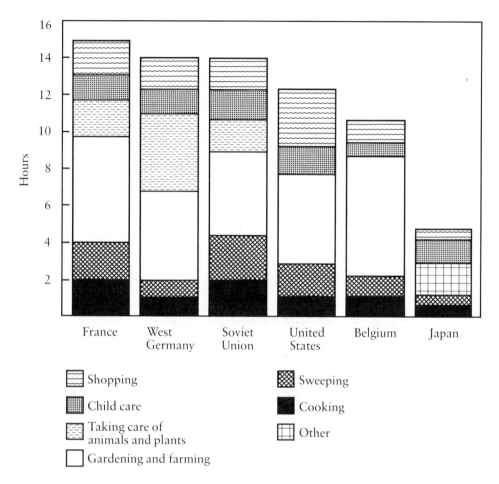

Figure 12-2
Husband's participation in childrearing and housework in six countries.

were deprived of maternal love and care as well as of educational and cultural stimulation, the new problem behaviors appear to be caused by affluence and parental overprotection. Children today are apt to encounter less frustration and to experience fewer difficulties; consequently, they are untrained to cope with demanding tasks by themselves. The result is poor tolerance of frustration. (Akō; Imaizumi). Cross-national data on children's lives reveal that, in one sense, Japanese children lead privileged lives, but, in another, the current situation has serious negative consequences for them (Prime Minister's Office, 1979). Some of these consequences are shown in Table 12.1. One reflection of the seriousness of the situation is the low degree of positive self-constitutes, in marked contrast to American children.

The new problem behaviors seem strongly related to a lack of paternal presence in children's education and home life. The idea of segregation by sex—expressed in "a man works outside, and a woman has to work inside (at home)"—is still quite popular and more widely accepted by the Japanese than by western countries (Prime Minister's Office, 1979). Furthermore, as is evident in Figure 12-2, the father's (husband's) participation in child rearing and housework is much more limited in Japan than elsewhere (Economic Planning Agency, 1978). Clinical psychologists point to the resulting "fatherless" home as one of the critical backgrounds for the new problem behaviors in adolescents (Inamura, 1980, 1983).

Issues of Self-Concept and Sex-Role Development in Japan

Several studies have observed significant differences between normal and delinquent adolescents in the development of self-concept and the degree of self-esteem (Miyano, Motoaki et al., 1978, 1979). Reflection on philosophic issues such as concepts of God, love, death, peace, and justice during adolescence may form an important basis for later personality development. Mugishima (1979) has presented data suggesting that such philosophic experiences at an early age are both less frequent and poorer in a delinquent group than in a nondelinquent or normal group.

Sociocultural factors affecting sex-role development—personal values, social norms, family structure, education, labor market, and such demographic variables as birth rate and life span—have had a massive influence upon sex-role development, and, through this, upon personality and adjustment. In particular, sex-role development in adolescence, which closely reflects socializing processes in the family and in the school, deeply influences a youngster's self-concept and adjustment. This paper focuses on sex-role development in Japanese adolescents and on some related problems including, self-concept and socialization processes. Recent trends in this field of research will be reviewed and examined, partly from a cross-cultural point of view, and some specific problems will be presented.

Self-Concept in Japanese Adolescents

Self-concept has been one of the focal points of psychology of adolescence ever since this science's introduction to Japan. One consistent characteristic of the development of self-concept and self-esteem is that of sex differences in self-concept.

Yamamoto, Matsui and Yamanari (1982) reported, in their study of college students, that self-evaluation by male subjects was significantly more positive than that by female subjects in various aspects of personality, such as in attitudes toward life and ability and confidence and satisfaction with one's own personality, as shown in Table 12.2. Similar tendencies were observed in cross-sectional data

Table 12.2

Means (SDs) of 11 Dimensions for Boys and Girls
and Significance Level of Sex Differences

	Boys	Girls	P
Sociability	3.00 (1.04)	3.22 (1.08)	.01
Athletic skills	3.04 (1.11)	2.60 (1.10)	.01
Intelligence	2.99 (0.92)	2.56 (0.89)	.01
Kindness and tenderness	3.49 (0.86)	3.43 (0.80)	.05
Sexuality	2.19 (0.96)	1.63 (0.87)	.01
Looks	2.76 (0.95)	2.58 (0.94)	.05
Way of living	3.21 (1.06)	2.84 (1.08)	.01
Economic capacity	2.54 (0.93)	2.70 (1.00)	.05
Hobby and special ability	3.30 (1.11)	3.02 (1.19)	.01
Earnestness	3.44 (0.82)	3.41 (0.86)	.05
Popularity of school	3.12 (1.08)	3.37 (1.10)	.01

SOURCE: Yamamoto, Matsui, & Yamanari, *Japanese Journal of Educ. Psych.* 30 (1982).

(Kajita, 1980; Kato, 1977; Miyazawa, 1978; Murase, 1973). Negative self-evaluations have been found in females, from adolescence to old age (Shimonaka & Murase, 1976).

Identity confusion of the type suggested by the psychoanalyst Erik Erikson, is another important characteristic in the development of self-concept. As with negative self-evaluation, it exists more predominantly among female than among many male adolescents. A close relationship was observed between identity confusion and a large disparity between two self-concepts, that of the real self and the ideal self, among female subjects (Matsuda & Hirose, 1982; Takeuchi, 1981).

In brief, most of the research conducted thus far almost unequivocally provides evidence of sex differences in self-concept, indicating low self-acceptance, negative self-evaluation and feelings toward self among females. This seems to be one of the characteristics peculiar to Japanese adolescents, for Maccoby and Jacklin (1974) give different data about American teen-agers. They report that out of thrity-nine studies on self-concept at various age levels reviewed, twenty-four showed no sex differences; only six reported higher self-esteem in boys, and nine found higher self-esteem in girls. This picture contrasts with that of consistent sex differences showing lower self-evaluation among females in Japanese samples.

How can the different results be explained? For Japanese adolescents, lower self-esteem in females might be assumed to be deeply related to difficulties in adjustment to their sex role, which is socially and traditionally defined more rigidly than in the United States. Not a few Japanese female adolescents are reluctant to accept norms of social expectations for women. Eventually, this reluctance leads to difficulties in integrating self-conceptions of sex role with sex-role norms in the society. Thus, the lower self-evaluation and identity confusion peculiar to Japanese female adolescents seem to be closely related with social norms concerning sex roles in Japan.

Sex-Role Development in Japanese Adolescents

Various aspects of the acquisition of sex roles in early childhood through adolescence have been investigated. Of these, cognitive aspects have received particular attention, and several consistent results have been obtained.

Kashiwagi (1967, 1972, 1974) has conceptualized social sex roles of males and females in two opposing dimensions; one, the *masculine* (M) dimension, characterized by activity, idependence, and dominance for males; and the other, *feminine* (F) dimension, characterized by elegance, loveliness, and calmness for females. In addition to these masculine and feminine dimensions, the qualities of brightness, warmth, and broad-mindedness, among others, are regarded as equally important for both sexes and are encompassed by the *humanity* dimension, as presented in Table 12.3 (Ito, 1978).

Sex differences in the conceptualization of sex roles have been identified by several researchers: male subjects tend to regard males and females on a nearly bipolar basis. Female subjects are more likely to minimize the difference between the roles of the two sexes.

In Ito's studies (1978, 1980), sex differences figured more prominently in the evaluation of desirable characteristics for subjects' own sex than in the evaluation of existing social sex roles. Males rated masculine and feminine dimensions

Table 12.3
List of Items in M-H-F Scale

Masculinity	Humanity	Femininity
ambitious	tolerant	cute
strong	broad-minded	elegant
bold	bright	sexy
a leader	cheerful	devoted
confident	warm	charming
dependable	sincere	speaks politely
active	healthy	delicate
self-assertive	candid	submissive
strong will	has one's own way of living	calm
quick in decision	has broad view	self-attentive

SOURCE: Ito, 1978.

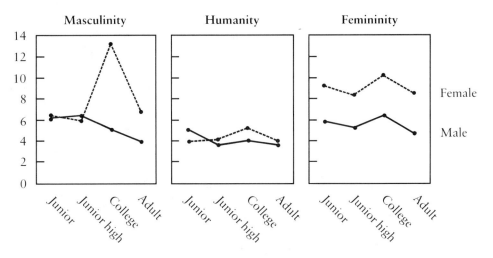

Figure 12-3
Discrepancy between conceptions of sex role and perceived social sex role in four age groups.

differently, and desirabilities for males in these two dimensions were clearly discriminated. In contrast, female subjects' conceptions of their own sex roles differed from their evaluation of the female social role. (They rated M traits higher on the M dimension and F traits lower on the F dimension for the female role; than their ratings existing for social sex roles (Figure 12-3).) Thus, discrepancies between conceptions of females' own individual sex roles and perception of the socially defined sex role were significantly larger in female subjects (Ito, 1981; Ito & Akitsu, 1983).

The largest discrepancies between the subject's own conception of sex role and his or her perception of social sex role were evident at the college level; such discrepancies, however, appeared consistently larger in female subjects through all age levels. (Inagaki, 1967; Kashiwagi, 1974). In adulthood, these discrepancies tended to decrease, as the conception of sex role gradually changed from the extremely unconventional pattern found in the college student to a moderate pattern of traditional sex-role steroeotypes (Inagaki, 1967). Cross-national comparisons of sex-role development have been few; however, discrepancies in conceptions of sex role have been pointed out in Japanese female adolescents compared with their American counterparts (Inagaki, 1967).

Self-Concept and Sex-Role Development

Studies in sex-role development suggest that Japanese female adolescents have considerable conflict in conceptualizing and accepting their own sex role and that this may cause some difficulty in their personality development and adjustment.

Table 12.4

Percentage of Agreement by Women to Question, "Which Do You Wish to be Born Next time, a Man or a Woman?"*

	United			Japan	
Answer	States	France	Sweden	(1973)	(1953)
To be a man	10.5	25.8	4.5	27	(64)
To be a woman	78.5	57.0	89.1	50	(27)
Ambiguous	11.0	17.2	2.7	23	(9)

* Data in the first four columns are from a 1973 survey. The last column presents data from a 1953 survey for Japan only.

In fact, a cross-national survey (Ministry of Education, 1975) revealed a lower degree of acceptance of their own sex in Japanese females: they are more reluctant to be women compared to the females in western countries (see Table 12.4). The results of this survey suggest that circumstances are apt to lead Japanese female adolescents to a lack of confidence in themselves and, hence, to identity confusion. Other evidence tends to support this hypothesis.

Several studies have examined the disparity of two self-concepts (the real and the ideal) in relation to acceptance of sex roles. Larger D-scores (disparity between real and ideal self-concepts) were found significantly in the female groups, indicating a negative, and sometimes rejecting attitude toward the subject's own sex (Takahashi, 1975). Significant positive correlations between identity confusion and D-scores were also observed among female adolescents. Lower self-esteem—lack of confidence, inferiority, and a passive and inactive attitude toward future life—has been suggested as a primary factor inhibiting the establishment of stable self-identity. In addition, girls with a high femininity score, as measured by a revised version of the MMPI, tended to accept the traditional female role and have, as a consequence, less conflict with social sex-role norms (Ito, 1980).

These data all suggest that acceptance of individual sex role is one of the critical determinants of self-concept in Japanese females adolescents. One factor that contributes greatly to low female self-esteem is the general trend in Japanese society for traits traditionally attributed to their role to be less valued than those attributed to the male role (Ito, 1978). Lower evaluations of the female role are clearly evident in Ito's study (see Table 12.5).

Relevant data have been presented by Spence, Helmreich, and Stapp (1975) concerning the relation between sex role and self-concept. According to their analysis, as shown in Table 12.6, high self-ratings on masculinity and femininity are significantly related to self-esteem in both men and women. In contrast to Japanese studies, consistent sex differences in self-esteem are absent from their

Table 12.5
Social Evaluation on Three Sex-Role Dimensions:
Masculinity, Humanity, Femininity

Gender	Dimension		
	Masculinity	Humanity	Femininity
Male	33.64	36.49	19.86
Female	32.15	36.92	20.90

SOURCE: Ito, 1978.

data. Instead, American women showed self-esteem. Strong associations of both masculinity and femininity with self-esteem in the United States (correlations of M and F and self-esteem ranged from .30 to .83) suggest that these two factors (M and F) may play an important role in determining an individual's self-esteem.

Relevant data comparable to Spence's are unavailable for Japanese samples. However, Ito's findings (1980) suggest a difference may exist. Female subjects with high scores on the F scale of MMPI tended to evaluate the F dimension highly as a female role; these subjects also seemed more likely to accept their own sex role than those with low F scores. (It may be proposed that this acceptance also leads to high self-esteem.) In contrast, subjects with low F scores and high M scores tended to evaluate the M dimension highly as a female role and appeared reluctant to accept their own female role.

The studies of Japanese adolescents described thus far have revealed that self-esteem is a quality found to be significantly lower in girls than in boys. In addition, greater discrepancies between female subjects' own sex-role concept and perceived social sex-role norms have been repeatedly found by various researchers using different measures.

Further examination is needed to clarify the mechanisms underlying the cognitive development of sex role and its relationship to self-esteem in Japanese

Table 12.6
Mean Self-Esteem in Four Groups Differing in
Masculinity and Femininity

	Groups			
	Low M	Low M	High M	High M
	Low F	High F	Low F	High M
Men	66.82	74.55	87.02	93.73
Women	69.66	75.41	92.17	98.73

adolescents. In addition to the cognitive domain, behavioral domains related to sex role in terms of masculinity and femininity as a duality present another topic for further examination. These studies should provide a better understanding of the characteristics and problems of the sex-role socialization process and self-concept in adolescents living in a changing society. Studies along this line merit cross-cultural research, for they will enable us to understand personality development and adjustment from a broad sociocultural point of view.

Sex-Role Socialization Processes and Their Consequences

Studies of child-rearing patterns have provided data suggesting that parental attitudes and behavior toward the child differ according to the sex of the child, the girl more frequently being trained to conform with her traditional sex role.

Aspects of sex-differentiated treatment by parents have been reported in several recent surveys. These include parental aspirations for the child's education, expectations of child's future life, assignment of chores, and attendance of *juku* ("after-school schooling") for sons and daughters (Economic Planning Agency, 1978; Ministry of Education, 1975, 1983; Prime Minister's Office, 1979, 1980). More detailed examinations of parental sex-differentiated disciplines reveal more complicated and confused pictures (Kashiwagi, 1975; Kashiwagi et al., 1976). Sex-differentiated discipline occurs in nearly 80 percent of Japanese homes, where girls are expected more to conform with their traditional role than boys (see Table 12.7). However, this discipline is not necessarily consistent with parental concepts

Table 12.7
Distribution of Mothers According to Types of Sex-Differentiated Discipline at Three Age Levels

	Age of children		
Types of mothers	10 years	12 years	14 years
Train children differently according to their sexes	37	30	35
Give sex-differentiated training only to sons	19	17	8
Give sex-differentiated training only to daughters	29	27	33
Train sons and daughters equally without any sex-differentiated training	15	26	23

SOURCE: Kashiwagi et al., 1976.

or opinions of sex roles; a large discrepancy between actual behavior and opinion was observed in nearly half of the parents. For instance, many mothers who expressed highly progressive opinions of the traditional sex-role stereotype, often trained their children according to conventional sex-role concepts. Incongruities between opinion and behavior was more frequently found among mothers with adolescents than among mothers with young children. It was also more prevalent among mothers of girls than of boys. On the other hand, children's attitudes toward such sex-differentiated discipline differed considerably between boys and girls. Boys, both in high school and college, showed more positive opinions of parental discipline; girls of the same age group were resistant to sex-typed training and exhibited more negative attitudes toward discipline.

In addition to discipline in the home, educational institutions and social settings play important roles as socializing agents in the development of traditional sex roles. Textbooks, curricula, and other aspects of elementary and secondary education have recently been criticized for bias in this respect (Sato, 1977). In but one of many examples, only girls are required to learn homemaking as a compulsory subject, but, other institutionalized methods affect children in the direction of sex-role differentiation.

Because of parental expectations and training based on the child's sex, highly biased distributions of males and females are found in university courses. In this respect, Japanese students appear strikingly different from students in other countries. As Figure 12-4 shows, this trend has been almost constant for the last decade.

As may be clearly seen in the divergent distributions of courses according to sex, sex-differentiated training has had a massive effect upon various aspects of child development. The influences of sex-typed socialization processes have been increasingly taken up by developmental psychologists, and detailed investigations have been reported by several researchers (Ito, 1980; Kashiwagi et al., 1976; Soeda & Kashiwagi, 1981).

Value, interest, life styles, academic achievement, and career patterns have been the main subjects of analysis in connection with sex-typed training by parents. What the research reveals, however, is a complicated picture of the impact of parental, sex-differentiated discipline upon sex typing in children. Boys, for example, show more sex-typed behavior at all ages. This suggests that parental training may function as direct reinforcement for their behavioral development. But in girls, no such direct impact could be detected. In fact, the results suggest a negative influence of parental, sex-typed training upon female adolescents.

Fear of success, conceptualized by Horner (1972), is considered to be related to sex typing in females. Several researchers discovered sex differences in relation to fear of success in Japanese adolescents. Though not evident through all age levels, these differences appeared substantially at the high-school level, a tendency which became increasingly striking as students grew older (Saito, Aoyagi & Kaneko, 1981). Qualitative differences were marked between males and females in

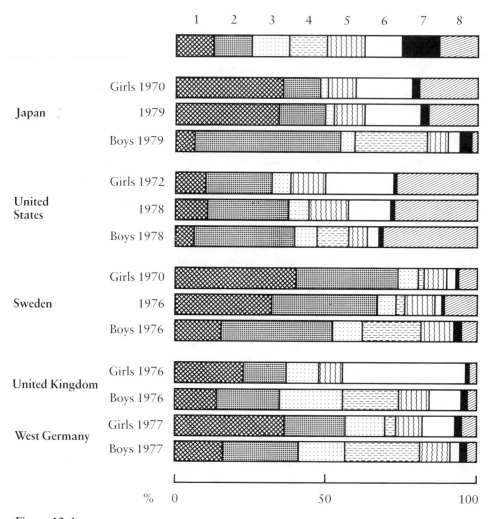

Figure 12-4
Distributions of students' selections of different courses in five countries. (1) humanities (2) social sciences (3) natural sciences (4) engineering (5) medicine (6) education (7) agriculture (8) miscellaneous.

the way in which each sex withdrew from achieving success (Okazaki, 1977). Based on content analysis of verbal responses, two types of motives were identified. One was withdrawal (avoidance) from success, due to negative evaluation of success itself. The other was fear of success, due to expectations of negative social criticism for assumption of an inappropriate female role. The former motive, withdrawal from success, was found in both sexes; the latter, fear of success, was present only among female subjects.

A preliminary analysis of Japanese and American data collected on maternal influences upon children's cognitive outcomes reveal a correlation between sex differentation and cognitive development. Since this study is not primarily concerned with sex differences, the sample numbers for each sex are insufficient to lead to firm conclusions. Despite this limitation, few cognitive performance measures show significant sex differences in both the United States and Japan, and general levels of cognitive functioning are nearly the same for both sexes in terms of mean scores of the cognitive measures. However, in Japan, the number of significant correlations is significantly higher in boys (36) than in girls (22). In the United States, on the other hand, the number of significant correlations is the same for boys as for girls (37, 36) (Kashiwagi & Azuma, 1981).

These data suggest that maternal variables play a more important role in the development of cognitive skills in Japanese boys than in Japanese girls. Moreover, Japanese boys tend to receive more educational stimulation, opportunities, and training advantageous to their later cognitive development than girls. Such differences between sexes in socialization processes are likely to be more prevalent in Japan than in America.

Finally, I would like to comment on the social values or norms underlying the socialization processes of sex roles, either explicitly or implicitly among the Japanese.

Kikuchi and Gordon (1970) have presented extensive cross-cultural data on value systems, mainly in adolescents. The data shows both male and female Japanese students put, among interpersonal values, significantly great emphasis upon "conformity" both at high school and college levels than did the American students. "Independence," an opposing value, was more highly valued by American students of both age levels and sexes than by their Japanese counterparts. Furthermore, Japanese students place higher value on "orderliness" and "goal orientation" among personal values than do their American counterparts. This suggests an inclination in the Japanese toward a well-organized life, systematic approaches to relatively well-defined goals, and resistance to change and diversity.

These findings seem to agree with anthropological observations and anecdotal writings on the Japanese national character (for example, Sobue, 1976; Research Committee on the Study of the Japanese National Character, 1982). The characteristics of personal and interpersonal values of the Japanese must be considered to understand sex-role socialization in Japan. Social norms concerning sex roles are not necessarily explicit; in fact, they are generally rather vague and implicit. Nevertheless, the pressure to conform to norms is more severe and pervasive for the Japanese than for westerners. Sex-differentiated training, frequently employed by Japanese parents and even by teachers, is one reflection of this strong sociocultural climate. Under the circumstances, discrepancies between self-concept concerning sex role and social norms attached to it are important issues in adolescents' development of self-identity. As such, the result is often serious conflicts for female adolescents in particular.

Another Perspective on Japanese Self-Concept

Negative evaluation of self, or strong awareness of weaker aspects of self, is sometimes pointed to as one of the general characteristics of self-concept among the Japanese. The scarcity of comprehensive cross-national studies precludes a definitive statement on this matter; however, several research findings seem to indicate the existence of such a national characteristic.

Thus, a study on anthropophobia, or social phobia (Ogawa et al., 1981), provides evidence concerning the negative self-evaluation of Japanese. Ogawa analyzed statements frequently made by patients of his who suffered from social phobia—a common syndrome in Japan—and identified, by means of factor analysis, eight common symptomatic features. Most of these features can be interpreted as pathological variations of excessively negative self-concept, such as "feeling of dissatisfaction with oneself," "anxiety concerning one's inability to deal with others," "anxiety concerning one's emotional instability," and so on. Ogawa devised a questionnaire to measure the degree of symptomatic tendency in his social-phobia patients when compared with three normal groups—one, Japanese and two, American. As might be expected, the pathological group recorded the highest scores on all dimensions; the Japanese group scored markedly higher than the two American groups on all dimensions.

Further support for the existence of this national characteristic comes from a cross-national survey carried out by the Japanese Prime Minister's Office in 1980. Elementary-school children in six countries were asked to rate themselves on eight statements concerning self. The results revealed a low degree of self-confidence among Japanese children. In marked contrast were the results of the American children, who gave highly positive responses to themselves.

Sometime earlier, Kimura, a Japanese psychiatrist, noted that predominance of self-punitive tendencies among depression patients in his book, *Between a person and a person* (1972). He suggested that cultural factors must be taken into account to explain this phenomenon. From Kimura's observations and Ogawa's clinical data, I infer that any adequate account of even a psychopathological issue must take into account cultural factors.

Do the Japanese really feel the way they describe themselves? I propose (a) that negative attitude toward self could be attributed to some inhibition against open acknowledgment by an individual of his or her positive traits, and (b) that this inhibition may be culturally induced, on the one hand, by the extremely high value placed on what is called "the virtue of modesty" and, on the other, by the strong social pressure for conformity. In this connection, locus of control, which is concerned with belief in or value of the self, is an issue worth attention from a sociocultural point of view.

Most studies agree that the Japanese tend to regard internal factors as more causally significant than external ones in cases of failure and to see the reverse in cases of success. In other words, the Japanese are more likely to attribute failure to lack of effort (or other internal factors), whereas they are more likely to attribute success to effective teaching, ease of task (or other external factors) (Shikauchi, 1978). It is not difficult to see in this pattern the reflection of a self-critical attitude or a modest self-evaluation.

In the paradigm of Internals-Externals, the former are postulated as indices of a competent self with a high degree of basic self-trust. Several cross-national studies on locus of control (Evans, 1981; Mahler, 1974; McGinnies et al., 1974) report that Japanese subjects assign a considerably higher degree of importance to "luck," as compared to subjects of other nations. Accordingly, Japanese subjects have been characterized as "dominantly externals." My own work, carried out in collaboration with a group of British researchers, confirms this tendency of the Japanese. Japanese samples attribute more value to "luck," both in failure and in success situations, than British samples. These characteristics in Japanese patterns cannot be accounted for except in cultural terms. If one believes that Japanese negative self-evaluation is culture biased—and thus may not really reflect all the attributes of the universal concept of negative self-evaluation—it is possible to assume that the same cultural forces induce a peculiarly Japanese pattern of locus of control.

Numerous researches on locus of control in the United States have clarified several developmental factors and correlates (Lefcourt, 1982). Internality is found to be positively associated with high levels of cognitive achievement, suggesting a close interrelationship between effort and achievement. Similarly, a significant relationship has been recognized between internality and self-esteem. In addition, most data based on cross-sectional samples show a general developmental trend indicating increasing internality with increasing age. These findings lead to the conclusion, therefore, that internality is a favorable state fostering high achievement and self-esteem. Change from "externals" to "internals" is either explicitly or implicitly regarded as part of a general developmental sequence.

Related studies in Japan present a different picture. A developmental tendency toward internality in Japanese children has not been found in most studies. Instead, perception of locus of control becomes more complicated, and different kinds of external factors become more influential, depending on the situation, with increasing age. Furthermore, the relationship of internality to high academic achievement, consistently positive in United States samples, is not appreciable in Japanese studies. Interestingly, internality is closely related to strictness (or modesty) in self-evaluation of performance in Japan (Hayami, 1981).

These findings, together with other comparative data referred to, raise a basic question about the interpretation of research findings. Earlier, in discussing cross-cultural studies on locus of control, I noted that the Japanese are categorized as "dominant externals," on the basis of high ratings on "luck." But should this high score be always interpreted as an indication of "externals?" In our research on Japanese and British students, Japanese rated "effort" as most important, both for success and for failure, but especially for the latter. They also rated "luck" considerably higher than did British students in both situations. In other words, these data show that Japanese students perceive the importance of effort in controlling the situation. At the same time, however, they think luck is a factor influencing the course of events. It seems that in the minds of the Japanese, "luck," usually considered an external cause, is not necessarily incompatible with "effort," an internal cause. Being "lucky" is sometimes seen as a personal trait, just like having a high level of ability.

"Do one's best and leave the rest to heaven (luck)," is a popular saying by which many prudent Japanese live. It contains no implication of defeat; far from meaning, "why bother to work hard when luck determines the outcome anyway," it expresses an individual's willingness to accept unforseen consequences once he or she has done the best that could be done.

Given a cultural climate where the viture of modesty is extolled, and self-assertiveness and even self-reliance are viewed unfavorably, it is not surprising the Japanese have developed a psychological structure which restrains them from positive self-evaluation. Such an internal organization makes them more aware of the limitations of human beings and more willing to entrust themselves to something beyond their own power to control. It should be noted, however, that this apparent fatalism is unaccompanied by the usual pattern of abandoning constructive actions. The Japanese rate effort highly; at the same time, they recognize the importance of luck. Nor is effort necessarily incompatible with luck. In sum, the higher externality and the negative self-evaluation found in the Japanese must be seen (and reconsidered) in the context of their view of life.

References

Akō, H. (1981). How can family violence be explained? *Psychology of Adolescense*, 27, 56–62.

Economic Planning Agency. (1978). *The cross-national survey on the time of living*. Tokyo: Printing Bureau, Ministry of Finance. (In Japanese)

Evans, H. M. (1981). Internal-external locus of control and word association: Research with Japanese and American students. *Journal of Cross-Cultural Psychology*, 12, 372–382.

Hayami, T. (1981). Causal attributions about poorly performing peoples, an approach by a case rating scale. *Japanese Journal of Educational Psychology*, 29, 80–83. (In Japanese)

Horner, M. S. (1972). Toward an understanding of achievement-related conflicts in women. *Journal of Social Issues*, 28, 157–176.

Imaizumi, N. (1982). Aggression and violence in recent juvenile delinquency. In K. Fujiwara (Ed.), *Advances in child psychology in Japan*. Tokyo: Kaneko-shobō. (In Japanese)

Inagaki, T. (1967). A cross-cultural study of the feminine role conecpt between Japanese and American college women. *Psychologica, 10,* 144–154.

Inamura, H. (1980). *Family violence—Pathology of Japanese parent-child relationships.* Tokyo: Shinyosha. (In Japanese)

————. (1983). *Adolescent collapse syndrome—A recent national disease.* Tokyo: Shinyosha. (In Japanese)

Ito, Y. (1978). Evaluation of sex-roles as a function of sex and role expectation. *Japanese Journal of Educational Psychology, 26,* 1–11. (In Japanese)

————. (1980). The impact of parental attitudes on the development of sex-role concepts in female adolescents. *Japanese Journal of Educational Psychology, 28,* 67–71. (In Japanese)

————. (1981). The structure of self-role concepts and attitudes in female adolescents. *Japanese Journal of Educational Psychology, 29,* 84–87. (In Japanese)

Ito, Y., & Akitsu, K. (1983). Perception of sex-role expectations in adolescence. *Japanese Journal of Educational Psychology, 31,* 146–151. (In Japanese)

Kashiwagi, K. (1967). The congitive development of sex-roles in female adolescents. *Japanese Journal of Educational Psychology, 15,* 193–202. (In Japanese)

————. (1972). The cognitive development of sex-role in female adolescents. *Japanese Journal of Educational Psychology, 20,* 45–58. (In Japanese)

————. (1974). The cognitive development of sex-role in female adolescents. *Japanese Journal of Educational Psychology, 22,* 205–215. (In Japanese)

————. (1975). Sex-differentiated discipline in childhood and adolescence. In A. Yoda (Ed.), *Recent trends of adolescents in Japan* (pp. 123–126). Tokyo: Kaneko-shobo. (In Japanese)

Kashiwagi, K., Kuno, Y., Monma, K., & Murayama, M. (1976). Sex-role learning process in children: Relations with maternal variables. *Essays and Studies,* Tokyo Women's Christian University, *23,* 73–98. (In Japanese)

Kashiwagi, K., & Azuma, H. (1981). Sex-typing in the cognitive socialization processes in Japan and the U. S. *Japanese Journal of Psychology, 52,* 269–300. (In Japanese)

Kashiwagi, K., & Little, A. Assessment oriented learning and adult work attitude in adolescence: A cross-cultural study on student learning orientations. Unpublished manuscript.

Kato, T. (1977). *Structure of self-consciousness* (adolescence). Tokyo: Tokyo University Press. (In Japanese)

Kajita, E. (1980). *Psychology of self.* Tokyo: Tokyo University Press. (In Japanese)

Kikuchi, A. & Gordon, L. V. (1970). Japanese and American personal values—Some cross-cultural findings. *International Journal of Psychology, 15,* 183–87.

Kimura, B. (1972). *Hito to hito no aida*. [Between a person and a person]. Tokyo: Kōbundō.

―――. (1973). *Ijo no kozo*. [English translation]. Tokyo: Kō-dasha.

Lefcourt, H. M. (1982). *Locus of control: Current trends in theory and research* (2nd ed.). Hillsdale: Lawrence Erlbaum Associates.

Maccoby, E., & Jacklin, C. N. (1974). *Development of sex-differences*. Stanford: Stanford University Press.

Mahler, I. (1974). A comparative study of locus of control. *Psychologia, 17*, 135–139.

Matsuda, K., & Hirose, H. (1982). Ego identity and self concept in the adolescence. *Japanese Journal of Educational Psychology, 30*, 157–161. (In Japanese)

McGinnies, E., Nordholm, L. A., Ward, C. D., & Bhanthumnarin, D. L. (1974). Sex and cultural differences in perceived locus of control among students in five countries. *Journal of Consulting and Clinical Psychology, 42*, 451–455.

―――(1983). *Statistical abstract of education, science and culture*. (In Japanese)

Ministry of Education (1975). *A basic survey on education in Japan*. (In Japanese)

Ministry of Justice. (1983). *A white paper on crime*.

Miyano, A. (1978, 1979). Self concept in delinquent boys. Papers presented at the 20th and 21st annual meetings of the Japanese Educational Psychology (mimeo, 454–455, 520–521). (In Japanese)

Miyazawa, S. (1978). A study of self-acceptance in adolescence. *Bulletin of the Faculty of Education*, University of Nagoya, *25*, 105–117. (In Japanese)

Motoaki, H., Soma, I., Kimura, Y., & Sako, Y. (1978, 1979). Socially-deviant behavior in adolescents. Papers presented at the 20th and 21st annual meetings of the Japanese Educational Psychological Association (mimeo, 428–429, 628–629). (In Japanese)

Mugishima, F. (1979). The process of delinquency and moral development. Paper presented at the Symposium held at the 43rd annual congress of the Japanese Psychological Association, Tokyo. (In Japanese)

Murase, T. (1973). Personality development and mental health revealed in SCT in junior high school boys—A three-year follow-up study. Paper presented at the 37th meeting of the Japanese Psychological Association (mimeo 574–575). (In Japanese)

Murase, T., Shimonaka, J., & Aral, H. (1974). A study on self-concept in female junior school students. Paper presented at 16th annual meeting of the Japanese Educational Psychological Association (mimeo, 236–237). (In Japanese)

Owaga, K., Hayashi, Y., Nagai, T., & Shiraishi, H. (1981). A study of negative self-awareness in interpersonal relationship, characteristics of anthropophobics from a cross-cultural point of view. *Bulletin of the Faculty of Education*, National University of Yokohama, *19*, 205–220. (In Japanese)

Okasaki, K. (1977). A study of fear of success—the relationship between achievement, motivation and sex-role concept. Paper presented at the 41st congress of the Japanese Psychological Association, Tokyo. (In Japanese)

Prime Minister's Office (1979). *Japanese adolescents in the world—a cross-cultural survey on adolescents' opinions and life.* Tokyo: Printing Bureau, Ministry of Finance. (In Japanese)

————. (1980). *Japanese children and their mothers.* Tokyo: Nihonhōsō Shuppan Kyokai. (In Japanese)

Saito, H., Aoyagi, H., & Kaneko, C. (1981). A developmental study on fear of success. *Bulletin of the Faculty of Tachikawa Junior College, 13,* 53–59. (In Japanese)

Sato, Y. (1977). *Report on sex-differentiated training in elementary and secondary schools.* Toyko: Shiraishi-shoten.

Sengoku, T. & Inaga, K. (1979). *Japanese elementary school children.* (In Japanese)

Shikauchi, K. (1978). Effects of self-esteem on attribution of success and failures. *Japanese Journal of Experimental Social Psychology, 18,* 35–46. (In Japanese)

Shimonaka, J., & Murase, T. (1976). Aging and sexual differences as major determinants of self-percepts of the aged. *Japanese Journal of Educational Psychology, 24,* 156–166. (In Japanese)

Sobue, T. (1976). *Bunka to pasonariti.* Tokyo: Kobundo and the Research Committee on the Study of the Japanese National Character of the Institute of Statistical Mathematics, 1982. (In Japanese)

Soeda, M., & Kashiwagi, K. (1981). The influences of child rearing upon the occupational activities in women. In *Essays and studies* (p. 31). Tokyo: Tokyo Women's Christian University. (In Japanese)

Spence, J. T., Helmreich, R., & Stapp, J. (1975). Ratings of self and personal sex-role attributes and their relation to self-esteem and conceptions of masculinity and femininity. *Journal of Personality and Social Psychology, 32,* 29–39.

Takahashi, M. (1975). Self-image of sex-role concept in early adolescence. Paper presented at 45th annual meeting of the Japanese Psychological Association, Tokyo. (In Japanese)

Takcuchi, N. (1981). A study on ego-identity and sex-identity in female college students. Paper presented at the 45th annual meeting of the Japanese Psychological Association, Tokyo. (In Japanese)

The Research Committee on the Study of the Japanese National Character of the Institute of Statistical Mathematics (1982). *Nihonjin no Koku minsei, No. 4.* Tokyo: Idemitsu shoten. (In Japanese)

Yamamoto, M., Matsui, Y., & Yamanari, Y. (1982). The structure of perceived aspects of self. *Japanese Journal of Educational Psychology, 30,* 64–68. (In Japanese)

Children's Social Development in Japan: Research Directions

Catherine Lewis

Why study child development in Japan? Brislin (1983) has recently listed general benefits of cross-cultural research, including: testing the universality of a construct, increasing the range of a variable under study, obtaining new variables, and unconfounding variables. I will discuss here aspects of Japanese child development which fit these criteria, and then explore one more reason for cross-cultural research: theory building. My examples focus on social development. Many are drawn from my own observational study of Japanese nursery schools, conducted in 1979. This study focused on classes of 5-year-olds, using timed spot observation, running accounts of behavior, unstructured observations, and teacher interviews (Lewis, 1984).

Increasing the Range of Variables under Study

Example: The Early Mother-Infant Relationship. If qualitative and some quantitative evidence on Japanese child rearing accurately reflect current practices, the exclusiveness of the Japanese mother-infant relationship and, perhaps, the responsiveness of mother to infant may frequently be in a range greater than in the United States (Benedict, 1946; Caudill, 1972; Caudill and Schooler, 1973; Doi, 1973; Shand, 1978; Vogel, 1963). There is evidence, for example, that Japanese mothers rarely use nonfamily baby-sitters or leave children during the early years of life (Takahashi, 1982). None of the twenty-four urban mothers studied by Takahashi had left their 2-year-olds with nonfamily baby-sitters during the previous month; only two of the mothers had used a relative (the father or grandmother) as a "baby-sitter" for the child during this time period. Only four of the twenty-four mothers had a friend who would take care of the child in the event of an unavoidable absence. Caudill and Schooler (1973), in an observational study of 3-month-olds, concluded that Japanese mothers spent more time with their infants than did American mothers. Researchers wishing to examine the impact of the early mother-infant relationship on subsequent attachment patterns, on effects of out-of-home care, or on stranger anxiety might profit from cross-national research. Such studies would expand the range of mother-child relationships studied on the variable of degree or exclusiveness of contact with the mother. For example, researchers interested in the relationship between separation history and adjustment to out-of-home care might use a Japanese sample to obtain mother-child pairs with few or no separations. An optimal design would be to study a range of mother-child relationships within each country. Replication across countries of conclusions pertaining to the shared range of a variable would strengthen the conclusion that differences are effects of the mother-child relationship, and not due to cultural factors or to the research methodology.

Obtaining New Variables

Example 1: Teaching Strategies. What teaching strategies facilitate learning and subsequent motivation to engage in tasks? That Japanese adults may use indirect teaching styles, not immediately focused on the child's correct performance, is suggested by the work of Hess and Azuma (this volume), Azuma (Note 1), Taniuchi (Note 2), Easley and Easley (Note 3), and Lewis (1984). These sources all suggest that teachers of young Japanese children may focus on eliciting and building their interest, and only secondarily on eliciting correct performance. For example, in a communication game, Japanese mothers devoted more time to indirect teaching, presumably designed to stimulate children's emotional involvement in the task, while American mothers adopted a directive teaching style, designed to help children briskly identify correct responses (Hess and Azuma, this volume). Taniuchi's (1985) study of preschool "talent education" suggests that some Japanese mothers may develop elaborate strategies to engage children emotionally in tasks. From observations of fifth-grade Japanese and American science lessons, Walberg and Azuma (this volume) find preliminary evidence that Japanese teachers may use an indirect approach designed to elicit and discuss the untutored beliefs initially held by students. In contrast, American teachers may use a directive approach, consisting of laboratory demonstration and elicitation of certain predetermined explanations.

Further evidence is needed to document the situations, if any, in which Japanese mothers and teachers adopt indirect teaching styles. This work should focus not on immediate performance, but on emotional climate-setting or on eliciting and discussing the child's beliefs about a problem. Two pieces of American evidence suggest that such indirect teaching strategies could facilitate learning. First, there is evidence that introducing a time for performance of a drawing task reduces the creativity of children's drawings (Amabile, DeJong & Lepper, 1976). It is possible to speculate that focusing children's attention on correct performance could have an effect similar to focusing it on a deadline, perhaps by drawing attention away from creative or other process components of the task. Second, Linn and Swiney's (1981) studies of scientific reasoning suggest that eliciting and discussing children's own incorrect intuitive theories about scientific phenomena effectively promotes their adoption of scientifically accepted assumptions. Surprisingly, actual visual demonstration of the scientific phenomenon in question was often *ineffective* in changing children's incorrect reasoning about scientific phenomena. Linn suggests that children's own intuitive scientific theories interfered with the ability to benefit from visual demonstration. Thus, eliciting and discussing children's own concepts may be a more effective means for achieving conceptual change than demonstrating correct results. In Linn's research, peers elicited and discussed each other's scientific reasoning during a classroom science lesson. We would benefit from knowing more about the nature, scope, and consequences of this pedagogical technique in both Japanese and American classrooms.

Example 2: Motivation. Taniuchi's ethnography of talent education in Japan describes techniques Japanese mothers and teachers may use to interest children, even infants and toddlers, in learning to play the violin. These techniques include forbidding the child to play the violin for the initial months of the "mother's" lessons, treating the violin as a special object to be touched and played only as a treat, and terminating each lesson *before* the child wishes to stop (in the case of toddlers, after 1 or 2 minutes). Several American colleagues with whom I have discussed these teaching techniques objected that adults should not labor to teach violin to a toddler "unless the child really wants to learn"—implying, in other words, that the initiative for learning should come from the child, not the parent. This suggests an interesting avenue of inquiry: how do adults conceptualize motivation, and to what extent do they believe the child's motivation to engage in a task can be increased by manipulation of the environment? Is lack of motivation viewed primarily as intrinsic to the child or as a result of poor task structure? If low motivation is viewed as intrinsic to the child, it would be interesting to know whether it is seen as relatively enduring—for example, as an inherited physiological predisposition—or as mutable. It would also be valuable to know whether the adult's view of motivation makes any difference in the teaching techniques which he or she chooses, or in the way a task is structured and presented. For example, an adult viewing motivation as largely intrinsic to the child may expend less effort attempting to engage the child or in structuring a task that would accomplish this. One interesting approach to the area of motivation would be a two-step inquiry, consisting of an ethnopsychology of motivation in both Japan and America, and an investigation of adults' behavior in structuring tasks, eliciting, and maintaining a child's interest, and in handling breakdowns in interest.

Example 3: Peer Discipline. The group's role for adults in Japanese society has received great attention (Nakane, 1972), but less is known about the role of peer groups in socializing Japanese children. My own ethnography of fifteen Japanese nursery schools (Lewis, 1984) suggests that teachers may cultivate stable, self-managing small groups, delegating to them responsibility for many aspects of classroom management, including conflict resolution, rule making, and rule enforcement. Frequently, I found that children were responsible for calling the class together, overseeing class projects, and even managing disagreements. For example, in one class thirty-eight 5-year-olds initiated preparations to go home on the basis of one quiet remark made by the teacher to a few children playing near her. Often teachers themselves did not attempt to find or involve children who did not appear for lunch, dismissal, or other class activities. Examples from observations and interviews suggest that teachers often encouraged children to manage their own and other children's problems without teacher intervention. For example, when a child reported rock throwing to a teacher, the teacher did not step in, but suggested that the child intervene. In one of the few aggressive episodes recorded in the field notes, two boys had a fight which progressed from sand throwing to hair pulling and hitting. The teacher did not directly attempt to stop them; in fact, she cheered on the smaller boy, saying, "Give it your best," and "Look, Taro's gotten strong; now he can fight without crying." She then encouraged bystanding children to become involved in settling the fight, telling them it was "everyone's problem."

Unfortunately, systematic comparative data on peer discipline are nonexistent. A worthwhile next step might be to sample educational settings in both the United States and Japan, to ascertain whether Japanese schools would indeed expand the range of the variable of peer management or reveal different divisions of peer and adult authority. A comparison of peer and adult authority raises a number of interesting theoretical issues. Although evidence exists on peer management of classroom behavior by older students, little is known about consequences of peer management in nursery schools (Bronfenbrenner, 1973). Research on children's moral judgments suggests that peer justice may be unduly harsh (Johnson, 1962), but little is known about how these moral judgments translate into actual behavior. We know little about peer-adult differences in the nature, timing, and consistency of sanctions. Nor do we know how children perceive the legitimacy of sanctions applied by the two groups, or how rule enforcement by teachers versus peers influences affective relationships with these two groups. Finally, we need to investigate the effect on the child's developing self-concept of behavioral demands and criticisms by adults versus peers.

Thus we know little about the effects of peer versus adult enforcement of rules on children's internalization of rules and their attitudes toward authority. Several speculative hypotheses might be considered. First, delegating authority to children may enable teachers to make few behavioral demands on them. In the Japanese schools I observed, peers assumed much of the authority for checking that other children completed their chores, finished their lunches, behaved responsibly toward each other, and so forth. This delegation of authority may have enabled the teacher to remain a benevolent figure to whom children had a strong, unconflicted positive attachment. A second speculation is that delegation of authority may allow children to experience negative sanctions as intrinsic consequences of their acts. When the group monitor fails to redirect his attention (to take an actual example from observations), the child may experience this very differently from a teacher's reprimand. Other children's sanctions may appear less contrived and external and more like the direct, natural consequences of the child's own acts, thus fostering greater behavioral change. Finally, it may be that peer criticism, in comparison with adult criticism, poses less of a threat to the child's identity as a good child. Research on moral judgment suggests that, in the mind of a 5-year-old, morality and adult authority are inextricably linked (Kohlberg, 1976). Thus, criticism by adults may, to a much greater degree than peer criticism, cause the child to feel like a bad child. The "good child" identity may, in turn, be a critical determinant of subsequent willingness to obey rules (Lepper, 1981). The fragile "good child" identity may fare better in an environment in which peers, not adults, bear messages that the child has misbehaved.

Unconfounding Variables

Teacher-student ratio may be a variable profitably unconfounded, or at least differently confounded, in Japan. Teacher-student ratio is typically as high as 1:40 for nursery school students and 1:50 for students in elementary and secondary schools (Cummings, 1980; Lewis, 1984). Superficial examination of Japanese educational outcomes, such as test scores, does not suggest that this high ratio is necessarily detrimental. While Japanese data may unconfound teacher-student ratio from certain variables confounded in the United States (such as school district income or degree of innovativeness), it may differently confound ratio with variables such as the presence of teaching techniques designed for large groups. Nevertheless, Japan may provide an important arena for testing and qualifying findings on student-teacher ratio.

Hypothesis Building: The Importance of Cross-Cultural Data. Recently, cognitive psychologists have made progress in understanding how individuals test hypotheses and have identified influences of intuitive heuristics, as well as subject matter knowledge, on hypothesis testing skills (Kahneman & Tversky, 1972; Linn & Swiney, 1981). Less well understood are the processes by which individuals *generate* hypotheses. Although the examples I have cited focus on the usefulness of cross-cultural research in *testing* hypotheses, its value in their generation should not be overlooked. Brislin (1983) cites evidence that cross-cultural experiences may promote understanding of the influence of social context, perhaps by making it easier for researchers to "remove" themselves from the cultures they are studying and to identify the multiple causes of others' behavior. This benefit of cross-cultural experiences has, I believe, had too little impact on psychological theory and research. Despite the prominent editorial note in *Developmental Psychology* that cross-cultural studies are "especially welcome," perusal of recent tables of contents suggests that only five articles during 1982, and one article during 1983, presented data from outside the United States. Almost all of these articles dealt with cognitive or language development.

Recent years have seen increasingly sophisticated cross-cultural research methods, such as instruments which are not simple, accurate translations, but which have comparable predictive value in more than one country (Stevenson et al., this volume). Nevertheless, cross-cultural tests of hypotheses remain fraught with difficulty. It is not possible to ensure cross-cultural identity of linguistic categories or of the research process—the effects of being observed, interviewed, or recorded. Research within a single foreign culture suffers from some of the same difficulties of linguistic and/or cultural interpretation. Such methodological untidiness may frighten off many potential cross-cultural research efforts.

Should cross-cultural or foreign research be limited to those problems for which methodological happenstance permits neat, definitive tests of hypotheses? I think not. An equally important role of cross-cultural or foreign research may be to stimulate questions and hypotheses and to challenge existing theories. Exposure to other cultures can provide a wealth of the sort of counterintuitive experiences on which theoretical advances are built. Limiting cross-cultural research to laboratory-neat tests of hypotheses could mean forfeiting data which may challenge thinking and promote within-culture progress.

The following examples describe areas of research in which Japanese data may provide an important stimulus to theory building in the United States. Some of these areas may not be amenable to neat cross-cultural investigation. The challenge, then, will be to develop methods of systematic, replicable within-culture description and ethnopsychological investigation which allow psychological theory to benefit from data collected in other cultures. Within-culture descriptive studies appear to be more common in the study of language and of cognitive development (for example, Hakuta, 1982; Saxe, 1982) than for social development. Ethnopsychological investigation which documents psychological theories of other cultures may challenge and enrich theories developed in our own culture. Kojima's history of Japanese child bearing ideology (this volume) suggest how fertile a field this can be. Data usually relegated to anecdotal status could be treated systematically, for example, by studying in this manner how individuals interpret children's behavior and adults' socialization strategies. It could also be illuminating to study how individuals in two cultures interpret their own behavior and that of members of the other cultures. For example, we might identify a parallel, on the cultural level, of the situation-person attributional bias: when looking at foreign cultures, we may attribute to personality behavior which, in our culture, we would attribute to situation.

Example 1: Locus of Control.   Kashiwagi (this volume) uses Japanese data to question the adequacy of American theory regarding locus of control. She suggests that American research often views internal locus of control as a variable state fostering high achievement. Studies of Japanese children generally find neither an increase in internality with age nor an association between internality and high academic achievement. Several cross-national studies find that the Japanese, in comparison to other nationalities, tend to attribute more importance to luck; these data may indicate that the Japanese concept of "luck" is not entirely external. Alternatively, attribution of luck may be seen as a way of maintaining high achievement in the face of success. Other evidence suggests that Japanese, in rating themselves, may tend to choose a more stringent standard of comparison than Americans (Kashiwagi, this volume). The factors governing choice of a standard of comparison, and the implications of this choice for motivation, are certainly key areas for research. Studies of Japan suggest the importance of group cooperation and group, not individual, achievement (for example, Nakane, 1972). Cooperative tasks, by nature, are not solely under one's own control. The importance of cooperative achievement in Japan points up the incompleteness of current theory relating internal control to achievement.

Example 2: Cooperation. The ability of Japanese adult groups to work together cooperatively has elicited the interest of many social scientists (for example, Nakane; Cole, 1979). While large cross-cultural differences in cooperation have been documented for numerous cultures and subcultures around the globe (for example, Kagan & Madsen, 1971; Madsen & Shapira, 1970), only a few studies have attempted to investigate *why* these differences in cooperation emerge (for example, Madsen & Lancy, 1981). We would profit from a thorough description of the settings and practices which may promote development of cooperation. Observations of Japanese nursery schools (Lewis, 1984) reveal practices which may influence the development of cooperation, such as provision of cooperative play materials, distribution of resources to necessitate cooperation, and creation of small, self-managing children's groups. For example, teachers deliberately provided fewer paintbrushes than there were children and withdrew toys as children grew older, to increase opportunities for contact among children. Teachers also designed tasks, such as joint playwriting, which required children within small fixed-membership groups to elicit and accommodate to each others' intentions. Further description of settings, which may influence cooperation, followed by theory building, and then perhaps by within-culture investigation of hypotheses, could promote our understanding in this area.

Example 3: Adult Control Strategies. American psychologists widely accept the view that firm control by parents (that is, consistent enforcement of clear rules) promotes internalization of values by children (for example, Baumrind, 1973). Observations of Japanese child rearing led me to question this view of firm control. Japanese mothers apparently do not make explicit demands on their children and do not enforce rules when children resist; yet diverse accounts suggest that Japanese children strongly internalize parental, group, and institutional values (Nakane; Vogel, 1963; Vogel, 1979). Challenged by the Japanese data on low parental control and high internalization, I reviewed the American data on firm control and reinterpreted them as revealing not the effects of parental firm control, but the effects of cooperation by the children (Lewis, 1981). This reinterpretation has stirred some theoretical interest (for example, Baumrind, 1983; Maccoby, 1980). What is important for our purposes is that the reinterpretation sprang from challenging data provided by Japan, even though the work is purely theoretical and nowhere mentions Japan.

Among the observations stimulating my interest in firm control were incidents in which teachers repeatedly declined to reprimand students or to enforce requests for behavior change. Teachers seemed to view the gaining of the child's understanding, and not his or her compliance, as the goal of intervention. Firm control may thus assume little importance. An incident from my field notes presents a good example: boys had been dropping clay "bombs" on the fish in an aquarium. The teacher explained that the clay could hurt the fish but did not specifically tell the boys to stop (nor did they). In her announcements to the whole class at the end of the school day, the teacher explained that some boys in the class thought they were "helping" the fish by throwing in clay "food," but that the boys were really harming the fish. When I subsequently interviewed the teacher about the incident, our exchange was as follows:

Interviewer: Did you really think the children were trying to help the fish by throwing the clay pellets?

Teacher: Yes.

Interviewer: Don't you think the boys understood they might hurt the fish by throwing the clay pellets?

Teacher: If they understood it was wrong, they wouldn't do it.

Kojima's study of Japanese child-rearing ideology (this volume), and Conroy et al.'s (1980) study of maternal control strategies also suggest that, as a goal in early socialization encounters, understanding may take priority over compliance. These data point up the need for research describing control strategies used by Japanese adults, perhaps thereby expanding the range of adult control techniques studied. An important facet of this research should be the exploration of variables, such as child's age, which may alter the relationship between adult control strategies and children's internalization.

Conclusion

The articles in this volume illustrate the importance Japanese data have already assumed in answering a wide range of research questions. How, then, should research on Japanese child development proceed? Given the expense, and potential for misinterpretation, inherent in cross-cultural research, the research process deserves careful attention.

Selecting Research Issues: A Systematic Approach.   Pooling the knowledge of many researchers may assume particular importance in the case of cross-cultural research. American researchers studying Japan are fortunate to have a community of Japanese colleagues who can help to identify and to prevent culturally inappropriate choices of research problems, methodology, or interpretation. Periodic meetings of groups of researchers to assess promising research issues in Japanese child development would also seem to be critically important. False starts are expensive, and the best way to avoid them may be to ensure that the research agenda is forged by a variety of individuals, Japanese and Americans, regional-area specialists, and specialists in theoretical areas.

It may prove more difficult to devise an equally binational format in which both Japanese and American researchers feel truly free to criticize proposed research and to suggest new research directions. Often, binational conferences are conducted solely in English. The cost of interpreters can be prohibitive. Nevertheless, exclusive use of English is bound to place nonnative speakers, however proficient their English, at a relative disadvantage. This is particularly true for discussions and other extemporaneous sessions. Some forethought about this problem may yield adequate solutions less expensive than a completely bilingual format. To lessen an English-centric bias, breaks could be provided during which Japanese participants can engage in Japanese-language discussion of controversial issues or of issues demanding some consensus. Alternatively, emphasis might be placed on previously formulated, rather than on spontaneous, critiques and comments. In addition, the periodic use of the Japanese language might remind non-Japanese speakers of the difficulty of communicating in a foreign language.

Research in Japan: Some Practical Considerations

Language. Beyond the obvious difficulties of learning any written and spoken foreign language, Japanese poses problems to the foreign researcher. Written Japanese is complex. Knowledge of 1850 ideographic characters and two alphabets composed of fifty-seven characters each is the minimum required for literacy. Well-educated individuals typically read two to three times the required number of ideographs.

The ideographic writing system can impose severe limitations on the functioning of foreign researchers. Telephone books, public transportation, and maps typically require reading knowledge of Japanese. Because of the complexity of the writing system, the typewriter has never come into widespread use in Japan, and business communication uses handwriting and typeset print (Pollack, 1984). Japanese-language word processing software is a rapidly developing new field. However, the fastest Japanese word processing systems still are less efficient than their American equivalents. Consequently, they have not achieved widespread use (Pollack, 1984) and can be very labor-intensive.

Relationships with Colleagues. The logistical difficulties posed by language differences often make the foreign researcher unavoidably dependent on Japanese colleagues. Volumes have been written on the nature of dependent relationships in Japan and on the nature of social relationships centered on debt, gratitude, and repayment (Benedict; Doi; Nakane). I will not attempt to summarize these works nor make claims for their general applicability. I will only attest that, in my own experience, issues of dependency, debt, and gratitude have at times made research in Japan bewildering and emotionally demanding. Paradoxically, my own most troubling experiences have stemmed from Japanese colleagues who have been *too* generous in providing me with time, resources, introductions, and so forth. My sense of indebtedness has sometimes inhibited my ability to make requests, to give veridical feedback that a task has been done improperly, and to express disagreement because of fear of conveying a lack of gratitude toward unstintingly generous hosts. My consequent self-censorship has sometimes limited the amount or quality of information I have collected.

Although I typically communicate in Japanese with Japanese colleagues, an issue more problematic than language itself may be certain metacommunication skills. For example, there may be indirect ways of making requests or giving negative feedback which are appropriate and comfortable in the context of a relationship of indebtedness. I know that some American colleagues who have done research in Japan have encountered similar self-imposed limitations. I do not know to what extent such problems are peculiar to Japan, and to what extent they inhere in research done outside one's own country. The frequency with which I hear Japanese describe Japan as a place where "interpersonal relations are complex" (*uningen kankei ga muzukashii*) and where it is necessary to "devote energy" to interpersonal matters (*ki o tsukau*) makes me suspect that even Japanese often find their interpersonal relations demanding.

Although I have been most concerned with the effects of relationships of indebtedness on my *own* behavior, I catch occasional glimpses of the impact of these relationships on my Japanese colleagues. Most of my relationships with them have been initiated through introductions from other Japanese or Americans. Often, the nature of the relationship between the introducer and introduced is unknown to me. I cannot be sure how much of the generosity extended has to do with intrinsic interest in me and my work and how much it has to do with details of the relationship between the other two individuals, about which I may know nothing. On one occasion, I discovered that a Japanese colleague's reluctance to provide clear feedback on my work was related to hiw own relationship with the person who had requested him to help me.

Difficulty obtaining frank, critical feedback from Japanese colleagues can be a major obstacle to research. A prominent Japanese intellectual suggests that the Japanese "esthetic sense" makes open confrontation "disagreeable to our sense of beauty" (Kunihiro, 1976). He suggests that in Japanese society there are "pressures at work against verbal commitment." American researchers must rely on their Japanese colleagues to point out any inadequacies in the cultural appropriateness of research concepts and methodology. Yet it may be very difficult to obtain such feedback once relationships are established. Mechanisms to increase critical feedback need to be considered and present an excellent topic of discussion for a bicultural conference. Speculatively, I would imagine that increased opportunities for feedback from socially unrelated individuals, increased anonymity of the feedback process, and increased status of the individual providing feedback (or decreased status of the person receiving it) might increase the likelihood of critical feedback. My impression is that researchers of great seniority or renown have an especially difficult time receiving candid feedback.

The Culture of Children

On Asking Questions.   For many social scientists, asking questions is the major means of obtaining data. But Japanese children may interpret question asking as a sign that they have misbehaved. I found that discipline by nursery school teachers frequently took the form of a series of questions which assumed that the child would not knowingly commit wrong. For example, a boy who hid the shoes of a boy washing his feet was questioned as follows: "Did Kenji ask you to move his shoes?" "What happens when you finish washing your feet and your shoes aren't there?" "Do you know it would be nicer to help Kenji?" Teachers' use of naive questions as a form of discipline may shape children's responses to interviewing. On occasions when I interacted informally with children, they apparently interpreted my (genuinely naive) questions about game rules as a signal that they were behaving improperly. I had the impression that direct question asking could be a stressful and inhibiting form of data collection, at least for children too young to correctly infer the motives of a researcher.

Uniforms and Uniformity.   Before undertaking observations of Japanese nursery schools, I read the few existing observational accounts. From these descriptions of daily ceremonies, school uniforms (including identical hats and handkerchiefs), and formal bows to the teacher, I gained the impression that children's behavior in nursery schools was somewhat regimented. The noise and chaos level of Japanese nursery schools was perhaps the single most astonishing aspect of my observations. Very high levels of spontaneous background noise (shouting, laughing, and so forth) partially obscured almost half the dictations of teacher activities that were made by an observer speaking directly into a hand-held tape recorder. It was dramatically demonstrated that identical uniforms and formal daily ceremonies imply nothing about the level of spontaneous play or the degree of discipline.

At the 1983 Conference on Child Development in Japan, sponsored by the Social Science Research Council, a similar discrepancy in views of Japanese education emerged. Although some conference members described Japanese education as emphasizing rote memorization of much information, with little room for individual deviation from the assigned task, others viewed Japanese education as child centered, emphasizing processes which allow the child to take the initiative in learning. As one conference member described the two views: "It's as if we're talking about two different countries." Interestingly, Japanese as well as Americans held both points of view. I suspect that some of the discrepancy had to do with the age of the children being considered, since older children probably receive more performance-oriented education (White and Pollack, Note 2). I suspect also that the discrepancy stems from unrealistic expectations of homogeneity. Performance-oriented drills may coexist with process-oriented teaching. This may be particularly true for the many Japanese children who are exposed to two educational systems; formal schools and afterschool "cram" schools for exam preparations.

Afterschool Schools.   I could locate little information on the exam-preparatory schools, although it is widely suggested that, even during the elementary school years, a substantial number of children attend such schools (White, 1984). Their very existence poses a problem for researchers, since it is difficult to assess the extent to which they, as opposed to the formal educational system, influence outcomes, such as test scores. The difficulty of studying the afterschool system is compounded by its lack of official status and its frequent perception as an embarrassment to Japan.

Improving Within-Culture Descriptive Research

I have suggested that an important function of research in other cultures may be to generate hypotheses and to stimulate reconsideration of current theories. Even when cross-cultural tests of hypotheses are methodologically difficult, within-culture descriptive and ethnopsychological research may provide the important benefit that Brislin terms "provoking insight into social contexts." For example, Japanese descriptive or ethnopsychological data may stimulate hypotheses regarding knowledge acquisition (Hatano and Inasaki, this volume), socialization techniques (Kojima, this volume), or locus of control (Kashiwagi, this volume). Cross-cultural research's hypothesis-generating function is often ignored, and hypothesis testing considered its legitimate purpose. Science may benefit as much from stimulation of hypotheses as from sites to test them. Refining methods of systematic, replicable descriptive research, and providing for a presentation of such research, could enliven theoretical developments in the United States.

Building Policy Support for
Cross-Cultural Research

Cross-cultural research is expensive and time-consuming. The research of Hess and Azuma (this volume) provides an egalitarian and economically promising model of projects independently funded and carried out in two countries. Studies of Japanese child development have been conspicuously absent from the recent proliferation of historical, economic, and political works on Japan. In part, this may be due to the expense of child development research—structured observations, measure development, computer analyses—compared to research in other disciplines. Foundations promoting regional area studies frequently offer grants which are grossly inadequate for behavioral science research. (On the other hand, agencies offering grants adequate to carry out cross-cultural behavioral science research often only fund research which proposes clean, definitive tests of hypotheses-generating research may not be considered scientifically acceptable.)

Cross-cultural research requires time as well as money. The time required for training in language and cultural background, for translating and back-translating instruments, may be prohibitive to the predoctoral or untenured researcher. Rarely is there much financial or peer support for the language and the cultural training which constitute the "infrastructure" of cross-cultural research.

Thus, the barriers to cross-cultural child development studies with Japan come in many shapes and sizes: they are methodological, linguistic, logistical, and economic. Yet the theoretical interest of the Japanese experience justifies a search for solutions. As the chapters in this volume suggest, Japanese data and theories can provide a fresh perspective and invigorate American thinking.

Footnotes

1. Azuma, H. Paper presented at the meetings of the Western Psychological Association, May, 1983.
2. Taniuchi, L. Qualifying paper presented to the School of Education, Harvard University, 1982.
3. Easley, J., and Easley, E. *Kitaemono school as an environment in which children study mathematics themselves.* Paper of the Bureau of Educations Research, University of Illinois, 1981.

References

Amabile, T., De Jong, W., and Lepper, M. (1976). Effects of externally-imposed deadline on subsequent intrinsic motivation. *Journal of Personality and Social Psychology, 34,* 92–98.

Baumrind, D. (1973). The development of instrumental competence through socialization. In A. D. Pick (Ed.), *Minnesota Symposia on Child Psychology, Vol. 7,* (pp. 3–46). Minneapolis: University of Minnesota Press.

———. (1983). Rejoinder to Lewis' reinterpretation of parental firm control effects: Are authoritative families really harmonious? *Psychological Bulletin, 94,* 132–142.

Benedict, R. (1946). *The chrysanthemum and the sword: Patterns of Japanese culture.* New York: Meridian.

Brislin, R. W. (1983). Cross-cultural research in psychology. *Annual Review of Psychology, 34,* 363–400.

Bronfenbrenner, U. (1973). *Two worlds of childhood: U.S. and U.S.S.R.* New York: Pocket Books.

Caudill, W., and Schooler, C. (1973). Child behavior and child rearing in Japan and the United States: An interim report. *Journal of Nervous and Mental Disease, 157,* 323–338.

Cole, R. (1979). *Work, mobility, and participation: A comparative study of American and Japanese industry.* Berkeley: University of California Press.

Conroy, M., Hess, R. D., Azuma, H., and Kashiwagi, K. (1980). Maternal strategies for regulating children's behavior: Japanese and American families. *Journal of Cross-Cultural Psychology, 11,* 153–172.

Cummings, W. (1980). *Education and equality in Japan.* Princeton, N.J.: Princeton University Press.

Doi, T. (1973) *The anatomy of dependence.* Tokyo: Kondansha International.

Hakuta, K. (1982). Interaction between particles and work order in the comprehension and production of simple sentences in Japanese children. *Developmental Psychology, 18,* 62–76.

Johnson, R. (1962). A study of children's moral judgments. *Child Development, 23,* 327–354.

Kagan, S., and Madsen, M. (1971). Cooperation and competition of Mexican-American and Anglo-American children of two ages under four instructional sets. *Developmental Psychology, 5,* 32–39.

Kahneman, D., and Tversky, A. (1972). Subjective probability: A judgment of representativeness. *Cognitive Psychology, 3,* 430–454.

Kohlberg, L. (1976). Morals and moralization: A cognitive developmental approach. In T. Lickona (Ed.), *Moral development and behavior* (pp. 31–53). New York: Holt, Rinehart and Winston.

Kunihiro, M. (1976). The Japanese language and intercultural communication. In (Japan Center for International Exchange, ed.), *The silent power: Japan's identity and world role;* essays selected from *The Japan Interpreter.* Tokyo: Simul Press. (In Japanese)

Lepper, M. (1981). Social control processes, attributions of motivation, and the internalization of social values. In E. T. Higgins, D. N. Ruble, and W. W. Hartup (Eds.), *Social cognition and social behavior: Developmental perspectives* (pp. 294–330). San Francisco: Jossey-Bass.

Lewis, C. (1981). The effects of firm control: A reinterpretation of findings. *Psychological Bulletin, 90,* 547–563.

———. (1984). Cooperation and control in Japanese nursery schools. *Comparative Education Review, 28,* 69–84.

Linn, M. D., and Swiney, J. (1981). Individual differences in formal thought: Role of expectations and aptitude. *Journal of Educational Psychology, 73,* 274–286.

Maccoby, E. (1980). *Social development: Psychological growth and the parent-child relationship.* New York: Harcourt Brace Jovanovitch.

Madsen, M., and Lancy, D. (1981). Cooperative and competitive behavior: Experiments related to ethnic identity and urbanization in Papua New Guinea. *Journal of Cross-Cultural Psychology, 12,* 389–408.

Madsen, M. and Shapira, A. (1970). Cooperative and competitive behavior of urban Afro-American, Anglo-American, Mexican-American and Mexican village children. *Developmental Psychology, 3,* 16–20.

Nakane, C. (1972). *Japanese society.* Berkeley: University of California Press.

Pollack, A. (1984). The keyboard stymies Japan. *New York Times,* June 6, 36–37.

Saxe, G. (1982). Developing forms of arithmetical thought among the Oksapmin of Papua New Guinea. *Developmental Psychology, 18,* 583–594.

Shand, N. (1978). Cultural factors in maternal behavior: Their influence on infant behavioral development in Japan and the U.S. In *Progress Reports I and II.* Topeka: Menninger Foundation.

Takahashi, K. (1982). Attachment behaviors to a female stranger among Japanese two-year-olds. *Journal of Genetic Psychology, 140,* 299–307.

Taninchi, L. (1985). Cultural continuity in an educational institution: A case study of the Suzuki Method of music instruction. In M. I. White, and S. Pollack (Eds.), *The cultural transition* (In press). London: Routledge and Kegan Paul.

Vogel, E. (1963). *Japan's new middle class.* Berkeley: University of California Press.

———. (1979). *Japan as number one: Lessons for America.* Cambridge, Mass.; Harvard University Press.

White, M. (1984). Japanese education: How do they do it? *The Public Interest, 76,* 87–101.

Achievement in Mathematics

Harold W. Stevenson
James W. Stigler
Shin-ying Lee

IN COLLABORATION WITH
**Seiro Kitamura
Susumu Kimura
Tadahisa Kato**

Students in Japan are consistently among the top performers in international studies of achievement in both mathematics and science (for example, Comber & Keeves, 1973; Glaser, 1976; Husen, 1967). Scores received by American children typically lag behind, and rarely is their average score among those of the top countries. In a recent study of high school students (Walberg, et al. 1984), for example, the average scores for Japanese students at each of three age levels (15, 16, and 17 and older) exceeded those of American students by more than 2 standard deviations. Because of the critical importance of mathematics as a core subject in all sciences, we need information about when such differences in performance begin and what factors are involved in producing high levels of achievement.

Cross-national studies usually have involved students in junior and senior high school. If differences in children's understanding and use of mathematics are found only after they attend school for a number of years, it would be obvious that school experience is a primary basis for cross-national differences in performance. If, however, differences appear early in children's schooling, experiences and training at home must also be considered as important variables.

We sought to provide such information about possible differences in performance during the early years of elementary school. First and fifth graders in Japan and the United States were tested in mathematics, reading, and cognitive abilities; additional information was obtained from their mothers, teachers, and the children themselves. Observations were made in the children's classrooms. Because such a large amount of data was obtained, only a portion can be discussed here.[1]

Constructing the Mathematics Test

Without an appropriate test it would be impossible to make meaningful cross-national comparisons of children's achievement in mathematics. What makes a test appropriate? It must tap concepts and skills to which the children have been exposed; the questions must be phrased clearly and be comparable in the different languages used; and the test itself must be reliable. There are other desirable characteristics, but these are some of the most important.

No mathematics tests now available taken into account the content of mathematics curricula in elementary schools of both Japan and the United States. Many Japanese and American achievement tests have been published, but translating them would hardly insure that the concepts and skills taught in one country would be represented in the tests from the other. Therefore, we found it necessary to construct our own test.

Our first step was to acquire an understanding of the content of the mathematics curricula in each country. We did this by analyzing textbooks used in grades one through six in each country. The Japanese Ministry of Education defines the national curriculum in great detail. Several textbook series exist, all based on it. We chose for analysis the most recent edition of *New mathematics* (*Atarashii sansu*), one of the most popular series. In the United States, where there is no national curriculum, a great deal of diversity is found in the mathematics textbooks used in elementary schools. We chose *Mathematics around us,* a series used in the majority of the schools in the Minneapolis metropolitan area, where we conducted our study.

A list was compiled, containing each concept and skill introduced and the grade level and semester in which it first appeared. The task was greatly simplified because Arabic numerals and an international system of mathematical notation are used in both countries. Entries were made in the list when the reviewers, fluent in both Japanese and English, agreed about what was being taught. In cases of disagreement, which were infrequent, the topics were discussed until a consensus was reached. (It should be noted that the study actually involved three cultures; Chinese children from Taiwan also were included. Data from the Taiwanese sample are not discussed in this report.)

A total of 320 concepts and skills were included in a master list. Of these, 78 percent appear in the United States series and 91 percent in the Japanese series. Or, looked at in another way, 71 percent appear in the series of both Japan and the United States; 20 percent appear in Japan, but not in the United States, and only 7 percent appear in the United States, but not in Japan. The Japanese list departs sharply in quality as well as in quantity from the American list. Many items on the Japanese list involve complex, advanced mathematical concepts. For example, "correspondence" in geometrical figures and statistical concepts such as population distributions, sampling, and probability—found in the Japanese texts—do not usually appear in American texts until high school or college.

Another way of organizing this information is to determine in which country a concept was first introduced. Among the 204 concepts common to the three countries, a concept appeared first in the Japanese textbooks 43 percent of the time; only 13 percent of the time did it appear first in the American textbooks. The two series of textbooks obviously differ greatly both in content and in rate of introducing mathematical concepts.

Because of differences in the mathematics curricula, we found it impossible to construct a useful test using only concepts that appeared simultaneously in all curricula. We sought, therefore, to sample broadly from what we believed to be the most important elements. The final test consisted of seventy questions. Of the concepts assessed in these questions, all but one appeared in the Japanese curriculum; all but four appeared in the American curriculum.

A rough index was calculated of the relative difficulty of the test for each country. If an item was introduced during the first semester of a year, the grade level was used (for example, 2.0); if the item was introduced during the second semester, a .5 was added (for example, 2.5). The index calculated in this manner for the items in the test was 2.85 for Japan and 3.26 for the United States. In other words, the concepts and skills generally tended to be introduced nearly a half-year earlier in Japanese texts. One possible explanation of the superiority of Japanese children at the later grades is that they are introduced to the content of mathematics earlier in their schooling than are American children. This possibility will be discussed later.

Verbal instructions for the test were carefully constructed in each language by native speakers, and the test was devised for individual administration. All questions were read by the examiner; thus, a child's score on the test was independent of reading skill. Examiners were residents of the cities in which the children lived. The test proved to be interesting and very reliable. Values of the Cronbach alpha statistic, computed separately by grade and country, ranged from .92 to .96.

Conducting the Study

A major problem arose in selecting appropriate samples of children. This was most acute in the United States. It would have been desirable to select children from a number of locations and to have included a broad range of ethnic, linguistic, and cultural backgrounds. Neither logistically nor financially was this feasible. It was necessary, therefore, to locate a single geographic area with a small minority population. Had we included large numbers of minority children, it would have been necessary to include minority status as one of the variables in our analyses. To do this we would have had to include representative samples of each minority group.

The Minneapolis metropolitan area, where the minority population is less than 4 percent, met our requirements. Our next task was to select the city in Japan most comparable to Minneapolis in size, and in cultural and economic status. From our experience and advice received from others, we chose Sendai. Both Sendai and Minneapolis are economically successful cities with little heavy industry and are considered to be more culturally traditional than many other large cities in each country.

Having selected our cities, the next step was to obtain representative samples of children. We did this by meeting with educational authorities in each city and selecting ten elementary schools judged to be a representative sample of elementary schools. We then randomly selected two first- and two fifth-grade classrooms in each school. From each of these classrooms we randomly selected twelve children, six boys and six girls. The final sample of children included 240 first graders and 240 fifth graders in each country.

The mathematics test was given to the children approximately 6 months after school opened for the year. The average ages of the children at the time of testing were identical for each country at both grades—7.0 years for the first graders and 11.2 years for the fifth graders.

Results of the Study

Japanese children scored significantly higher than American children at both first and fifth grades. The cross-national differences in the achievement scores in mathematics clearly are not a phenomenon of the later years of schooling, for they appear as early as first grade. Variability of performance did not differ markedly in the two countries, nor did the scores of boys and girls differ significantly in either country. These data are summarized in Table 14.1.

We can also look at these data in terms of the scores obtained by children in the different classrooms. These data appear in Figure 14-1. The height of the line represents the average score for the classroom and the width of the line, the range of scores within the classroom.[2] Since first graders received lower scores

Table 14.1
Average Performance for Boys and Girls
on the Mathematics Test

Country	Boys		Girls	
	M	SD	M	SD
Grade one				
Japan	20.7	5.7	19.5	4.6
United States	16.6	5.5	17.6	5.2
Grade five				
Japan	53.0	7.5	53.5	7.5
United States	45.0	6.5	43.8	5.9

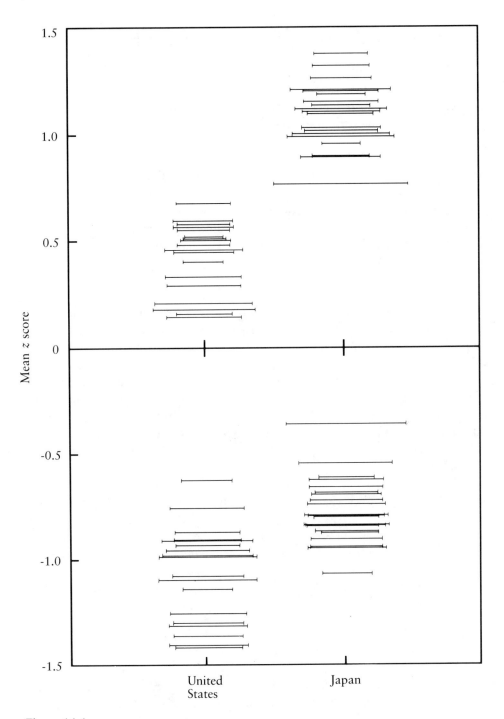

Figure 14-1
Scores on the mathematics test (standard scores) presented for first- and fifth-grade classrooms in Japan and the United States.

than fifth graders, the results for first graders appear in the lower half of the graph.

There is some overlap in the scores for the two sets of twenty first-grade classrooms. By the fifth grade, the difference is dramatic. The mean of the American classroom with the *highest* average level of performance lies *below* that of the *worst* performing fifth-grade classroom of Japanese children.

Possible Bases of the Differences

Differences in achievement as striking as these and in prior studies must be influenced by a great many cultural factors. Some are discussed in the following paragraphs. We shall concentrate primarily upon variables related to schooling.

The Curriculum

One reasonable hypothesis is that the differences in performance are due in part to differences in the curriculum of each country. However, several tests of this hypothesis make it appear unlikely that this in itself offers a convincing account of the results.

Looking at the first grade, fifteen of the early items in the test appeared in the first grade curricula in both countries. Nearly all were introduced in the first semester of the first grade. American children performed more poorly on the fifteen items than did the Japanese children. The percentage of the Japanese children who responded correctly to all of these items was 28.8 percent in comparison to 23.2 percent of the American children.

Similar effects were found at the fifth grade. All fifth graders were given items 35 through 38 of the mathematics test. The average grade placement of these four items in the American and Japanese textbooks was 2.6 and 3.2, respectively—far below the fifth grade. Even so, the American children again performed significantly more poorly than did the Japanese. The percentage of American children who answered all four items correctly was 7.3 percent; among Japanese children, it was 36.1 percent. Obviously, we must look elsewhere than the elementary school curriculum for an explanation of the differences in performance.

Educational Status of the Parents

Parents' educational status is typically found to be related to children's levels of achievement. It is possible that the Japanese families exceeded the American families in their educational status. This, however, proved not to be the case. Over half of the American mothers, for example, had attended college or graduate school. In Sendai, only 22 percent of the mothers had attained this level of education. Among the fathers, 66 percent of the Americans, but only 39 percent of the Japanese were college graduates. Educational status of the parents, then, cannot account for the differences in children's achievement between the two countries.

Teachers' Experience

A similar argument can be raised about the teachers: Japanese teachers may have had a higher level of education than American teachers. This again was not the case. The American teachers were all university or college graduates. Ten of the forty teachers had an M.A. degree, and one, a PH.D. Nearly all had majored in education as undergraduates; 76 percent in elementary education. Of the Japanese teachers, 68 percent had a bachelor's degree, and 70 percent of these had majored in elementary education. The remaining teachers in Japan had attended other types of teacher-training institutions. Although important differences may have existed in the content of the teachers' education, the amount of education received by the American teachers was greater than that of their Japanese counterparts.

The average years of teaching experience was similar: 15.4 years for the Minneapolis teachers and 17.4 years for the Japanese teachers. Because of the broad ranges of experience in each country, the difference was statistically insignificant.

Children's Intellectual Level

A positive relation between children's intellectual level and their academic achievement has been frequently found. Perhaps the Japanese children simply were brighter than the Americans, and differences in achievement reflected this higher level of intelligence. This possibility can be evaluated, for all children were given a battery of ten cognitive tasks constructed for this project. Many of these tasks were adaptations of subtests commonly included in scales of intelligence. Included were tests of verbal ability: vocabulary, general information, verbal memory, serial memory for words, and serial memory for numbers—and non-verbal tests: coding, spatial relations, perceptual speed, auditory memory, and spatial representation.

There were differences in the scores on some of the individual tasks, but they tended to be in the opposite direction from those in the mathematics test. In the first grade, American children received higher scores than Japanese children on six tasks; Japanese children received higher scores on one task; and no significant difference existed between the two groups of children on the remaining three tasks. In the fifth grade, there was no significant difference between the scores of the two groups of children on five of the tasks; American children received higher scores on two, and Japanese children received higher scores on two. Although the correlations between individual cognitive tasks and the mathematics scores were all significant and positive, ranging between .20 and .62, differences in mathematics achievement cannot be explained by reference to cross-national differences in general intelligence.

Time Spent in Mathematics Classes

The Japanese school year includes 240 days of instruction, and there are $5\frac{1}{2}$ days in each school week. In contrast, the American school year typically includes 178 days of instruction, and schools are in session only 5 days a week. The children's teachers reported that American first graders spent an average of 29.9 hours each week in school and Japanese first graders, an average of 30.7. There was a marked difference in the fifth grade, where Japanese children were reported to spend 37.3 hours and American children, 30.4. Overall, therefore, children in Japan received many more hours of instruction each year than did children in the United States.

We are able to provide a detailed picture of how the children spent their time in school. Among the many variables coded in the observations made in their classrooms, one was the subject being taught. Since the children were observed for large amounts of time—1200 hours in Sendai and over 1300 hours in Minneapolis—and the periods for the observations were randomly determined—highly reliable estimates of the proportion of time devoted to various subjects can be obtained. These proportions appear in Figure 14-2. According to these data, American first-grade teachers devoted about half as much time to instruction in mathematics as did Japanese first-grade teachers. At the fifth grade, the difference decreased, but remained significant. In contrast, language arts—reading, spelling, and writing—received much more emphasis in American than in Japanese classrooms.

The data related to subject matter are summarized in a second way in Figure 14-3. Here, the proportions of time devoted to each subject are plotted according to the mean proportion for each classroom. As can be seen, variability among Minneapolis classrooms is much greater than among those in Sendai. This can be readily explained. There is a precisely defined national curriculum in Japan, and teachers are expected to adhere closely to it. In constrast, American teachers, especially in elementary schools, may organize the curricula of their classrooms—as long as they adhere to the general policies of their school. Guidelines published by state and local school districts typically define general goals for elementary school education, rather than the specific manner in which time is to be organized or a curriculum is to be followed.

Language arts and mathematics had very similar ranges in Sendai. In Minneapolis, however, the range is greater for language arts than for mathematics. The time spent in fifth-grade classrooms on language arts ranged from 4 percent to 80 percent. For mathematics the range was more truncated. Although some teachers spent as much as 40 percent of their time in activities related to math-

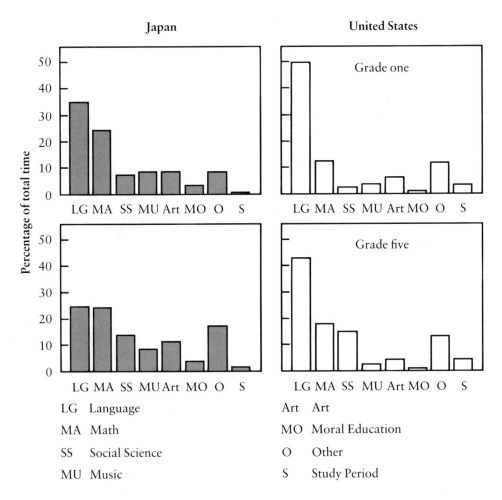

Figure 14-2
Proportion of time spent in first and fifth grades in language, mathematics, social science, music, art, moral education, and "other" classes.

ematics, others spent practically no time at all. In the first grade, children in one-third of the American classrooms spent less than 10 percent of their time on mathematics; at the fifth grade, children in three classrooms were never seen engaged in mathematics during the many days observers were present.

Instructing children does not insure they will learn. The teacher must have the children's attention. We found strong evidence that Japanese children were much more likely to be attentive to their teachers than were American children. Children in Minneapolis were coded as attending to the teacher or to the leader of an activity 46 percent of the time and children in Sendai, 65 percent of the time. The percentages were similar at the two grade levels (see Figure 14-4). Not

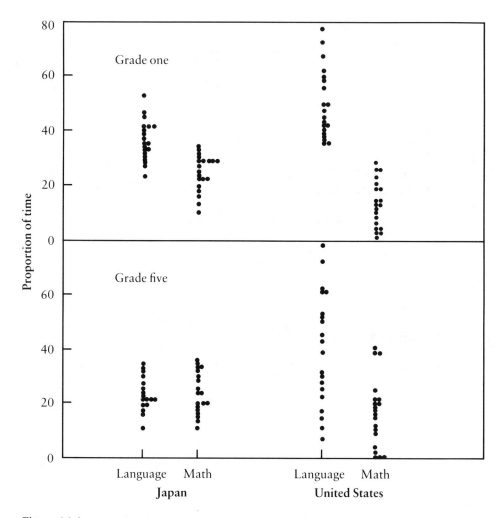

Figure 14-3
Proportion of time spent in language arts and mathematics classes for each of the class-rooms in first and fifth grades.

surprisingly, children spent a greater proportion of time attending to teachers in some classrooms than in others. Even so, there were large cultural differences in these proportions for different classrooms. The great majority of American classrooms were below the mean of the Japanese classrooms at both grades one and five.

Children engaged in inappropriate activities much less frequently in the Japanese classrooms, as shown in Figure 14-5. An activity was coded as being inappropriate when the child was not doing what he or she was expected or sup-

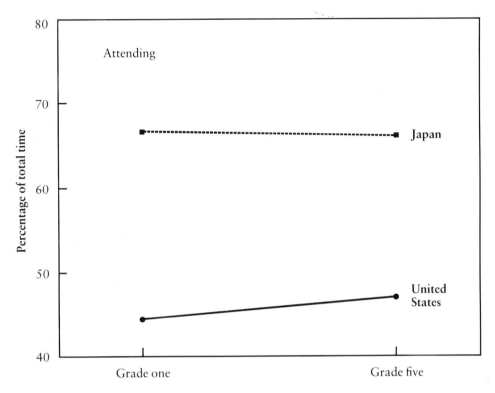

Figure 14-4
Proportion of time spent attending to the teacher in teacher-led activities.

posed to be doing—for example, talking to peers, asking inappropriate or irrelevant questions, wandering about the room, or staring into space. Since these activities are inappropriate, low z scores are more desirable. Low average z scores were found for many more Japanese than for American classrooms, reflecting a lower incidence of irrelevant activities.

Thus, not only was less time spent in instructing American children in mathematics, but they, in turn, spent less time attending to the teacher and more time engaging in inappropriate activities which interfered with or precluded learning.

Homework

Learning occurs not only in school, but also at home. Part of the learning at home occurs as children practice their lessons through homework. From their responses in interviews, we have many indications that neither American parents nor teachers consider homework of great value. This attitude is in marked contrast

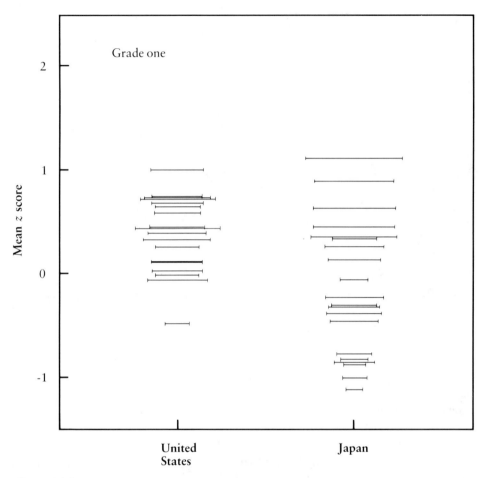

Figure 14-5
Proportion of time spent in inappropriate activities. (a) Grade one.

with that of parents and teachers in Japan. Consequently, American children spend much less time on homework than do Japanese children. Each mother was asked to estimate the time her child typically spent on homework each weekday and during each day of the weekend. The z scores for Japanese and American children are plotted by classroom in Figure 14-6. There is great homogeneity in the mothers' estimates at grade one but somewhat greater diversity at grade five. In no case was the average as high in American as in Japanese first-grade classrooms. Although some overlap exists at grade five, again, the overall mean is clearly higher for Japanese children.

During weekdays, American first-grade children were estimated to spend an average of 14 minutes a day on homework and fifth graders, 46 minutes. The

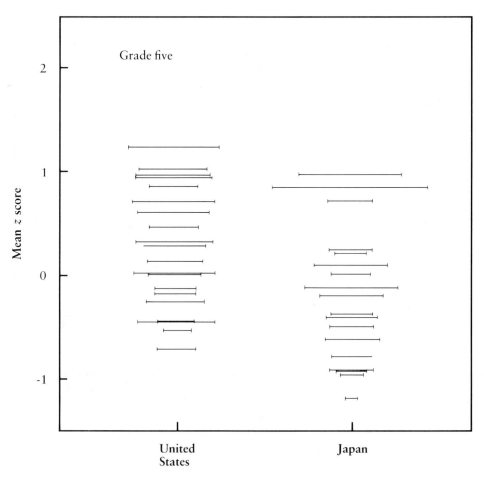

Figure 14-5
(*b*) **Grade five.**

corresponding averages in Japan were 37 and 57 minutes. On weekends, American children studied even less—an estimated 7 minutes on Saturday and 11 minutes on Sunday. Corresponding values for the Japanese children, who spend half of each Saturday in school, were 37 and 29 minutes.

Homework was not limited to times school was in session. During the summer vacation—the longest vacation during the school year in Japan—68 percent of the teachers made homework assignments. Before Christmas vacation in Minneapolis—the American children's longest vacation—only 12 percent of the teachers gave their pupils homework to complete over the holidays. In sum, according to all indications, American children spend less time on homework than do Japanese children.

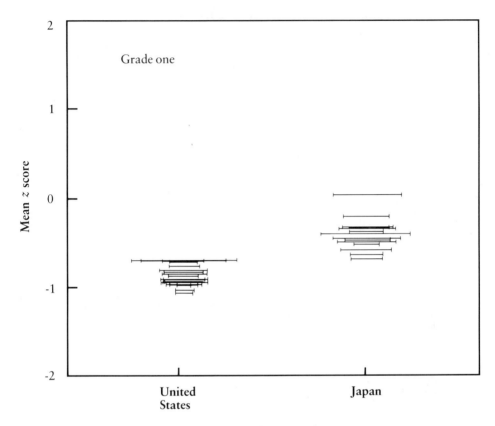

Figure 14-6
Average amounts of time spent in homework in each classroom according to mothers' estimates for children at first and fifth grades. (a) Grade one.

Conclusions

We found many other differences between home and school in Japan and in the United States which help us understand the bases for differences in mathematics achievement. Parental factors cannot be underestimated, for differences in achievement in mathematics were apparent before the children had finished their first year in school. When we look at the contributions of schooling, measures related to time are of special interest. Not surprisingly, American children perform less well in mathematics than Japanese children since, during their elementary school years, they spend less time in school. Moreover, proportionally less time is spent in American schools on mathematics instruction and children are less attentive, engage in more irrelevant activities, and devote less time outside of school on homework than do their Japanese counterparts. Nor is it surprising

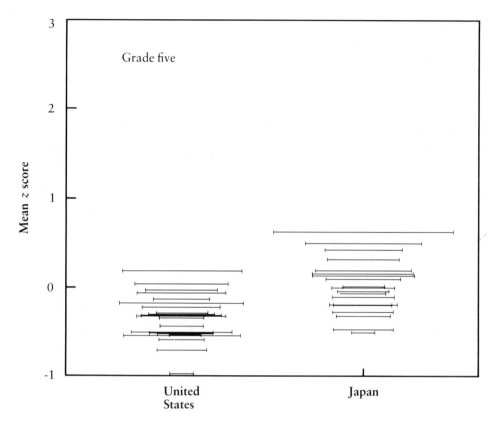

Figure 14-6
(*b*) **Grade five.**

that the gap between the two cultures increases between the first and fifth grades. These are important clues about differences in academic achievement. Learning requires time and practice. When either is reduced, it is impaired.

Footnotes

1. This report presents data from a larger project on children's achievement in Japan, Taiwan, and the United States supported by a grant from the National Institute of Mental Health (MH 30567).

2. A brief explanation should be provided of how this graph was generated. The scores on the mathematics test obtained by the children in the three cultures were transformed into z scores by forming a single distribution containing all of the children's scores. The z scores for each child were then combined to form new distributions for each of the twenty classrooms at each grade in each country. The average score for each classroom is represented by the height of the lines in the graph, and the range of scores (mean $\pm$ 3 standard deviations), by the length of the line.

References

Bolster, L. C. (1978). *Mathematics around us*. Glenview, Ill.: Scott-Foresman.

Comber, L. C., & Keeves, J. P. (1973). *Science achievement in nineteen countries*. New York: John Wiley & Sons.

Glaser, N. (1976). Social and cultural factors in economic growth. In H. Patrick & H. Rosovsky (Eds.), *Asia's new giant* (pp. 813–896). Washington, D.C.: Brookings Institution.

Husen, T. (1967). *International study of achievement in mathematics: a comparison of twelve countries*. New York: John Wiley & Sons.

New Mathematics. (1978). (Rev. ed.) Tokyo: Shoseki Kabushiki Kaisha, 1978.

Walberg, H. J., Harnisch, D. L., & Tsai, S. L. (1984). Mathematics productivity in Japan and Illinois. Unpublished manuscript, University of Illinois at Chicago.

Learning to Read Japanese

Harold W. Stevenson
Shin-ying Lee
James Stigler

IN COLLABORATION WITH

Seiro Kitamura
Susumu Kimura
Tadahisa Kato

This chapter describes the reading ability of Japanese and American elementary school children. The data to be discussed were derived from a large project concerned with Japanese, Chinese, and American children's early achievement in reading. To our knowledge, this is the first comparative study of the performance of children in reading these three writing systems. We will restrict our discussion here to the achievement of Japanese and American children.

A major problem in learning to read Japanese arises because Japanese is written not with one orthographic system, as are languages such as English and Chinese, but with three. Before we can go further, therefore, it is necessary to briefly introduce the characteristics of the Japanese writing systems. More thorough descriptions are available elsewhere (for example, Hatano, Kuhara, & Akiyama, 1981; Saito, 1981; Sakamoto & Makita, 1973; Taylor & Taylor, 1983).

Written Japanese

Until the Japanese began to import Chinese characters (*kanji*) many hundreds of years ago, there was no written form of Japanese. Chinese characters were given Japanese pronunciations, thus making written communication possible. Not only were Chinese characters imported, but adaptations of the Chinese pronunciations of the characters were also incorporated into the Japanese language. Consequently, nearly every character used in written Japanese has both a Japanese (*kun*) and a Chinese-based (*on*) pronunciation. Because it is difficult to know which pronunciation is appropriate in a particular context, a major problem arises in translating the written symbol into the spoken word.

Besides confusion over pronunciations, another problem resulted from borrowing a writing system developed for a language very different structurally from the one for which it was used. As often happens with something borrowed, the fit was less than ideal. In Chinese, the speaker is able to differentiate among different characters with the same pronunciation by means of four (or more, depending upon the dialect) differentiating tones. Japanese, however, has no tones. This means that different characters, each with a distinctive tone but the same pronunciations in Chinese, often have one *on* pronunciation in Japanese. The result is that Japanese is a language with a great many homonyms.

Change in the Chinese pronunciation of various characters over successive Chinese dynasties compounded these difficulties. Since Chinese characters were imported over a period of many centuries, successive Chinese pronunciations were often incorporated into Japanese. Thus, many characters have multiple *on* pronunciations, whereas a single character may have several *kun* pronunciations. It is, obviously, almost impossible at times, without seeing a character, to infer its meaning; knowing or hearing the correct pronunciation is insufficient.

Here, then, are two major problems in learning to read Japanese: there are single characters with multiple pronunciations and multiple characters with the same pronunciation. Both increase the difficulty of going from symbol to sound in reading *kanji*, and from sound to symbol in writing *kanji*. Interestingly, however, the meaning of a word usually can be directly discerned from seeing the characters that constitute it, even though deciding without instruction how the characters should be pronounced might be difficult.

In addition to the problems associated with pronouncing *kanji*, another set arose from the entirely different grammatical systems of Japanese and Chinese. For example, word order is important in Chinese; it is less important in Japanese. When word order is unimportant, some means of noting parts of the sentence, such as the subject and object, is necessary. Within a Japanese sentence, the subject is noted by a particle (*ga*) and the object by a different particle (*o*). Chinese lacks such particles. An important component of the Japanese sentence is tense. This is missing in Chinese and usually must be inferred from the context in which the word is embedded. After adopting Chinese characters for use in writing Japanese, early efforts to overcome these problems were made by placing small, additional characters at particular points around the periphery of a character to represent particles and inflection. This proved awkward, and soon the *kana* were developed. Certain Chinese characters were simplified and were assigned readings that corresponded to the elements of the Japanese syllabary. For example, the character 安 became あ and was always pronounced *a*; 加 became か and was always pronounced *ka*.

The invention of *kana* was a great advance in increasing the accessibility of the written language. *Hiragana*, a cursive *kana*, was assigned for the use of women, and *katakana*, a more linear form, was developed for priests and men. Gradually, the function of the two *kana* changed, so that particles, some nouns and verbs, and all endings denoting adjectives, adverbs, and the tense of verbs are now written in *hiragana*. *Katakana* is used primarily for transliterated foreign words and where emphasis is desired. Small *hiragana* called *furigana* are written alongside difficult or new characters to assist the reader in pronunciation.

Both types of *kana* contain forty-six symbols, each corresponding to a distinct syllable. The symbols are increased by twenty-five through the use of diacritic marks to yield a total of seventy-one *hiragana*. The young child who has learned the *hiragana* can read correctly any sentence in Japanese written in *hiragana*. This is a great advantage. However, except for the most simple texts for preschoolers, written Japanese always employs both *kanji* and *kana*. The young Japanese child is faced, therefore, with the awesome task of mastering each of these orthographies. Texts of any complexity are not written solely in *hiragana* for the same reason that the use of roman letters (*romaji*) in writing Japanese makes it so difficult to comprehend: although the sentences can be read easily, their meaning is often difficult to discern.

By the end of the first grade, the Japanese child is expected to have learned seventy-six *kanji*, including those for such single-character words as rain, flower, middle, or book and such two-character words as teacher and school. Introduction of *kanji* into the Japanese elementary school curriculum is carefully planned. From grades two through six the numbers of new *kanji* to be learned each year are 145, 195, 195, 195, and 190. These are known as the *jyoyo kanji*. During the succeeding three years of middle school, approximately 850 additional *kanji*, the *toyo kanji*, are taught. By the end of this time the student can read all 1846 *kanji* considered necessary for a literate person. Since only a modest proportion of Japanese words are represented by a single character, combinations of the 1846 characters are used to form many thousands of words.

Theoretical Interpretations

Theoretical discussions of the role of orthography in reading often have greatly oversimplified the tasks faced by the Japanese child in learning to read. The presence in Japanese of whole characters composed of distinctive patterns of strokes, along with a syllabary with constant symbol-sound correspondence, has been cited as a great advantage of Japanese over other orthographies. Gleitman and Rozin (1977), for example, have expressed the point this way:

> A script that represents meanings only (a logography) cannot ultimately serve the purpose of effortless recognition of rare or novel items. And on the other hand, a script that represents sounds only (a phonology) poses problems for the rapid reconstruction of meanings from text. . . . The Japanese writing system, from this point of view, seems ideal. (p. 36)

Others, such as Martin (1973), have contrasted Japanese and English orthographies to explain the difficulties of American children in reading. In a paper, "Learning to read: Why Taro finds it easy and Johnny finds it hard," Martin concluded that the difference between learning to read Japanese and learning to read English is related to the nature of the writing systems and their correspondence to the sound system of the language. His conclusion is based, in part, on the following argument:

> It appears to be true that what the human ear extracts from the speech signal is not, in the first instance, the phonemes or their components, but rather the syllables. And here is where Taro gets his big break. For the linguistic structure of Japanese is such that the syllable is virtually identical with the morphophoneme, that is with the phonetic units that make up the morphophonemes; moreover, the number of syllables in Japanese is quite small—no more than a hundred or so, even if we include a few odd types. It is an easy job for Taro to learn the kana syllabaries, because he immediately recognizes their linguistic basis in the syllable. In Johnny's case, the major hurdle seems to be breaking the syllable up into smaller entities.

If learning to read Japanese were as easy as such analyses imply, only a few Japanese children of normal itelligence should be poor readers, and reading disabilities should be very rare. Such an argument has been proposed by Makita (1968) in his well-known discussion of the apparent lack of reading disabilities among Japanese children. Many writers have found his observations compelling, and there has been a widespread belief that Japanese children do not display reading disabilities. Unfortunately, this belief has been perpetuated on the basis of argument rather than of data. Before we began our study, no one had directly tested large samples of Japanese children to determine whether or not reading disabilities actually would be found among them. Nor had it been directly tested whether Japanese children were better readers than, for example, their American counterparts, who read an alphabet.

Part of the reason for the lack of cross-cultural data is that comparable instruments have been unavailable in English and in Japanese. Although many reading tests have been published in each language, there were no directly comparable tests in vocabulary, grammatical structure, and content of the items. Our first task in undertaking comparative research was to construct such a test.

Constructing the Reading Test

We devised a reading test which contained items testing sight reading of vocabulary, reading of meaningful text, and comprehension of text. We began by compiling lists of each vocabulary word introduced in Japanese, American, and Chinese elementary school textbooks. For this purpose we selected the current editions of two of the most popular text series in Japan and in the United States. Lists were created by entering words into the computer in English and, in the case of Japanese, entering transliterations of Japanese in *romaji*. Accompanying each word were the grade and semester of its first appearance. For Japanese, it was also noted whether all or part of the word was written in *kanji, hiragana,* or *katakana,* the number of *kanji* used, and the English translation. Upon completion, there were approximately 7000 entries for each language. By the end of the sixth grade, therefore, children were reading approximately the same number of words in each language.

Preparation also included summarizing all the stories in the texts and identifying the grades at which various grammatical structures appeared. With this information we were able to construct relevant items of comparable difficulty and equivalent grammatical complexity.

Items were constructed simultaneously in all three languages. Decisions about their acceptability were made through group discussion by persons from each culture who were familiar with at least two of the languages. All items were reviewed by professionals in each culture to insure that they were satisfactory for children of the ages included in our study, culturally appropriate, and written in standard forms of the language.

The test was composed of four parts arranged according to grade level:

Kindergarten Items. The kindergarten test involved matching, naming, and identifying *hiragana* in Japanese and letters in English (Figure 15-1a).

Vocabulary. The vocabulary portion of the test was designed to assess the child's ability to sight-read single, isolated words (Figure 15-1b). In grades one to three, the words were common to all three languages, but grades four to six had an insufficient number of new vocabulary items common to the three languages. It was necessary, therefore, to use different words in the three forms of the test at grades four to six. To insure comparability, words selected for the test at grades four to six appeared for the first time at a particular grade level and had a similar frequency of usage as determined by reference to frequency counts of words in English and of characters in Japanese. Words appeared in the form included in the children's texts; that is, in single or multiple *kanji* or in *kanji* with *hiragana.*

Reading and Comprehending Text. These portions of the test provided an index of the child's ability to read meaningful text presented in clauses, sentences, and paragraphs, as well as to respond to true-false and multiple-choice questions about the text. Three types of item were included: (a) phrases or sentences describing one of three pictures (Figure 15-1c and d); (b) sentences in which certain key words were omitted, but for which three alternatives were available; and (c) paragraphs about which questions were asked (Figure 15-1e).

Examples of the four portions of the test are shown in Figure 15-1. There were separate booklets for each language, but items in both the Japanese and English versions have been combined in this figure for purposes of illustration.

English	q	w	t	m	o	i	u	j	z

Japanese

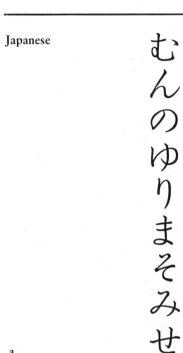

a

Figure 15-1
Examples of items from the reading test. (a) Kindergarten items.

English	tobacco	couple	fiery

Japanese

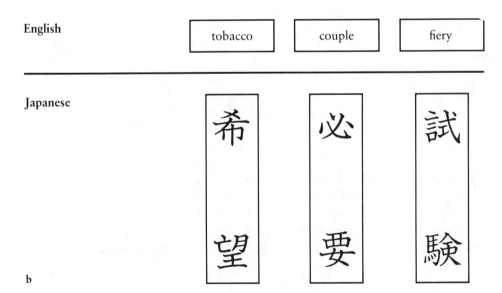

b

Figure 15-1
Examples of items from the reading test. (b) Vocabulary items.

English   The day we went on a picnic was a cloudy day.

Japanese

みんなが　遠足に　行った　日は、
くもり　でした。

c

Figure 15-1
Examples of items from the reading test. (c) Sentence reading and comprehension (item from second-grade level).

English   The kitten is sitting under the table.

Japanese

下に すわって います。 小さい ねこが、 テーブルの

d

Figure 15-1
Examples of items from the reading test. (d) Sentence reading and comprehension.

All three forms of writing, *hiragana, katakana,* and *kanji,* appear in the first-grade Japanese sentence. The stem of the first word, "small," is written with a single *kanji,* followed by two *hiragana* denoting an adjective; "table," a foreign word incorporated into Japanese, is written in *katakana;* "below" is written in *kanji,* and the rest of the sentence, "is sitting," is written in *hiragana.* The mixture of *hiragana* and *kanji* is also evident in the sentences at the other grade levels.

The subjects for the study were children from the first and fifth grades of elementary schools in Sendai, Japan, and in the Minneapolis metropolitan area. (Some children in this study also participated in our study of mathematics achievement described in the preceding chapter.) The children attended twenty classrooms representative of the range of classrooms in each city; all the children enrolled in each classroom visited were tested. Thus, the data to be reported are based upon a total of 789 Japanese and 410 American first graders, and 775 Japanese and 453 American fifth graders. (The different sizes of the samples is due to the different numbers of children enrolled in Japanese and American

English

Ages ago, people depended on hunting to survive. In the autumn of each year they went out to hunt game. When they returned with their catch they smoked the meat and used the fur and skins to make clothing. In this fashion, they provided themselves with food and clothing for the winter.

Japanese

むかし、ひとびとはえものをとって生活していました。毎年秋にはりょうにでかけました。とった動物をころしたあと、肉はかんそうしてとっておき、毛がわで着る物をつくりました。このようにして、ひとびとは冬にそなえて、食べ物と着る物を用意することができたのです。

e

Figure 15-1
Example of items from the reading text. (e) Paragraph reading and comprehension.

elementary school classrooms.)

The reading test was administered approximately 4 months after the school term began. The test was given individually to each child by examiners who were residents of the city in which the child lived.

Reading Scores

There are many ways in which children's performance on the reading test can be summarized: the percentage reading above or below grade level, the average level of performance, and the percentage in each country who were in the upper and lower portions of distributions of reading scores combined across the three cities where data were collected. We shall look at each of these in turn.

Relation to Grade Level. The percentages of first-grade children reading *above* grade level in Minneapolis and in Sendai were, respectively, 56.6 percent and 85.6 percent. As Figure 15-2 shows, nearly 70 percent of the Japanese first-graders passed the first-grade items and were able to continue to the second-grade level of the test but stopped there. The American children were more likely to be reading at a first-grade level. However, there were first graders both in Minneapolis and in Sendai who were reading at fourth-, fifth-, and sixth-grade levels.

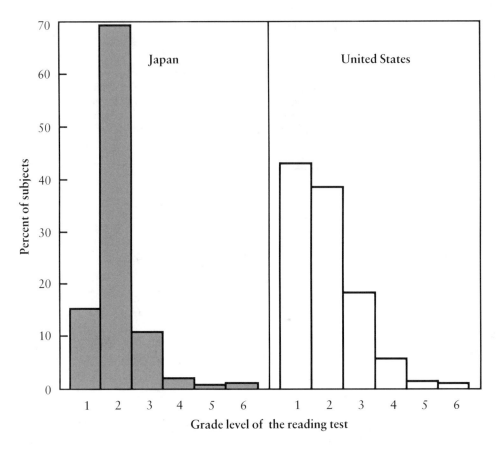

Figure 15-2
Percentages of first-graders reaching each grade level of the reading test.

As can be seen in Figure 15-3, a surprisingly large percentage of the fifth graders were reading below grade level. In both cities there were fifth graders whose reading skill was equivalent to that of first- and second-grade children. At the same time, reasonably large proportions were able to read successfully at above the fifth-grade level. Significantly more American than Japanese fifth graders were able to do this.

Overall Scores. Overall distributions of vocabulary and comprehension scores are plotted in Figure 15-4. Scores for reading of text follow essentially the same pattern as those for reading comprehension and are not presented graphically. Statistical comparisons indicate that the American children received significantly higher scores on vocabulary items than Japanese children at first grade, $p < .001$, but not at fifth grade. The respective mean scores of first graders were 9.9 and 7.2, and at fifth grade, 48.4 and 46.9. Scores for reading comprehension and reading of text did not differ significantly between Japanese and American children at either grade.

The data are presented in a different way in Figures 15-5 and 15-6. Here,

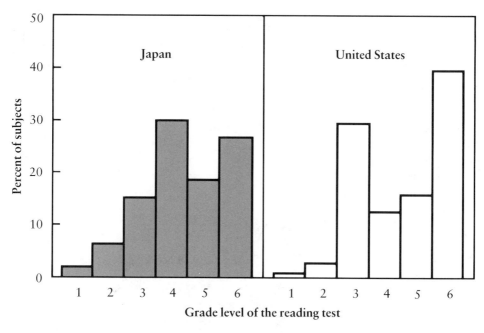

Figure 15-3
Percentages of fifth-graders reaching each grade level of the reading test.

the average raw scores on the reading test are plotted for children who were at various percentiles of reading ability. On vocabulary items, first graders below the fiftieth percentile received very similar scores in Sendai and in Minneapolis. Among the more advanced readers—those who continued on to higher levels of the test—the American children received notably higher scores. On comprehension items, Japanese first graders received higher scores than their American counterparts, except among the best readers, where the American children again achieved the higher scores.

Differences between the scores of Japanese and American children at various levels of reading skill were smaller at the fifth-grade level, but the pattern remained the same. Among the better readers, the Americans tended to receive the higher raw scores.

High and Low Scores. In order to determine the relative frequency of high and low scorers on the reading test, we combined the data for the Japanese, American, and Chinese children. We then selected the 100 children who received the top scores and the 100 children who received the lowest scores. These selections were made from a total of approximately 240 children from each grade in each country. If children in each country performed comparably, there should be approximately 33 Japanese, 33 American, and 33 Chinese children among those receiving the 100 highest scores. Similarly, there should be approximately 33 children from

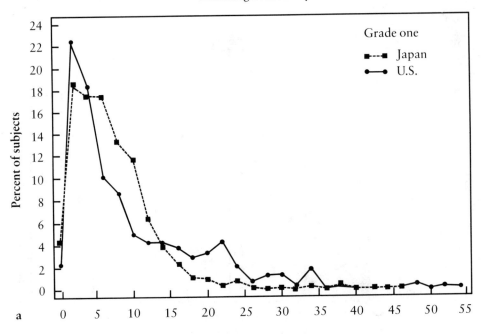

Reading vocabulary

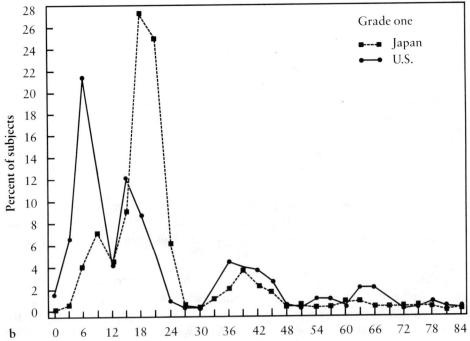

Reading comprehension

Figure 15-4
Distributions of scores obtained on the vocabulary and the comprehension parts of the reading test.

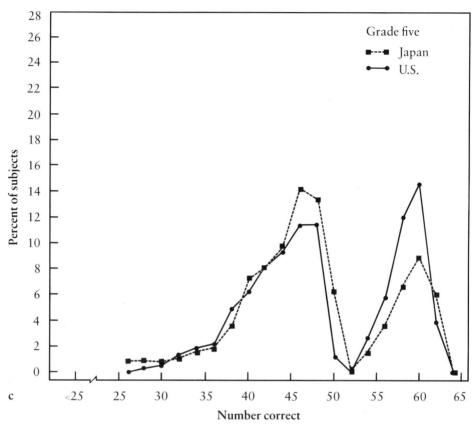

Figure 15-4 (*continued*)

each country receiving the 100 lowest scores.

There were 47 American and 43 Japanese children among the 100 first graders receiving the lowest vocabulary scores. Among those receiving the highest vocabulary scores were 47 American and 13 Japanese children. Since the vocabulary items were written primarily in *kanji*, obviously, many Japanese first-graders were unable to read the *kanji* appearing in their first-grade readers. Many of the first-grade vocabulary items appeared in the children's textbooks after the reading tests were given. The young readers of English have the possibility of "sounding out" these new words; children reading *kanji* do not have this advantage.

The picture is somewhat different in the case of reading comprehension. Among the 100 first graders with the lowest scores, 56 were American and 9 were Japanese. Among the 100 children with the highest scores, there were 32 Americans and 25 Japanese. We interpret these results to indicate that in reading meaningful text, the presence of *hiragana* proved to be advantageous to the Japanese children. A remarkably small number of Japanese first graders were among those with the poorest reading comprehension.

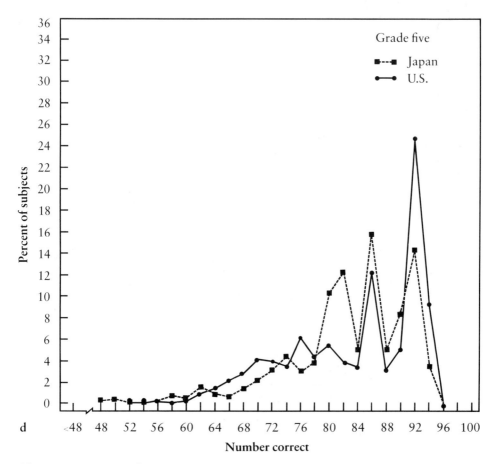

Figure 15-4 (*continued*)

Results were much the same on vocabulary items for low scorers at grade five as at grade one. Again, there was overrepresentation of both Japanese and American children: 48 Japanese and 44 American children were among the 100 fifth graders receiving the lowest scores. There were somewhat more high scorers among the Japanese fifth graders than there were at first grade: 34 versus 13. The number of American children represented among the top 100 scorers declined slightly: 47 at first grade and 41 at fifth grade.

The advantage of the Japanese children in reading comprehension was lost by fifth grade. There were 35 Japanese children among the 100 lowest scorers and only 24 among the highest scorers. The American children were overrepresented both among those with the lowest scores (47 children) and among those with the highest scores (55 children). The large number of American children with low scores is surprising in view of the much greater amount of time spent

Grade one

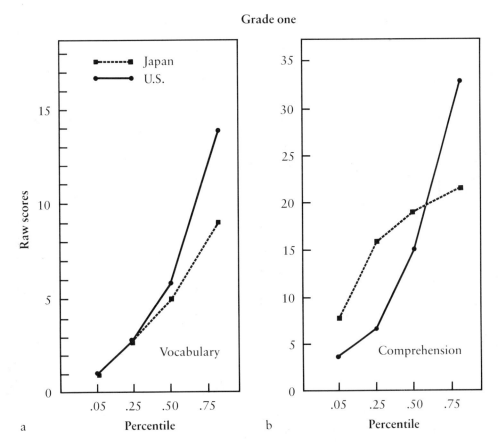

Figure 15-5
Mean raw scores on the vocabulary and the comprehension parts of the reading test for first-graders plotted according to percentile level.

on language arts in the American classrooms than in the Japanese.

The interpretation of the findings discussed thus far seems to be relatively straightforward. There is ample evidence that Japanese children know *hiragana* well from an early age; in fact, the average child knows a high proportion of the *hiragana* before entering school (Muraishi, 1972). Thus, simple texts with a high density of *hiragana*, such as those found in the first grade, can be read with high comprehension. But when there is a high density of *kanji*, as by fifth grade, the children have increasing difficulty not only in decoding, but also in ascertaining the meaning of sentences. The advantages of *hiragana* are obvious, but so are the problems resulting from their use. Why, the child may wonder, is it necessary to commit to memory the many complex *kanji* if everything can be written in *hiragana*? The Chinese child is never faced with this question. Without a ready knowledge of characters, reading a Chinese text is impossible.

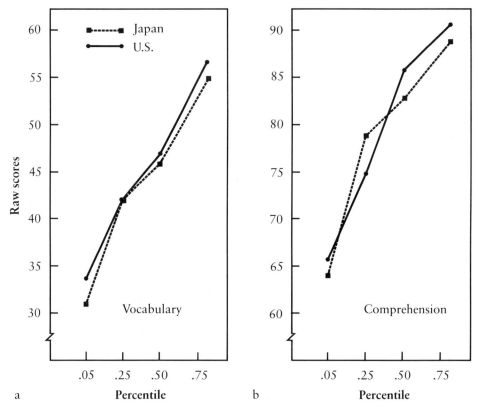

Figure 15-6
Mean raw scores on the vocabulary and comprehension parts of the reading test for first-graders plotted according to percentile level.

The data also provide some support for the phonetic recoding hypothesis advanced in discussions of reading an alphabetic system. Differences between Japanese and American children are most notable among good readers, that is, among children in the top quartile in reading scores. These children appear to have caught on that it is possible to sound out words. With such an insight, words written in an alphabet can be decoded, even though they have never before been encountered in print—an advantage denied to children who read a logographic form of writing such as Japanese. Unless the Japanese child has been taught the pronunciation and meaning of a new character, it is very difficult, if not impossible, to guess what the meaning and pronunciation might be.

As is evident from the numbers of children in the 100 best and worst readers, Japanese children are not as fluent in reading *kanji* as are Chinese children in reading characters. (The excellent performance of the Chinese children can be easily seen by subtracting the total numbers of Japanese and American children represented in the preceding data from 100.) As mentioned, the same characters appeared in the Japanese and the Chinese versions for the first three grades of the reading test. At the later grades, characters differed in the two versions, but were comparable in terms of the year they were introduced and of their frequency of usage. The difference between Japanese and Chinese children in their skill at reading Chinese characters may be a matter of practice. It seems more likely, however, that it is a result of the greater apparent necessity for mastering Chinese characters in reading Chinese than in reading Japanese.

Poor Readers. We have still another way of comparing the reading skill of the Japanese and the American children. All fifth-graders started on the fifth-grade items of the reading test. If they were unsuccessful on three-fourths of these items, they were required to go to the fourth-grade items. If they were unsuccessful on three-fourths of these items, they were required to go to the third-grade items. In this way, a child could be forced to go back as far as the first grade. The results indicate that 8 percent of the Japanese children and 3 percent of the American children failed to meet the criteria for success at grade three and were therefore reading at least three years below their grade level—a common criterion for reading disability.

In Figure 15-7 a & b, the scores at each grade level of the test presented according to the children's level of reading ability. Looking first at the hatched column, we see that the fifth-grade items of the test were effective in separating children at various levels of reading ability; that is, children who eventually were required to return to the first- or second-grade levels received lower scores than those who returned to the third-grade level, and so forth. A similar hierarchy emerged for items at each grade level of the test. Scores on the vocabulary portion were consistently lower among the Japanese than among the American children, but, as might be guessed from the data already discussed, their performance was more similar on the comprehension items at all grade levels.

These data offer no support for the belief that reading disabilities are absent among Japanese children or for the hypothesis that the orthographic systems of Japanese preclude the development of reading disabilities. There *are* Japanese children with serious difficulties in learning how to read, and the severity of their problems is at least as great as that of American children.

Conclusions

The results turned out to be quite different from what would be predicted from current theoretical discussions of the role of orthography in reading. Rather than demonstrating a superiority in performance by the Japanese children, as would be predicted from many current theoretical discussions of the usefulness of a syllabary and of characters in learning to read, Japanese children performed no more effectively than did American children. The early advantage of a syllabary was rapidly lost as the proportion of *hiragana* to total text decreased. This is an initial study and, naturally, further comparative research is needed. Nevertheless,

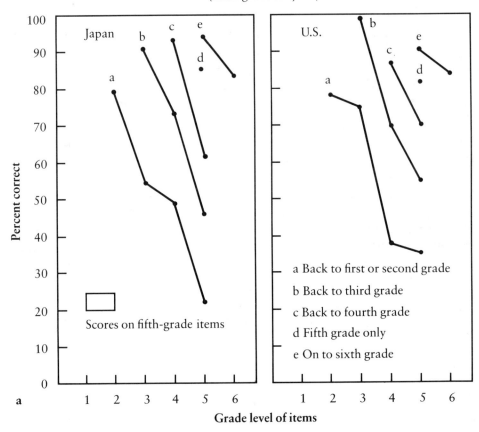

Figure 15-7
Percent correct responses made by fifth-graders who were reading at fifth-grade level, sixth-grade level, and who were required to return to earlier grade-levels of the test

these data do a great deal to dispel notions emerging from *a priori* considerations rather than from the results of research, about the relative difficulties of reading alphabetic, logographic, and syllabary forms of writing.

Footnote

The research discussed in this paper was supported by a grant from the National Institute of Mental Health (MH 30567).

References

Gleitman, L. R., & Rozin, P. (1977). The structure and acquisition of reading. I. Relation between orthographies and the structure of language. In A. S. Reber & D. L. Scarborough (Eds.), *Toward a psychology of reading*. Hillsdale, N. J.: Lawrence Erlbaum.

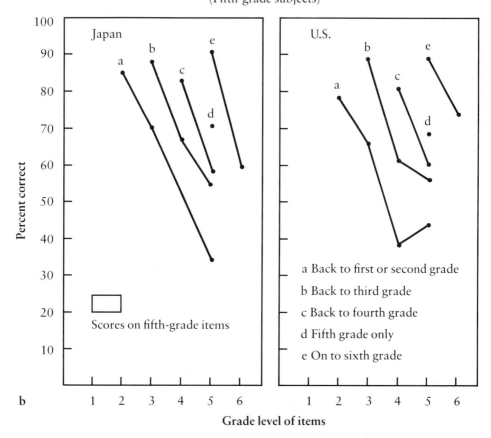

Reading comprehension
(Fifth-grade subjects)

Japan

U.S.

Percent correct

Grade level of items

a Back to first or second grade

b Back to third grade

c Back to fourth grade

d Fifth grade only

e On to sixth grade

Scores on fifth-grade items

Hatano, G., Kuhara, K., & Akiyama, M. (1981). *Kanji* help readers of Japanese infer the meaning of unfamiliar words. *The Quarterly Newsletter of the Laboratory of Comparative Human Cognition, 3,* 30–33.

Makita, K. (1968). The rarity of reading disability in Japanese children. *American Journal of Orthopsychiatry, 38,* 599–614.

Martin, S. E. (1973). Learning to read: Why Taro finds it easy but Johnny finds it hard. Paper presented at the Second Japan-U.S. Joint Sociolinguistic Conference, Tokyo.

Muraishi, S. (1972). Acquisition of reading Japanese syllabic characters in preschool children. Paper read at the meetings of the International Congress of Psychology, Tokyo.

Saito, H. (1981). Toward comparative studies in reading *Kanji* and *Kana. The Quarterly Newsletter of the Laboratory of Comparative Human Cognition, 3,* 33–36.

Sakamoto, T., & Makita, K. (1973). Japan. In J. Downing (Ed.), *Comparative reading.* New York: Macmillan.

Taylor, I., & Taylor, M. M. (1983). *The psychology of reading.* New York: Academic.

PART THREE

CONCEPTUAL ISSUES

Issues in Socioemotional Development

Kazuo Miyake
Joseph J. Campos
Jerome Kagan
Donna L. Bradshaw

Recently, dramatic changes in the conceptualization of socioemotional development and a resurgence of interest in emotions have emerged in psychology, pointing to important new directions for cross-cultural comparison of Japanese and American children. One of these new directions results from the appreciation that human emotions acquire their significance to a large extent because of their social communicative functions. Increasing interest in the social facets of emotions has generated novel research in the field of emotional communication. This research has centered on the identification of facial, vocal, and gestural patterns that have social regulatory functions, the description of how emotional expressions and feelings become socialized with age, and the consequences of emotional communication for the development of later compliance, conscience, and personality (Campos et al. 1983; Kagan, 1984).

Moreover, the recognition that emotions have social functions has led to a new understanding of the critical role they play in the development of social relationships, especially parent-infant attachment. The mother-child relationship is now conceptualized in terms of the felt security provided by mother to child, rather than in terms of the amount of physical stimulation or the extent of drive reduction she brings about (Sroufe & Waters, 1977). This felt security has profound psychological consequences, motivating the child's exploration of the social and nonsocial world and influencing his or her later engagement in both cognitive tasks and peer relations.

Furthermore, the child's endogenous disposition to react emotionally (that is, his or her temperament) has become significant because it is an important influence on the behavior of social partners, as well as on cognitive and perceptual development (Goldsmith & Campos, 1982). The concept of temperament in contemporary theories of socioemotional development balances the previous emphasis in psychoanalytic theory—and later, social-learning theory—on the role of the parent as the exclusive socializing influence on the child. The result is a more dyadic and transactional approach to early development.

Finally, in contemporary approaches to the psychology of emotion, the interactional processes constituting the core of the study of socioemotional development are no longer divorced from the values and goals of the parents and the culture in which the family lives (Lewis & Michalson, 1983). These values determine what expressions and feeling states are encouraged or suppressed, what aspects of independent behavior are encouraged, and how discipline is administered. Because values are important, parental attitudes must be considered in order to interpret correctly any social-emotional interactions, especially when comparing cultural groups. Researchers dealing with socialization have thus become less concerned with broad descriptions of child-rearing practices, and more skeptical of social variables that are postulated inevitably to determine later personality. Instead, they have become more concerned with describing the processes by which multiple factors, such as temperament, parental attitudes, emotional communication, and the cultural context of behavior interact to produce development.

Historically, the study of the social development of infants and young children has had an honored place in cross-cultural psychology and in anthropological field studies of any culture (for example, Whiting & Child, 1953). Classic accounts of Japanese psychology from an anthropological perspective, such as Ruth Benedict's (1946) *The Chrysanthemum and the Sword*, devote much attention to the socialization practices of parents which attempt to shape the child to meet the specific social demands of Japanese culture, and which consequently reflect more directly than almost any other area of psychological study its goals and values. Heavily influenced by Freudian theory, research in this tradition has tried to explain the development of the modal "Japanese personality" through examination of practices concerned with breast-feeding, toileting, and other aspects of early experience emphasized in psychoanalytic theory.

In addition, anthropologists have frequently described both the content and methods of child discipline, along with the parents' attitudes about what constitutes a socially appropriate occasion and manner of expression of one or another emotion. However, the level of description and explanation in this classic work is typically very broad, and generalizations derived from interviews and naturalistic observations have rarely been subjected to quantitative analyses or corroborated by more controlled experimentation.

The study of emotions in genral also has a rich history in cross-cultural research, especially the investigation of the issue of universality versus cultural specificity of the reception and the production of expressions of emotions (for example, Ekman, 1973). In this regard, studies of the Japanese have been of interest because of the traditional Japanese emphasis on nonverbal modes of communication (Morsbach, 1973) and because of the extensive control apparently exercised over the expression of negative emotions such as anger and distress (Ekman, 1973). Although research on this topic has included careful experimental studies, such as those of Ekman (1972), most studies have been conducted only with adults, whereas systematic research on the *development* of either the understanding or expression of emotions has been neglected until recently.

In this chapter, we will begin by reviewing some of the classic work on early social and emotional development in Japan, including a few studies contrasting maternal behavior and child development between Japan and the United States. Then, we will illustrate some of the new conceptual and methodological approaches to the study of socioemotional development both intraculturally and cross-culturally by describing recent research from our laboratories dealing with emotional communication, maternal attachment, temperament, and parental attitudes.

The Role of Emotional Processes in the Development of the Japanese Child

Interest of American scientists in the study of Japanese child-rearing practices was mainly inspired by American experiences with Japan in World War II. Beginning with Ruth Benedict's classic work, the goal of early studies was to describe the relationship between culture and personality. Through its broad descriptions of many aspects of the socialization of Japanese children, this body of literature has provided many interesting observations and hypotheses which have been very influential in suggesting important directions for more focussed research. Some of the observations most interesting from the perspective of current trends in socioemotional development will be highlighted in this brief survey of the most influential English-language studies dealing with social and emotional development in Japan.

Doi: Emotional Interdependence in Japanese Mother-Child Dyads

The Japanese psychoanalyst Doi (1973) has attempted to explain much of Japanese personality development as a reflection of a single concept, *amae*. *Amae* is roughly translated as "dependency"; however, it has no precise English equivalent. Doi has described a two-stage process of social development in Japanese infants. Prior to 7 months of age, infants experience what Doi has called a sense of "perfect oneness" with their social environment, an experience similar to what American psychoanalyst Mahler has called "symbiosis" (Mahler, Pine & Bergman, 1975). Doi goes on to argue that the Japanese mother encourages in her infant the development of the unique characteristic of "*amae*," by fostering the self-indulgent tendency to expect—and even to take advantage of—the help and support of individuals and groups close to him or her.

Amae does not begin until the age of 7 to 8 months, when the infant starts to become aware that his or her mother exists as a separate entity. Not only does the Japanese infant long for a return to the state of "perfect oneness" with the mother, he or she also longs to preserve the state of *amae*. The mother's encouragement of *amae* and the child's contentedness with it combine to motivate the Japanese child strongly to prevent any separation from the mother. Doi asserts that this motive serves as a basis for, and colors, all subsequent human relationships and has profound implications for the later personality of Japanese individuals.

It should be noted here that although Mahler et al.'s theoretical model of "symbiosis" is similar to that of "*amae*," the stress in the former theory is much more on the processes of separation and individuation than on the desire to maintain a symbiotic state of oneness and closeness. In Mahler's model, such excessive closeness and interdependency is a sign of psychopathology after the first few months of infancy. Mahler et al. do not believe that the longing for oneness characteristic of *amae* and the anxiety accompanying its inevitable frustration could actually become a major motivating force for later development, as Doi's model hypothesizes.

Vogel: Emotional Bonding of Japanese Infants to the Family

The importance of a close mother-child relationship and the nature of maternal communiations concerning the child's relation to the outside world were stressed in a now classic participant-observer study of families in Tokyo conducted by Vogel and Vogel (1961; Vogel, 1967). They reported; Japanese children and their mothers spent little time apart and that the American custom of babysitting was practically nonexistent. This was true even in more contemporary nuclear Japanese families. Moreover, physical contact was seen by Japanese families as a natural expression of affection, necessary and desirable for the proper rearing of children.

In addition, the Vogels reported that mothers communicate to their children from an early age fear of the world outside the family, especially strangers. At the same time, mothers demonstrate to their children that they will be there for comforting fears and distress, thereby encouraging the children to remain close and dependent. Perhaps as a consequence, Vogel and Vogel (1961) remarked, many Japanese children, although curious, are fearful of unfamiliar situations and are often extremely shy and inhibited on entering school.

With regard to child compliance, the most important concern of the Japanese mother is not absolute obedience, but rather, the preservation of closeness between mother and child. According to Vogel (1967), "One of the principles implicit in the attempt to get the child to understand is that one should never go against the child" (p. 245). This attitude suggests that Japanese mothers should work very hard to avoid direct expression of negative emotions or verbal evaluations of the child, even when he or she misbehaves. In sum, the descriptions of child-rearing practices in Japan provided by Vogel and Vogel reinforce Doi's theoretical statements concerning the close and dependent nature of the mother-child affective bond, especially the stress on physical contact. They also point out the consequent strong desire on the part of the mother to circumvent negative emotional expressions by her child. Further description of maternal behavior which seems to reflect these values is provided by Lebra (1976).

Lebra: Maternal Discipline in the Context of Emotional Interdependence

Lebra describes the relationship between maternal care practices and infant behavior as basically one of interdependence, exemplified by prolonged breast-feeding, cobathing, cosleeping, communicating physically, carrying the child on the mother's back, and toilet training the child by holding him or her above the toilet. Lebra's writings imply that a Japanese mother tries to sensitize her child to the negative effects of feelings of loneliness. According to Lebra, she tries to train the child to avoid these feelings by increasing the child's dependence on her. One goal of the Japanese mother is thus to keep the child in close physical contact with the adult social world to the greatest extent possible.

Lebra further describes the discipline techniques of Japanese mothers. These include, on the one hand, threats of abandonment, ridicule and embarrassment, and, on the other, appeals for empathy, with the mother presenting herself as a victim of the child's misbehavior. These strategies are significant because they emphasize the child's relationship to the mother; they keep the child allied with the mother against the outside world. In this connection, Lebra reports that Japanese mothers rarely directly embarrass or ridicule their children themselves; instead they talk about how *others* will laugh or tease the child and how not only the child but the mother too will suffer.

Lanham: The Positive Emphasis of Compliance Training of Japanese Children

Lanham (1956, 1962) did her field study in an urbanizing city of 35,000 first, in 1951 to 1952 and, again, in 1960. Combining questionnaires, interviews, and participant observation, she studied parents of children aged from 3 years to the early teens. Lanham emphasized the extremely positive nature of child training in Japan.

> The least one can say is that parents believe that proper training of children is positive rather than negative. . . . Children are told that they are good, *ii*, great or wonderful, *erai*, and clever, *orikoo* . . . . The strongest negative sanction used to enforce compliance is the verbal threat of sickness. . . . (1962, pp. 144–65)

Regarding socialization goals, she states:

> The mother's efforts are therefore not directed toward herself or the achievement and status of her offspring, but rather to the training of her children in proper interpersonal relationships. She will internalize and blame on herself her children's failure. (1962, p. 197).

Japanese mothers' concern with compliance stems from their fear that the child will not do well outside of the family and may hurt the feelings of other persons. In the United States, Lanham believes, maternal concern about compliance stems from a fear of disobedience. By contrast, for Japanese mothers, obedience itself is not considered a desired goal. These mothers deeply understand the reason why a child does not comply and do not feel the need for authoritarian control. They also believe that harsh punishment for noncompliance and misbehavior may lead to weakening of the mother-child emotional tie.

Important Observational Studies Making Japan-United States Comparisons

The descriptions and generalizations reviewed regarding goals and methods of socializing children in Japan compared with those in the United States remain to be supported by carefully designed cross-cultural studies. The classic research of Caudill and his associates (Caudill & Weinstein, 1969) on early mother-infant interaction in both Japan and the United States and a recent study by Hess and Azuma of Japanese and American families are examples of steps in the needed direction (Azuma, Kashiwagi & Hess, 1981; Conroy et al. 1980).

Caudill's Studies of Mother-Infant Interaction

Early observational studies directly examining mother-infant interaction in Japan and comparing it with mother-infant interaction in the United States suggest major differences between the interactional styles of the two cultures and provide some empirical support for the hypothesis that the mother-child relationship in Japan is extremely close. Caudill and Weinstein present data suggesting that American mothers rely more on verbal modes of interaction, whereas Japanese mothers more often emphasize close, physical contact. They note that American mothers act as if they want a vocal, active baby and Japanese mothers as if they want a quiet, contented baby.

According to Caudill (1971), an American mother views her baby as a separate and autonomous being. Therefore, she helps the infant to learn ways of actively expressing his or her needs and wishes. In contrast, a Japanese mother views her baby much more as an extension of herself (complementing the baby's sense of oneness postulated by Doi) and feels that she knows what is best for him or her. Thus, she has less need for encouraging *distal* expressive communication, and with the constant physical proximity between the two, there is much less need for *verbal* communication.

Caudill conducted a follow-up study of his original subjects when the children were 2½ and 6-years-old to determine whether the differences in behavior observed in Japan and in the United States during infancy led to parallel differences at later ages (Caudill and Schooler, 1973). The following statement summarizes the conclusions of the follow-up study.

> Compared to Japanese, Americans are more active, more vocally and physically emotional, more independent, and more likely to manipulate functionally both their social and physical environment. . . . (Caudill and Schooler, 1973, pp. 335–36).

With a sample of only twenty American and twenty Japanese children, Caudill and his colleagues were able to demonstrate meaningful and consistent cross-cultural differences in the behavior of children and their caretakers which persist from infancy through early childhood. They argued that the differences observed in infant behavior in the two cultures were most easily explained by early learning in response to differing maternal expectations and behaviors and were not due to genetic differences between the groups. A later study by Caudill and Frost (1973) attempted to substantiate this interpretation by replicating Caudill's methods with a sample of twenty-one Japanese-American mothers and infants.

The mothers that Caudill and Frost studied were third generation Japanese-Americans (Sansei), a group well integrated into the American middle class. Their behavior with their fourth-generation, genetically pure Japanese infants (Yonsei) was therefore expected, on the basis of Caudill's environmentalist hypothesis, to resemble that of other middle-class American mothers more closely than that of middle-class mothers in Japan. For the most part, Caudill and Frost's findings accorded with their expectations: Japanese-American mothers, like other American mothers, chatted more to their 3 to 4 month-old infants than did Japanese mothers. Their infants were also more active and vocalized happily more frequently, and unhappily less frequently, than babies observed in Japan. Thus, Caudill and Frost concluded that differences found by Caudill and Weinstein between infants in Japan and in the United States were primarily the result of culturally determined social interactions rather than of genetic factors, such as racial differences in emotionality.

Caudill and Weinstein's study, based on data collected more than twenty years ago, has been replicated recently by Sengoku, Davitz, and Davitz (1981). However, some cohort differences were found: according to these researchers, contemporary Japanese mothers are more likely to play with their infants, and American mothers are more likely to indulge their infants' negative states than were their counterparts two decades earlier. Nevertheless, basic differences between the two groups still remained.

Hess and Azuma

Although the primary focus of this study was the influence of maternal variables on the cognitive development of elementary-school children, Robert Hess, Hiroshi Azuma, and their colleagues did collect important interview and questionnaire data on social and emotional variables as well (Azuma et al.; Conroy et al.). Furthermore, as mentioned above, theirs is one of the few studies to date (besides those by Caudill and his followers) to directly compare Japanese and American parents and children using identical methods of data collection.

With regard to child-rearing goals, they reported that the developmental tasks mothers believe should be mastered before age 6 differ between the two countries. Japanese mothers are more likely to value emotional maturity, compliance to adult authority outside the home and courtesy in social exchange, whereas American mothers believe verbal assertiveness and social skills deserve more attention. Japanese mothers are more concerned than American mothers with the child's ability to relate appropriately to others and to control his or her emotions.

Japanese and American mothers also differ greatly in their strategies for regulating the behavior of their children. Japanese mothers are more likely to base their requests on appeals to feelings and the consequences of the particular behavior (for example, "that makes your dad angry"). American mothers, on the other hand, tend to base their appeals to the child on the authority of their role as mother. Again, these data seem to indicate that the Japanese mother wishes to avoid confrontation. Instead, in attempting to gain compliance, she assumes that the close bond with her child will bring him or her to conform with her wishes.

Summary

The theoretical and empirical work concerning the socioemotional development of the Japanese child surveyed thus far contains a number of consistent observations concerning the nature of mother-child interaction, maternal attitudes, and early social development in Japan. Many of the observations we have highlighted are very relevant to the emerging trends in the study of socioemotional development defined earlier. For example, most investigators have remarked on the Japanese mother's emphasis of nonverbal means of communicating with her child, for example, through physical contact and efforts both to avoid expressing negative feelings toward the child and to prevent eliciting negative emotions in him or her by her own actions. The Japanese mother's nonverbal communication style and her attitudes and socialization goals have been hypothesized to account for many of the profound differences in subsequent personality, group allegiance, and school behavior existing between Japanese and American children. A significant area of future research will be to confirm these early anthropological and psychological hypotheses about the relationship between early mother-child emotional communication styles and subsequent individual and group behavior.

In addition, the repeated descriptions of the closeness of the mother-child bond and the rarity with which infants are apart from their mothers suggest that empirical study of the development of the attachment relationship, separation reactions, and stranger distress in Japanese children is of particular significance.

The reports of Caudill and Weinstein and others indicate that Japanese infants are less active, less expressive of positive affect, and more expressive of negative vocal effect than American infants. The Vogels' reports that Japanese children are often shy and inhibited in new situations suggest potentially important child characteristics to consider in the current, transactional approach to social development.

We will devote the remainder of this chapter to a description of ongoing research on a number of the major issues in socioemotional development, discussing theoretical and methodological advances which have given them particular significance both in the study of the Japanese child and in developmental psychology in general.

The Study of Emotional Communication in Japanese and American Infants

Emotions: From Dependent to Independent Variables

One of the new directions in the contemporary study of emotion involves consideration of the role of emotions as determinants of both social and intrapersonal processes (Campos et al. 1983). For many years, the study of emotions was dominated by the search for the pattern of emergence of discrete emotional states. Numerous studies investigated when phenomena, such as the social smile, laughter, anger, stranger, and separation anxiety, fear of heights, fear of looming stimuli, and attachment could first be identified. This search for times of onset typified the study of emotions as dependent variables. Moreover, it reflected a widespread belief of the time—that emotions were processes secondary to more fundamental perceptual or cognitive phenomena and were epiphenomenal, or noncausal, byproducts. The presupposition that emotions were epiphenomenal prevented psychologists from exploring the possibility that *receptive* aspects of emotional behavior may have crucial importance in the regulation of behaviors of human infants, children, and adults.

Several factors have led researchers to balance their interest in emotions as *outcomes*, with exploration of emotions as *determinants*. In recent years, strong evidence has been obtained showing emotional expressions are not cultural constructions, as was once believed, but are biologically adaptive patterns with an evolutionary history (Ekman, 1973; Izard, 1971). The most important evidence for the biological basis of certain emotional states has been the cross-cultural research showing that recognition of the facial expressions of anger, joy, fear, surprise, sadness, disgust, contempt, and possibly a few other states was apparently universal. The recognition of emotional expressions was evident even in preliterate cultures with minimal exposure to films, photographs, and other representations of facial expressions of members of literate societies (Ekman, So-rensen & Friesen, 1969).

There were two immediate implications of this work. One was to provide behavioral researchers with a metric specific to discrete emotional states, such as anger, joy, fear, surprise, sadness, disgust/contempt, and, possibly, interest. The other implication was to shift the role of facial expressions from *response patterns* to *social signals* with possibly universal behavior regulatory consequences.

The Study of Mother-to-Infant Emotional Communication: Japan and the United States

There are several reasons for studying similarities and differences in the conse-quences of emotional expressions for Japanese and American infants. First, it should be remembered that the personal space of the mother and child differs in the two countries. Japanese mothers are much closer physically to their infants, carrying them for longer periods of time each day and until a much later age in the baby's life than do American mothers (Caudill & Weinstein; Lebra). In ad-dition, Japanese mothers frequently carry their infants in a different position than many American mothers—on their backs rather than in front of them. These differences in amount and type of physical proximity are likely to influence the channels used for emotional communication, with tactile and low-intensity vocal expressions being used by the Japanese mother more frequently than by the Amer-ican mother.

Moreover, according to Doi (1971) and Vogel (1967), the Japanese mother emphasized indulgence of the child's emotional states more than does her Amer-ican counterpart. Child-rearing practices in Japan are not directed toward eliciting obedience as a goal in itself, but toward maintaining positive interaction between mother and child, with infrequent use of punishment (Lanham, 1962; Lebra). Compared with American mothers, Japanese mothers less frequently use appeals to maternal authority and more frequently employ appeals for empathy (Conroy et al.). Accordingly, there may be differences evident in anger expression even in infancy between the two cultures. Specifically, the reception of anger signals must be a rarer event for the Japanese child than for the American.

As a first step in the study of differences between the two cultures in emo-tional regulation, we investigated the consequences of vocalic expression of emo-tions directed toward the infant. Our sample consisted of infants in Denver, Colorado, and in Sapporo, Hokkaido. Both groups were 11 months of age and from middle- and upper-middle class families. Different groups of infants were presented with vocal expressions of joy, anger, or fear when an interesting but somewhat abruptly moving toy entered the room. Dependent variables included the latency to resume movement following the utterance of the vocal affect signal, the distance moved to approach the mother following each signal, and the ten-dency to approach another similar toy on a subsequent trial.

The results of this study reveal quite striking differences between Japanese and American infants in their responses following the mother's utterance of an *anger* vocal expression. However, there are no cross-national differences following the mother's utterance of either joy or fearfulness. For instance, the latency to resume locomotion toward the toy in Japanese infants following vocalizations of joy (N = 11) was 8.08 seconds, following fear (N = 4), was 17.50 seconds, and following anger (N = 10), it was 48.89 seconds. For 11-month-old American infants, the corresponding figures were: for joy (N = 12), 8.00 seconds, for fear (N = 12), 14.65 seconds, and for anger (N = 12), 17.50 seconds.

Thus, the Japanese infants showed far greater behavioral inhibition following maternal vocalization of an anger expression when they moved toward a toy than did the American infants. This finding suggests that by 11 months of age, the vocal expression of anger has already assumed much greater behavior regulatory control among the Japanese infants (for whom it may be a signal reserved only for extreme occasions of discipline) than it is for the American infants (who may hear anger expressions much more frequently, thus attenuating their effectiveness). The study raises a number of other unanswered questions, however. Is the Japanese infant more prone to seek emotional information from the mother than is the American infant? Is the long-lasting effect of the emotional communication from the mother likely to be greater in the Japanese infant than in the American infant? Is the use of vocal expressions of emotion more effective in Japanese mother-infant dyads than the use of facial expressions? At what age is the Japanese infant's greater responsivity to anger vocalizations first evident?

Differences in Manifestation of Attachment in Japan and in the United States

Studies of emotional communication stress the immediate effects of emotional signals by the mother and other significant social figures in the regulation of the infant's behavior. However, there are also significant long-lasting consequences of emotional communication. Perhaps the most important of these arises from the mother's responsiveness to the *infant's* social signals. According to ethological attachment theory (Ainsworth et al. 1978; Bowlby, 1969; 1973; 1980), such maternal responsiveness shapes the quality of the attachment relationship, teaching the child trust in the caregiver's availability and confidence in the child's own efficacy (Lamb, 1981).

Ethological attachment theory proposes that the quality of the attachment relationship is manifested in two general ways: by the infant's use of the mother as a secure base for exploration and by seeking her proximity as a haven of safety when in a state of fear or distress. To measure these individual differences, Ainsworth and her colleagues devised a paradigm called that Strange Situation (Ainsworth et al.). This paradigm has become the most widely used method of assessing the individual differences in attachment behaviors in infancy. In the United

States, these individual differences in Strange Situation performance have been reported to reflect differences in the mother-infant interaction, as assessed in the home (for example, Ainsworth et al.), to be stable over significant periods of time, given a stable social and economic family context (Waters, 1978). The differences in performance also predict individual differences in social interaction, peer relationships, problem-solving competence, and preschool teacher ratings of problem behavior (Sroufe, 1983). The Strange Situation consists of an 8-episode procedure involving an opportunity for the child to play with toys in the mother's presence, two separations from the mother, two entrances by a stranger, and two reunions with the mother.

Based principally upon the infant's reactions to reunions with the mother, three broad classifications of individual differences are obtained and designated as A, B, and C. Group A (or "avoidantly attached") babies are characterized by conspicuous avoidance of the mother upon reunion, by failure to cling to her when held, and by minimal differences in their reactions to reunions with the mother and the stranger. Group B (or "securely attached") babies tend to seek proximity to, and contact with, the mother when distressed, especially during reunions. Finally, Group C (or "ambivalently attached") infants, like B infants, manifest strong contact-maintaining and proximity-seeking behavior, but, unlike B infants, tend to resist interactions and contacts with their mothers upon reunion. They are also difficult to console and prone to excessive crying. In the United States, the A and the C classifications are often assumed to reflect poor mother-infant interaction and "insecurity" of attachment, while the B classification is assumed to reflect a "secure" mother-infant relationship.

There are at least two ways in which paradigms like the Strange Situation can be used to study attachment cross-culturally. One way is the literal application of scoring rules and procedures developed in one culture to the scoring of infant performance in the other culture. The second way is the use of the paradigm as a rich source of individual differences in emotional and attachment-related behaviors without assuming that morphologically-similar behavior patterns in the two cultures imply similar quality of attachment. We will now describe a line of research comparing Japanese and American infants' attachment behaviors in the Strange Situation which, initially using the Strange Situation in the former way, will shift to treating the attachment assessment in the latter way upon acquiring a sufficient body of longitudinal data (Miyake, Chen & Campos, in press).

We earlier described how in Japan the interactive relationship between the infant and the mother is one of close physical contact and infrequent separation. The mother-infant interaction is also one in which the mother encourages strong ties by her infant and in which she strives to avoid harsh discipline or unnecessary frustration. This suggests that Japanese infants will have an attachment relationship qualitatively different from that typically seen in American mother-infant dyads. Specifically, American mother-infant relationships involve less physical contact and more distal interaction. Furthermore, Japanese mothers use baby-sitters so infrequently, and are so rarely separated from their infants, that the context of testing infants in standard attachment paradigms like the Strange Situation is also likely to be much more stressful to the Japanese infant than to western babies accustomed to brief separations from their mothers.

For these reasons, Miyake, Chen, and Campos predicted that the attachment classifications of Japanese infants in the Strange Situation would be very different from those in the United States. On the basis of previous findings, which suggested that the more distressing the Strange Situation is for a child, the more likely he or she is to be classified as a C infant and the less likely he or she is to be classified as an A infant (Campos et al. 1983, Miyake, Chen & Campos in press), they specifically predicted a much higher proportion of C babies in the Japanese sample than in normative American ones.

This prediction was strongly supported. In the United States and several other western countries such as Sweden, the distribution of A, B, and C infants is approximately 20 percent, 65 percent, and 15 percent. By contrast, Miyake, Chen, and Campos reported in two separate cohorts that there were *no* A infants and approximately 35 percent C infants in the Japanese, the rest being classified either as B infants or as a separate classification termed "pseudo-C." (The latter category was used because in a few cases infants met some, but not all, of the criteria required for classification into the C group). The expected behavior pattern of strong attachment of the Japanese infant to the mother and the desire to prevent separation thus seemed to be confirmed in this study.

The Miyake, Chen, and Campos study revealed another important finding relevant to assessment of Strange Situation behavior. Because the study was longitudinal from birth, it was possible to determine whether emotional reactivity in the neonatal period predicted later Strange Situation performance. As was mentioned earlier, previous work with the Strange Situation had suggested that any factor likely to make it more stressful to the infant is likely to result in the infant being classified as a C baby. Besides the context of testing, another factor influencing the stressfulness of the paradigm is the child's own endogenous threshold for distress (i.e., irritability). Individual differences in irritability have proven to be stable in the first year of life (Korner et al. 1981), and in some studies (for example, Crockenberg, 1981; Waters et al. 1980), neonatal irritability has predicted subsequent C-like behavior. Accordingly, irritability was targeted for study in the neonatal period, with the expectation that irritable infants will be likely to be categorized as C babies at 1 year of age.

The measurement of irritability took place when the infant was assessed in the hospital on the second and fifth day of life and used Bell, Wellor, & Waldrop's (1971) response to the interruption of sucking procedure. This task was chosen because it permits estimation of threshold to distress, a parameter linked closely to infant temperament (Goldsmith & Campos, 1982).

Once again, the prediction of Miyake, Chen, and Campos was confirmed. There was a statistically significant trend for more babies who cried as neonates on the interruption of sucking task to be classified as C or pseudo-C infants when tested in the Strange Situation 12 months later. In contrast, no meaningful predictions were obtained on a noncry index, the latency to any observable (noncry) response on the same task. These data thus show an infant's disposition to become irritable can make an important contribution to patterns of attachment behavior.

In summary, research on attachment classifications to date has documented the existence of major differences in the Strange Situation performance of Japanese infants relative to those in other countries. However, the greater incidence of "C" infants in Japan does not in any way imply that the Japanese infant is more likely to be "ambivalently attached" than is the American infant. Rather, it points out the importance of taking into account the cultural context of testing—especially the much greater stress produced among Japanese infants by even brief separations from the mother. In this regard, it is interesting that Durrett, Otaki, and Richards (1984) recently reported a study of Japanese infants in Tokyo in which distributions of Strange Situation classifications were found similar to those obtained in the United States. It is thus not inevitably the case that Japanese infants will be overrepresented in the "C" classification. It will be necessary to review the total pattern of home and Strange Situation behavior in this study before it will be possible to determine which patterns of attachment behaviors in the Strange Situation in Japan reflect emotionally unstable or problematic mother-infant interactions in the first year of life and which patterns predict subsequent social and cognitive competence.

Temperament: Inhibition and Irritability in American and in Japanese infants

The findings relating neonatal irritability to attachment assessments highlight the importance of the topic of temperament. There has been a renaissance of interest in this concept of conjunction with the move toward more transactional conceptions of human development. Temperament refers to relatively stable individual difference dispositions which are particularly evident in the intensity and temporal patterning of emotional arousal and expression. Although many researchers feel temperament is genetically or constitutionally determined, we believe that temperamental dispositions can not only influence the parent-child interaction, but also can be affected by it. The bidirectionality of influence of temperamental dispositions is reflected in the popularity of the concept of "goodness of fit" (for example, Lerner & Lerner, 1983).

A number of important dimensions of temperament have been shown to be stable, to influence the parent-infant interaction, and to affect engagement in cognitive tasks. These dimensions include activity level (Goldsmith & Gottesman, 1981), irritability (Korner et al.; Crockenberg), and fearfulness (Rothbart, 1981).

Recently, another temperamental disposition having these characteristics has been identified: inhibition or lack of inhibition to unfamiliar social and nonsocial events.

Inhibition and Lack of Inhibition to the Unfamiliar

Inhibition to the unfamiliar is evident in the first year of life in the infant's reactions to a number of events: to the approach of strangers, to a dishabituation stimulus, to novel environments, and to other unfamiliar events. Inhibition is especially clear after the first birthday when the child encounters an unfamiliar peer (Kagen et al. 1984b). About 10 percent of American 2-year-olds consistently show an extreme degree of inhibition to nonthreatening but unfamiliar events, for example, an unfamiliar woman talking to them. Inhibited children stop playing, become quiet, and assume a wary facial expression, although they may recover after 10 to 20 minutes and eventually play with the stranger in a relaxed manner. In contrast, other infants will quickly smile, talk to the adult stranger, and allow her to play with them within a few seconds. Inhibited children are usually characterized by their parents as shy, cautious, or timid, whereas uninhibited children are usually called sociable, bold, exploratory, or fearless.

The temperamental dimension of inhibition is significant for at least four reasons. First of all, it shows remarkable stability. In one study of Chinese American infants tested in a day-care setting, significant stability was obtained between 7 and 21 months on cardiac indices of this temperamental disposition (Kagan, Kearsley, & Zelazo, 1978). In another study of children falling into the top and bottom 10 percent on assessments of inhibition as toddlers, stability has been evident between 21 months and 5.5 years of age on indices of both heart rate and behavior (Kagan, 1984).

Second, individual differences in inhibition have been shown to have physiological correlates: inhibited children show higher levels of sympathetic nervous system activation, especially during mild cognitive stress. Signs include high and steady heart rate levels, greater pupillary dilatation, higher secretion of cortisol levels, and decreased sinus arrhythmia. (Sinus arrhythmia refers to the tendency of heart rate to increase and decrease either synchronously or slightly out of phase with the inhalation and exhalation phases of the respiratory cycle.) They also show an increase in fundamental frequency and decrease in variability of the pitch periods of the vocal spectrum when they are speaking single words under mildly stressful conditions (Kagan et al., 1984a,b).

Third, the concept of inhibition links infant temperament to research on the adult personality dimension of introversion-extraversion. Like inhibition, introversion-extraversion has a physiological underpinning (Eysenck, 1967) and overlaps strongly with sociability (Scarr & Kidd, 1983). It also shows a strong genetic loading (Scarr & Kidd), like that which is hypothesized for temperamental inhibition.

Fourth, inhibition shows important external correlates, being related to cognitive tasks, disturbances in body function, and compliance. For instance, Reznick (1982) reported that infants with high and stable heart rates during a baseline period preceding the presentation of stimuli in a category extraction task are extremely vigilant. They were more likely to show maximal dishabituation of fixation to a dishabituation stimulus than were uninhibited infants. Temperamental inhibition has also been reported to be related to the likelihood of experiencing nightmares and sleep disturbances in early childhood. Inhibited infants are also more likely to be constipated and to show frequent and unusual fears. In addition, parents of inhibited children are very likely to report their infants are obedient (Kagan et al., 1984b).

The concept of temperamental inhibition has important implications for understanding Japanese mother-child interaction. Many have noted that Japanese children seem to learn social rules very easily, like Kagan's inhibited children. Moreover, Vogel has commented on the hesitancy of Japanese children in novel situations such as entrance to school. The impression is that Japanese children are on the whole more inhibited in these circumstances than comparable groups of American children. Because it is unclear whether such differences between Japanese and American infants are biologically or environmentally determined, it is important to determine whether this characteristic is already partly evident in very early infancy, whether the parent-child interaction brings it about, or whether both endogenous and environmental factors interact to create the disposition.

There is a body of evidence suggesting that some temperamental differences between Japanese and American infants are already observable in the neonatal period. For example, Kosawa (1980) reported that 8 of 26 items on the Brazelton Neonatal Behavioral Assessment Scale were significantly different in Japanese newborns than in the American standardization sample for that scale. Orientation to voice and rattle were much higher in American than in Japanese neonates. Japanese infants also showed more lability of states, more startle, less tremulousness, less cuddliness, less consolability, and less motor readiness (pull-to-sit) than did American infants. In addition, Shand (personal communication) has reported that Japanese infants show greater activity levels in the first 3 months of life than do American infants.

The studies to date have not controlled important contextual factors (such as perinatal medical practices) that may confound differences in neonatal behavior between the two cultures. It is unclear, therefore, whether the observed differences between Japanese and American neonates reflect endogenously based racial differences in temperament or result from the mother-infant transaction. Moreover, there have to date been no studies on the important temperamental dimension of inhibition. To test whether Japanese and American children differ on this dimension, they need to be studied under comparable circumstances involving mild cognitive and social stress, while cardiac, respiratory, vocal and pupillary reactions are measured.

Japanese and American Social-Class Differences in Child-Rearing Attitudes

The attitudes of the mother about the importance of certain behaviors in herself or her child and about the appropriateness of different techniques for dealing with her child are important considerations in the interpretation of her interactive behavior with the child, especially when comparing behavior across cultures or subcultures such as social classes. Recently, Kagan has applied an innovative measurement technique based upon selective recall to the comparison of Japanese and American mother's attitudes regarding three issues frequently highlighted in our discussions of emotional communication and mother-child interaction in Japan: expression of affection, importance of emotional independence for the child, and restrictive versus permissive approaches to child rearing.

The traditional procedures designed to assess the attitudes of adults, both within and across cultures, have been limited largely to direct verbal report obtained either through questionnaire or interview. These traditional methods are more likely to be valid when a particular belief does not have an alternative, is relatively free of an evaluative dimension, and is easily accessible to conscious report than when the attitude has an opposite with which it is incompatible, a strong value attached to it, and no accessibility to conscious report. Direct questioning is likely to be more valid when a person is asked to judge, for example, the desirability of one soap over another than when asked to judge the desirability of a law permitting or denying federal funds for abortion.

For more controversial issues, it is necessary to have other indices of the degree to which a person is committed to a particular attitude. One possibility for the evaluation of differential commitment is the selective recall of information favoring one or the other of two complementary attitudes presented simultaneously. The use of selective recall is based on the hypothesis that when the amount of information favorable or in opposition to an attitude is equal, than a person's recall will be better for the information that supports his or her preferred belief.

This method has been used to measure the differences that exist between middle- and working-class mothers on child-rearing attitudes. Briefly, mothers listened to recorded essays on three different themes—expression of affection, encouragement of independence, and restrictiveness of child rearing. Each essay contained balanced arguments favorable to or opposing the two sides of each theme.

The first essay, on the importance of giving infants a great deal of physical affection, argued either that kissing and hugging would make the child more secure or that too much physical affection can spoil the child and make him or her too dependent upon the parents for approval. The second essay contrasted the importance of the child attaining emotional independence from the family with the desirability of retaining a close dependent tie to his or her parents throughout adolescence and early adulthood. The third essay compared a restrictive and a permissive socialization regimen. The argument for the former was based on the desirability of rearing a child who will be reasonably obedient to authority and, as a result, will do well in school and gain job security. The argument for permissiveness was based on the desirability of socializing a child who is not overly fearful of parents and other authority figures and, hence, is resistant to coercion and free to pursue gratification of his or her motives. The measure obtained from these essays was the number of words recalled that favored each side of the argument, after tangential comments and successive repetitions of words had been eliminated.

Data obtained on American samples revealed that middle-class, in contrast to working-class, mothers recalled more of the proaffection than the antiaffection theme, and more of the prorestrictive than the antirestrictive theme. There were no class differences with respect to the essay on independence.

When this procedure was replicated on twenty middle- and twenty working-class Japanese mothers living in Hokkaido, it was found that, as in the United States, middle-class Japanese mothers recalled more words from the proaffection than the antiaffection theme, whereas working-class mothers showed the opposite profile. This suggests that across both cultures middle-class status is associated with a more favorable attitude toward physical affection. Like the Americans, the Japanese showed no class differences with respect to the essay on independence. By contrast, there was a social-class effect on attitudes toward restrictive versus permissive child rearing, in the direction opposite to that found in the United States. Middle-class mothers in Japan were more likely to recall words favoring permissiveness than were working-class Japanese mothers. This finding is consistent with previous reports discussed earlier, indicating that middle-class Japanese mothers want to avoid creating anger and fear in their child, for these emotions impede the establishment of the interdependent relation which is the goal of socialization. On the other hand, many more working- than middle-class Japanese mothers believe the child must be prepared for the difficult challenges of life, especially the financial pressures associated with economic disadvantage. As a result, working-class mothers feel they should not spoil their children with too much affection or yield to their demands for material gifts.

These results suggest that the use of selective memory is a potentially useful tool in cross-cultural studies of parental attitudes. They already demonstrate that the belief in a universal Japanese maternal interactional style favoring permissiveness may be incorrect. Future research needs to address the question of how attitudes influence child-rearing practices, emotional communication, and the child's characteristic social dispositions.

General Conclusions

In this chapter, we have reviewed some of the classic and contemporary work on the socioemotional development of Japanese infants, especially as it differs from that of American babies. We have noted several consistent themes in both the anthropological and psychological literature pointing to the physically closer, less verbal, and less conflictual nature of the relationship Japanese mothers and infants maintain. These observations have been borne out in recent empirical studies. We have seen how Japanese infants, possibly because of the rarity of anger expressions from their mothers, are by 11 months of age already very sensitive to the expression of that emotion. We have also presented evidence that Japanese infant attachment classifications can differ dramatically from those typically seen in western cultures like the United States, apparently reflecting the great impact separations from the mother have for the Japanese baby. We have reviewed work suggesting that temperamental tendencies, such as irritability and inhibition, play an important role in the behavior of both American and Japanese infants and suggested these temperamental traits may be evident very early in life. Finally, we have documented how the mother's attitudes toward child rearing differs in significant ways within cultures as a function of social class.

Numerous issues important for contemporary theories of emotion remain to be investigated. These issues deal with the origins of expression and perception of emotion in the two cultures, the comparative investigation of endogenous temperamental differences between Japanese and American infants, and how these differences condition the mother-infant interaction. Additional issues relate to the development of more complex emotions, such as shame and guilt, and how the expressions of more basic emotions, such as anger, become socialized in the course of the first few months of life. Research is also needed on questions, such as that on the differential effectiveness of different emotional expressions in eliciting child compliance and self-regulation and on how attitudes toward school tasks and academic performance may differ as a result of the mother's emotional-communicational style.

Given the rapid advances currently being made in the technology of assessment of facial and vocal expressions of emotion, in the physiology of both emotional and temperamental states, and in the quantification of social interactions, we feel the time is ripe for major collaborative research efforts involving both Japanese and American investigators on the cross-national investigation of socioemotional development.

References

Ainsworth, M., Blehar, M., Waters, E., & Wall, S. (1978). *Patterns of attachment: A psychological study of the Strange Situation*. Hillsdale, N.J.: Lawrence Erlbaum Associates.

Anderson, J. W. (1972). Attachment behavior out of doors. In N. Blurton-Jones (Ed.), *Ethological studies of child behavior* (pp. 199–215). Cambridge: Cambridge University Press.

Azuma, H., Kashiwagi, K., & Hess, R. (1981). *The influence of maternal teaching style upon the cognitive development of children.* Tokyo: University of Tokyo Press. (In Japanese)

Bell, R. Q., Weller, G., & Waldrop, M. (1971). Newborn and preschooler: Organization of behavior and relations between periods. *Monographs of the Society for Research in Child Development, 36* (Serial No. 142).

Benedict, R. (1946). *The chrysanthemum and the sword: Patterns of Japanese culture.* Cleveland, OH: World.

Boccia, M., & Campos, J. (1983, April). *Matenral emotional signaling: Its effect on infant's reaction to strangers.* Paper presented at the meeting of the SRCD, Detroit.

Bower, G. (1981). Mood and Memory. *American Psychologist, 36,* 128–148.

Bowlby, J. (1969). *Attachment and loss. Vol. 1. Attachment.* New York: Basic Books.

———. (1973). *Attachment and loss. Vol. 2. Separation: Anxiety and anger.* New York: Basic Books.

———. (1980). *Attachment and loss. Vol. 3. Loss.* New York: Basic Books.

Campos, J. J., Barrett, K. C., Lamb, M. E., Goldsmith, H. H., & Stenberg, C. (1983). Socioemotional development. In M. M. Haith & J. J. Campos (Vol. Eds.), *Handbook of child psychology. Vol. 2. Infancy and psychobiology* (pp. 783–915). New York: John Wiley & Sons.

Campos, J. J., Emde, R. N., Gaensbauer, T. J., & Henderson, C. (1975). Cardiac and behavioral interrelationships in the reactions of infants to strangers. *Developmental Psychology, 11,* 589–601.

Campos, J. J., & Stenberg, C. (1981). Perception, appraisal, and emotion: The onset of social referencing. In M. E. Lamb & L. R. Sherrod (Eds.), *Infant social cognition: Empirical and theoretical considerations* (pp. 273–314). Hillsdale, N.J.: Lawrence Erlbaum Associates.

Carr, S. J., Dabbs, J. M., & Carr, T. S. (1975). Mother-infant attachment: Importance of the mother's visual field. *Child Development, 46,* 331–338.

Caudill, W. (1971). Tiny dramas: vocal communication between mother and infant in Japanese and American families. In W. Lebra (Ed.), *Mental health research in Asia and the Pacific,* Vol. II. Honolulu: East-West Center Press.

Caudill, W., and Frost, L. A. (1973). A comparison of maternal care and infant behavior in Japanese-American, American, and Japanese families. In W. Lebra (Ed.), *Mental health research in Asia and the Pacific,* Vol. III. Honolulu: East-West Center Press.

Caudill, W., and Weinstein, H. (1969). Maternal care and infant behavior in Japan and America. *Psychiatry, 32* (1), 12–43.

Caudill, W., and Schooler, C. (1973). Child behavior and child rearing in Japan and the United States: An interim report. *The Journal of Nervous and Mental Disease, 157*(4), 323–339.

Conroy, M., Hess, R. D., Azuma, H., & Kashiwagi, K. (1980). Maternal strategies for regulating children's behavior: Japanese and American families. *Journal of Cross-Cultural Psychology, 11,* 153–72.

Crockenberg, S. B. (1981). Infant irritability, mother responsiveness, and social support influences on the security of infant-mother attachment. *Child Development, 52,* 857–865.

Doi, T. (1973). *The anatomy of dependence.* Tokyo: Kodansha International.

Durrett, M. E., Otaki, M., & Richards, P. (1984). Attachment and the mother's perception of support from the father. *International Journal of Behavioral Development, 7,* 167–176.

Ekman, P. (1972). Universals and cultural differences in facial expressions of emotion. In J. Cole (Ed.), *Nebraska symposium on motivation.* Lincoln, Neb.: University of Nebraska Press.

———. (1973). Cross-cultural studies of facial expressions. In P. Ekman (Ed.), *Darwin and facial expressions: A century of research in review* (pp. 169–222). New York: Academic Press.

Ekman, P., Sorensen, E. R., & Friesen, W. V. (1969). Pan-cultural elements in facial displays of emotion. *Science, 164,* 86–88.

Eysenck, H. J. (1967). *The biological basis of personality.* Springfield, Ill.: Charles C Thomas.

Goldsmith, H. H., & Campos, J. J. (1982). Toward a theory of infant temperament. In R. Emde & R. Harmon (Eds.), *The development of attachment and affiliative systems.* New York: Plenum Press.

Goldsmith, H. H., & Gottesman, I. I. (1981). Origins of variation in behavioral style: A longitudinal study of temperament in young twins. *Child Development, 52,* 91–103.

Hara, H., & Wagatsuma, H. (1974). *Shitsuke* [Child rearing]. Tokyo: Kobundoh.

Holden, G. W. (1983). Avoiding conflict: Mothers as tacticians in the supermarket. *Child Development, 54,* 233–240.

Izard, C. E. (1971). *Human emotions.* New York: Plenum Press.

Kagan, J. (1974). Discrepancy, temperament and infant distress. In M. Lewis & L. Rosenblum (Eds.), *The origins of fear.* New York: John Wiley & Sons.

———. (1984). *The nature of the child.* New York: Basic Books.

Kagan, J., Kearsley, R., & Zelazo, P. (1978). *Infancy: Its place in human development.* Cambridge, Mass.: Harvard University Press.

Kagan, J., Reznick, J., & Snidman, N. (1984, April). *Behavioral inhibition to the unfamiliar.* Paper presented at the meetings of the International Conference on Infant Studies, New York.

Kagan, J., Reznick, J., Clarke, C., Snidman, N., & Garcia-Coll, C. (1984a). Cardiac correlates of behavioral inhibition in the young child. In M. Coles, J. Jennings, & J. Stern (Eds.), *Psychophysiological perspectives: Festschrift for Beatrice and John Lacey* (pp. 216–228). New York: Van Nostrand Reinhold.

Kagan, J., Reznick, J., Clarke, C., Snidman, N., & Garcia-Coll, C. (1984b). Behavioral inhibition to the unfamiliar. *Child Development, 55,* 2212–2225.

Korner, A. F., Hutchinson, C. A., Koperski, J. A., Kraemer, H. C., & Schneider, P. A. (1981). Stability of individual differences of neonatal crying patterns. *Child Development, 52,* 83–90.

Kosawa, Y. (1980). *The influentiability of the infant upon the early development of mother-child relationships.* Unpublished doctoral dissertation, University of Tokyo.

Lamb, M. (1981). The development of trust and perceived effectance in infancy. In L. P. Lipsitt (Ed.), *Advances in infancy research* (Vol. 1). Norwood, N.J.: Ablex.

Lanham, B. (1956). Aspects of child care in Japan: Preliminary report. In D. Haring (Ed.), *Personal character and cultural milieu.* Syracuse: Syracuse University Press.

Lanham, B. (1962). Aspects of child-rearing in Kainan, Japan. Unpublished doctoral dissertation, Syracuse University.

Lebra, T. S. (1976). *Japanese patterns of behavior.* Honolulu: The University Press of Hawaii.

Lerner, J. V. & Lerner, R. M. (1983). Temperament and adaptation across the lifespan: Theoretical and empirical approaches. In P. B. Baltes & O. G. Brim (Eds.), *Life-span development and behavior* (Vol. 5), pp. 197–231.

Lewis, M., & Michalson, L. (1983). *Children's emotions and moods.* New York: Plenum Press.

Mahler, M., Pine, F., & Bergman, A. (1975). *The psychological birth of the human infant.* New York: Basic Books.

Miyake, K., Chen, S., & Campos, J. J. (in press). Infant temperament, mother's mode of interaction, and attachment in Japan: An interim report. In I. Breterton & E. Waters (Eds.), Growing points of attachment theory and research. *Monographs of the Society for Research in Child Development.*

Morsbach, H. (1973). Aspects of nonverbal communication in Japan. *Journal of Nervous and Mental Disease, 157,* 262–277.

Reznick, J. S. (1982). *Development of perceptual and lexical categories in the human infant.* Unpublished doctoral dissertation. University of Colorado.

Rothbart, M. K. (1981). Measurement of temperament in infancy. *Child Development, 52,* 569–578.

Schaffer, H. R. (1971). Cognitive structure and early social behavior. In H. R. Schaffer (Ed.), *The origin of human social relations* (pp. 247–261). New York: Academic Press.

Scarr, S., & Kidd, K. K. (1983). Developmental behavior genetics. In M. M. Haith & J. J. Campos (Vol. Eds.), *Handbook of child psychology. Vol. 2. Infancy and developmental psychobiology.* New York: John Wiley & Sons.

Sengoku, T. (1981, September 29–October 10). The changed infant: A Japanese-United States comparison of the 3-month-old infants. *Yomiuri Shimbun.* (In Japanese).

Sorce, J., Emde, R. N., Campos, J. J., & Klinnert, M. (in press). Maternal emotional signaling: Its effect on the visual cliff behavior of one-year-olds. *Developmental Psychology.* (In press).

Sorce, J., Emde, R. N., & Frank, (1982). Maternal referencing in normal and Down's syndrome infants: A longitudinal study. In R. N. Emde & R. J. Harmon (Eds.), *The development of attachment and affiliative systems: Psychobiological aspects.* New York: Plenum Press.

Sroufe, L. A. (1983). Individual patterns of adaption from infancy to preschool. In M. Perlmutter (Ed.), *Minnesota symposium on child psychology* (Vol. 16), Hillsdale, N.J.: Lawrence Erlbaum Associates.

Sroufe, L. A., & Waters, (1977). Attachment as an organizational construct. *Child Development, 48,* 1184–1199.

Vogel, E. (1967). *Japan's new middle class: The salaryman and his family in a Tokyo suburb.* Berkeley: University of California Press.

Vogel, E., and Vogel, S. (1961). Family security, personal immaturity, and emotional health in a Japanese sample. *Marriage and Family Living, 23,* 161–166.

Waters, E. (1978). The reliability and stability of individual differences in infant-mother attachment. *Child Development, 49,* 483–494.

Waters, E., Vaughn, B., & Eyelard, B. (1980). Individual differences in infant-mother attachment behavior at age one: Antecedents in neonatal behavior in an urban, economically disadvantaged sample. *Child Development, 51,* 208–216.

Whiting, J., & Child, I. (1953). *Child training and personality.* New Haven: Yale University Press.

Zajonc, R. (1980). Feeling and thinking: Preferences need no inferences. *American Psychologist, 35,* 151–175.

Two Courses of Expertise

Giyoo Hatano
Kayoko Inagaki

Several aspects of cognitive development can be conceptualized as processes of spontaneous expertise.[1] Starting with little or no documented declarative knowledge or rules, children—through accumulated experience—acquire domain-specific knowledge enabling them to solve various problems in the target domain. After briefly discussing the significance of this conceptualization, we shall propose three issues related to the processes of spontaneous expertise. These issues, we believe, are not only theoretically interesting in developmental research, but can be studied profitably through cross-cultural analysis.

What is significant about conceptualizing processes of cognitive development as processes of spontaneous expertise? It has been asserted that developmental or adult-child differences in cognition are similar to expert-novice differences (Brown & DeLoach, 1978). This would imply that adults and children differ primarily in the amount and structuredness of knowledge in the target domain; in other words, in explaining adult-child differences, maturational and/or domain-general cognitive variables are, at most, secondary. Thus, this assertion gives an answer to the question, "What develops?" It is domain-specific knowledge that develops.

To conceptualize the *processes* of cognitive development as those of spontaneous expertise goes a little further. It suggests an answer to the question, "How does it develop?" Undoubtedly, the processes of expertise are based upon the accumulation of experience, which consists largely of solving problems in a given domain. In achieving expertise, individuals, supervised by more capable members, solve increasingly complex problems in the domain, using relevant prior knowledge which is, in turn, gradually enriched and integrated. In Piagetian terminology (Piaget, 1950): a new problem situation is assimilated into preexisting knowledge; this results in accommodation of the knowledge. According to this conceptualization, the key concern in developmental research is thus, the analysis of relationships between problem solving and acquisition-integration of knowledge in a domain.

From Procedural to Conceptual Knowledge

Our first issue concerns the processes through which novices become adaptive experts—performing procedural skills efficiently, but also understanding the meaning and the nature of their object. In comprehending the object's nature, what role is played by repeated practice in daily life of the procedural skills involved? This issue seems quite similar to the one Piaget (1976, 1978) attempted to examine, but as will be seen, there are important differences.

In any society, less mature members acquire a body of procedural knowledge, that is, decision-rules as well as executive strategies, along with the skills necessary for applying that knowledge. Both the knowledge and its attendant skills comprise an important part of the culture. They are useful to their possessor in solving frequently encountered problems, thus increasing his or her competence as a member of the society. Such skills are therefore performed repeatedly. In a familiar environment, people behave quite effectively with only procedural knowledge, even without understanding. Usually they acquire procedural knowledge and skills without undue difficulty, through direct observation, verbal instructions, corrective feedback, and/or supervision. In this way, knowledge is transmitted from culture to individual, though individual selectivity also operates in the process.

However, since human beings have an intrinsic motivation to understand, we assume they are dissatisfied with any procedural competence they might achieve; they also want to understand, that is, to find the meaning of the pro-cedural skill. What is the distinction between the performance with and without such understanding? When do we consider that a skill is performed with under-standing? It is when the performer can explain why it works, that is, verbalize the principle involved. Or it is, at the least, when he or she can judge, not only the conventional version of the skill, but its variations as appropriate or inap-propriate and/or can modify it according to changes in constraints (Greeno, 1980).

These explicit and implicit forms of understanding seem possible only when the performer has more or less comprehensive knowledge of the nature of the object of the procedure and its surrounding "world." This knowledge gives mean-ing to each step of the skill and provides criteria for selection of possible alter-natives for each step within the procedure. It may even enable the performer to devise new procedures and to make new predictions. We will term this, *conceptual knowledge*. One form of conceptual knowledge is the so-called mental model (Gentner & Stevens, 1983), with which people can run mental simulations and make predictions or explanations about an unfamiliar object or situation that extends beyond their experience. By constructing conceptual knowledge, indi-viduals can go beyond the culturally given. Without it, when the original version of the skill appears to reach its limits of effectiveness, all that is possible is trial-and-error or empirical minor adjustment.

People may ask themselves why a skill works, or why each step is necessary after accumulated practice has freed them from monitoring the skill consciously. Questioning of this nature can be the initial step toward the constructing of the relevant conceptual knowledge, but by itself alone, it is insufficient. Two kinds of component knowledge are also needed.

First, the individual needs *data*, or empirical knowledge. He or she must observe covariations of variables, that is, corresponding changes between actions and consequences or among dimensions of consequences. Variations in key variables may be produced "naturally"—by factors beyond intended control—or "socially," in a collective enterprise of performing the skills. Otherwise, people must intentionally vary the procedure to collect the data necessary for construction of conceptual knowledge. Said differently, they must examine versions of the skill other than the conventional one, an option which is "risky," to successfully solve the problem.

Second, they need to have a *model*—or preconceptual knowledge—even if only a tentative and implicit one.[2] Without this model, it is impossible to determine what variables are to be chosen for consideration from among an almost infinite number of candidates. A model may be obtained primarily through perception, as a somewhat vague "image" of the object—what it is like. It may also be derived indirectly, especially when mechanisms are invisible, on the basis of its functions or reactions to external stimulation. In the latter, it is often borrowed from another domain through analogy. Prior knowledge of constituent parts, if available, is also used in this derivation.[3]

These two types of component knowledge are reciprocally selective: the observed data suggest what model should be adopted, and the adopted model constrains what kind of data are to be observed.

It is likely that a farmer, starting with conventional farming skills, will acquire much conceptual knowledge about plants by observing "naturally produced" covariations while growing rice or corn. Because of this knowledge, tentative though it is, an experienced farmer can deal effectively with various changes in constraints, like unusual weather or plant disease. Eventually, the farmer may even serve as a consultant for less experienced farmers, and as such, can be legitimately called an adaptive expert (Hatano, 1982a).

Similarly, children may sometimes ask, while performing a procedural skill and receiving feedback: "How does A lead to B?" "Why is doing X necessary to produce Y?" (Karmiloff-Smith & Inhelder, 1975). As Condry & Koslowski (1979, p. 246) put it, a child, having found regularity, "seeks to know why and how." In other words, he or she looks for "causal explanations for the way the world is organized." From these questions, the child is likely to construct conceptual knowledge. Motoyoshi's observation (1979) suggests that children can incorporate observed data into a model, even when they cannot see the inside: after accumulated experience in attempting to grow a flower and then comparing her results with her friends', a 5-year-old girl stated: "Flowers are like people. If flowers eat nothing, they will get weak of hunger. If they eat too much, they will get sick." (p. 136)

To summarize, it can be assumed that people—children are no exception—can construct corresponding conceptual knowledge by performing a procedural skill, and with that conceptual knowledge they can be flexible and adaptive, for example, they can "invent" other procedural knowledge.

Do we overestimate children's capacity, since Piaget (1976, 1978) demonstrated a delay of several years between the guided, successful solution of a problem and understanding how and why the solution procedure works? We do not think so. His findings will be replicated if we give children novel, nonsignificant problems and adopt a rigorous criteria for assessing their understanding (for example, stating coherent justifications according to formal logic). What should be emphasized here is that even young children can construct some conceptual knowledge through repeated practice of a procedural skill in a "meaningful" context. Once obtained, this conceptual knowledge can not only invest the procedure with meaning (the how and the why), but it also enables children to make predictions in unfamiliar situations and to invent new strategies.

In a sense, what we have formulated here represents an attempt at a revival of the Piagetian spirit. Though we have placed greater emphasis on the constraints of eco-social settings and on the domain-specificity of cognitive competence, two of his basic ideas are intact. The first is that human beings have an intrinsic motivation for understanding; the second is that an important part of knowledge acquisition is endogenous; that is, achieved through reflexive abstraction. It is indirectly dependent upon external feedback, which serves only as a cue for interpretation, whereas internal feedback is brought about by reorganizing pieces of prior knowledge. Therefore, studying this first issue of adaptive expertise may shed light on an often-neglected aspect of Piagetian theory.

Since some procedural knowledge and skills are specific to a particular culture or subculture, it should be rewarding to use cross-cultural comparison to examine what conceptual knowledge results from practice in a particular culture-specific skill.

A promising attempt at this has been studies examining whether repeated application of culture-specific skills would result in the enhanced acquisition of substance-weight conservation of clay, an aspect of conceptual knowledge about the object of these skills (Adjei, 1977; Price-Williams, Gordon & Ramirez, 1969; Steinberg & Dunn, 1976).

It would also be interesting to examine whether children's spontaneous process of constructing conceptual knowledge is universal across cultures. Similarities in thinking have frequently been observed among children in a variety of cultures and between children and primitive people; this suggests a universal process is involved. On the other hand, historical differences between western and Japanese science suggest there can be different routes to the elaboration of the conceptual knowledge we call science. Although physics, with its atomistic and mechanistic ideas, has played a central role in western science, Japanese endogenous science evolved until the Meiji Restoration, with medicine, which was holistic and vitalistic, as its core (Yasunaga, 1976). Children too may construct different conceptual knowledge according to the availability and the conspicuousness of models in their culture.

Generalized Consequences of Routine Expertise

Adaptive expertise is not the only course of spontaneous development, however. Sometimes, in solving a large number of problems, people learn merely to perform a skill faster and more accurately, without constructing or enriching their conceptual knowledge (even after this might be possible because the procedure had become automatized). For example, many amateur gardeners have repeatedly grown Saint Paulia flowers as prescribed in a greenhouse, where both temperature and humidity can be automatically controlled, without understanding the nature of these flowers, the conditions under which they grow best, or the contents of the fertilizers. Our lives are filled with procedures we carry out simply to get things done; if we repeat them hundreds of times, we can become quite skillful at them. However, our skill is useful only as long as the object and its constraints are constant, that is, the same set of materials and devices is available. Thus, we may become routine experts, but not adaptive ones; routine experts are outstanding in speed, accuracy, and automaticity of performance but lack flexibility and adaptability to new problems. Nevertheless, people unhesitatingly call them experts, since their procedural skills are highly effective for solving everyday problems in a stable environment.

Clearly, even young children can become routine experts. The processes of routine expertise have been fairly well conceptualized (Anderson, 1981). We propose, therefore, that another challenging issue to study is not the processes of routine expertise themselves, but their "generalized consequences."

Two examples of such consequences are found in the studies of abacus operation and the processing of *kanji*, conducted by Hatano and his associates, which we shall describe next.

It is generally agreed a procedural skill is often efficient but only for a limited type of problem. This is mainly because the information embedded in the skill cannot be easily recombined to form other procedural skills (Rumelhart, 1979). However, practice in a procedural skill will facilitate the development of other procedural skills in the same domain. Thus, it will have some generalized consequences by transfer of training in the classical sense, that is, through shared components. We found that after-school training in abacus made third graders' paper-and-pencil addition-subtraction of multidigit numbers faster and more accurate primarily through the shared component skills of basic computation (for example, use of the number facts of single-digit addition and subtraction, and of complementary-numbers-to-10) (Hatano & Suga, 1981). Though this practice did not improve pupils' understanding of principles of carrying or borrowing, it reduced the number of "bugs," that is, the consistent application of wrong algorithms, as well as careless errors in paper-and-pencil computation. This probably occurred because these learners had little difficulty in executing the right procedure.

Moreover, routine expertise in a procedural skill often produces as byproducts strategies or consolidated sequences of behaviors by which the skill can be even more efficiently performed. These byproducts are essentially cultural learning sets. Thus, routine experts often show a capacity remarkably different from that of ordinary people in tasks which, though apparently very different, induce these sequences of behaviors. Scribner and Cole (1981) demonstrated that literacies developed and used in different contexts tend to produce a correspondingly differentiated pattern of cognitive competence. It has also been shown that experienced readers of Japanese can quickly infer the meaning of unfamiliar *kanji* compound words appearing in a discourse by combining prototypal meanings of the component *kanji*. This is because readers are so accustomed to retrieving the meaning directly from *kanji* and relying on compounding schemata (Hatano et al. 1981). A study still in progress suggests this skill for inferring meaning can be generalized to "artificial" words, components of which are new, experimentally introduced symbols with verbally given prototypal meanings.

Finally, routine expertise may produce new mental devices convenient for performing a given task. Abacus experts have interiorized the operation; thus, they can calculate without an abacus as accurately as, and often faster than, with it (Hatano et al. 1977). Grand experts of this abacus-derived mental arithmetic have a mental abacus of an expanded size on which they can represent a number of many digits. We found that such grand experts can rapidly reproduce a series of 15 digits either forward or backward. It might be added that these experts' span of memory for English alphabet letters or for names of fruit is not different from 7 ± 2. Also, their memory for digits is stable, and partially compatible with verbal input and output, but vulnerable to visuo-spatial interference (Hatano & Osawa, 1983). They still hold digits in working memory, not in the rehearsal buffer but in visuo-spatial storage, and do not transmit them to long-term memory. By this powerful mental device of representation, they can mentally calculate a series of large numbers in an algorithmic fashion. A recent developmental study (Hatano, Amaiwa & Shimizu, 1984) demonstrated that even lower-intermediate abacus operators, who can mentally add and subtract numbers of 2 to 3 figures only, rely to some extent on a mental abacus for memorizing digits. As abacus operators become experts at abacus and mental calculation, the mental abacus plays an increasingly dominant role.

In sum, routine expertise may, in fact, produce more or less "generalized consequences," not through understanding, but through well-established patterns and modes of processing. It should prove rewarding to examine, by cross-cultural comparison, what generalized consequences are brought about by practice in a culture-specific skill, which is necessitated by the eco-social environment or fostered by cultural tradition. Since it takes thousands of practice hours to become a grand expert, it is impossible to assign subjects randomly to either the experimental or the control condition. Therefore, cross-cultural comparison is often the only realistic research strategy. The more closely we observe the target skill and context for its use, the more likely we will be to assess the subtle characteristics of its experts, that is, the generalized consequences of the skill.

Factors Differentiating Adaptive and Routine Expertise

If, then, there are two courses of expertise, adaptive and routine, what factors differentiate them? With the present scanty empirical evidence, a comprehensive answer is impossible, but we would like to discuss our speculations in greater detail, deriving our basic ideas from Piaget (1950). As has been discussed, Piaget believed human beings are intrinsically motivated to understand the world. At the same time, he pointed out that, to understand, it is necessary to examine systematically the effects of variations in action upon outcome. This can be achieved by either actively manipulating certain variables or observing naturally occurring variations. However, we know that people are not always engaged in such active experimentation. What encourages someone to engage in such experimentation? We would like to propose three factors.

The first concerns the nature of the object which the procedural skill deals with and the constraints for successfully obtaining the desired outcome. More specifically, it concerns to what degree such a system of object and constraints contains built-in "randomness." If a skill concerns a "natural" object, a variation in critical parameters, which often occurs because of the system's built-in randomness, may make the original version of the skill ineffective, thereby motivating some modification of the skill. In other words, the person applying the skill has many opportunities for observing the effects of modification of the skill on the outcome. Consequently, repeated application of the procedure with variations is likely to lead to adaptive expertise. On the other hand, if the system the procedural skill deals with is highly standardized or is without built-in randomness, there is no necessity for even minor modification of the skill. Here, repeated application of it without variation is unlikely to lead to adaptive expertise. For example, in traditional agriculture, because of individual differences in the nature of a plant (for example, growth rate, vulnerability to disease) and weather conditions that change to some degree from year to year and are, moreover, beyond human control, people are obliged to modify their skill, depending on feedback received during the performance of it. Similarly, in preparing home-cooked meals, the chef's available ingredients may not always be the ones listed in the recipe. In short, people need to adapt a procedural skill according to the amount or kind of materials or devices available to them at the time of performance. In these instances, the performer will probably acquire conceptual knowledge, that is, the how and the why of each step. However, in modernized agriculture, such as greenhouse plant growing, where performers can choose a highly specified variety of plants and easily control weather conditions like temperature and humidity, skill flexibility is not essential. In the same way, cooking with an automatic device (for example, an electronic oven) and a detailed recipe involving precise quantification may ensure a standard dish, but people doing it will have less opportunity to acquire the related conceptual knowledge. As these examples show, modern technology, which aims at reducing built-in randomness in the system, by no means facilitates the acquisition of conceptual knowledge. If we can empirically confirm the above prediction in cross-cultural studies between technologically more advanced and less advanced societies, it may have a strong social impact.

The second factor concerns the context in which the procedural skill is used. When the results obtained through performing it have no vital importance or usefulness, performers tend to produce minor variations in procedural skill and to examine their effects, often playfully. That is, they are willing to engage in active experimentation which, in turn, creates a greater possibility of acquiring conceptual knowledge. In contrast, when a procedural skill is performed primarily to obtain rewards, people are reluctant to risk varying the skill, since they believe safety lies in relying on the "conventional" version. This observation has been supported, though indirectly, by recent studies suggesting the expectation of reward, either tangible or symbolic, decreases quality of performance and intrinsic motivation (Lepper & Greene, 1978). In reviewing these studies, Inagaki (1980) suggests that expectation of reward may prevent learners from understanding things deeply. It changes the "goal structure" of the activity, and thus leads learners to shift from "heuristic" strategies, such as "examining possibilities of alternative solutions" or "seeking a more universal solution beyond the present successful one," to "algorithmic" strategies, ensuring steadier and often quicker solutions within a given time. It is suggested, then, that to maximize an expected external reward a learner may adopt an orientation toward success or efficiency rather than toward understanding.

Inagaki and Hatao (1984) confirmed that when college students, expecting an external evaluation of their performance, were required to translate a letter from English into Japanese, they adopted a "safety strategy." These students spent more time in translation and more frequently checked the dictionary for uncertain words than did control students who had been given no such expectation. Yet, despite the longer time spent, the "expectant" group elaborated less on expressions which required inference by them to be fully understood. The study suggests that the subjects tended to stay within the imposed task of translation, instead of proceeding toward coherent interpretation of the content of the letter. It also suggests that the externally rewarding performance—a frequent occurence in schools—may prevent students from seeking the understanding through which conceptual knowledge is acquired.

The third factor concerns the degree to which understanding a system of the objects-constraints of procedural skills is valued by reference group members. A culture, where understanding the system is a goal, encourages individuals in it to engage in active experimentation. That is, they are invited to try new versions of the procedural skill, even at the cost of efficiency. They are also often required to explain the appropriateness of the skill, largely in relation to others, but sometimes to themselves. In explaining, individuals tend to try to select, integrate, and elaborate potentially relevant pieces of preconceptual knowledge, probably relying on mental experimentation. By contrast, a culture, which highly values the prompt performance of a procedural skill and its outcome, discourages individuals to seek explanations or examine new variations in the skill. Such a culture regards asking why or forming corresponding conceptual knowledge through experimentation as extraneous or even detrimental to performance efficiency. Hunt and Love (1972) suggest that few great mnemonists—like their subject "VP"—can be found in American society, where asking why as opposed to practicing memorizing is encouraged. We suggest accumulated practice of procedural skill is likely to lead to adaptive expertise under an understanding-oriented culture, whereas it is likely to result in routine expertise under a promptitude-oriented culture. A culture, comprising the shared beliefs of the "developed" people in it, would be internalized by its "developing" members because their metacognitive goals of knowing would be acquired through joint activities with developed members (see Wertsch, 1979).

Since Japanese schools and homes are said to be efficiency oriented rather than understanding oriented (Hatano, 1982b), it will be interesting to examine whether Japanese children are in fact inferior to members of an understanding-oriented culture in the flexibility and the adaptability of their procedural knowledge.

Footnotes

1. We recognize that there are other courses of expertise. For example, one may proceed from a well-defined set of declarative knowledge or rules to proceduralization and automatization (see Anderson, 1981).

2. This is, in other words, the structure which can integrate the observed covariations. We avoid the term *structure* because it may be interpreted to connote a general one like Piaget's structure of coordination.

3. There can be, therefore, intermediate stages in the construction of conceptual knowledge, where pieces of partial knowledge are not well integrated into a whole or where different models coexist. For example, a person may know that object A is similar to object B in its construction without being able to specify the difference between the two; he or she may know that it has parts a and b without grasping how they are connected.

References

Adjei, K. (1977). Influence of specific maternal occupation and behavior on Piagetian cognitive development. In P. R. Dasen, (Ed.), *Piagetian psychology: Cross-cultural contributions* (pp. 227–256). New York: Gardner Press.

Anderson, J. R. (Ed.) (1981). *Cognitive skills and their acquisition.* Hillsdale, N.J.: Lawrence Erlbaum Associates.

Brown, A. L., & DeLoache, J. S. (1978). Skills, plans and self-regulation. In R. Siegler (Ed.), *Children's thinking: What develops* (pp. 3–35). Hillsdale, N.J.: Lawrence Erlbaum Associates.

Condry, J., & Koslowski, B. (1979). Can education be made intrinsically interesting to children? In L. G. Katz, (Ed.), *Current topics in early childhood education*, Vol. II, pp. 227–260. Norwood, N.J.: Ablex.

Gentner, D., & Stevens, A. L. (1983). *Mental models.* Hillsdale, N.J.: Lawrence Erlbaum Associates.

Greeno, J. G. (1980). *Forms of understanding in mathematical problem solving.* Paper presented at the 22nd International Congress of Psychology, July, 1980, Leipzig.

Hatano, G. (1982a). Cognitive consequences of practice in culture specific procedural skills. *Quarterly Newsletter of Laboratory of Comparative Human Cognition, 4,* 15–18.

———. (1982b). Should parents be teachers too? A Japanese view. *Dokkyo University Bulletin of Liberal Arts, 17,* 54–72.

Hatano, G., Kuhara, K., & Akiyama, M. (1981). Kanji helps readers of Japanese infer the meaning of unfamiliar words. *Quarterly Newsletter of the Laboratory of Cognitive Human Condition, 3,* 30–33.

Hatano, G., Miyake, Y., & Binks, M. G. (1977). Performance of expert abacus operators. *Cognition, 5,* 57–71.

Hatano, G., & Osawa, K. (1983). Digit memory of grand experts in abacus-derived mental calculation. *Cognition, 15,* 95–110.

Hatano, G., & Suga, Y. (1981). *Abacus learning, digit span and multi-digit addition/subtraction skills among 3rd-graders.* Paper presented at the American Educational Research Association Annual Meeting, April, 1981, Los Angeles.

Hatano, G., Amaiwa, S., & Shimizu, K. (1984). *Formation of "mental abacus" for computation and for memorizing digits: A developmental study.* Paper presented at the

American Educational Research Association Annual Meeting, April, 1984, New Orleans.

Hunt, E., & Love, T. (1972). How good can memory be? In A. W. Melton & Martin (Eds.), *Coding processes in human memory.* (pp. 237–260). Washington, D. C.: Winston.

Inagaki, K. (1980). Effects of external reinforcement on intrinsic motivation. *Japanese Psychological Review, 23*, 121–132. (In Japanese with an English summary)

Inagaki, K., & Hatano, G. (1984). *Effects of external evaluation on reading comprehension and intrinsic interest.* Paper presented at the American Educational Research Association Annual Meeting, New Orleans.

Karmiloff-Smith, A., & Inhelder, B. (1975). If you want to get ahead, get a theory. *Cognition, 3*, 195–212.

Lepper, M. R. & Greene, D. (Eds.) (1978). *The hidden cost of reward.* Hillsdale, N.J.: Lawrence Erlbaum Associates.

Motoyoshi, M. (1979). *Essays in education for day care children: Emphasizing daily life activities.* Tokyo: Froebel-Kan. (In Japanese)

Piaget, J. (1976). *The grasp of consciousness.* London: Routledge & Kagan Paul.

———. (1978) *Success and understanding.* London: Routledge & Kagan Paul.

———. (1950). *The psychology of intelligence.* New York: Harcourt Brace & World.

Price-Williams, D. R., Gordon, W., & Ramirez, M. (1969). Skill and conservation: A study of pottery-making children. *Developmental Psychology, 1,* 769.

Rumelhart, D. E. (1979). *Analogical processes and procedural representations.* CHIP Report No. 81. Center for Human Information Processing, University of California, San Diego.

Scribner, S., & Cole, M. (1981). *The psychology of literacy.* Cambridge, Mass.: Harvard University Press.

Steinberg, B. M., & Dunn, L. A. (1976). Conservation competence and performance in Chiapas. *Human Development, 19*, 14–25.

Wertsch, J. V. (1979). From social interaction to higher psychological processes: A clarification and application of Vygotsky's theory. *Human Development 22*, 1–22.

Yasunaga, T. (1976). *Ando Shoyeki.* Tokyo: Heibon-Sha. (In Japanese)

18 | The Search for Cross-Linguistic Invariants and Variation in Language Development

Kenji Hakuta
Lois Bloom

The goal of this chapter is to present some of the interesting and important aspects of cross-linguistic comparisons which can be made between the acquisition of Japanese and of English. We do not attempt an exhaustive review of the literature (see, for example, Clancy, in press; Iwata, 1979; Murata, 1968, 1972; Sato, 1978 for reviews of the Japanese literature). We focus instead first on the basic theoretical issues underlying the study of language development in general. Then we selectively describe research that seeks invariants as well as interesting variations in the cross-linguistic circumstances of language development in Japanese and in English.

Among the areas of child psychology, language development is perhaps one of the least understood by those outside the specialty. Developmental psycholinguists frequently find themselves forced to explain the major issues in the field, even to their colleagues in developmental psychology. This confusion exists in part because the questions asked by linguists (for an immediate example, see Kuno, this volume) ordinarily have considerable influence on the questions asked by developmental psycholinguists. In an interdisciplinary volume such as this, then, it behooves us to consider these issues. Therefore, we should ask why developmental psycholinguists study child language in general and cross-linguistic child language acquisition in particular. Such a discussion is a prerequisite for any consideration of specific research findings from comparative studies of the acquisition of Japanese and of English, the topic that comprises the second part of this chapter.

Why Study Language Development?

The basic reasons for studying language development in children have endured throughout the history of child language. Linguists have been fascinated with the developing language of children as it bears on the diachronic question of language history and the synchronic question of the form and function of the linguistic system. Psychologists have been motivated by their desire to understand the mind, the nature of learning, and the relation between the individual and society. Of prime importance are the issues of the relation between language and thought and between biological and social influences on language. (For brevity, we omit from this discussion the more abstract relation between linguistic and psycholinguistic theories, although serious readers are urged to consult relevant sources, such as Wexler, 1982.)

Language and Thought

One important contemporary issue is that of the mental representation of the form and the function of language and how each element is related to general cognition. Two distinct points of view are associated with two of the most influential theorists of our time: Jean Piaget and Noam Chomsky. Their views differ about the relation between the mental representations of language and of reality. They also differ about whether language is learned and develops according to universal developmental laws or is a matter of the maturation of biologically determined and universal grammatical mechanisms.

According to Piaget, language is a part of general cognition; the same symbolic capacity underlying the development of language also underlies the development of other aspects of thought. Moreover, language development depends upon cognitive development. The meaning of children's language derives from the representation of reality—objects, events, and relations between them developed in infancy. Subsequent development of language continues to depend on the logical development of thought. The existence of language universals (for example, Comrie, 1981) is the reflection of the universality of human development more generally.

In contrast, for Chomsky the syntax of language is an autonomous cognitive system which is biologically determined, with no causal chain existing between it and thought. The child is born with a specifically linguistic mechanism which somehow makes it possible to discover the particular grammar of the language on the basis of only a limited sample of speech from the environment. Language acquisition is a matter of maturation. What is mentally represented is an abstract system of rules and the mechanisms for their discovery. These rules cannot be learned from the environment. They bear no relation to the representation of reality in everyday events, constituting instead a core "universal grammar" which forms a part of an innately determined human mental capacity.

The tension between these two points of view has permeated efforts to explain language development (Piattelli-Palmarini, 1980). In linguistic terms, the question concerns whether the semantic or the formal aspects of language are primary in determining the contrasts children learn. To what extent do children depend on semantic categories, derived from their understanding of the world, for arriving at syntactic categories? Or are the syntactic categories somehow given as a priori structures, waiting for their maturational time of ascendence? In cognitive terms, the question is whether and how the processes involved in language learning are specific to language or extend as well to other kinds of problem-solving.

Much of the debate concerning the relation between language and thought has centered on the influence of thought on language. However, we have also come to recognize that the course of language acquisition is equally influenced by the nature of the linguistic system the child is learning. The importance of language for language development—or linguistic determinism—has been described in several ways (see Bloom, 1981). According to the theory of generative transformational grammar, language acquisition is determined by the innate linguistic universals which decide basic grammatical categories (Chomsky, 1965). Another view holds that children discover underlying grammatical categories by learning to pay attention to the surface forms of speech which mark the part of speech (such as *-ing* on verbs in English, and *-te-ru* in Japanese). Noticing the endings of words helps the child to discover whether a word names an object or an action (Brown, 1957) and to discover the grammatical categories to which the word belongs (Maratsos, 1982). And according to Slobin (1973), children growing up in different environments are similar both in their cognitive development and in the cognitive strategies they use in language acquisition. Nevertheless, researchers have observed different sequences of development among children learning different languages. These sequences, in which different children learn to express similar ideas about the world, are determined in large part by the accessibility of the surface forms of the language expressing those ideas.

Languages that differ from one another in their surface forms can still be similar in their underlying universal principles. In the same way, the children learning these different languages can also be similar in the cognitive strategies they use in acquisition. Thus, although sequences of acquisition can differ in the particulars of surface form, they may still have much in common. One such example is the similarity in how the verb system influences acquisition of different languages. Verbs are prominent in both Japanese and English. For example, they are very resistant to deletion in adult Japanese (Kuno, 1973) and are the most frequently expressed constituents in Japanese child-language (Clancy; Rispoli, 1984) and in English child-sentences (Bloom, Miller & Hood, 1975). In the acquisition of both languages, pro-verbs (for example, *do* in English, *suru* in Japanese) are ubiquitous in early sentences. Before children acquire a store of more semantically specific verbs, they learn to use pro-forms to maintain the structural integrity of their speech (Bloom, 1981; Rispoli). Thus, the same principles, whether specifically linguistic or more generally cognitive in nature, can influence the acquisition of different languages in similar ways.

Language, the Individual, and Society

Different theorists have conceptualized language differently with respect to its role in the relation between the individual and society. Both Piaget and Chomsky, despite their differences, conceive of language as a faculty of the individual mind. Although neither would deny that social interaction provides the context, each holds that language develops within the individual.

In contrast, others conceive of language as, first and foremost, a social phenomenon. Language is an activity taking place between rather than within individuals and existing in society rather than in the mind. Children acquire words and syntactic structures through social activities of negotiation and interaction with an adult (Bruner, 1983; Dore, 1984; Vygotsky, 1962, 1978). This second theoretical tension concerns the relative contributions of the child and the social context to the process of acquisition. The debate over this is a contemporary version of the nature-nurture issue.

The initial attraction of Chomsky's nativist view of language, on its introduction a generation ago, was the corrective it offered to the environmental emphasis created by the dominance of behaviorism. However, in the last decade, with the increased attention to the importance of interaction between the child and the social context, the balance has tipped once again toward the environment in the effort to explain acquisition. Communication, rather than language structure or cognitive development, has emerged as the salient factor in child language.

However, social interaction and communication do not explain language (Bloom, 1983; Shatz, 1982). Even after we understand the development of communication and the ways children learn to use it in context, we will still need to explain how the forms they use are acquired. Both biology and society will have to be implicated in any theory hoping to explain acquisition to anyone's satisfaction.

We have also become aware that affect—emotions and drives—is another nonlinguistic factor in development. From the beginning of infancy, exchanges between infants and their caregivers are heavily endowed with feeling. Mothers are adept at interpreting and giving meaning to their infants' affective expressions. This is, no doubt, the basis upon which communication develops between them. However, whereas affect is the content of communication in infancy, we still do not know how infants' expression of it and adult responses to it relate to the acquisition of language. We do know that children are very different from one another in the frequency and intensity of their affective displays. During the period of transition from prelinguistic to linguistic forms of communication—roughly the last quarter of the first year and first quarter of the second year—affective and linguistic expression coexist as two parallel and complementary communication systems, differing in form as well as content (Bloom & Capatides, 1985).

Since affective displays and their influence on the communicative interaction between infant and caregiver have only begun to emerge as factors in development, we know little about cross-cultural differences in this respect (see Campos et al., this volume). Western research has emphasized the dyadic model of communication, perhaps because it is characteristic of western communication patterns (see, for example, Bruner; Stern, 1977). However, the dyadic model of communication in infancy is hardly universal. In two nonwestern cultures, New Guinea and Samoa, mothers avoid face-to-face contact with their infants. They also refrain from elaborate interpretations of their baby's facial expressions and vocalizations (Ochs and Schieffelin, 1982). Thus, while important for communication in some societies, the relevance of affective displays in infancy for language acquisition is unknown. Since Japanese is a language in which affect plays a prominent role in grammar (for example, see the following discussion and Kuno, this volume, about point of view, camera angle, and empathy in Japanese grammar), comparison of the development of these aspects of language should be promising.

Why Study Language Development Cross-Linguistically?

Cross-linguistic reseach is conducted for three major reasons related to the goals of developmental psycholinguistics in general. First, the researcher may want to test the claim for universality of a developmental phenomenon which has been formulated on the basis of a single language—typically, English. By looking for invariants in development across languages having different structural characteristics, one can determine whether the principle should be formulated as a universal about all human languages or as specific to the particular configurations of particular languages.

A second reason arises when the findings in a given language may be consistent with a particular theoretical (linguistic) interepretation, but the pattern of results might be confounded with alternative interpretations. The cross-cultural developmental psycholinguist is excited if another language can unconfound the alternative explanations.

A third reason is that the researcher might want to determine which aspects of the process are governed by formal linguistic constraints, and which by other "nonlinguistic" factors, such as the cognitive and the social development of the child. As Slobin (1973, 1982) has pointed out, the pacesetter of language development is best seen as a combination of cognitive development and of the formal difficulty of the linguistic system.

In the remainder of this chapter, we describe some representative efforts which fit into these categories in the comparison of Japanese and English acquisition.

Universality

Take a specific principle formulated on the basis of English. Bever (1970) reported that children acquiring English develop a heuristic strategy based on the regularity of word order-meaning correlation found in English. Since most sentences, such as *Frogs are eating the princes* are semantically of the form AGENT-ACTION-OBJECT, children develop a heuristic taking the sequence NOUN-VERB-NOUN and labeling the corresponding interpretation. This accounts, for example, for the fact that at a certain point in development (somewhere around age 4) children learning English systematically misinterpret passive sentences such as *Frogs are being eaten by the princes* to mean the consumption of royalties by amphibians. This hypothesis can be generally stated as proposing that children will formulate an order-based interpretive heuristic which capitalizes on the basic order of the target language. That hypothesis can be projected to Japanese to test its universality.

Word order in Japanese does not play the kind of key grammatical signalling role it does in English. The basic and preferred word order of Japanese is Subject-Object-Verb (SOV). Postposed particles (markings appearing on the ends of words) serve the key function of signalling whether, for example, a particular noun is the subject or the object of a sentence. Since the predominant order for their target language is AGENT-OBJECT-ACTION, do Japanese children, then, construct an analogous strategy sensitive to word order? Such a finding would amount to a straightforward generalization of Bever's English-based claim. An alternative possibility is that, because Japanese uses particles to indicate the grammatical roles of the words (*-ga* for subject and *-o* for object), children may ignore the order of words in the sentence.

Studies of comprehension and production of sentences containing these particles support neither of these possibilities. Rather, children acquiring Japanese formulate an interpretive strategy taking *both* order and particles into account (Hayashibe, 1975; Hakuta, 1982). That is, they come to expect particular particles to appear in particular locations in the sentence. They take a noun marked by *-ga* to be the agent of the proposition only if it is on the first noun of the sentence. Otherwise, they ignore it. Thus, they correctly interpret *Inu-ga neko-o name-ta* ("the dog licked the cat"), they perform randomly on *Neko-o inu-gan-ame-ta* (the same meaning, but in the Object-Subject-Verb order), and systematically misinterpret *Neko-ga inu-ni name-rare-ta* (the same propositional meaning but in the passive). In the last sentence, they are fooled because the first noun is marked by *-ga*.

The type of approach thus described enables two things. First, it permits a stringent test of a hypothesis. In this instance, it has shown any claim about the primacy of word order in language acquisition cannot be universal. It must be tempered by the extent to which different languages recruit word order as a device to signal grammatical structure. Second, this approach tells us something about

Japanese children's language acquisition: their development is best characterized as the broadening of the expectancy of particles with respect to position. Particles are first bound to specific locations in the sentence. Development then consists of broadening the range of locations where they may be found.

Another area where English-based hypotheses about universality has been tested is sentence verification. Generally speaking, in English, one responds *yes* or *no* to a proposition, depending on whether it is stated negatively or affirmatively. *The ball game was terrific* is responded by *Yes, it was* or *No, it wasn't*. *The ball game wasn't worth going to* is responded by *Yes, it was* or *No, it wasn't*. In Japanese, yes (*hai*) or no (*iie*) depend on the speaker's agreement with the truth value of the proposition regardless of whether it is stated with a negative or not. An obviously false negative statement such as *President Reagan is not a Republican* in English requires *Yes, he is,* whereas in Japanese it requires *Iie, chigai masu.* ("No, it is different.") In response to an obviously true negative statement, such as *Drinking water from the Sumida River is not good for your health*, (prescriptive) English requires *No, it is not*. In contrast, Japanese requires *Hai, sou desu.* ("Yes, it is so.") Thus, the Japanese affirmation indicates agreement with the proposition.

Akiyama (1984) has examined this system in a series of studies from the information-processing perspective (see especially, his review prepared for a Japanese audience in Akiyama, 1981). He has adpated the sentence-verification paradigm (Carpenter & Just, 1975; Clark & Chase, 1972) developed with English-speaking children and applied it to Japanese children. The details of the study are too complicated to address here. However, Akiyama has shown different patterns of response times for English- and Japanese-speaking children which are predictable, in part, by the grammatical differences between the two languages we have outlined. His research points to the value of the strategic use of cross-linguistic comparisons to modify claims about universality.

Other researchers have looked at sentence coordination [sentences conjoined, for example, by "and" (-*te* for verbs, -*to* for nouns)] in Japanese, to test for the generality of models of their development in English (Hakuta, de Villiers & Tager-Flusberg, 1982; Lust & Wakayama, 1979). The theoretical orientations of these studies are different. Lust and Wakayama take a generative grammar perspective and look for the operation of relatively abstract constraints. Hakuta et al. take into account the surface, linear properties of the sentences. However, both find it difficult to extend the English-based model directly onto Japanese.

Unconfounding Hypotheses

We now turn to a case where Japanese can be used to sort out hypotheses that are confounded in English. Research with this goal is a sophisticated variant of the test of universality mentioned previously. The particular example we raise concerns relative clauses. Relative clauses may not, on the surface, appear to be a thrilling topic of investigation. Yet, in fact, they are centrally important in the description of languages because they are a manifestation of their power to embed one proposition within another.

The literature on relative clauses deals mostly with English. As such, it is filled with studies that argue between two competing explanations for what determines their difficulty of comprehension. One class of explanations is based on an abstract description of the sentence in terms of the grammatical relations. The theories are built on units such as "subject" and "object." These are somewhat "deep" and abstract relations. A second class of explanations is pitched at the more concrete aspects of the sentence. It takes as units the surface, linear sequence of words appearing in the sentence. These two competing classes of theories say different things about why the following sentences differ in their difficulty of comprehension:

1. The philosopher [that the psychologist admired] hated eggs.
2. The philosopher [that admired the psychologist] hated eggs.

For the first class of explanations, a simplified version of the argument goes as follows: what is important is the relationship between the two grammatical roles played by the *head noun* of the relative clause (the philosopher in both sentences). In (1), the head noun is the object within the relative clause (the psychologist admired the philosopher). However, it is the subject in the main sentence (the philosopher hated eggs). In (2), the head noun is the subject both within the relative clause and in the main sentence. Sentence (2) is easier than (1) because the head noun plays the same grammatical role in both its functions in (2), whereas it plays different roles in (1).

The second class of explanations says the following: what is important is the order in which nouns and verbs appear in a linear sequence. The central burden for the listener is to assign appropriate relationships between the nouns and the verbs as they come in. Sentence (1) is more difficult than (2) because two nouns are followed by two successive verbs, and this sequence taxes memory.

English is not a good language for separating out these two classes of explanations because it relies heavily on word order for the determination of grammatical roles. Any explanation based on grammatical roles and their relationships is confounded with a specified linear order of elements in the sentence. This confounding can be sorted out in Japanese because of its flexibility of word order. Thus, a sentence with a given grammatical description can appear in at least two forms:

3. Haitatsuya-ga [keikan-o nagu-tta kosodoro-o] oikake-ta.
   deliveryman-subj police-obj hit-past thief-obj chase-past
4. [Keikan-o nagu-tta kosodoro-o] haitatsuya-ga oikake-ta.
   police-obj hit-past thief-obj deliveryman-subj chase-past

Experiments with such types of sentences, when performed with Japanese children, show the linear order of the elements, rather than their grammatical descriptions, determines difficulty of comprehension (Hakuta, 1981; Harada et al. 1976). Thus, a sentence of a given grammatical description varies, depending on the order in which the constituents appear. Now, when interpreting back to English, by virtue of having ruled out the class of explanations using only grammatical descriptions as their vocabulary, one can conclude the explanation based on the linear order of constituents is more likely to be correct.

We would like to emphasize that very few studies have explicitly unconfounded hypotheses through cross-linguistic comparison (Bowerman, 1980). It would seem appropriate, for example, for Japanese researchers to use English as a way of unconfounding variables in Japanese, such as the intricate interweaving of linguistic forms with affective expression. We are unaware of any such studies.

Linguistic and Nonlinguistic Factors in Development

We now turn to the third important function of cross-linguistic research: the sorting out of linguistic from nonlinguistic contributions to the patterns of language development. Unlike the functions already discussed, the research reported here has not necessarily been directed toward cross-linguistic comparison. Rather, it is based on observations of independent reports on the acquisition of English and of Japanese. Thus, more rigorous research is needed to substantiate the generalizations offered here.

Furthermore, the further one gets from the relatively sharply defined linguistic issues, the more difficult it becomes to relate particular areas to theoretical concerns. In some ways, these phenomena may be seen as worthy of description and comparison because they are simply interesting, not necessarily because they resolve some theoretical dilemma—cognitive, linguistic, or otherwise. In our discussions with Hiroshi Azuma and Harold Stevenson at the Center for Advanced Study in the Behavioral Sciences, we referred to this aspect of cross-linguistic comparison as the "freak show" approach. Unusualness invites display.

Of particular interest are cases where particular meanings are expressed by children learning one language earlier than children learning another language because of the differences in the grammars of the languages. For example, Japanese divides demonstrative pronouns, adjectives, and adverbs in a more complex way than does English. While English uses *this* and *that*, Japanese brings a third dimension into play, *kore* ("this"), *are* ("that over there, away from both the speaker and listener"), and *sore* ("that over there, next to the listener"). According to Okubo's (1967) diary study, the child was using the three forms by age 2;6 (pp. 72–73). From such data, one can infer (pending verification through experiments rather than through naturalistic observation alone) that children as young as 2 can make distinctions involving the location of the listener.

In another remarkable early achievement in children's development of Japanese, Clancy reports discriminating use of Japanese sentence-final particles -*yo* and -*ne*, which mark whether the information conveyed in the sentence is old or new to the listener. To illustrate the distinction, imagine two first-time customers in a *fugu* ("globefish," a delicacy which requires careful preparation because its blood is poisonous) restaurant:

Situation One: Kore, oishii-yo
this, taste good-emph
Situation Two: Kore, oishii-ne
this, taste good-agr

In the first situation, we can infer the speaker has not yet tasted his stew and that he is transmitting information he knows is privy to him. In the second situation, we infer both speakers have tasted the stew and the speaker is seeking agreement.

Clancy reports routine use of these emphatic forms by children. For example, a child aged 2;4, watching a garbage truck from a window, saw it drive away and reported to adults sitting inside the room: *itchatta-yo.* ("It went away.") Systematic experimental elicitation of these structures would be valuable in determining the productive use of forms that suggest an early form of perspective-shifting in the Japanese child.

Kuno (this volume) suggests that Japanese is constrained by a variable, which he calls an explicitness requirement for source of information. With it, "the speaker can make an affirmative statement about a past, present or future action or state only if he has the firsthand non-hearsay knowledge about it. Otherwise, the speaker must make his source of information explicit." For example, imagine a situation where a child is privy to the knowledge that mother has gone out shopping, but either (1) has direct knowledge of the information, or (2) was told by her father of it. Now her older brother is looking for mother and asks,

mama doko?
mama where

the appropriate reply would be:

(1) kaimono-ni i-tta
shopping-to go-past
(2) kaimono-ni i-tta-tte
shopping-to go-past-I hear

The *-tte* ending is translated as "I hear" indicating the source of information is indirect. According to Clancy (in press), this form of reportative speech is commonly found in Japanese children before age 2. Her data are consistent with reports from Fujiwara (1977) and Okubo. A child of 1;10 was heard to say the following: *jiichan-ga atsui-tte* ("Grandfather said it's hot") (Fujiwara, 1977: p. 142, reported in Clancy).

Reportative functions do not appear in the speech of children acquiring English until much later. This might lead to the conclusion that the cognitive complexity of the meaning contained in such utterances constrains the development of these functions. However, the early appearance of these forms in the speech of Japanese children suggests this would be an erroneous conclusion. Clancy suggests that Japanese children acquire these forms early because they are linguistically simple—they are marked morphologically, rather than syntactically, and they appear at the end of the sentence. He further observes such reportative forms are commonly found in mother's speech to children. (We must allow for the possibility, however, that they may be embedded in, and constrained by, the conversational context.)

These studies suggest surprisingly precocious developments in language when looked at from the perspective of cognitive complexity. In contrast, there are also cases where it appears that cognitive development serves as the pacesetter of linguistic development. Clancy, for example, notes that concessive conjunctions (*-temo*/"even though," "although") and conditional conjunctions (*-tara*/"when," "if") appear quite early in Japanese child speech. This fact is anomalous with reports of English, Italian, German, and Turkish, where they are reportedly late acquisitions (Bloom et al., 1980; Clancy, Jacobsen & Silva, 1976). However, the early appearance of these forms in Japanese appear constrained by the conversational context in which they are used. Clancy finds that, in her data, children and parents use these forms exclusively for the function of conveying permission and prohibition. In other words, they are not used in the full adult range of functions. Japanese children pick up these forms because they are linguistically simple and use them in restricted conversational contexts. Their use in full adult contexts presumably must await appropriate cognitive grasp of the functions signalled therein.

In her comprehensive review of the literature on the acquisition of Japanese, Clancy highlights several additional areas for a fruitful exploration of the relationship between linguistic and nonlinguistic development. For example, the obligatory use of numerical classifiers in Japanese may force the early acquisition of concepts related to object's shape and class. Clancy also emphasizes the complex sociolinguistic rules of Japanese, including sex and status appropriate forms. In addition, Kuno (this volume) suggests that the use of appropriate forms that take into acocunt the "camera angle" of the speaker might be interesting to study developmentally.

Expanding the Data Base

Data from individuals who serve as the locus of contact between the two languages: namely, bilinguals and second-language learners, should supplement the comparative study of the acquisition of Japanese and English such as we have described. There are now a few studies of Japanese speakers learning English (for example, Hakuta, 1976; Itoh & Hatch, 1977; Milon, 1974). But we know of no studies of the acquisition of Japanese by English speakers.

One of the interesting outcomes of recent research in second-language acquisition is that interference from the native language is quite selective. In many respects, Japanese speakers learning English will resemble speakers of other languages learning English. Still, there are also some characteristics unique to Japanese speakers, attributable to the unique combination of Japanese and English. We propose that studies of second-language learners, both Japanese learning English and speakers of English learning Japanese, will provide glimpses into some profound differences between the mental sets created by the two languages.

To take one example, the English article system for marking definite and indefinite reference (*a* and *the*) presents inordinate difficulty for Japanese speakers. Observers have noted this difficulty even in children as young as 5 (Hakuta). It is not observed in learners of English, whose native language has an article system, such as Spanish (Hakuta and Cancino, 1977). This suggests that, in the course of learning Japanese, the child becomes entrenched in a linguistic system focusing, not on distinctions based on definiteness, but on some other system. We suspect that the Japanese system is based more on the discourse system which keys in on such variables as "theme of the sentence" and "exhaustive listing" (see Kuno, 1972). Somehow entrenchment in this system throws a hurdle in the way of the Japanese learner coming to grips with the English system of definiteness. Going in the other direction, from English to Japanese, common observation of second-language learners of Japanese suggests these learners have difficulty with appropriate markings on nouns with -*wa* (typically a topic marker) and -*ga* (typically a subject marker), which variables of the discourse system seem to govern.

Discourse style is also an area that can be investigated in second-language learners. Japanese speakers, for example, will tend to construct sentences of the following sort: *In America, there are many kinds of people. But Japan there are not many kinds.* Such forms reflect the tendency, based on Japanese to bring the topic of the sentence to the front of the sentence. It is also interesting to note that Japanese speakers avoid the use of relative clauses in English written compositions in comparison to speakers of, say, Arabic and Spanish (Hakuta; Schachter, 1974). At this point, it is unclear whether such characteristic stamping of English patterns by Japanese is attributable to relatively low-level transfer from Japanese—such as the order in which words and phrases are arranged in sentences—or to higher-level differences, such as the ordering of units of thought independent of language.

A study of second-language learners brings sociolinguistics into consideration in a hurry, since errors of this kind are perhaps the most salient made by such subjects. American businessmen who think that they can get their Japanese lessons the easy way, from bar hostesses at night, are in for a shock when they later try to use their learnings. It is evident, although unstudied, that language forms appropriate to the sex and social status of the speaker and the audience present one of the largest stumbling blocks for learners of Japanese.

Conclusion

We have only touched the surface of issues that arise in cross-linguistic comparisons of the acquisition of English and Japanese. While we could not treat the grammatical differences between the two languages in sufficient depth in this chapter, we would like to point to some reasons why Japanese and English are particulary well suited for systematic comparative study.

First, they are unrelated languages. Second, they differ in many characteristics used in classifying languages. For Greenberg (1963), it is basic word order (Japanese is SOV, English is SVO). For Li and Thompson (1976), it is the degree to which the notions of subject and topic are recruited. (Japanese is topic-prominent; English is subject-prominent.) For Chomsky (1982), it is whether or not the structures rely on the configurational order of constituents (English is configurational, whereas Japanese is nonconfigurational.) And although Kuno (this volume) does not relate his analysis to language typology, Japanese is a language whose insightful description requires more use of notions related to the affect of the speakers (such as their point of view, empathy, and camera angle) than does English. Third, both languages have been well described linguistically. Because many of the Japanese linguists have received training in the United States, these descriptions have focused on aspects of language where English and Japanese critically differ (Inoue, 1976; Kunihiro, 1980; Shibatani, 1976). And fourth, there is sufficient contact between speakers of the two languages such that there are Japanese speakers learning English and English speakers learning Japanese. These individuals can provide important clues to the key characteristics on which the languages can be fruitfully compared.

References

Akiyama, M. (1981). Gengo kakutoku ni okeru nippongo to eigo [Japanese and English language acquisition]. *Jidoo shinrigaku no shimpo (Progress of Child Psychology)*. 283–306.

———. (1984). Are language-acquisition strategies universal? *Developmental Psychology, 20*, 219–228.

Bever, T. G. (1970). The cognitive basis for linguistic structures. In J. R. Hayes (Ed.), *Cognition and the Development of Language*. New York: John Wiley & Sons.

Bloom, L. (1981). The importance of language for language development: Linguistic determinism in the 1980s. *Annals of the New York Academy of Sciences, 379*, 160–171.

———. (1983). Review of *Language acquisition: The state of the art. Science*, May 15.

Bloom, L., & Capatides, J. (1985). Development from affective communication in infancy to communication with language. Unpublished manuscript, Teachers College, Columbia University.

Bloom, L., Lahey, M., Hood, L., Lifter, K., & Fiess, K. (1980). Complex sentences: Acquisition of syntactic connectives and the semantic relations they encode. *Journal of Child Language, 7*, 235–261.

Bloom, L., Miller, P., & Hood, L. (1975). Variation and reduction as aspects of competence in language development. In A. Pick (Ed.), *Minnesota symposia on child psychology*, Vol. 9. Minneapolis: University of Minnesota Press.

Bowerman, M. (1980). Cross-cultural perspectives on language development. In H. C. Triandis (Ed.), *Handbook of cross-cultural psychology*, Vol. III. Boston: Allyn & Bacon.

Brown, R. (1957). Linguistic determinism and part of speech. *Journal of Abnormal and Social Psychology, 55*, 1–5.

Bruner, J. (1983). *Child's talk: Learning to use language.* New York: W. W. Norton.

Carpenter, P. & Just, M. A. (1975). Sentence comprehension: A psycholinguistic model of sentence verification. *Psychological Review, 82*, 45–73.

Chomsky, N. (1965). *Aspects of the theory of syntax.* Cambridge, Mass.: MIT Press.

———. (1982). *Lectures on government and binding.* Dordrecht, Netherlands: Foris Publications.

Clancy, P. (in press). The acquisition of Japanese. In D. I. Slobin (Ed.), *The crosslinguistic study of language acquisition.* Hillsdale, N.J.: Lawrence Erlbaum Associates.

Clancy, P., Jacobsen, T. & Silva, N. (1976). The acquisition of conjunction: A cross-linguistic study. *Papers and Reports on Child Language Development, 12*, 71–80.

Clark, H. H. & Chase, W. G. (1972). On the process of comparing sentences against pictures. *Cognitive Psychology, 3*, 472–517.

Comrie, B. *Language universals and linguistic typology.* Chicago: University of Chicago Press, 1981.

Dore, J. (1984). Holophrases revisited: Their "logical" development from dialog. In M. Barrett (Ed.), *Children's single-word speech.* London: John Wiley & Sons.

Fujiwara, Y. (1977). *Yooji no gengo hyoogen nooryoku no hattatsu [The development of language expression ability of children].* Hiroshima: Bunka Hyooron Publishing Co.

Greenberg, J. H. (1963). Some universals of grammar with particular reference to the order of meaningful elements. In J. H. Greenberg (Ed.), *Universals of language*. Cambridge, Mass.: MIT press.

Hakuta, K. (1976). A case study of a Japanese child learning English. *Language Learning, 26*, 321–351.

————. (1981). Grammatical description versus configurational arrangement in language acquisition: The case of relative clauses in Japanese. *Cognition, 9*, 197–236.

————. (1982). Interaction between particles and word order in the comprehension and production of simple sentences in Japanese children. *Developmental Psychology, 18*, 62–76.

Hakuta, K. & Cancino, H. (1977). Trends in second-language-acquisition research. *Harvard Educational Review, 47*, 294–316.

Hakuta, K., de Villiers, J. & Tager-Flusberg, H. (1982). Sentence coordination in Japanese and English. *Journal of Child Language, 9*, 193–207.

Harada, S. I., Uyeno, T., Hayashibe, H., & Yamada, H. (1976). On the development of perceptual strategies in children: A case study on the Japanese child's comprehension of relative clause constructions. *Annual Bulletin of the Research Institute Logopedics Phoniatrics. University of Tokyo, 10*, 199–224.

Hayashibe, H. (1975). Word order and particles: A developmental study in Japanese. *Descriptive and Applied Linguistics, 8*, 1–11.

Inoue, K. (1976). *Henkei bunpoo to nihon-go [Transformational grammar and Japanese]*. (2 volumes). Tokyo: Taishu-kan.

Itoh, H. & Hatch, E. (1977). Second language acquisition: A case study. In E. Hatch (Ed.), *Second language acquisition: A book of readings*. Rowley, Mass.: Newbury House Publishers.

Iwata, J. (1979). Gengo kinoo [Language faculty]. *Jidoo shinrigaku no shimpo [Progress of Child Psychology]*, 121–144.

Kunihiro, T. (Ed.) (1980). *Nichieigo hikaku kooza [Japanese-English contrast forum], Volume 2: Bunpoo* [Grammar]. Tokyo: Taishukan Shoten.

Kuno, S. (1972). Functional sentence perspective: A case study from Japanese and English. *Linguistic Inquiry, 3*, 269–320.

————. (1973). *The structure of the Japanese language*. Cambridge, Mass.: MIT Press.

————. (1974). The position of relative clauses and conjunction. *Linguistic Inquiry, 5*, 117–136.

Li, C. & Thompson, S. (1976). Subject and topic: A new typology of language. In C. Li (Ed.), *Subject and topic*. New York: Academic Press.

Lust, B. & Wakayama, T. (1979). The structure of coordination in the first language acquisition of Japanese. In F. Eckman & A. Hastings (Eds.), *First and second language learning*. Rowley, Mass.: Newbury House Publishers.

Maratsos, M. (1982). The child's construction of grammatical categories. In E. Wanner & L. Gleitman (Eds.), *Language acquisition: The state of the art*. New York: Cambridge University Press.

Milon, J. (1974). The development of negation in English by a second language learner. *TESOL Quarterly, 8,* 137–143.

Murata, K. (1968). *Yooji no gengo hattatsu [Language development of children]*. Tokyo: Baifukan.

Murata, K. (1972). *Yoochienki no gengo hattatsu [Language development in the kindergarten period]*. Tokyo: Baifukan.

Ochs, E., & Schieffelin, B. (1982). Language acquisition and socialization: Three developmental stories. In R. Bauman, & J. Sherzer (Eds.), *Working Papers in Sociolinguistics*. Austin: Southwest Educational Laboratory.

Okubo, A. (1967). *Yooji gengo no hattasu [Development of child language]*. Tokyo: Tokyoodoo.

Piatelli-Palmarini, M. (1980). *Language and learning: The debate between Jean Piaget and Noam Chomsky*. Cambridge, Mass.: Harvard University Press.

Rispoli, M. (1984). Operating principles and processing constraints in the acquisition of Japanese verb morphology. Paper presented to the International Conference on Child Language, Austin, Texas.

Sato, I. (1978). Gengo kakutoku [Language acquisition]. *Jidoo shinrigaku no shimpo [Progress of Child Psychology]*, 83–110.

Schachter, J. (1974). An error in error analysis. *Language Learning, 24,* 205–214.

Shatz, M. (1982). On mechanisms of language acquisition: Can features of the communicative environment account for development? In E. Wanner & L. Gleitman (Eds.), *Language acquisition: the state of the art*. New York: Cambridge University Press.

Shibatani, M. (Ed.) (1976). *Syntax and semantics: Japanese generative grammar*. New York: Academic Press.

Slobin, D. I. (1973). Cognitive prerequisites for the development of grammar. In C. A. Ferguson & D. I. Slobin (Eds.), *Studies of child language development*. New York: Holt, Rinehart and Winston.

———. (1982). Universal and particular in the acquisition of language. In E. Wanner & L. Gleitman (Eds.), *Language acquisition: state of the art*. New York: Cambridge University Press.

Stern, D. (1977). *The first relationship*. Cambridge, Mass.: Harvard University Press.

Vygotsky, L. S. (1962). *Thought and language*. Cambridge, Mass.: MIT Press.

———. (1978). *Mind in society*. Cambridge, Mass.: Harvard University Press.

Wexler, K. (1982). A principle theory for language acquisition. In E. Wanner & L. Gleitman (Eds.), *Language acquisition: State of the art*. New York: Cambridge University Press.

Child Development in Japan and the United States: Prospectives of Cross-Cultural Comparisons

George DeVos

WITH THE COLLABORATION OF

Marcelo M. Suarez-Orozco

The range and variety of data and issues touched on in this volume illustrate, in effect, both the promises and the limitations of cross-cultural comparisons for social science. Underneath a diversity of methods and conflicting theoretical contentions within the social and behavioral sciences, one can discover a basic unity of purpose. The social sciences are slowly transcending the limitations of western cultural traditions which gave them birth. The invigorating interactive effort of behavioral scientists from a diversity of present-day societies, illustrated in this volume, should overcome the unexamined assumptions each social group takes for human universals. Gradually we shall come closer to a science dependent on collaborative explorations of psychological universals—operative not only within individuals, but between and among humans as social beings living in organized systems.

An overreaching conceptual framework in the behavioral sciences must contend with the issue of levels of analysis of human action. Anthropologists, for example, have come to recognize a difference of approach between the *emic* and the *etic*, roughly, between the experiential and the external, between objective observation of "meaning" in human behavior and human expression of intent and purpose. The interfaces of emic experience, between the social and the psychological, occur simultaneously and are operative in all human behavior. Anthropologists have come to recognize that an understanding of the dynamic effects of human intentionality—the perception of "meaning"—can be attained only by an observer's getting "inside" a society. What a given individual then perceives as his or her reality gives us a better understanding of behavioral causality.

With sufficient inquiry, patterns of human motives begin to appear in any given society. Indeed, from an etic perspective, all human behavior is more frequently seen as patterned by social structure or by psychological structuring than is apparent to ordinary awareness. Such structural influences in any society are indeed not perceived by its actors with objectivity. The single actor will only seldom totally comprehend his or her own actions on all possible levels of analysis. This is especially true when behavior in one culture is perceived by members of another culture. In the future, then, I believe social and behavioral research will have to deal more systematically with both emic and etic approaches as two interrelated, irreducible aspects of reseach into human behavior.

Rather than attempt to review the content of the chapters appearing in this volume, I would like to comment on a number of issues that have emerged and to discuss some of the implications of what is now known for what we must learn in the future.

Child Rearing

Japanese society is changing with great rapidity. A number of pertinent questions thus arise for future research. How will child-rearing practices be influenced by new trends in modern Japanese city life? What will be the further adaptation to apartment-house living with the increased work patterns of the mother in occupations outside the house? Further sociological forces may radically alter the nature of parent-child relationships within the present generation of Japanese. What will happen in the present generation: will some of the social and economic factors interfere with the adequate functioning of traditional child-rearing methods? Put another way, will social and economic pressures to attain higher levels of consumption become more salient concerns than remaining at home with the child, regardless of the Japanese woman's strong motives to assume the role of ideal mother?

Newly pressing social motivations can contravene other ideal considerations of parental supervision in regard to child-rearing practices. There is continuity of expectations in Japan about the exemplary behavior to be enacted in training a child. However, the reality for many children today is an absence of parental direction and supervision during critical stages of development.

These are some of the emerging questions which will require systematic consideration. Parallel changes in other societies, including the United States, will provide fertile ground for further comparison, collaboration, and theory building.

Adolescence

Psychologists and anthropologists studying adolescence have come to consider this developmental phase in terms of a social, not a biological definition. Nevertheless, given that different cultures define the transition from childhood to adulthood differently, there is still much to be learned by further research into the interaction between social expectations and physiological development. There are notable differences, even within a society, in the execution of similar social expectations, regardless of individual variability in time of onset of physiological puberty.

It should be noted that during the earlier periods in Japan there was no concept of adolescence. Moreover, extreme class differences existed among the samurai, farmers, and townspeople in their interpretation of the onset of adult status. By the end of the Tokugawa era (1868), the samurai expected their youth to comport themselves as adults at a far earlier age than was true for their contemporaries in the merchant and the artisan classes. Thus, for example, at the age of 15, a member of the Tokugawa family headed a Japanese delegation sent to a World's Fair in Paris. Today, it would be inconceivable in the United States—or in Japan—to have a 15-year-old lead a diplomatic delegation. In this instance, the social status of the youth's family proved more important than his chronological age in the expectation of adult, responsible behavior.

Life-Course Perspectives

Morioka (this volume) points to the importance of a life-course perspective in understanding what happens in adolescence and beyond. Timing is an important factor in events with an impact upon occupational attainments and earnings in later adult years, such as school completion, a first job, and marriage. It is noteworthy, for example, that women who become pregnant at an earlier age have less education and, throughout the life span, a lower level of income and occupational status than women who postpone the birth of their first child. The statistical relationship between the individual and certain life events, however, cannot be removed from its cultural context. For example, in some groups or populations, families intervene to ameliorate negative effects of early childbirth.

Similar patterns exist between contemporary Japan and the United States in many of these aspects. The degree to which occupational career or family role has greater saliency than domestic marital interrelationships may be a characteristic of some cultures more than others. This may attest to the particular forms of emphasis on occupational attainment in Japan and in the United States (Hogan, 1980).

Locus of Control

In American data, what is termed *internality* is found to be positively associated with high cognitive achievement; that is, when the locus of control tends to be internal, there is a close interrelationship between effort and achievement. However, the data also recognize significant relationships between internality and self-esteem. In the cross-national data, a general developmental trend indicates increasing internality with increasing age.

Although at present no theoretical or conceptual connection exists between the two bodies of work, I find a suggestive similarity here to the work of Witkin and others, reporting the maturational and developmental progression from a "field dependent" cognitive style toward "field independence" (DeVos, 1980). There has been no notable systematic cross-cultural comparison of Japanese and American research techniques; yet American studies show that school achievement is higher in children who manifest an ability to trust the perceptual cues from within themselves rather than remaining dependent on cues from the outside environment.

An assumption, derived from the American studies, is that internality is a favorable state fostering both achievement and self-esteem. However, recent studies done in Japan are anomalous compared with previous studies, and they present a somewhat inconsistent picture. Most Japanese studies fail to find an appreciable relationship between a developmental tendency toward *internality* and high academic achievement. In the Japanese studies, it is closely related to strictness or modesty and self-criticism in the evaluation of one's own performance. Japanese of both sexes place greater emphasis on self-reflection and self-criticism than do Americans.

I suggest that these findings are related to ethnocentrism in the research. The correlation found in the American results is culturally specific. Some comparative research on the methods and variables used to rate internality or field independence presumes connections which do not hold true for the Japanese. In Japan there is evidence of an internalization pattern occuring within the context of a pattern of socialization that increases sensitivity to the feelings of others. Achievement motivation and field independence thus coexist with a strong need for group affiliation and a delicate sensitivity to the feelings of others.

In Japan, role expectations downplay personal assertions and individuality within the social context. The Japanese assessment of what constitutes accomplishment places a consistently high emphasis on *effort*. Their ratings of *luck* as equally helpful in accomplishment does not negate the belief in the necessity of a great deal of effort. Luck is not perceived as an excuse; it is seen as something that helps you at times when you have done your best. Indeed, whereas effort may prove unsuccessful if your luck is bad, you cannot succeed without it. It is an ethnocentric convention in research method which equates high ratings on luck with negatively correlated attitudes toward effort. In the Japanese case, these implicit relationships break down.

Achievement

There is a rich field of research in the comparison of formal education, teaching, and learning patterns in Japan and in the United States. Some of the present research here concerns itself with improving methods of instruction or the setting of specific goals. For example, a critical attitude exists among some Japanese scholars toward what they consider a lack of individuality or creativity fostered in Japanese youth. In contrast, their American counterpart's are concerned with the lack of learning of basic skills now evident in primary and secondary education, as well as with the alarming disorganization and lack of discipline prevalent in many classrooms. Each society can learn from the other in observing the effects of attempted policy changes in educational procedures. However, attempts at change in either setting must take into account certain deeply ingrained cultural attitudes in teachers, parents, and pupils, who are socialized in characteristic cultural patterns by the time of their first contact with the educational system.

Moreover, policy changes in educational practice involve political and social patterns, which may prevent necessary research or subsequent utilization of objective research, should such work run counter to deeply held social attitudes. The comparative approach between Japan and the United States occurs between two contemporary democratic cultures. Nevertheless, there remain societal and ideological inhibitory constraints on research in both countries. Hopefully, comparative, collaborative work may facilitate the entering of "dangerous" areas of social sensitivity. Conversely, some mutual reluctance may inhibit particular forms of possible comparative research. Minority school failure, whether the minority are Mexican Americans and blacks in the United States or *burakumin* and Koreans in Japan, is one such sensitive area of exploration which would benefit from further systematic comparisons.

Given the degree of public alarm and political attention paid to the relative failure of the American educational experiences compared with that in other industrial societies, this comparative approach should have considerable effect on attempts to change educational procedures. The basic premises of American social ideology would suggest that educational problems put American industry, with its need for trained personnel, at a distinct competitive disadvantage. Turning to Japanese forms of discontent, we note some Japanese scholars question the implicit pressure toward conformity of thought they believe to be reinforced by the Japanese educational system. Japanese discontent reveals a presumption that more individualistic forms of thought should be welcomed—by some at least—as a goal of education.

Another concern, in looking at differences in the formal educational experiences in Japan and in the United States, is not only the measurement of positive accomplishment, but, the possible cost of this accomplishment, either in emotional and characterological problems or in malaise. For example, critical assessment by a student is praised in the United States, where in Japan it is discouraged. In the Japanese school system, assertiveness receives no positive evaluation and is not seen as a desirable outcome of effective education; hence, the fear on the part of some Japanese that their system leads to too much docility and conformity.

I would emphasize that the trait of self-criticism, both as to *what* one is doing, and *how*, is more apparent among Japanese than Americans. Japanese are, it appears, more willing to be self-critical about their system or, at least, to countenance the criticism of outsiders. Americans, on the other hand, are more apt to be defensive and to contend more easily that their system "is best." This is not to say that the modesty of some Japanese does not conceal deeply held attitudes of superiority, especially in respect to minorities—a topic I have studied at length (DeVos & Wagatsuma, 1967; Lee & DeVos, 1981). However, such an attitude does not seem to interfere with continual self-criticism, both of accomplishment and of personal inadequacies.

Contending with a recent pattern of open discontent with schooling by Japanese youth, researchers are turning increasingly to comparative and collaborative approaches to analyze and formulate responses. It should be noted all evidence pointing to a high degree of field independence in the cognitive patterns of Japanese also relates in Japan to the generally high levels of scholastic achievement. It should also be noted that internality and field independence are unrelated variables, although in the assumptions of many writers, they tend to be confused.

Delinquent Behavior

In my judgment, an unnecessary gap in communication remains between behavioral scientists, including developmental psychologists studying normative behavior and those more concerned either with mental illness or social deviance. In this context, one should note that a very large body of work already exists, by Japanese psychologists and sociologists, dealing with juvenile delinquency and poor school performance of deviant youth.

A number of Japanese scholars have concerned themselves with traumatic early childhood separation from the mother and subsequent forms of deviance, a topic emerging in American studies as well. For example, as early as 1956, Abe discussed how faulty socialization may lead to the development of deviant ego mechanisms which, in turn, are influenced by delinquent values of the peer group. Abe tried to provide an interface between structural variables in personality and adaptational variables in social areas.

Similarly, much recent Japanese research has focussed on poor family interaction and separation from parents as influential in the appearance of juvenile delinquency (see Wagatsuma & DeVos, 1983). Poor school performance has also been linked to subsequent delinquent behavior.

My own studies of minority status and deviance provide another example. In my extensive work with minorities, I found that, in the two Japanese minority groups, the *burakumin*—the descendants of the former pariah, untouchable caste of Japan (DeVos & Wagatsuma, 1966)—and the Korean minority (DeVos, 1981), patterns of deviance resembled patterns of social alienation found in some American minorities, such as Mexican-Americans and Afro-Americans. Children belonging to socially disparaged groups face difficulties in internalizing the acceptable standards of the majority; hence, there is a greater appearance of delinquency among these minority groups.

A number of other culture-specific patterns also deserve attention. One Japanese example is the issue of sibling position. It is evident that the sibling position of the Japanese parent is related to the later appearance of delinquency in the child. A commonly observed phenomenon in Japan is that elder sons are indulged to a greater degree than are subsequent children in the family. Thus, second sons and daughters of rural families are the ones who more often leave home and migrate to the city. It seemed likely, therefore, that sibling position would be related to possible manifestations of delinquency. This hypothesis did hold true: delinquent children proved significantly more often to be the children of second sons and younger daughters in large families.

Future Research

Two prospectives may be most provocative to pursue in future research: socialization by status and socialization for achievement.

Socialization of Status. Perhaps the most neglected aspect of comparative studies being conducted in Japan and in the United States is systematic research of how status difference is socialized. Concern with status varies so markedly in the two cultures that one cannot help but consider how status and authority are systematically socialized differently in dissimilar social systems. Despite the modern ideology shared by both countries of "democratic equality" as a political and social goal, there are different traditions of social stratification characterizing Japan and the United States. These traditions are still observable as cultural continuities. America still bears witness to the acute observations of de Tocqueville more than a century ago of social discomfort with any status differences. Yet it struggles to overcome the effects of a racial caste system and seeks to erase status differences accorded to various ethnic minorities. American society, both in its schools and legal institutions, is committed to a satisfactory incorporation of all groups constituting the contemporary population. Its various social institutions self-consciously seek the best modes of including the continual flow of immigrants to the United States.

In Japan, there is an overtly hierarchical tradition, with highly articulated forms of status deference. The society as a whole, however, shares with the United States the illusion of total homogeneity, arising from an ideology uniting the "nation" as an unbroken historic continuity. Three diverse, religious traditions, which have harmonized and blurred into one another have nurtured the Japanese national entity. As Prince Shotoku Taishi suggested, Shinto roots draw sustenance from the native soil nourishing the trunk of Confucian principles which hold aloft the flowering branches of Buddhism. There has been little modern concern with religious doctrine per se in Japan, but in its own way, each of the Japanese religious traditions emphasizes the status difference between men and women and between the young and the old. This age and sex differentiation is not only acknowledged but permeates all interactional behavior. Thus, for example, they are inherent in body posture and in the relative forms of politeness which signal all forms of verbal address. Deference or superiority are part of interpersonal experience in Japan.

The socialization of status position must be distinguished from patterns of decision making. Parental status is not simply an instance of one person in authority exercising his or her will over that of a child. Rather, parenthood is a mentorship teaching causality in behavior and the consequences of action. A sense of morality is thus inculcated through increasing realization of the consequences of individual actions. By setting an example—such as demonstrating deference towards others—the parent leads the child to conform to social expectations. This social constraint directs the child toward endurance as a means to the ultimate realization of goals and objectives.

Americans find receptivity to such "mentorship" dangerous and the appearance of passivity and dependence shameful. The Japanese feel no such discomfort. In sum, then, questions remain as to how status behavior is socialized in both societies. Are there notable changes in the definition of authority and deference behavior now appearing in Japan? Has a shift occurred from an age-graded, sex-linked interpersonal system to one showing more concern with the symbolic expression of autonomy, if not the actively rebellious flouting of authority? One future prospective for comparison is the observation of a possible change in child rearing: a convergence of behavior toward authority socialized in the posture and the language of children as well as in the social comportment of adults.

Socialization for Achievement. Another, more specific prospect for research is an exploration of the relationship of studies of cognitive ability to processes of internalization. A systematic relationship is found between the type of discipline encountered at given ages of childhood and the development of self-regulation within the individual. There is a developmental progression in internalization, related somehow to a cognitive progression noted in school performance and in other forms of learning. The work of Azuma and Hess is most suggestive in spelling out cultural differences in disciplinary measures. Of course, there is overlap in the type of disciplinary techniques used by American and Japanese mothers; but definite tendencies distinguish them.

These studies can be related to children's acquisition of a deepening sense of causality through their implicit understanding of intentionality in social interaction. The Japanese are more apt to emphasize the consequences of one person's actions on another as a reason for self-constraint. By emphasizing feelings, the Japanese mother appeals to the child's capacity for empathy; he or she learns that some behaviors have harmful consequences. The negative consequences of the child's disruptive behavior on the loving mother can induce, at times, strong feelings of guilt. The intrinsic relationship is yet to be explored between guilt and the need to achieve as a means of reducing parental suffering.

In contrast, discipline in American families more often centers on the assertion of parental will and authority rather than on the consequences of the child's actions. A Japanese mother sensitizes her children to the interpersonal consequences of action; an American mother makes behavior a resultant of a prevailing will. The Japanese mother supports but deemphasizes the authority role. She neutralizes the interpersonal confrontational possibilities of constraint, whereas the American mother's battle with her child over proper behavior often results in a contest of wills.

In Japan, there is an emphasis on affiliative, nurturant, expressive behavior as well as instrumental achievement. The Japanese child becomes increasingly socially sensitized to the feelings of others in interdependent relationships. As noted, this is not counterindicative to the development of cognitive independence. The Japanese example suggests a need to separate out cognitive approaches to achievement motivation from interpersonal patterns within a social milieu.

Writers in the field of need-achievement assume, perhaps too readily, a universal for the American pattern of individualistic goals related specifically to high achievement motivation. The Japanese cultural milieu continually emphasizes mutual social goals, especially within the family or an in-group, without sacrificing achievement and accomplishment. Obviously, the American pattern of individualism is not a paradigm for all forms of understanding human motivation.

Hess, Azuma, and their associates (this volume) demonstrate a clear correlational relation between efficiency of communication and maternal expectations for achievement and disciplinary strategy. The maternal teaching style and expressions of appreciation, the mother's praise and the emotional climate created in her relationship with her child are singular for the Japanese context. More studies of cross-cultural preschool patterns can be conducted not only in Japan and in the United States, but in other social settings as well. My own use of the Thematic Apperception Text, for eliciting fantasy material has consistently shown that a concept of effort and the necessity to overcome difficulty through it is a predominant Japanese fantasy related both to cognitive styles and to patterns of internalization.

Longitudinal Sequences

One must emphasize the increasing capacity for longitudinal research in the retesting of previously contrasted samples in both countries. We hope for many such opportunities to test samples over periods of time, comparing the systematic continuity of given similarities and differences. Now that Japanese and American social scientists have established collaborative associations, we look forward with confidence to further fruitful results in comparative research.

References

Abe, J. (1958). *Shakai shinrigaku*. Tokyo: Kyoritsu Shuppan.

DeVos, G. A. (1960). Ethnic adaptation and minority status. *Journal of Cross-cultural Psychology, 7*, 101–125.

DeVos, G. A., & Wagatsuma, H. (1966). *Japan's invisible race: Caste in culture and personality*. Berkeley: University of California Press.

Hogan, D. (1980). The transition into adulthood as a career contingency. *American Sociological Review, 45*, 261–276.

Lee, C., & DeVos, G. A. (1981). *Koreans in Japan: Ethnic conflict and accommodation*. Berkeley: University of California Press.

Contributors

Hiroshi Azuma majored in psychology at the University of Tokyo and received his Ph.D. from the University of Illinois in 1960. He is currently Professor at the University of Tokyo, where he began as Assistant Professor in 1964. His specialty is in education, learning, and developmental psychology. He is interested in the problems of cognitive development and culture. Address: University of Tokyo, 7-3-1, Hongo, Bunkyo-ku, Tokyo.

Harumi Befu is Professor of Anthropology at Stanford University, where he has been since 1965. He received his Ph.D. from the University of Wisconsin (Madison). His area of interest is in social organization and cultural change, which is reflected in his publications, such as *Japan, an anthropological introduction* (Harper & Row, 1971) and *The challenge of Japan's internationalization: Organization and culture* (coedited with Hiroshi Mannari, Kodansha International, 1983). Address: Department of Anthropology, Stanford University, Stanford, CA 94305.

Lois Bloom is Professor of Psychology and Education at Teachers College, Columbia University. Her research in language development has been concerned with the integration of meaning and discourse factors in the child's construction of basic sentence grammar and the beginnings of complex syntax. She is author of *Language development: Form and function in emerging grammars* (The MIT Press, 1970), which was translated and published in Japan (Taishukan Publishing Co., 1981). Address: Box 5, Teachers College, Columbia University, 525 West 120th Street, New York, NY 10012.

Joseph J. Campos received his Ph.D. in 1966 from Cornell University. After a 2-year postdoctoral research fellowship at the Albert Einstein College of Medicine in New York City, he became Professor of Psychology at the University of Denver. His interests are focused on the nature and measurement of emotions, especially emotional development. At present, he is investigating from a cross-cultural vantage point the processes of emotional communication in infancy and toddlerhood. Address: Department of Psychology, University of Denver, Denver, CO 80208.

George DeVos is Professor of Anthropology at the University of California (Berkeley). He received his Ph.D. from the University of Chicago and is well known for his work on the culture of Japan. His interests include the study of culture and personality, ethnic problems, social deviancy, and cultural change. Address: Department of Anthropology, University of California, Berkeley, CA 94720.

W. Patrick Dickson is Associate Professor of Child and Family Studies and Faculty Associate in the Wisconsin Center for Education Research. He received his Ph.D. in Child Development from Stanford University. His fundamental research interest is in the environmental influences on the development of intelligence, with special emphasis on the role of parent-child communication. Address: School of Family Resources and Consumer Sciences, University of Wisconsin, 1300 Linden Drive, Madison, WI 53706.

Kenji Hakuta is Associate Professor of Psychology at Yale University. He received his B.A. and Ph.D. from Harvard University. He has conducted studies of language acquisition in Japanese and American children, with emphasis on grammar. His other interests include bilingualism and second-language acquisition. He has recently completed *The mirror of bilingualism* (Basic Books, 1985). Address: Department of Psychology, Yale University, Box 11A Yale Station, New Haven, CT 06520.

Giyoo Hatano is Professor of Psychology and a fellow at the Center for Data Processing and Computer Sciences at Dokkyo University, Saitama, Japan. He received his Ph.D. from the University of Tokyo. He is interested in cognitive and developmental psychology and has published studies of abacus expertise and *kanji*. Currently, he is developing a general theory of expertise, incorporating cognitive, motivational and sociocultural factors. Address: Dokkyo University, 600, Sakae-cho, Souka-shi, Saitama, Japan.

Robert Hess is a psychologist interested in the relationship of individual behavior to culture and social institutions. He has been collaborating with Professor Hiroshi Azuma and others in Japan on a comparative study of family influences on school readiness and later school achievement. He has a Ph.D. in Human Development from the University of Chicago, where he was on the faculty until 1967. Since that time he has been the Lee L. Jacks Professor of Child Education at Stanford University. Address: School of Education, Stanford University, Stanford, CA 94305.

Susan Holloway is an Assistant Professor at the University of Maryland at College Park. Her work concerns parental socialization of social and cognitive skills, including the effects of parental beliefs about child rearing on children's own beliefs and behaviors. She is also interested in how multiple caregiving contexts affect preschool children. She has pursued research on these themes in Mexico and Japan, as well as in the United States. Address: Institute for Child Study, College of Education, University of Maryland, College Park, MD 20742.

Kayoko Inagaki is Associate Professor on the Faculty of Education at Chiba University. She has also served on the Faculty at Izumi Junior College. Her current interests include theories of motivation for understanding and the acquisition of information about biology in everyday life. Address: Chiba University, 1-33, Yayoicho, Chiba-shi, Chiba.

Tadahiko Inagaki is interested in the history of teaching, with particular emphasis on Japanese education. Along with studying historical aspects of western influences and their subsequent transformation in Japan, he has conducted research on teaching in collaboration with teachers. During the past 10 years, he has observed American and British classrooms and is interested in conducting comparative research in the hope of elucidating characteristics of Japanese education. Address: University of Tokyo, 7-3-1, Hongo, Bunkyo-ku, Tokyo.

Jerome Kagan is Professor of Psychology at Harvard University. He received his Ph.D. from Yale University in 1954 and spent 7 years at the Fels Research Institute. After coming to Harvard in 1964, Kagan initiated a series of longitudinal studies concerned first with the ontogeny of cognitive processes and, later, with stability and change in temperamental styles. His recent books include *The second year* (Harvard University Press, 1981) and *The nature of the child* (Basic Books, 1984). Address: Department of Psychology and Social Relations, Harvard University, Cambridge, MA 02138.

Keiko Kashiwagi majored in psychology at Tokyo Women's Christian University and completed graduate training at the University of Tokyo. She is currently professor at the Tokyo Women's Christian University, where she has been since 1960. Her specialty is in developmental psychology, with particular interests in role development and the development of self-regulation, especially in its relation to culture. Address: Tokyo Women's Christian University, 2-6-1, Zempukuji, Suginami-ku, Tokyo.

Tadahisa Kato is Assistant Professor of Psychology at Tohoku Fukushi College. He received his master's degree from Tohoku University. His main fields of research are in physiological psychology and counseling psychology. Address: Tohoku Fukushi Daigaku, Kunimi 1-8-1, Sendai, Japan.

Susumu Kimura is Professor of Psychology at Tohoku Fukushi College. His interests include development in early childhood and are focused mainly on children with various mental handicaps. He spends a portion of his time as a supervisor of the education of young handicapped children in nursery schools and institutions. Address: Tohoku Fukushi Daigaku, Kunimi 1-8-1, Sendai, Japan.

Seiro Kitamura is Emeritus Professor of Psychology at Tohoku University in Sendai, and honorary member of the Japanese Psychological Association. He currently serves as a lecturer at Tohoku Fukushi College. His Ph.D. is from Tohoku University. His recent books include *Psychology of self* (Seishin-shobo, 1977), *Psychology of mental imagery* (Seishin-shobo, 1982), and *Psychology of hope* (Kaneko-shobo, 1984). Address: Tohoku Fukushi Daigaku, Kunimi 1-8-1, Sendai, Japan.

Hideo Kojima received his undergraduate degree and his Ph.D. at Kyoto University. He is Professor in the School of Education at Nagoya University and has also taught at Kanazawa University. He is interested in the analysis of three-person relationships within the family (for example, parent, child, infant; father, mother, child), historical aspects of child development, and life stages. Address: Nagoya University, Furocho, Chikusa-ku, Nagoya-shi, Aichi.

Susumu Kuno is Professor of Linguistics at Harvard University. He specializes in theory of grammar, discourse analysis, Japanese and English syntax, as well as in computational linguistics. He is author of *The structure of the Japanese language* (MIT Press, 1973) and several other books. He received a B.A. and an M.A. in Linguistics from Tokyo University, and a Ph.D. in Linguistics from Harvard University in 1964. Address: Department of Linguistics, Harvard University, Cambridge, MA 02138.

Shin-Ying Lee is a doctoral student in Developmental Psychology at the University of Michigan. She received her B.A. from National Taiwan University. Her research interests include cultural influences on children's belief systems and the relation between the belief systems and academic performance. Address: Department of Psychology, University of Michigan, Ann Arbor, MI 48109.

Robert Levine is a social anthropologist and developmental psychologist who teaches at Harvard University, where he is Roy E. Larsen Professor of Education and Human Development and Professor of Anthropology. An African specialist, he has long been interested in the creation of a cross-cultural psychology unbiased by western conceptual frameworks, and sees Japanese research as the most vigorous contributor to this process at present. Address: Harvard Graduate School of Education, 705 Larsen Hall, Appian Way, Cambridge, MA 02138.

Catherine Lewis is Assistant Professor of Psychiatry and Research Psychologist in Pediatrics at the University of California, San Francisco. She has served as a Congressional Science Fellow, and has worked and conducted research in Japan for 3 years. Her major research interests include the development of children's health behavior and concepts, adolescents' decision making and adult-child control strategies. Address: University of California at San Francisco, Hospitals and Clinics, A-205, San Francisco, CA 94143.

Teresa M. McDevitt is a doctoral student in Education at Stanford University. Her research interests include children's listening skills, family influences on children's cognitive and communicative abilities, and patterns of authority in the family and their consequences for children. Address: School of Education, Stanford University, Stanford, CA 94305.

Kazuo Miyake is Director, Research and Clinical Center for Child Development at the University of Hokkaido, where he has been Professor of Developmental Psychology since 1970. From 1964 to 1965, he was a visiting scholar at the Harvard-Yenching Institute. His current interests include the role of early temperamental disposition in child development and the socialization of emotion. Address: University of Hokkaido, Nishi-5, Kita-8-jo, Kita-ku, Sapporo-shi, Hokkaido.

Kiyomi Morioka is Professor of Cultural History and Director of the Institute of Folklore Studies at Seijo University in Tokyo. Prior to that, he was Professor of Sociology at Tokyo University of Education. He is especially interested in the changes that have taken place in family life in Japan over the past 100 years in the process of industrialization. Address: Institute of Folklore Studies, Seijo University, 6-1-20, Seijo, Setagaya-ku, Tokyo.

Gary Glen Price is Associate Professor of Early Childhoold Education at the University of Wisconsin-Madison. He received his Ph.D. from Stanford University in 1976. His research on environmental influences on intellectual abilities is tied to the cognitive and neuropsychological elucidation of psychometric abilities. Address: Department of Curriculum and Instruction, University of Wisconsin-Madison, 225 North Mills Street, Madison, WI 53706.

Harold W. Stevenson is Professor of Psychology at the University of Michigan. He received his Ph.D. from Stanford University and, before coming to Michigan, was Director of the Institute of Child Development at the University of Minnesota. He has had a long-term interest in Japan, and with colleagues in Japan, Taiwan, and the United States, has recently completed a large project on the correlates of children's achievement in elementary school. Address: Department of Psychology, University of Michigan, Ann Arbor, MI 48109.

James W. Stigler is an Assistant Professor in the University of Chicago's Committee on Human Development. His primary interests are in cognitive development and he has studied these from a cross-cultural perspective. He has a special interest in mental calculation and in the use of the abacus. Address: Committee on Human Development, University of Chicago, 5730 South Woodlawn Avenue, Chicago, IL 60637.

Marcelo M. Suarez-Orozco is a teaching associate and research assistant at the Institute of Human Development, University of California, Berkeley. His interests include culture and personality migration, ethnicity and educational anthropology. He has worked among Mexican and Central American immigrants and has studied the adaptation to school by Hispanic immigrants. Address: Department of Anthropology, University of California, Berkeley, CA 94720.

Keiko Takahashi is Professor of Psychology at Soka University in Tokyo. Her Ph.D. is from the University of Tokyo. Her interests include the development of attachment relationships from infancy to adulthood. Recently, she has been concerned with the analysis of infants' adaptation to strange situations. Address: Soka University, 1-236, Tangicho, Hachioji-shi, Tokyo.

Merry I. White is a lecturer at the Harvard Graduate School. She is the author of *Stranger in his native land* (forthcoming), a study of cultural and social issues in the internationalization of Japan, and coauthor with Robert A. LeVine of *Human conditions: The cultural basis of educational development* (Routledge and Kegan Paul, 1986). Address: Harvard Graduate School of Education, 601 Larsen Hall, Appian Way, Cambridge, MA 02138.

Yoshiaka Yamamura received his degrees from the Tokyo University of Education. He is currently Professor at Tsukuba University. His research theme is how a child is socialized into becoming a Japanese, particularly through the family and school. He has written *The Japanese and mother* (Toyokan, 1971), *The Japanese parent, the Japanese home* (Kanekoshobo, 1983), and articles on economic socialization. Address: Rikkyo University, 3-34-1, Nishi-Ikebukuro, Toshima-Ku, Tokyo.

Acknowledgments

This book is the product of a special project group formed at the Center for Advanced Study in the Behavioral Sciences at Stanford, California, to explore issues related to comparative child development. The group, whose members were Hiroshi Azuma, Kenji Hakuta, and Harold Stevenson, spent the 1982–1983 academic year at the Center. Their major purpose was to review and synthesize information about child development in Japanese and American societies. One of the year's activities was a conference to which leading researchers in Japan and the United States were invited. The organization of the conference took shape in a planning meeting to select topics and participants. John Flavell, Robert Hess, and Eleanor Maccoby of Stanford University, Keiko Kashiwagi of Tokyo Women's University, and Giyoo Hatano of Dokkyo University joined Azuma, Hakuta, and Stevenson for this meeting.

The conference was held in April, 1983. Participants, in addition to the organizers, included scholars from Japan and the United States. The Japanese participants included Tadahiko Inagaki, Hideo Kojima, Kazuo Miyake, Kiyomi Morioka, Shigefumi Nagano, Yutaka Saeki, and Keiko Takahashi. The American participants were Harumi Befu, Lois Bloom, Joseph Campos, Michael Cole, George DeVos, Dennis Hogan, Jerome Kagan, Susumu Kuno, Robert LeVine, and Herbert Walberg. Rapporteurs for the conference were Catherine Lewis and David Crandall. Financial support for the conference was provided by the Social Science Research Council's Committee on Japanese Studies, and by the Center for Advanced Study in the Behavioral Sciences. Lonnie Sherrod of the Council, and many members of the Center staff, including Gardner Lindzey, Katherine Holm, Alan Henderson, Muriel Bell, and Frances Duignan were of great help to us in organizing and managing the conference.

The information and ideas presented at the conference were fresh and for the most part unavailable to Western readers. It seemed appropriate, therefore, to share this information with a broader audience than could be present at the conference. The participants agreed to rewrite their papers for publication. In addition, several papers were written especially for the volume.

Many people helped us to put the volume together. We have been assisted in editing the papers by Catherine Arnott, Muriel Bell, and David Crandall. Keiko Kashiwagi has worked diligently in facilitating communication between us and the Japanese authors. We are grateful, too, to the foundations that provided the partial financial support that enabled us to spend the year at the Center: the Alfred P. Sloan Foundation for Azuma; the Exxon Education Foundation, the Alfred P. Sloan Foundation, and the Spencer Foundation for Hakuta; and the

John D. and Catherine T. MacArthur Foundation for Stevenson. In addition, Stevenson received partial support as a Fellow of the John Simon Guggenheim Foundation. Support for the conference and the preparation of this volume also was provided by the Center/FFRP Fund.

Author Index

Subject Index